New York City 2008

A Selection
of **Restaurants** & **Hotels**

Manufacture française des pneumatiques Michelin
Société en commandite par actions au capital de 304 000 000 EUR
Place des Carmes-Déchaux – 63000 Clermont-Ferrand (France)
R.C.S. Clermont-Fd B 855 200 507

Dépot légal Octobre 2007
Printed in Canada
Published in 2007
Cover photograph : Eisinf, Susie M./Stockfood

Please send your comments to:
Michelin North America, Inc.
Travel Publications
One Parkway South – Greenville, SC 29615 USA
Phone: 1-800-423-0485
Fax: 1-800-378-7471
www.michelintravel.com
Michelin.guides@us.michelin.com

Dear reader

We are thrilled to present the third edition of our Michelin Guide New York City. Our teams have made every effort to update the selection to fully reflect the rich diversity of the restaurant and hotel scene in the Big Apple.

The Michelin Guide provides a comprehensive selection and rating, in all categories of comfort and prices. As part of our meticulous and highly confidential evaluation process, Michelin's American inspectors conducted anonymous visits to restaurants and hotels in New York City. Michelin's inspectors are the eyes and ears of the customers, and thus their anonymity is key to ensure that they receive the same treatment as any other guest. The decision to award a star is a collective one, based on the consensus of all inspectors who have visited a particular establishment.

Our company's two founders, Édouard and André Michelin, published the first Michelin Guide in 1900, to provide motorists with practical information about where they could service and repair their cars, and find quality accommodations and a good meal. The star-rating system for outstanding restaurants was introduced in 1926. The same system is used for our American selections.

We sincerely hope that the Michelin Guide New York City 2008 will become your favorite guide to the city's restaurants and hotels. On behalf of all our Michelin employees, we wish you the very best enjoyment in your Big Apple dining and hotel experiences.

Contents

Where to **stay**

Contents

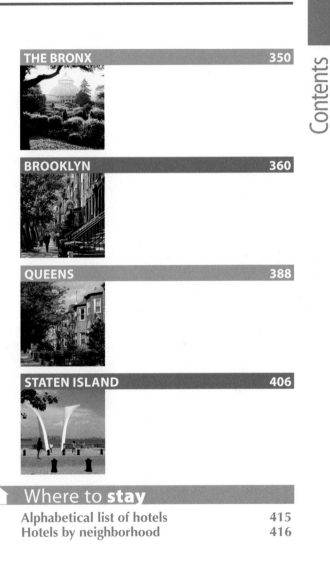

How to use this guide

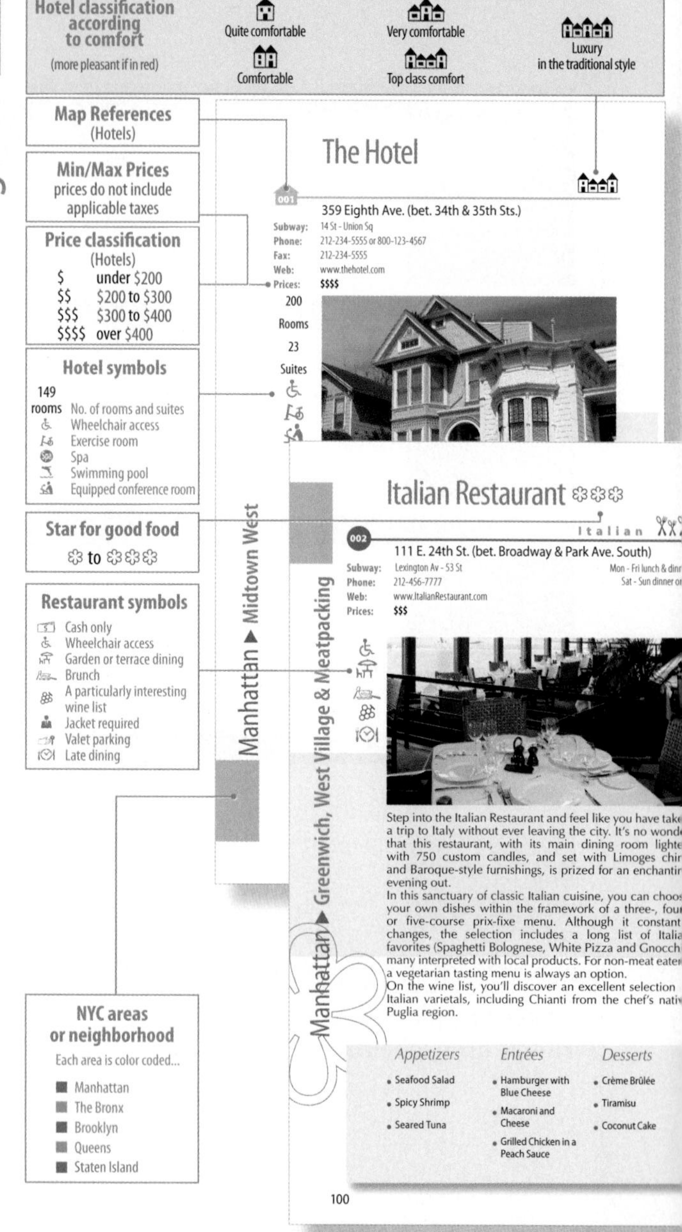

Hotel classification according to comfort
(more pleasant if in red)
Quite comfortable
Comfortable
Very comfortable
Top class comfort
Luxury in the traditional style
Map References (Hotels)
Min/Max Prices prices do not include applicable taxes
Price classification (Hotels)
$ under $200
$$ $200 to $300
$$$ $300 to $400
$$$$ over $400
Hotel symbols
149 rooms No. of rooms and suites
Wheelchair access
Exercise room
Spa
Swimming pool
Equipped conference room
Star for good food
to
Restaurant symbols
Cash only
Wheelchair access
Garden or terrace dining
Brunch
A particularly interesting wine list
Jacket required
Valet parking
Late dining
NYC areas or neighborhood
Each area is color coded...
Manhattan
The Bronx
Brooklyn
Queens
Staten Island
The Hotel
001
359 Eighth Ave. (bet. 34th & 35th Sts.)
Subway: 14 St - Union Sq
Phone: 212-234-5555 or 800-123-4567
Fax: 212-234-5555
Web: www.thehotel.com
Prices: $$$$
200 Rooms
23 Suites
Manhattan ▶ Midtown West
Italian Restaurant
Italian
002
111 E. 24th St. (bet. Broadway & Park Ave. South)
Subway: Lexington Av - 53 St
Phone: 212-456-7777
Web: www.ItalianRestaurant.com
Prices: $$$
Mon - Fri lunch & dinr
Sat - Sun dinner or
Manhattan ▶ Greenwich, West Village & Meatpacking
Step into the Italian Restaurant and feel like you have tak
a trip to Italy without ever leaving the city. It's no wond
that this restaurant, with its main dining room light
with 750 custom candles, and set with Limoges chir
and Baroque-style furnishings, is prized for an enchantir
evening out.
In this sanctuary of classic Italian cuisine, you can choo
your own dishes within the framework of a three-, fou
or five-course prix-fixe menu. Although it constant
changes, the selection includes a long list of Itali
favorites (Spaghetti Bolognese, White Pizza and Gnocch
many interpreted with local products. For non-meat eate
a vegetarian tasting menu is always an option.
On the wine list, you'll discover an excellent selection
Italian varietals, including Chianti from the chef's nati
Puglia region.
Appetizers
Seafood Salad
Spicy Shrimp
Seared Tuna
Entrées
Hamburger with Blue Cheese
Macaroni and Cheese
Grilled Chicken in a Peach Sauce
Desserts
Crème Brûlée
Tiramisu
Coconut Cake
100

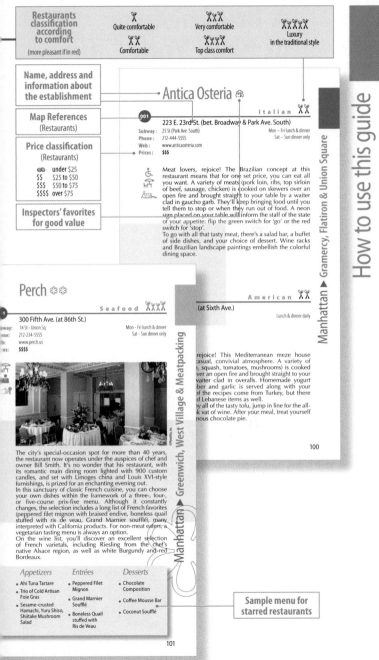

Restaurants classification according to comfort

(more pleasant if in red)

- Quite comfortable
- Comfortable
- Very comfortable
- Top class comfort
- Luxury in the traditional style

Name, address and information about the establishment

Map References (Restaurants)

Price classification (Restaurants)

- under $25
- $$ $25 to $50
- $$$ $50 to $75
- $$$$ over $75

Inspectors' favorites for good value

Antica Osteria

Italian

901

223 E. 23rd St. (bet. Broadway & Park Ave. South)

Subway: 25 St (Park Ave. South)
Phone: 212-444-5555
Web: www.anticaosteria.com
Prices: $$$

Mon – Fri lunch & dinner
Sat – Sun dinner only

Meat lovers, rejoice! The Brazilian concept at this restaurant means that for one set price, you can eat all you want. A variety of meats (pork loin, ribs, top sirloin of beef, sausage, chicken) is cooked on skewers over an open fire and brought straight to your table by a waiter clad in gaucho garb. They'll keep bringing food until you tell them to stop or when they run out of food. A neon sign placed on your table will inform the staff of the state of your appetite: flip the green switch for 'go' or the red switch for 'stop'.
To go with all that tasty meat, there's a salad bar, a buffet of side dishes, and your choice of dessert. Wine racks and Brazilian landscape paintings embellish the colorful dining space.

American

(at Sixth Ave.)

Lunch & dinner daily

rejoice! This Mediterranean meze house casual, convivial atmosphere. A variety of , squash, tomatoes, mushrooms) is cooked ver an open fire and brought straight to your vaiter clad in overalls. Homemade yogurt ber and garlic is served along with your of the recipes come from Turkey, but there d Lebanese items as well.
y all of the tasty tofu, jump in line for the all-k vat of wine. After your meal, treat yourself nous chocolate pie.

Manhattan ▸ Gramercy, Flatiron & Union Square

100

Perch

Seafood

1

300 Fifth Ave. (at 86th St.)

Subway: 14 St - Union Sq
Phone: 212-234-5555
Web: www.perch.us
Prices: $$$$

Mon - Fri lunch & dinner
Sat - Sun dinner only

©PhotoDisc, Inc.

The city's special-occasion spot for more than 40 years, the restaurant now operates under the auspices of chef and owner Bill Smith. It's no wonder that his restaurant, with its romantic main dining room lighted with 900 custom candles, and set with Limoges china and Louis XVI-style furnishings, is prized for an enchanting evening out.
In this sanctuary of classic French cuisine, you can choose your own dishes within the framework of a three-, four-, or five-course prix-fixe menu. Although it constantly changes, the selection includes a long list of French favorites (peppered filet mignon with braised endive, boneless quail stuffed with ris de veau, Grand Marnier soufflé), many interpreted with California products. For non-meat eaters, a vegetarian tasting menu is always an option.
On the wine list, you'll discover an excellent selection of French varietals, including Riesling from the chef's native Alsace region, as well as white Burgundy and red Bordeaux.

Appetizers	Entrées	Desserts
• Ahi Tuna Tartare	• Peppered Filet Mignon	• Chocolate Composition
• Trio of Cold Artisan Foie Gras	• Grand Marnier Soufflé	• Coffee Mousse Bar
• Sesame-crusted Hamachi, Yuru Shiso, Shiitake Mushroom Salad	• Boneless Quail stuffed with Ris de Veau	• Coconut Soufflé

Manhattan ▸ Greenwich, West Village & Meatpacking

101

Sample menu for starred restaurants

How to use this guide

A brief history of New York City

Introduction to New York City

Cultural magnet, economic powerhouse—so what? New York is first and foremost one great place to eat. With over 17,300 restaurants in 320 square miles, there's practically an eatery on every corner of this consummate food town.

Rum, Riches, Red Sauce

From its trade-post beginnings in 1624, New York banked on business. As it expanded, so did the number of boardinghouses, chophouses, oyster bars, cafes, and—of course—taverns that fed workers. Places along Wall Street, especially, were known for drinks, dinner and deals. Dinner was hearty and plenteous (as was the drink), but even as early as the 1790s, French gastronome Brillat-Savarin commented favorably on the quality and variety of food he enjoyed in the city. Business boomed in the 19th century, and those reaping the profits were eager to eat them up in style. A few grand hotels accommodated, but America's first non-hotel restaurant set the standard for years to come. Coupling European sophistication with American innovation, Delmonico's introduced the *à la carte* menu and dishes that still evoke luxury: baked Alaska, lobster Newburg, and eggs Benedict.

Yet those who powered New York's success with their sweat also did the most to define its cuisine. These new immigrants brought dreams and family recipes to share in the red-sauce joints of Little Italy, Lower East Side Kosher delis and Chinatown's Cantonese places. As old foodways blended in this new melting pot, ethnic foods became quintessential New York fare. A German sausage

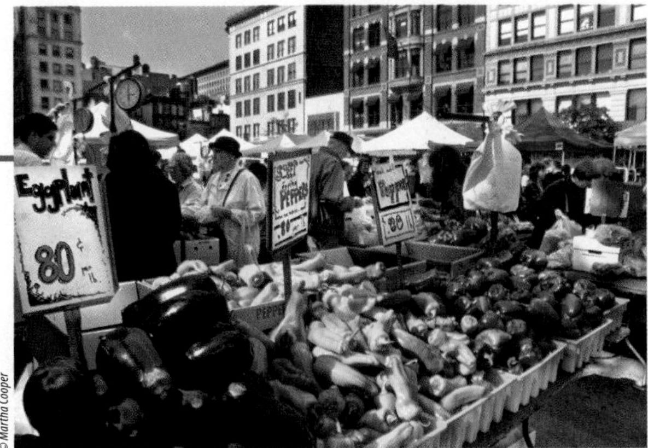

© Martha Cooper

evolved into the hot dog; a Polish bread became the New York bagel, served with lox and a schmear.

World on a Plate

Prohibition in the early 20th century brought the demise of elite restaurants as humbler places catering to the average Joe (and Joann, as women entered the work force) flourished. Diners, often run by Greek immigrants, offered American comfort foods like meatloaf, and macaroni and cheese. African Americans from the South brought new riffs on soul food, like fried chicken and waffles, to jazz-age Harlem. Two subsequent international migrations became nothing less than culinary tidal waves, the aftershocks of which still reverberate through the city's kitchens.

A few plucky French chefs stayed on after the raves about their cooking at the 1939 World's Fair. Those chefs and the ones who followed made New York into the New World outpost of haute cuisine, and eventually nouvelle cuisine, not to mention the casual bistro, exalted as it had never been in France. *Cucina italiana* was revisited, too, going regions beyond red sauce. Immigration restrictions relaxed after 1965, beckoning Southeast Asians, Indians, and many others who continue to bring zesty new flavors to the city. The century's last decades introduced "New American" cuisine and a farm-fresh focus to city dining.

Such are the happy paradoxes that make New York a dynamic, distinctive food town, where Bubbie's heirloom bread recipe might be revived by a Korean artisan baker, some of the most accomplished "French" cooks are Mexican, and macaroni and cheese has gone gourmet. Who knows what's next, but from the oyster bars and chophouses of old to today's sushi temples and steak palaces, diners have always been able to count on the Big Apple for a juicy bite.

Where to **eat**

Alphabetical list of restaurants

Peter L. Wrenn/MICHELIN

Restaurants by Cuisine Type

American

American Grill	410
Barbuto	131
Beacon	235
BG	237
Blue Hill	133
Blue Smoke	104
Boathouse Central Park	306
Bridge Cafe	94
Café Cluny	134
Carol's Cafe	411
Cookshop	51
Craft	109
Diner	370
Dressler	371
DuMont	372
Four Seasons (The)	201
Good	140
Good Enough to Eat	340
Harry's Cafe	95
Henry's End	376
Home	143
J.G. Melon	316
Kitchenette	297
Métrazur	210
New Leaf Café	171
Nicole's	213
Odeon (The)	300
PicNic Market & Café	346
Sardi's	263
Taste	330
Telepan	347
21 Club	269
Union Square Cafe	122
Water's Edge	404
West Bank Café	270

Asian

Aja	186
Cendrillon	277
Chance	369
China Grill	239
Garden Court Café	314
Kampuchea Noodle Bar	178
Kuma Inn	179
Momofuku Noodle Bar	88
Momofuku Ssäm Bar	88
Monkey Bar	211
Spice Market	158
Tao	225

Austrian

Blaue Gans	291
Café Sabarsky	308
Danube	294
Thomas Beisl	386
Wallsé	162

Barbecue

Daisy May's BBQ	241
Dinosaur Bar-B-Que	168
Smoke Joint (The)	385

Basque

Euzkadi	78

Brazilian

Malagueta	398

Cajun

Bayou Restaurant	411

Caribbean

MoBay Uptown	170

Chinese

Contemporary

Deli

Egyptian

Ethiopian

European

French

Fusion

Gastropub

German

Greek

Indian

Italian

Jamaican

Japanese

Korean

Latin American

Malaysian

Mediterranean

Mexican

Middle Eastern

Moroccan

Persian

Pizza

Portuguese

Puerto Rican

Russian

Scandinavian

Seafood

Southern

Southwestern

Spanish

Alcala	187
Bolo	105
Boqueria	105
Casa Mono	107
Degustation	78
El Cid	137
El Faro	137
La Paella	84
Las Ramblas	145
Picasso	217
Sevilla	157
Suba	182

Sri Lankan

Sigiri	89

Steakhouse

Ben Benson's	236
Benjamin Steak House	191
Blair Perrone	192
BLT Prime	103
BLT Steak	193
Bobby Van's Steakhouse	193
Bull and Bear	195
Capital Grille (The)	196
Craftsteak	51
Del Frisco's	242
Frankie & Johnnie's	245
Gallagher's	246
Keens Steakhouse	248
Maloney & Porcelli	210
MarkJoseph Steakhouse	96
Michael Jordan's	211
Morton's	212
Nebraska Beef	97
Nick & Stef's	256
Old Homestead	149
Peter Luger	381
Porter House	260
Ricardo Steakhouse	172
Smith & Wollensky	222
Sparks Steak House	222
Staghorn Steakhouse	264
Strip House	158
Wolfgang's Steakhouse	228

Thai

Arharn Thai	394
Chao Thai	395
Jaiya	115
Kittichai	280
Pongsri Thai	70
Prem-on Thai	157
Sea	384
Sripraphai	401
Zabb Queens	404

Turkish

Antique Garage	274
Beyoglu	306
Pera	216
Sip Sak	221
Taksim	225
Turkish Kitchen	121
Zeytin	348

Vegetarian

Gobo	140
Pure Food and Wine	118

Vietnamese

Nam	299
Nha Trang Centre	67
Omai	56
Pho'Hoang	398
Sapa	119
Thai So'n	72

At finer restaurants in Los Angeles, Melbourne, Cape Town and of course, Positano.

Restaurants by Neighborhood

Harlem & Washington Heights

Lower East Side

Midtown East & Murray Hill

Russian

Firebird	XXX	244
Russian Samovar	X	262

Seafood

Blue Fin	XX	237
Esca	XXX	243
Le Bernardin	✿✿✿ XXXX	251
Sea Grill (The)	XX	263

Steakhouse

Ben Benson's	XX	236
Del Frisco's	XXX	242
Frankie & Johnnie's	XX	245
Gallagher's	XX	246
Keens Steakhouse	XX	248
Nick & Stef's	XX	256
Porter House	XXX	260
Staghorn Steakhouse	XX	264

SoHo & Nolita

Asian

Cendrillon	X	277

Contemporary

Blue Ribbon	X	276
Mercer Kitchen	X	281
Salt	X	284
Savoy	X	284
Tasting Room	XX	285
Zoë	X	286

French

Balthazar	X	275
Jean Claude	X	279
L'Ecole	XX	280
Raoul's	X	283

Fusion

Public	X	283

Greek

Snack	☺ X	285

Italian

Ama	X	274
Downtown Cipriani	XX	278
Giorgione	XX	279
Mezzogiorno	X	282
Peasant	X	282

Japanese

Blue Ribbon Sushi (SoHo)	X	276

Korean

Woo Lae Oak	XX	286

Mexican

Café El Portal	X	277

Seafood

Aquagrill	XX	275
Ed's Lobster Bar	X	278
Lure Fishbar	XX	281

Thai

Kittichai	XX	280

Turkish

Antique Garage	X	274

TriBeCa

American

Kitchenette	X	297
Odeon (The)	XX	300

Austrian

Blaue Gans	X	291
Danube	✿ XXX	294

Contemporary

Dennis Foy	XXX	295
Dylan Prime	XX	295
Harrison (The)	XXX	297
Tribeca Grill	XX	301

French

Bouley	✿✿ XXXX	292
Capsouto Frères	XX	293
Chanterelle	XXX	293
Landmarc	XX	298

Italian

Acappella	XXX	290
Arqua	XX	290
Bread Tribeca	X	291
Gigino Trattoria	XX	296
Pepolino	X	300
Scalini Fedeli	XX	301

Japanese

Megu	XXX	298
Nobu	XX	299

Seafood

Fresh	XX	296

Vietnamese

Nam	X	299

Upper East Side

American

Boathouse Central Park	XX	306
J.G. Melon	☺ X	316
Taste	X	330

Asian

Garden Court Café	☺ X	314

Austrian

Café Sabarsky	X	308

Chinese

Philippe	XX	325
Shanghai Pavilion	XX	327

Contemporary

Aureole	✿ XXX	305
Carlyle (The)	XXXX	308
Davidburke & Donatella	XXX	309
Etats-Unis	✿ X	312
Frederick's Madison	XX	313
JoJo	✿ XX	317

Upper West Side

Bronx

Starred Restaurants

Within the selection we offer you, some restaurants deserve to be highlighted for their particularly good cuisine. When giving one, two or three Michelin stars, there are a number of things that we judge, including the quality of the ingredients, the technical skill and flair that goes into their preparation, the blend and clarity of flavors, and the balance of the menu. Just as important is the ability to produce excellent cooking time and again. We make as many visits as we need, so that our readers can be sure of quality and consistency.

A two- or three-star restaurant has to offer something very special in its cuisine; a real element of creativity, originality or "personality" that sets it apart from the rest. Three stars – our highest award – are given to the very best restaurants, where the whole dining experience is superb.

Cuisine in any style, modern or traditional, may be eligible for a star. Because we apply the same independent standards everywhere, the awards have become benchmarks of reliability and excellence in more than 20 European countries, particularly in France, where we have awarded stars for almost 80 years, and where the expression "Now that's real three-star quality!" has entered into the language.

The awarding of a star is based solely on the quality of the cuisine.

Exceptional cuisine, worth a special journey.

One always eats here extremely well, sometimes superbly. Distinctive dishes are precisely executed, using superlative ingredients.

Jean Georges	XXXX	341
Le Bernardin	XXXX	251
Per Se	XXXXX	259

Excellent cuisine, worth a detour.

Skillfully and carefully crafted dishes of outsanding quality.

Bouley	XXXX	292
Daniel	XXXXX	310
Del Posto	XXXX	53
Gordon Ramsay at The London	XXXX	247
Masa	XX	253
Picholine	XXXX	345

A very good restaurant in its category.

A place offering cuisine prepared to a consistently high standard.

Annisa	XX	127
Anthos	XXX	233
Aureole	XXX	305
A Voce	XX	101
Babbo	XX	130
Blue Hill	XX	133
Café Boulud	XXX	307
Café Gray	XXX	240
Country	XXXX	108
Cru	XXXX	136
Danube	XXX	294
Dévi	XX	110
Dressler	XX	371
Etats-Unis	X	312
Fleur de Sel	XX	113
Gilt	XXX	203
Gotham Bar and Grill	XXX	141
Gramercy Tavern	XXX	114
Jewel Bako	X	82
JoJo	XX	317
Kurumazushi	X	206
L'Atelier de Joël Robuchon	XX	207
Modern (The)	XXX	255
Oceana	XXX	214
Perry Street	XXX	155
Peter Luger	X	381
Saul	XX	383
Spotted Pig	X	159
Sushi of Gari	X	328
Veritas	XX	123
Vong	XX	227
Wallsé	XX	162
wd~50	XX	183

Bib Gourmand

This symbol indicates our inspector's favorites for good value. For $40 or less, you can enjoy two courses and a glass of wine or a dessert (not including tax or gratuity).

Where to eat for less than $25

Where to have brunch

Where to have a late dinner

Allison M. Simpson / MICHELIN

Peter L. Wrenn/ MICHELIN

Manhattan

Chelsea

Center of New York's art world and gay community, Chelsea is situated west of Avenue of the Americas (Sixth Avenue) between 14th and 30th streets. It's a place of stark contrasts—busy commercial avenues intersect quiet residential side streets, and tiny neighborhood cafes abut gargantuan dance clubs. You'll find restaurants in this eclectic neighborhood cater to a wide range of tastes, from French bistros and old-fashioned Spanish places to sushi bars and authentic Mexican eateries.

Check out **Chelsea Market** *(75 Ninth Ave., between 15th & 16th Sts.; 212-243-6005; www.chelseamarket.com)*. This 1898 Nabisco factory (where the Oreo cookie was first made, in 1912) was reopened in 1997 as an urban food market. Interspersed with stores selling flowers, meats, cheeses and other gourmet essentials are cafes, bakeries, and several soup-and-sandwich shops.

A Bit of History

Chelsea got its name in 1750, when British army captain Thomas Clarke bought a farm here (bounded by 21st and 24th streets, Eighth Avenue and the Hudson River) and named it after his London neighborhood. In 1813 the property passed to Clarke's grandson **Clement Clarke Moore**, a scholar and literary figure best known for writing *A Visit from St. Nicholas* aka *The Night before Christmas*. In the 1820s Moore helped shape the development of the district by setting aside land for park-like squares, giving the neighborhood a distinctly English feel, even as its population increasingly hailed from Germany, Italy, Scotland and Ireland. He also specified that residences had to be set back from the street behind spacious front yards.

The Hudson River Railroad opened along 11th Avenue in 1851, spawning slaughterhouses, breweries and tenements. From about 1905 to 1915, several motion-picture studios operated here. Dock activity along the Hudson River began to decline in the 1960s, opening up warehouses and industrial spaces for new uses. Slowly artists moved in, and town houses began to be refurbished.

Chelsea's Gallery Scene

More than 100 world-class **galleries** now occupy garages and lofts on the district's western flank (concentrated between 20th and 30th streets, west of Tenth Avenue), offering museum-quality exhibitions alongside up-and-coming group shows. Be sure to pick up a **Gallery Guide**, which contains a fold-out map locating all the galleries in the area. The guide also lists opening receptions, a fun way to drink in the scene. On 20th, 21st, and 22nd streets, a lovely **historic district** preserves Clement Clarke Moore's vision of elegant city living in some of Chelsea's loveliest brownstones. While you're in the neighborhood, check out the ever-evolving waterfront area, home to the mammoth Chelsea Piers recreation complex and the Hudson River Greenway.

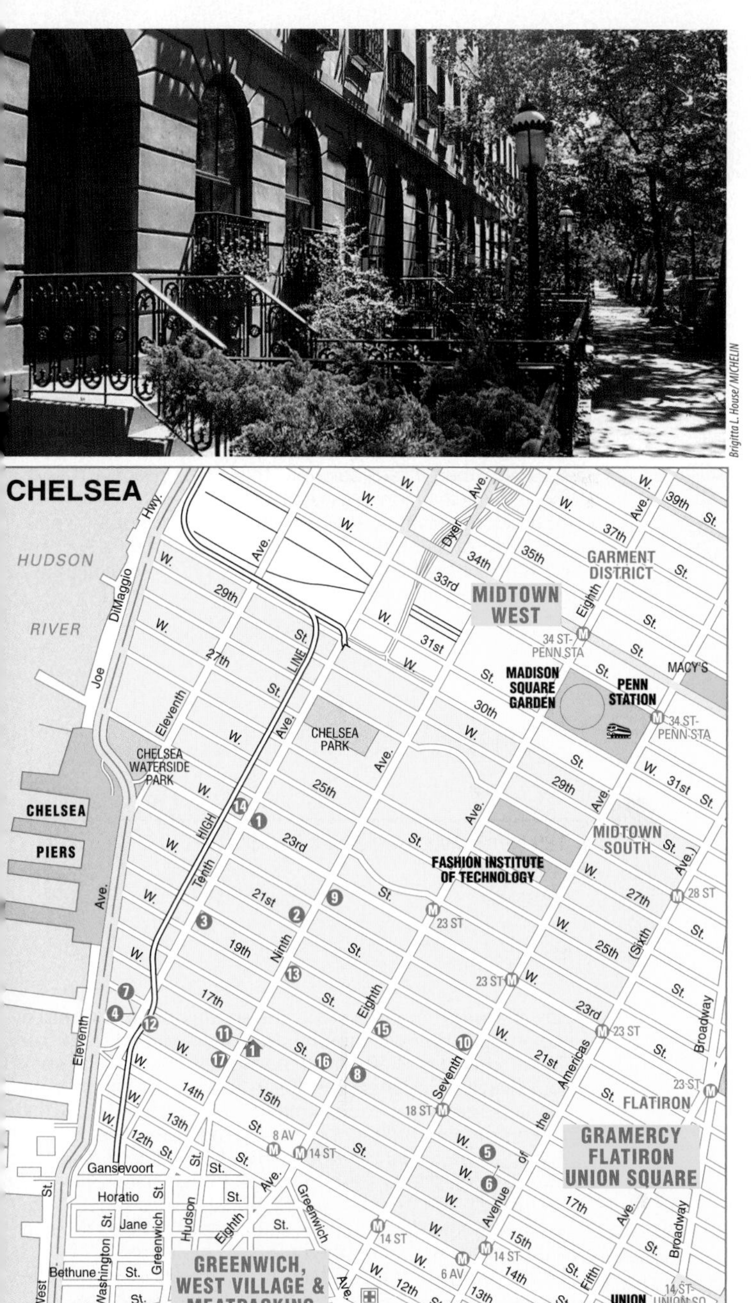

Brigitta L. House/ MICHELIN

Bette

Contemporary XX

001

461 West 23rd St. (bet. Ninth & Tenth Aves.)

Subway: 23 St (Eighth Ave.) — Mon – Sat dinner only
Phone: 212-366-0404
Web: www.betterestaurant.com
Prices: $$$

This stylish low-key setting, hidden away on 23rd Street (look for the apple doorknob), comes alive in the evening. That's no surprise, since owner Amy Sacco is well known as the queen of the New York City nightlife scene. Sacco has decked out her restaurant with pop-style portraits of glamorous women, dark wood wainscoting and sultry lighting. A panel of glass separates the elegant bar from the dining room, lucky for those trying to enjoy a peaceful meal.

At lunch the fashion and publishing crowds come to pick at salads. At night, the Beautiful People pour in to see and be seen while they sample the likes of lobster spaghetti, grilled meats and fish.

Bombay Talkie

Indian X

002

189 Ninth Ave. (bet. 21st & 22nd Sts.)

Subway: 23 St (Eighth Ave.) — Dinner daily
Phone: 212-242-1900
Web: www.bombaytalkie.com
Prices: $$

Street food from India steals the spotlight at this Chelsea restaurant. Owner Sunitha Ramaiah named Bombay Talkie after the 1970 film that inspired her, and Thomas Juul-Hansen designed the dining space accordingly with painted murals of Indian movie stars and an LCD flat screen running Bollywood films in the downstairs bar.

Styled as an Indian teahouse, Bombay Talkie divides its menu into sections dubbed "Street Bites," "Dinner by the Roadside" and "Curbside." Regional dishes range from Kathi rolls and dosas to pork vindaloo. East meets West in a mesmerizing mix on the house cocktails list.

Don't skip dessert here; the delicate flavors of Mariebelle cardamom ganache or carrot halwa will leave you with sweet dreams.

Cookshop

American XX

003

156 Tenth Ave. (at 20th St.)

Subway: 23 St (Eighth Ave.) Lunch & dinner daily
Phone: 212-924-4440
Web: www.cookshopny.com
Prices: $$

This Chelsea spot from the husband-and-wife team behind Five Points, wins rave reviews from a sophisticated crowd. Soft lighting, warm design and closely spaced tables lend an intimate air, while thoughtful service makes regulars out of first-timers.

Large blackboards bearing the daily changing menu highlight the chef's passion for market-fresh products. The roster reads like a geography lesson, with items like Catskill duck, Montauk squid and Vermont quail grouped by cooking method. The wine list offers a fine selection at sensible prices.

Cookshop remains popular as ever for it's delicious cooking, thus reservations suggested—unless you prefer to dine at the bar or one of the bar tables, in which case it's first-come, first-fed.

Craftsteak

Steakhouse 

004

85 Tenth Ave. (at 15th St.)

Subway: 14 St - 8 Av Dinner daily
Phone: 212-400-6699
Web: www.craftsteaknyc.com
Prices: $$$$

Opened in 2006, Craftsteak was yet another addition to Tom Colicchio's growing restaurant empire. A cavernous space on the edge of the Meatpacking District, this urban-chic steakhouse creates a dramatic ambience, complete with a spacious dining room and separate bar and lounge area. Diners from all over come here, and the boho-banker crowd is an attractive one.

The kitchen turns out flawless fare, high in quality and simplicity. Ingredient-focused, the dishes wow foodies, celebrities and fashionistas alike. An extensive raw-bar menu rounds out the first-course selections, while Hawaiian grass-fed Angus beef, corn-fed Hereford and Australian Wagyu beef are main-course standouts. Prices are high, though, so come on an expense account.

Crema

Mexican X

005

111 W. 17th St. (bet. Sixth & Seventh Aves.)

Subway: 18 St — Tue – Sun lunch & dinner
Phone: 212-691-4477
Web: www.cremarestaurante.com
Prices: $$$

Monterrey-born chef Julieta Ballesteros showcases the regional cuisine of her homeland at her newest venture, Crema. Already carrying a loyal following from sibling Mexicana Mama in the West Village, Crema is as artsy as the crowd it draws. Inside, it's pure Mexico City from the colorful décor to the upbeat music. An open kitchen brings the space to life.

Equal parts upscale and casual, vibrant presentations of flavorful dishes show off the chef's creative flair. Choose the spicy grilled scallop tostadas with mango salsa, smooth *empanadas de huitlacoche* or the succulent ribeye with homemade mole. The prix-fixe lunch menu, which includes a choice of soup or salad, an entrée with a side dish and a soft drink, is a particularly good value.

da Umberto

Italian XX

006

107 W. 17th St. (bet. Sixth & Seventh Aves.)

Subway: 18 St — Mon – Fri lunch & dinner
Phone: 212-989-0303
Web: N/A
Prices: $$

There's something to be said for tried and true. Da Umberto's inviting bar and natural-light-filled dining room fill nightly with power brokers and others who often rely on expense accounts. There are no surprises here, but consistently good food and attentive service keep a well-heeled crowd of regulars coming back for more.

Start with a selection from the tantalizing array of antipasti displayed on a rustic wooden table. Then choose among house-made pasta, grilled fish, and meat offerings such as the veal chop or *bistecca alla Fiorentina*, a Porterhouse steak for two. Italian dishes, which stay true to their roots while accommodating American tastes, are complemented by a dizzying list of daily specials.

Del Posto ✿✿

Italian XXXX

007

85 Tenth Ave. (bet. 15th & 16th Sts.)

Subway: 14 St - 8 Av
Phone: 212-497-8090
Web: www.delposto.com
Prices: $$$$

Wed – Fri lunch & dinner
Sat – Tue dinner only

Lydia Gould Bessler

Grand design often acts as a distraction for less-impressive food, but in the case of Del Posto, it's simply a complement. Spacious balconies on three levels overlook the stunning first-floor dining room, while dark paneled walls, exquisite fabrics and glittering chandeliers complete the opulent Old World décor.

A project by the blockbuster partnership between Mario Batali and the Bastianich family, Del Posto was getting press long before it opened, simply because of its provenance. As it turns out, the praise is well deserved—so prepare to be wowed. What may sound rustic on the menu turns out lusciously delicate, from spaghetti with crabmeat, chive blossoms and spicy habañero peppers to notable versions of traditional dishes like young fried chicken cacciatore. Even the wine list impresses with its tremendous spectrum of regional Italian producers and varietals.

Appetizers

- Spaghetti with Spicy Crab, Saffron and Caramelized Shallots
- Garganelli Verdi al Ragù Bolognese
- Risotto with Morels

Entrées

- Veal Chop for Two with Black Trumpets and Watercress
- Cacciucco with Red Mullet and Green Onion Crostino
- Pork Loin with Cipolla Ripiena and Preserved Figs

Desserts

- Chocolate-Caramel Bar, Caramel Popcorn, Salted Caramel Gelato
- Raspberry Millefoglie, Ice Wine Granita, Lychee Sorbet
- Chocolate-Peanut Butter Semifreddo, Toasted Marshmallow

Gascogne

French

008

158 Eighth Ave. (bet. 17th & 18th Sts.)

Subway: 14 St - 8 Av
Phone: 212-675-6564
Web: www.gascognenyc.com
Prices: $$

Tue – Sun lunch & dinner
Mon dinner only

A jewel in the heart of Chelsea, Gascogne sparkles with rustic fare from southwestern France. Fine cassoulet, foie gras and veal kidneys flamed with Armagnac are examples of the carefully prepared dishes. In true French fashion, the bar stocks a good selection of aged Armagnac for after-dinner sipping.

If you're on a budget, go for the prix-fixe pre-theater menu, which is offered all evening on Monday. Weekend brunch is also a good bet, with a set offering that might include rabbit terrine with black truffles, or roast pork loin with white bean ragout. In cold weather, ask for a table by the window overlooking the charming, flower-filled garden—complete with a Christmas tree in season; in summer you can dine outside in this shady space.

Klee Brasserie

Contemporary

009

200 Ninth Ave. (bet. 22nd & 23rd Sts.)

Subway: 23 St (Eighth Ave.)
Phone: 212-633-8033
Web: www.kleebrasserie.com
Prices: $$

Thu – Sun lunch & dinner
Mon – Wed dinner only

Chelsea's new darling, Klee Brasserie fills nightly with Beautiful People, all clad in the latest fashions, down to their designer bags. Playful interiors are simple, yet striking: a mix of warmth and industrial chic. Foodies will enjoy peeking behind the scenes through the big square window that frames the kitchen, while those who prefer to people-watch can use the swivel seats to keep track of who's who in the dining room.

Ranging across the culinary map, the menu steers toward artisan ingredients (Kurobuta pork, Nova Scotia halibut, Wagyu beef) in appealing preparations with heavy Mediterranean accents.

Here's hoping that Klee (meaning "clover" in German) continues to strike the fancy of the denizens of this often fickle neighborhood.

Le Zie 2000

Italian XX

172 Seventh Ave. (bet. 20th & 21st Sts.)

Subway: 23 St (Seventh Ave.) — Lunch & dinner daily
Phone: 212-206-8686
Web: www.lezie.com
Prices: $$

Wholesome is as wholesome does, and Le Zie 2000 does it well. Italy's Veneto culinary region stars in this pastel dining room. Start your meal by sharing the *cicchetti*, an antipasto that includes the likes of sardines in *saor* (a sweet and sour preparation), marinated zucchini, octopus with celery, stuffed fried olives, cod mousse and more—served with grilled polenta, the region's signature starch. Then move on to the hearty homemade pastas or stay in the Venetian vein with traditional calf's liver. Heading the dessert menu is creamy tiramisu, a confection that originated in Venice.

All of Italy's viticultural regions are represented on the wine list, which cites some 200 labels.

Outside, Le Zie's small patio is a fine place to while away a sunny day.

Matsuri

Japanese XX

369 W. 16th St. (bet. Eighth & Ninth Aves.)

Subway: 14 St - 8 Av — Dinner daily
Phone: 212-243-6400
Web: www.themaritimehotel.com
Prices: $$

Matsuri is a place to soak up the scene, and what a scene it is! True to its name ("festival" in Japanese), Matsuri exudes a party vibe. Housed in a cavernous space underneath the Maritime Hotel *(see hotel listing)*, the multilevel dining room is decorated with large Japanese lanterns that hang like bright moons from the dark vaulted ceiling. And the stars are here, too, in a galaxy of celebrities and models who frequent this trendy place.

Sushi and classical Japanese dishes shine with top-quality ingredients—many flown in from Japan—prepared in a way that only emphasizes their flavors. Order a parade of small courses to share, and be sure to sample some of the 200 different types of sake, which include Matsuri's own house brew.

Morimoto

Fusion

012

88 Tenth Ave. (at 16th St.)

Subway: 14 St - 8 Av — Mon – Fri lunch & dinner
Phone: 212-989-8883 — Sat – Sun dinner only
Web: www.morimotonyc.com
Prices: $$$

From the A-list crowd that frequents this hotspot to the kitchen's artful presentations, it's all about looks at Morimoto. Philadelphia restaurateur Stephen Starr bet on New York and built another stage here for Iron Chef Morimoto. The knockout interior design is defined by a large-scale artwork composed of glass bottles that divides the dining room.

Adding to the big-city buzz, the open kitchen turns out innovative, colorful courses peppered by a mix of Japanese, Asian and European influences. Dishes double as eye candy, with a modern panache applied to the cooking method and even more so to the presentations. Every dish that arrives at the table seems to manifest a more dazzling display than the one before it.

Omai

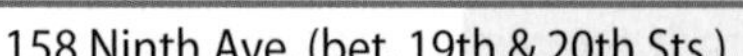

Vietnamese

013

158 Ninth Ave. (bet. 19th & 20th Sts.)

Subway: 23 St (Eighth Ave.) — Dinner daily
Phone: 212-633-0550
Web: www.omainyc.com
Prices: $$

Don't look for a sign to identify this little Chelsea restaurant—there isn't one. Once you find the place, though (look for the pots of bamboo outside), you'll step into a space tastefully underdecorated with Southeast Asian accents.

Vietnamese dishes here manage to be creative while staying true to their roots. Omai's takes on entrées such as roasted duck, jumbo shrimp and sautéed chicken are perfumed with tamarind, curry and coconut, and lemongrass. Want something lighter? The menu offers options from spring rolls to rice and vegetables to noodle dishes. Finish your meal with a tempting dessert, such as the coconut pyramid with tapioca pandan sauce. Hint: avoid the middle row of tables if you don't want to be jostled while you eat.

The Red Cat

Contemporary XX

014

227 Tenth Ave. (bet. 23rd & 24th Sts.)

Subway: 23 St (Eighth Ave.) — Dinner daily
Phone: 212-242-1122
Web: www.theredcat.com
Prices: $$

With its wood-paneled walls, and red-and-white color scheme enlivened by contemporary art, The Red Cat's dining room has a New England-meets-the-big-city air. A stylish crowd adds to the ambience; this is the kind of place you can tell is cool, but not so cool that you'd rather be elsewhere.

Innovative American fare here often includes varying preparations of a sautéed Chatham cod, or a pan-roasted organic chicken. It's the kind of menu that has wide appeal, as the food is creative enough to be unusual, but not so weird that Mom can't enjoy it. A classic example is the lobster and potato chip salad, a highlight of the chef's irreverent culinary style.

The restaurant's location makes it convenient to browsing Chelsea's tony art galleries.

Rocking Horse

Mexican 

015

182 Eighth Ave. (bet. 19th & 20th Sts.)

Subway: 14 St - 8 Av — Lunch & dinner daily
Phone: 212-463-9511
Web: www.rockinghorsecafe.com
Prices: $$

From its elegant design to its upscale cooking, Rocking Horse Cafe is not your run-of-the-mill Mexican restaurant. The sleek dining room is the perfect match for the contemporary Mexican-accented cuisine.

Niman Ranch pork, free-range chicken and fresh vegetables provide the filling for burritos, quesadillas and enchiladas at lunch, while the likes of black tiger prawns with caramelized papaya and poblano chiles, and Chiltepe chile-crusted tuna take the stage at dinner. The house-made guacamole is flavorful and mild, served with warm corn tortilla chips. Save room for the *tres leches* cake, topped with sliced bananas and banana cream.

Snag a seat by the retractable wall and take in the lively street scene while you sip a margarita.

Sueños

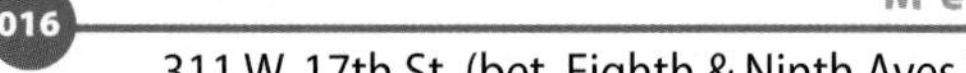

Mexican

016

311 W. 17th St. (bet. Eighth & Ninth Aves.)

Subway: 14 St - 8 Av — Tue – Sun dinner only
Phone: 212-243-1333
Web: www.suenosnyc.com
Prices: $$

Sueños ("dreams" in Spanish) is a literal dream come true for chef/owner Sue Torres. Formerly of Rocking Horse Cafe, also in Chelsea, Torres supervises the kitchen and the dining room at this restaurant, which is tucked away down an alley.

There's nothing timid about the place; from the brightly painted magenta and orange brick walls to the bold chile tasting menu, Sueños celebrates the best of Mexico. Dining spaces center on a glass-enclosed patio, complete with a fountain and flowers. This place has a festive spirit, with flavor-packed signatures like tequila-flamed rock shrimp with avocado and black bean salad, and fun "make your own taco and tostado" menus. Do try this at home, but not before you attend cooking classes in the restaurant.

202

Contemporary

017

75 Ninth Ave. (bet. 15th & 16th Sts.)

Subway: 14 St - 8 Av — Tue – Sun lunch & dinner, Mon lunch only
Phone: 646-638-1173
Web: N/A
Prices: $$

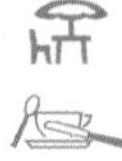

Set in Chelsea Market, 202 gives shoppers in the Nicole Farhi boutique a respite from difficult fashion decisions (Black skirt or blue?). Grab a table—there's no separation between shop and restaurant—and order a guiltless tuna burger, bright fish tacos, or a crisp seasonal salad. While these dishes are shopping-friendly, there is enough hearty fare on the menu—created by British chef Annie Wayte—to satisfy more ravenous appetites. And if you felt any angst over the crispy fish and chips you inhaled, by the time you finish that last luscious bite of chocolate pot de crème, you'll wonder why you ever fretted over such a silly thing.

Sister to Nicole's in Midtown *(10 E. 60th St.)*, 202 offers a classy vibe and service sans attitude.

ROEDERER
en 1776

Chinatown & Little Italy

As different as chow mein and chicken cacciatore, these two districts are nonetheless neighbors. In recent years, their borders have become blurred, with Chinatown gulping up large parts of Little Italy.

CHINATOWN

Sprawling Chinatown is a veritable city within a city. Markets here stock everything from lychee to lipstick, while storefront restaurants serve up 20 distinct Asian cuisines in more than 200 restaurants. Especially crowded on weekends, the area marked by pagoda-roofed buildings bursts its seams at **Chinese New Year** (first full moon after January 19), when dragons dance down the streets accompanied by costumed revelers and fireworks.

The first Chinese came to New York in the 1870s from the California goldfields or from jobs building the transcontinental railroad. In 1943, following the repeal of the 1882 Chinese Exclusion Act, a new influx of immigrants arrived in New York. They set up garment factories, Chinese laundries, shops and restaurants in the quarter, which has inexorably spread into Little Italy and the Lower East Side.

Today Manhattan's Chinatown holds one of the largest Chinese immigrant communities outside Asia. Mulberry and Mott streets teem with shops and food markets, the latter hawking exotic items like duck eggs and durian fruit. When you get hungry, head for Mott Street, and be sure to experience dim sum—a multicourse meal of small buns, pastries, dumplings and more, served from rolling carts.

LITTLE ITALY

Little Italy, which once ran from Canal Street north to Houston and from Lafayette Street west to the Bowery, may now be more aptly called Micro Italy. Mulberry Street is the main drag and the tenacious heart of the neighborhood, which is quickly being swallowed up by Chinatown. The onetime stronghold of Manhattan's Italian-American population has dwindled to a mere corridor—Mulberry Street between Canal and Broome streets—that caters mainly to hungry tourists, though you can still find some authentic delis, bakeries and gelato shops in the quarter. Devotees still frequent Mulberry Street for authentic Italian fare, then walk down to Ferrara's bakery *(195 Grand St.)* for Italian pastries and a cup of strong espresso.

On weekends from May to mid-October Mulberry Street is closed to vehicular traffic, making Little Italy one big alfresco party—the **Feast of San Gennaro** in mid-September is particularly raucous. Although these days, you can get better Italian food elsewhere in the city, you still can't beat the ambience on Mulberry Street.

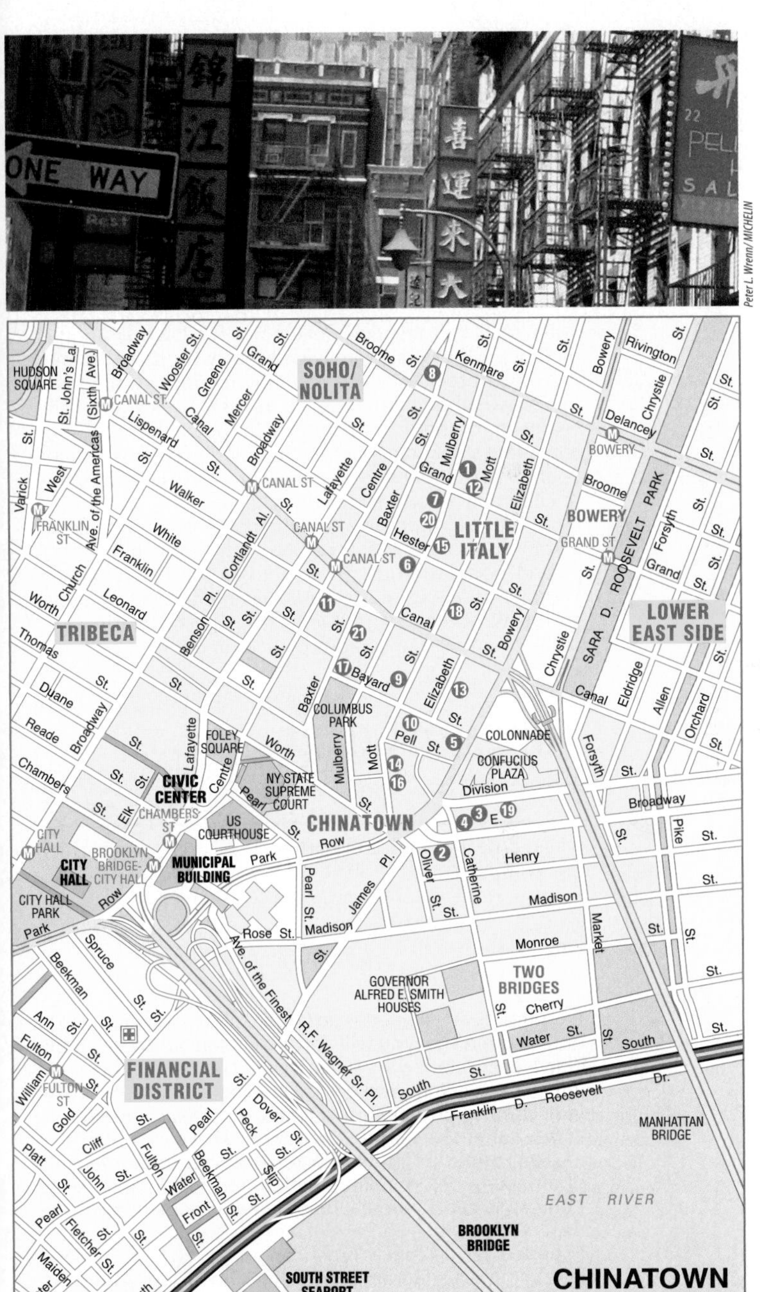

Peter L. Wrenn/ MICHELIN

Da Nico

001  Italian

164 Mulberry St. (bet. Broome & Grand Sts.)

Subway: Canal St (Lafayette St.) — Lunch & dinner daily
Phone: 212-343-1212
Web: www.danicorest.com
Prices: $$

Sister to Il Palazzo and Pellegrino, Da Nico is another member of the Luizza family's Mulberry Street restaurants. Although the interior was recently refurbished, the place to sit—weather permitting—is on the back patio. This enclosed outdoor terrace, which nearly doubles the restaurant's seating space in summer, provides a quiet, countryside ambience, seemingly far from the commotion of Little Italy's commercial thoroughfare.

From the coal-fired pizza oven come a variety of pizzas, all of which are made using a crust recipe that has been passed down through generations of the Luizza family. Shrimp *fra diavolo*, calamari Luciana, chicken cacciatore and steak Fiorentina—not to mention pasta and risotto—number among the copious choices at dinner.

Dim Sum Go Go

002 Chinese

5 East Broadway (at Chatham Sq.)

Subway: Canal St (Lafayette St.) — Lunch & dinner daily
Phone: 212-732-0797
Web: N/A
Prices: ⊖⊖

Despite the name, you won't find dancers in white go-go boots here. What you will find is a simple but comfortable place decorated with sleek metal chairs and red voile lining the ceiling. Servers offer good advice about the vast number of dim sum choices, which are served à la carte, rather than from steam carts. That fact makes this a good restaurant to introduce neophytes to the delights of dim sum, before taking them to more authentic Hong Kong-style spots where it helps to know something about the cuisine.

Founded by French-American food writer Colette Rossant, this restaurant serves dim sum all day. There are 24 different types of dumplings alone here; go for the dim sum platter if you want a well-priced sampling.

Fuleen Seafood

Chinese

11 Division St. (bet. Catherine & Market Sts.)

Subway: Canal St (Lafayette St.)

Lunch & dinner daily

Phone: 212-941-6888

Web: N/A

Prices:

If you fancy Chinese food, you won't dig up a better lunch special in Chinatown—or perhaps all of Manhattan—than the lunch deal (daily from 11am to 3pm) at Fuleen Seafood. Less than $5 here buys your choice of an entrée, and they throw in rice and soup on the house. It seems unbelievable, but the locals and those on break from jury duty at the nearby courthouse, who crowd the large, round tables here, know where to go for a good filling meal for an incredibly low price. The long list of main courses offers something for everyone: seafood, shellfish, chicken, beef, pork and vegetable dishes.

The simple décor is typically no frills, but the patrons who come here for good food at a good value aren't looking for hip styling or a cool crowd.

Golden Unicorn

Chinese

18 East Broadway (at Catherine St.)

Subway: Canal St (Lafayette St.)

Lunch & dinner daily

Phone: 212-941-0911

Web: N/A

Prices: $$

You enter the Golden Unicorn through a commercial building in the underbelly of eastern Chinatown. If it's a weekend, you'll have to elbow your way through the mob to get a number from the woman who runs the show. When she calls your number, she'll direct you to take the elevator to either the second or third floor, where you're in for a dim sum treat at lunch.

Family-size tables leave just enough space for the waitstaff to roll carts of delectable little jewels past each diner. Choose from a mouthwatering array of shrimp and leek dumplings, shu mai, barbecue pork buns, crispy duck, and more. Just don't fill up before your favorites have wheeled your way. Dinner brings Cantonese fare, but it's the dim sum that really packs 'em in.

Great N.Y. Noodletown

005 **Chinese**

28 Bowery (at Bayard St.)

Subway: Canal St (Lafayette St.) — Lunch & dinner daily
Phone: 212-349-0923
Web: N/A
Prices:

If you're looking for fancy décor or friendly service, keep on walking. But if it's tasty, inexpensive Chinese food you seek, at almost any hour, stop right here. Great N.Y. Noodletown is a casual place: the menu is displayed under the pane of glass that tops the tables, they don't serve beer, and they only take cash.
Although noodles dominate the menu (get them pan-fried, Cantonese-style or in Hong Kong-style lo mein), they aren't the high point of the menu. There's also a choice of salt-baked dishes—the soft-shell crab being one of the better choices—and best of all are the barbecued meats that you can see hanging in the restaurant's window. Roast duck and pork are fantastic here, and the prices are unbelievably low.

Il Cortile

006 **Italian**

125 Mulberry St. (bet. Canal & Hester Sts.)

Subway: Canal St (Lafayette St) — Lunch & dinner daily
Phone: 212-226-6060
Web: www.ilcortile.com
Prices: $$

Several dining rooms at Il Cortile each have their own ambience, but the most pleasant space is the airy garden room (*il cortile* is Italian for "courtyard"), more like an atrium with its glass-paneled ceiling, brick walls and abundant greenery. Statues may be plentiful here, but this restaurant's décor is among the most restrained in this often over-the-top neighborhood.
Chef Michael DeGeorgio presents a wide array of pastas, meat and seafood dishes, including his *ragù del Macellaio,* a rich tomato sauce simmered like *nonna* used to make with pork, meatballs, braciola and sausage—offered only on Sundays. More than 30 years of sharing family recipes have made Il Cortile a favorite of city politicians, neighbors and tourists.

Il Palazzo

007

Italian XX

151 Mulberry St. (bet. Grand & Hester Sts.)

Subway: Canal St (Lafayette St.)

Lunch & dinner daily

Phone: 212-343-7000

Web: N/A

Prices: $$

Located on Little Italy's main thoroughfare, Il Palazzo dishes up authentic Italian fare to a host of regulars, especially at dinnertime. The main dining room recalls a winter garden with its flowering plants and well-spaced tables, while the menu lists a generous and varied selection of Old World classics such as veal saltimbocca, chicken cacciatore, rigatoni alla vodka, linguine with clam sauce, and shrimp scampi. The specials are the reason to come here, though, so be sure to check with your server as to the day's additions.

If you just can't eat another bite at the end of your meal, you can always skip the sweet course and end your meal with a glass of potent grappa or smooth vintage port instead.

La Esquina

Mexican 

008

106 Kenmare St. (bet. Cleveland Pl. & Mulberry St.)

Subway: Spring St (Lafayette St.)

Lunch & dinner daily

Phone: 646-613-7100

Web: N/A

Prices: $$

Given all the hype La Esquina received, it's remarkable that the food is as good as it is. This trendy spot divides its space and parcels its cool clientele into three distinct dining sections, each sharing the same kitchen. The first is a take-out window with sidewalk seating, the second a cozy corner cafe, and the third a lively subterranean dining room (open for dinner only) that requires booking well in advance.

The latter is still perpetually packed, since La Esquina remains a hotspot. Now, though, the buzz has calmed a bit and the food can finally take center stage, where it deserves to be. Flavors from the kitchen are carefully balanced; the cocktails are tasty, and desserts are influenced by the fruits of the season.

Mandarin Court

009 — Chinese

61 Mott St. (bet. Bayard & Canal Sts.)

Subway: Canal St (Lafayette St.) — Lunch & dinner daily
Phone: 212-608-3838
Web: N/A
Prices: 

Dim sum is not just for weekend brunch anymore. At Mandarin Court, dim sum is served every day from 8am to 4pm. The presentation is Hong Kong-style; the waitresses roll carts full of dumplings, buns, wontons and other savories past your table so you can take your pick. There's even sweet dim sum for dessert (egg custard; coconut-flavored gelatin; sesame ball).

If you're really hungry, try one of the entrées, which include steaming bowls of broth brimming with noodles, vegetables, meat or seafood. The dining room may not look like much, and it may be a bit noisy with your neighbors a little too close for comfort, but the regulars don't come here for the atmosphere. They're attracted by good Cantonese fare at reasonable prices.

New Yeah Shanghai

010 — Chinese

65 Bayard St. (at Mott St.)

Subway: Canal St (Lafayette St.) — Mon – Fri lunch & dinner
Phone: 212-566-4884 — Sat – Sun dinner only
Web: N/A
Prices:

Just off the bustle of Bayard Street in the heart of Chinatown, New Yeah Shanghai offers a taste of its namesake city. Live plants, arched ceilings and Asian decorative accents lend a cave-like, Pacific Rim feel to this otherwise casual restaurant. Decision-making may be difficult here, where an extensive menu features Shanghai favorites, dumplings galore, all sorts of noodles and many daily specials, as well as seasonal items created specifically for holidays throughout the year. The carefully cooked food is served as promptly as it is prepared by the capable staff, and the large portions are ideal for family-style gatherings (with leftovers to go).

New Yeah Shanghai's loyal crowd of regulars, locals and tourists feel equally at home here.

Nha Trang Centre

Vietnamese

011

148 Centre St. (bet. Walker & White Sts.)

Subway: Canal St (Lafayette St.) Lunch & dinner daily
Phone: 212-941-9292
Web: N/A
Prices: ⊜

Amid a clutch of Vietnamese restaurants in Chinatown, Nha Trang Centre draws a loyal crowd from nearby City Hall. They judge the assortment of *pho*—the beloved Vietnamese noodle soup—the crispy pork spring rolls, and the wealth of seafood, beef, chicken and pork specialties on the extensive bill of fare to be some of the best around. Preparations are authentic; portions are copious, and prices are low enough to get out for under $15 at lunch. For aficionados of this type of cuisine, a special menu section devotes itself to traditional Vietnamese dishes, including barbecued beef, crispy squid, and frogs' legs. The jury's still out regarding the ambience, but the staff makes up for any aesthetic weakness with speedy and pleasant service.

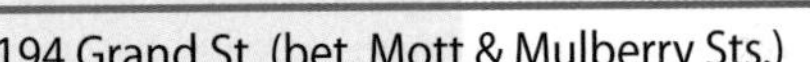

Nyonya

Malaysian

012

194 Grand St. (bet. Mott & Mulberry Sts.)

Subway: Canal St (Lafayette St.) Lunch & dinner daily
Phone: 212-334-3669
Web: N/A
Prices: ⊜

$

Now for something completely different: Malaysian food in Little Italy. A surprising addition to the neighborhood's red-sauce joints, Nyonya is worth seeking out for unique dishes at prices that won't blow your budget. A fusion cuisine that resulted from the intermarriage of Chinese and Malaysians in order to strengthen early trade ties between the two countries, Nyonya (a word that refers to the woman in such a marriage) pairs traditional Chinese ingredients with Malay herbs and spices.
You're bound to find something you like on the extensive menu, which lists everything from Nyonya seafood rice noodles to curried pork spareribs. Even dessert is interesting with dishes like *pulut hitam*, a sweet treat made from black rice and coconut milk.

Oriental Garden

013 — Chinese 

14 Elizabeth St. (bet. Bayard & Canal Sts.)

Subway: Canal St (Lafayette St.) — Lunch & dinner daily
Phone: 212-619-0085
Web: N/A
Prices: ⊜

You'll know what the food focus is here as soon as you walk through the door. On either side of the entrance, two aquarium tanks swim with live fish and lobsters, awaiting your order (actually, they may not be anticipating it quite so fondly, since they're the ones that will soon be on the plate).

Adventurous palates are rewarded here, where barbecued eel on a stick is one of the intriguing selections. If you're not a fish lover, there are plenty of other dishes on the menu, including an extensive selection of classic Chinese fare. The walls of the room are lined with framed Chinese characters, the service is attentive, and the place is always hopping. Just be sure to bring cash; Oriental Garden doesn't accept credit cards for bills under $60.

Peking Duck House

014 — Chinese XX

28 Mott St. (bet. Chatham Sq. & Pell St.)

Subway: Canal St (Lafayette St) — Mon – Fri lunch & dinner, Sat – Sun dinner only
Phone: 212-227-1810
Web: www.pekingduckhousenyc.com
Prices: $$

Round up a few friends and go for the specialty of the house—you guessed it: Peking Duck. The slow-roasted duck comes out juicy inside with pleasingly crispy skin, and it's a surefire crowd pleaser (the dish, which consists of a whole duck or the traditional mulitcourse meal, is better enjoyed by two or more). In ceremonial fashion, the chef slices the bird tableside and serves it with house-made pancakes, scallions, cucumbers and hoisin sauce.

Don't care for duck? There's a full roster of other selections, from Szechuan-style prawns to "volcano" steak, flamed with Grand Marnier. Those who want a similar dining experience outside Chinatown should visit the restaurant's Midtown sister *(236 E. 53rd St.)*.

Pellegrino's

Italian

015

138 Mulberry St. (bet. Grand & Hester Sts.)

Subway: Canal St (Lafayette St) — Lunch & dinner daily
Phone: 212-226-3177
Web: N/A
Prices: $$

On a warm summer day, the view from one of Pellegrino's sidewalk tables takes in the heart of Little Italy. You're likely to find a good number of out-of-towners here, since the long, narrow dining room is attractive, the umbrella-shaded outdoor tables are inviting and the service is courteous. Children are welcome at Pellegrino's; in fact, the restaurant offers half-portions for smaller appetites.
The food, which stays true to its roots in sunny Italy, includes a balanced selection of pasta, meat and fish. Linguini alla Sinatra, the signature dish named for the beloved crooner, abounds with lobster, shrimp, clams, mushrooms and pine nuts in red sauce. Large portions of tasty food make Pellegrino's a good value in this touristy neighborhood.

Ping's

Chinese

016

22 Mott St. (bet. Chatham Sq. & Pell St.)

Subway: Canal St (Lafayette St) — Lunch & dinner daily
Phone: 212-602-9988
Web: N/A
Prices: ©©

Discreet Asian décor highlights this hectic yet fun place in the middle of Chinatown. The menu, as overseen by chef/owner Chuen Ping Hui, offers tremendous variety and concentrates on Hong Kong-style dishes characterized by their light sauces and simple preparations. You can't go wrong with the seafood (stack of tanks near the entrance display a variety of sea creatures) paired with black-bean, garlic-ginger or pungent XO sauce; or the tender, juicy, roasted poultry dishes, such as Ping's crispy chicken. Prices are very reasonable given the quality of the cuisine, and generous portions are meant for sharing, family-style.
A second location in Queens *(8302 Queens Blvd., Flushing)* proves that Ping's has a recipe for success.

Pongsri Thai

017 — Thai

106 Bayard St. (at Baxter St.)

Subway: Canal St (Lafayette St.) — Lunch & dinner daily
Phone: 212-349-3132
Web: N/A
Prices: ¢¢

Popular at lunchtime with the City Hall crowd, Pongsri Thai (also known as Thailand Restaurant, per the sign out front), serves up a taste of traditional Thai cuisine with its hot, sour, sweet and tangy elements. The value at midday is good, and the service is speedy. Fish choices run the gamut from spicy fried whole fish to steamed mussels; for vegetarians, there's a wide selection of vegetable curries, as well as noodle dishes. To whet your appetite, try the traditional soups and salads or sample some of the extensive array of appetizers.

While the Chinatown location is the longstanding original, there are two additional outposts in Manhattan: in the Theater District at 244 West 48th Street, and in Gramercy at 311 Second Avenue.

Shanghai Café

018 — Chinese

100 Mott St. (bet. Canal & Hester Sts.)

Subway: Canal St (Lafayette St.) — Lunch & dinner daily
Phone: 212-966-3988
Web: N/A
Prices: ¢¢

Head to this Chinatown cafe when you're craving good Shanghai-style cuisine at a fair price in a pleasing, contemporary setting. Dumpling assemblers add these little gems to the enormous steamers in the front window, beckoning diners for an authentic meal.

The enormous menu cites a decision-defying array of dim sum, soups, noodles and rice dishes. Standouts are the tiny, succulent soup buns. Filled with crabmeat and/or pork, these juicy little jewels explode with flavor in your mouth. A hands-down favorite, "steamed tiny buns," as the menu calls them, appear in steamer baskets on nearly every occupied table. Once you taste them, you'll agree that Shanghai Café ranks a bun above the usual Chinese fare on this stretch of Mott Street.

Sunrise 27

Chinese XX

019

27 Division St. (bet. Catherine & Market Sts.)

Subway: Canal St (Lafayette St.) — Lunch & dinner daily
Phone: 212-219-8498
Web: N/A
Prices: ⊜

Large windows face the street at Sunrise 27, beckoning diners into this understated restaurant, where golden dragons sprawl across a screen at the back of the room.

At lunch, you have a choice of the regular menu or the cart of tempting dim sum. For dinner, you'll be hard-pressed to decide among the pages of offerings, which include casseroles filled with the likes of fresh frog with ginger and scallions, or sliced eel. Several chicken dishes (salt-baked or crispy fried) are offered as half or whole portions, catering to a variety of appetites.

The pleasant waitstaff is well-organized, always accessible and thoughtful, providing hot towels between messy courses for guests who can't get enough of the deliciously sweet and sticky sauces.

Taormina

Italian XX

020

147 Mulberry St. (bet. Grand & Hester Sts.)

Subway: Canal St (Lafayette St.) — Lunch & dinner daily
Phone: 212-219-1007
Web: N/A
Prices: $$

Named for a scenic resort town that towers above the sea on the east coast of Sicily, Taormina remains one of the few culinary strongholds of the city's disappearing Little Italy. The restaurant's contemporary style showcases exposed brick, light varnished woods and a windowed façade overlooking Mulberry Street. Taormina's elegant ambience makes it a good alternative to the sensory overload experienced at most of the competition.

Pastas like pappardelle with porcini and *linguine della casa* (tossed with shellfish, calamari and garlic in a fresh tomato sauce) are homemade and offer an authentic taste of *Italia*. There's a tempting selection of antipasti, and the balanced menu nods to its namesake with a good array of seafood offerings.

Thai So'n

021 Vietnamese

89 Baxter St. (bet. Bayard & Canal Sts.)

Subway: Canal St (Lafayette St.)

Lunch & dinner daily

Phone: 212-732-2822

Web: N/A

Prices: ⊜

Set on busy Baxter Street, Thai So'n is known in the neighborhood for serving high-quality Vietnamese fare at a great value. The place has a dining-hall-like atmosphere and comfort is minimal, but that's not why folks come here. They come for the contrasting flavors and textures that form the basis of the the huge menu of flavorful cuisine, which incorporates fresh vegetables, fiery peppers, and herbs like basil, coriander, mint and lemongrass. If it's cold out, try a steaming bowl of *pho* (beef or chicken broth full of rice noodles and your choice of other ingredients) to chase away the chill.
The casual atmosphere makes this spot a prime choice for groups or families dining with children; takeout and delivery are also available.

East Village

The neighborhood bounded by 14th and Houston streets, and Bowery and the East River is the center of alternative culture in New York—rock concerts, poetry readings, and Off-Off Broadway theater productions take place here nightly. Not only does the East Village have a highly developed cafe culture, it's also one of the best places in the city to shop for used books and records and vintage clothes. In general the East Village caters to a very young crowd—almost all the cafes, bars and boutiques attract patrons in their twenties and thirties who, if they're not living on a limited budget, like to pretend they are.

A Bit of History

In 1651 **Peter Stuyvesant**, the Dutch-born director-general of the New Netherland colony, purchased the land bounded by today's 17th Street, 5th Street, Fourth Avenue, and the East River from the Indians for use as a farm. After surrendering to the English in 1664, Stuyvesant withdrew from public affairs and moved to his manor house on present-day Stuyvesant Street.

Briefly in the early 1800s, the district west of Second Avenue boasted fashionable town houses, home to a social elite that included **John Jacob Astor**, the fur-trade and real-estate magnate who helped develop the surrounding neighborhood starting in 1825, and railroad tycoon **"Commodore" Cornelius Vanderbilt**. The working-class neighborhoods farther east were home to Polish, Ukrainian and German immigrants until the early 20th century. The term "East Village" was coined in the early 1960s to distinguish the neighborhood from the rest of the Lower East Side. The glory days of the East Village were the 1980s, when rock bands like the B-52's, the Talking Heads, and the Ramones made names for themselves at the legendary club CBGB & OMFUG (a.k.a. Country, Bluegrass, Blues and Other Music for Uplifting Gourmandizers).

A Taste of East Village

The East Village today contains vestiges of almost all chapters of its history. Laid out in 1834, ten-acre **Tompkins Square Park**, sits roughly at the center of the village. Its 150-year-old elms, flowers and fountains, make the park one of downtown Manhattan's most attractive public spaces. Most of the village's side streets are lined by 19th-century brownstones, spiffed-up tenements, and lush trees. **St. Mark's Place** is the most densely commercial street in the East Village, drawing hordes of students and hippies to its sushi bars, jewelry and sunglass stalls, record stores and head shops. **Second Avenue** is really the district's spine. Here you'll find an astounding variety of ethnic eateries—Italian, Russian, Korean, Thai, Jewish and Mexican among them. Sixth Street between First and Second avenues is known as **Little India** for the many super-cheap Indian and Bangladeshi restaurants that line the block.

Amy Moskowitz/ MICHELIN

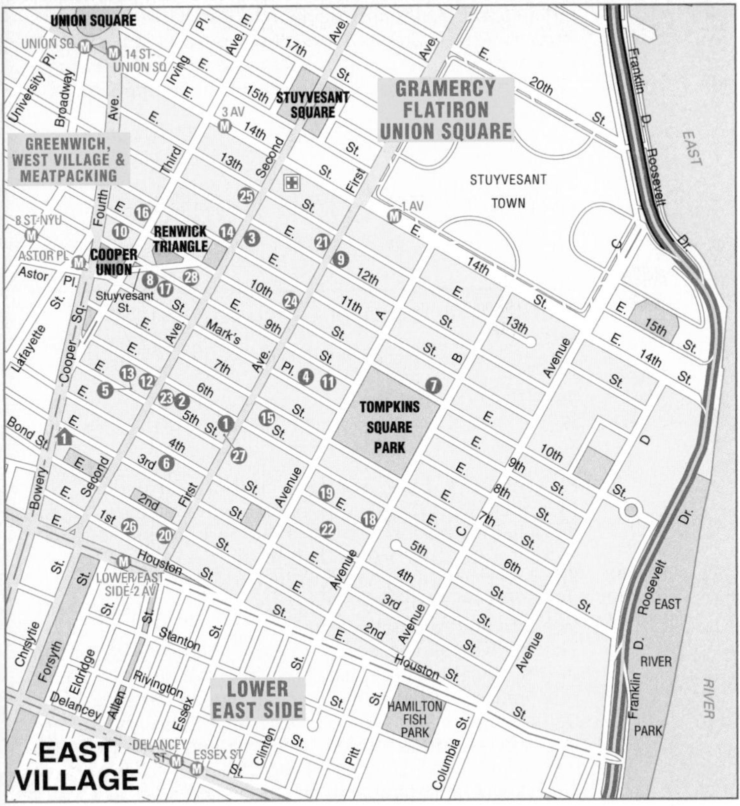

EAST VILLAGE

Banjara

001 **Indian**

97 First Ave. (at 6th St.)

Subway: Lower East Side - 2 Av — Lunch & dinner daily
Phone: 212-477-5956
Web: www.banjarany.com
Prices: $$

Named for the Banjara gypsy tribe of Eastern India, this restaurant stands out among the numerous other Indian eateries that mark this Little India section of the East Village. Banjara isn't flashy like most of its Curry Row competition; the dining room is decorated with fresh flowers and rich-hued Indian tapestries gracing the back wall of the bar area and creating an exotic ambience.

Spices add robust flavor, but Banjara eschews the heavy-handed fiery spicing sometimes found in other nearby Indian spots. Authentic regional dishes fill the menu here, from clay-oven-fired tandooris to *dumpakht*, a traditional stew that is sealed in its cooking vessel under a dome of pastry (think of it as the aromatic Indian version of a potpie).

Brick Lane Curry House

002 **Indian**

306-308 E. 6th St. (bet. First & Second Aves.)

Subway: Astor Pl — Lunch & dinner daily
Phone: 212-979-2900
Web: www.bricklanecurryhouse.com
Prices: $$

Fans of Brick Lane, London's historic Curry Row, will love this East Village curry house, which stands out for its delicious northern Indian food and gracious service. Nods to the Brits are evident in the décor—brick walls lined with charming London metro signs—as well as in the selection of perfectly tapped and poured brews, sure to warm any Anglophile's heart.

The kitchen allows guests to take liberties with Indian dishes, mixing and matching ingredients in classic preparations. For instance, you can request *tikka masala*—traditionally made with chicken—with shrimp, tofu or vegetables instead. Curries, *saag*, and tandoori entrées can be similarly altered. Excellent yogurt-based *lassi* provides a cooling accompaniment to any of the fiery dishes.

Cacio e Pepe

Italian 

182 Second Ave. (bet. 11th & 12th Sts.)

Subway: 3 Av — Dinner daily
Phone: 212-505-5931
Web: www.cacioepepe.com
Prices: $$

Lower Second Avenue has its share of Italian restaurants, but this one is worth seeking out. Run by a Roman expatriate, Cacio e Pepe focuses on Roman regional specialties, presenting a generous variety of choices on its seasonally changing menu. For example, the signature Tonnarelli Cacio e Pepe combines house-made tonnarelli tossed in pasta water, olive oil, abundant pecorino cheese and cracked black pepper; the dish is presented in a hollowed-out pecorino wheel. The wine list is short but carefully selected to highlight less-familiar producers in the most notable Italian regions.

In warm weather, the garden behind the restaurant makes a perfectly lovely setting for dinner. Any time of year, expect service that is warm and attentive.

Café Mogador

Moroccan 

101 St. Mark's Pl. (bet. First Ave. & Ave. A)

Subway: 1 Av — Lunch & dinner daily
Phone: 212-677-2226
Web: www.cafemogador.com
Prices: 

In the heart of East Village, Café Mogador adds a North African note to the neighborhood's ethnic restaurant mix. Moorish lanterns, jars of spices and black-and-white photographs of Morocco lend an exotic air to this little cafe, where prices are approachable and service is cheerful and attentive.

A staple of Moroccan cuisine, couscous is interpreted here with an array of veggies (turnips, carrots, cabbage, zucchini and pumpkin) and topped with chickpeas, onions and raisins. Traditional *bastilla* fills layers of crispy filo with shredded chicken, eggs, almonds and cinnamon, and *tagines* (meat, poultry or lamb stewed with fruit or vegetables) are always popular. The menu adds hints of the Mediterranean with the likes of hummus and charmoula.

Degustation

005 — **Spanish**

239 E. 5th St. (bet. Second & Third Aves.)

Subway: Astor Pl — Mon – Sat dinner only
Phone: 212-979-1012
Web: N/A
Prices: $$

Jack and Grace Lamb have done it again with Degustation. This contemporary spot in the grungy-hip East Village (next door to the Lambs' Jewel Bako) is not your average tapas bar. Leave it to the Lambs to marry unusual flavors and textures with European and Asian influences.
Dimly lit, the tiny space with its slate-lined walls has an industrial-chic feel. The kitchen takes center stage, and the 16 seats all cozy up to a counter around it. Here the chef prepares such tongue-tantalizing dishes as tortillas with shallot confit and quail egg, crispy pork belly with hon shimeji mushrooms, and squid stuffed with braised short ribs. Dessert is equally inventive, boasting the likes of blowtorch-grilled strawberries, ginger granita and basil-mint foam.

Euzkadi

006 — **Basque**

108 E. 4th St. (bet. First & Second Aves.)

Subway: Lower East Side - 2 Av — Dinner daily
Phone: 212-982-9788
Web: www.euzkadirestaurant.com
Prices: $$

Haven't heard of Euzkadi? Maybe you've been living in a cave. While some restaurants dish out great food but disappoint in the décor department, this one-of-a-kind place delivers both. With textured, exposed walls painted with prehistoric-style cave drawings, thick velvet curtains shutting out all sunlight, and soft low lighting, diners can be cave dwellers—even if just for the evening. This cocoon-like restaurant is a great find, despite its cramped quarters.
Of course, no caveman ever ate this well. The menu covers all the bases of traditional Basque cooking, including tapas and the house specialty, *paella Mariscos*. Loaded with fish and shellfish, and redolent of saffron, the paella comes sized for two in a traditional cast-iron pan.

Gnocco

007 Italian

337 E. 10th St. (bet. Aves. A & B)

Subway: 1 Av — Mon – Fri dinner only
Phone: 212-677-1913 — Sat – Sun lunch & dinner
Web: www.gnocco.com
Prices: $$

Gnocco's decidedly comfortable, light-filled front room with its brick walls and paintings of oversize Georgia O'Keefe-style flowers makes this a popular neighborhood hangout. Floor-to-ceiling windows overlook Tompkins Square Park, while the shady back terrace with its vine-covered walls is a great place to sit in nice weather.

Don't leave without sampling the signature gnocco, crispy deep-fried pillows of dough served with thin slices of prosciutto di Parma and coppa. Well-executed homemade pastas, including the more familiar gnocchi, make a fitting first course; then there's a small selection of meat and fish dishes. If you don't have room for dessert, the cantucci accompanied by a glass of *vin santo* makes a light ending to the meal.

Hasaki

008 Japanese

210 E. 9th St. (bet. Second & Third Aves.)

Subway: Astor Pl — Wed – Sun lunch & dinner
Phone: 212-473-3327 — Mon – Tue dinner only
Web: N/A
Prices: $$

On weekends, you'll recognize this sushi bar by the line that snakes out the door onto the sidewalk. Hasaki doesn't take reservations, but that doesn't seem to deter the devotees of this little place. The lively sushi bar is where the action is; step up and see what all the fuss is about.

Sashimi (buttery yellowtail, King crab, tuna—not to mention the list of daily specials) is carefully presented and served with soba noodles, a bowl of rice and the requisite wasabi and pickled ginger. Ocean trout carpaccio and fried softshell crab are among the newest additions to the menu. Aside from sashimi and sushi, the menu offers tempura, chicken teriyaki and grilled salmon, among other cooked selections—all at prices that won't break the budget.

Hearth

009 **Mediterranean** XX

403 E. 12th St. (at First Ave.)

Subway: 1 Av — Dinner daily
Phone: 646-602-1300
Web: www.restauranthearth.com
Prices: $$$

A joint venture by chef Marco Canora and partner Paul Grieco, Hearth emphasizes Mediterranean-inspired cuisine (the chef's family has roots in Tuscany) on its tempting seasonal menu. If you're lucky enough to grab one of the handful of stools that overlook the well-run, open kitchen, you'll have the pleasure of watching your meal being prepared. Hearth's market-driven menu changes with each season and features premium organic ingredients prepared elegantly, but with little fuss. Even hard-core oenophiles will get a chuckle out of the wine list here; furnishing an amusing education in varietals, the list is worth reading for its descriptions alone.
Members of the engaging and professional staff not only aim to please, they succeed in doing so.

Hiro

010 **Japanese** X

84 E. 10th St. (bet. Third & Fourth Aves.)

Subway: Astor Pl — Mon – Sat lunch & dinner
Phone: 212-420-6189 — Sun dinner only
Web: www.hironyc.com
Prices: ⊜

Sushi reigns at Hiro. This relaxed East Village Japanese place has simple interiors with slate floors, redwood furnishings and Asian accents. The focus here is on the sushi bar, manned by several chefs. The polite staff ensures that guests are always satisfied, and reasonable prices and a laid-back attitude entice both professionals and students from nearby NYU (who tend to take their sushi to go).
Hiro offers a wide selection of typical Japanese dishes, such as tempura and teriyaki, along with specialty sushi rolls displaying creative combinations not often found in similar restaurants. Bento boxes are also available at lunch or dinner, but with the unique maki, colorful presentations and large portions, sushi is the main attraction here.

Itzocan

Mexican

011

438 E. 9th St. (bet. First Ave. & Ave. A)

Subway: 1 Av — Lunch & dinner daily
Phone: 212-677-5856
Web: N/A
Prices: $$

This little hole in the wall near Tompkins Square Park packs a big punch for its tiny size. Inside there are seats for less than 20 people, but the authentic Mexican food at inexpensive prices (dinner entreés from $10 to $15) and the lively vibe make up for the cramped quarters.
Start your meal with the wonderfully fresh house-made guacamole, which has just the right amount of heat, and a seemingly bottomless pitcher of their terrific sangria. For lunch, you'll find an assortment of burritos and quesadillas. At dinner the choices go upscale (flank steak in chile pasilla; semolina epazote dumplings with roasted poblano peppers) and include several specials. Save room for the moist chocolate mole cake—accented with a whisper of chile pepper.

Jack's Luxury Oyster Bar

Seafood

012

101 Second Ave. (bet. 5th & 6th Sts.)

Subway: Lower East Side - 2 Av — Mon – Sat dinner only
Phone: 212-253-7848
Web: N/A
Prices: $$$

Like its predecessor, Jewel Bako Makimono (now closed), this slip of an oyster bar with its narrow rows of tables may be tiny, but its charm is huge. You can thank owners Jack and Grace Lamb for that.
The chef's tasting menu is the way to go here. Items tend toward fresh seafood—including oysters, of course. You can also order à la carte, or choose from the extensive raw bar list. It's easy to craft a delightful meal out of the shellfish alone, but then you'd miss tasty small plates like Coho salmon tartare and peekytoe crab tart. Oh, and that's not to mention the chef's tasting menu.
The short dessert list changes regularly, but if it's offered the day you're there, try the satisfying baba au rhum cake, served warm with whipped cream.

Jewel Bako ✿

013 — Japanese

239 E. 5th St. (bet. Second & Third Aves.)

Subway: Astor Pl — Mon – Sat dinner only
Phone: 212-979-1012
Web: N/A
Prices: $$$

Jewel Bako/Swee Phuah

Jewel Bako—the name means "jewel box"—is the flagship of husband-and-wife restaurateur team Jack and Grace Lamb. And a jewel box it is, with its tables strewn beneath a pair of striking backlit bamboo arches. Even though a recent expansion has doubled the capacity, the space remains intimate, and a seat at the sushi bar here is highly coveted.

Each piece of sushi sparkles, from a silky sweet scallop to chopped mackerel topped with a shiso leaf that serves as a light herbal foil to the richness of the fish. Rare varieties like Japanese spotted sardine, golden cuttlefish and live octopus come fresh from the Tsukiji Market in Tokyo. To brighten the taste further, wasabi is grated fresh at the table.

Known for their warm welcome, the Lambs divide their time between their handful of restaurants (including Jack's Luxury Oyster Bar, and Degustation).

Appetizers

- Mushrooms "En Papillote" with Sake and Yuzu
- Usuzukuri: Sashimi of Live Fluke with Ponzu and Shiso Flowers
- Yellowtail Sashimi: Hamachi, Kanpachi, Hiramasa and Shima Aji

Entrées

- Trio of Tartares: Blue Fin, Salmon and Yellowtail, with Lotus Root Chips
- Crispy Scorpion Fish, Soy Radish and Ginko Reduction
- Anago with Asparagus, Shiitake and Sea Salt

Desserts

- Green Tea Profiteroles with Tofu Cream and Green Tea Powder

Kanoyama

014 — Japanese ✗

175 Second Ave. (at 11th St.)

Subway: 3 Av — Dinner daily
Phone: 212-777-5266
Web: www.kanoyama.com
Prices: $$

The young staff at Kanoyama caters to a clientele that is fanatical about sushi but prefers the mellow East Village vibe to the power-surge of Midtown. Take your place at the sushi bar with the regulars if you want to watch the chefs' amazing knife work and enjoy the warm banter. The energy in the tiny dining room is contagious.
Daily fish specials display incredible variety at top quality, and the daily menu supplements with even more choice. It's not inexpensive, but the quality stands up to the price. After all, it's how much of the buttery toro or creamy uni you consume that determines the final tab.
Kanoyama does not accept reservations on Friday and Saturday nights but there are plenty of fun bars nearby for a drink to pass the time.

Kyo Ya

015 — Japanese ✗✗

94 E. 7th St.

N/APhone: 212-982-4140 — Tue – Sun dinner only
Web: N/A
Prices: $$$

Mystery pervades this unmarked East Village newbie, located below street level down a modern stairway lined with slate. Little expense was spared to fashion this elegant Zen lair and every stone was a careful choice.
The same attention to detail paid to the décor is applied to the food. The chef's specialty is *kaiseki* cuisine, whose origins lie in the traditional Japanese tea ceremony. Seasonality is key to any *kaiseki* meal, which progresses through a specific flow of courses with most ingredients flown in from Japan. To experience this, you must order in advance to give the kitchen ample time to prepare. Or order from the lovely menu of small plates, where the same philosophy of articulate cooking applies and top-quality products change daily.

Lan

016 **Japanese**

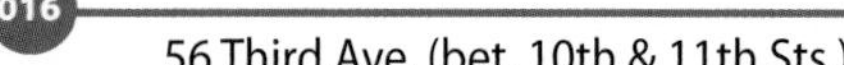

56 Third Ave. (bet. 10th & 11th Sts.)

Subway: 3 Av — Dinner daily
Phone: 212-254-1959
Web: www.lan-nyc.com
Prices: $$

Behind its red awning, Lan reveals a candlelit haven of white-cloth-covered tables and exposed brick accented by orange walls. In addition to the normal menu of sushi, sashimi and rolls, Lan also features entrées (such as broiled black cod marinated in Saikyo miso sauce), which change according to the season.

Appetizers, like steamed Chilean sea bass with simmered lotus roots, show off the chef's creativity, while meat dishes—a house specialty—combine top-quality products (Kobe beef, prime ribeye, organic chicken) with Asian techniques. Try the hot pots for two; they come with everything you need to cook your meal at the table. Shabu shabu (thin slices of prime ribeye with assorted market vegetables and dipping sauces) is a favorite.

La Paella

017 **Spanish**

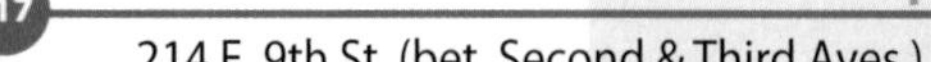

214 E. 9th St. (bet. Second & Third Aves.)

Subway: Astor Pl — Tue – Sun lunch & dinner
Phone: 212-598-4321 — Mon dinner only
Web: www.lapaellanyc.com
Prices: $$

Bring some friends to La Paella, so you can sample a wider array of the well-prepared vegetable, meat and seafood tapas. Recalling an Old World Iberian inn with its gold-toned walls, wrought-iron accents and wooden ceiling beams draped with dried flowers, the dining space can get crowded in the evening. The romantic setting makes it a great date place, as long as you don't mind the noise.

The specialty is—you guessed it—paella, and they serve several types of the traditional Spanish dish, including a vegetarian and an all-seafood preparation, as well as a Basque version, made with chorizo, chicken, shellfish and squid atop a bed of saffron rice. Keep the party going with a pitcher of fruity sangria or a bottle of Rioja from the wine list.

Lavagna

Italian

018

545 E. 5th St. (bet. Aves. A & B)

Subway: Lower East Side - 2 Av — Dinner daily
Phone: 212-979-1005
Web: www.lavagnanyc.com
Prices: $$

Little sister to Le Tableau (just down the street), Lavagna seems to be going strong, if the crowds that pack the place on weekends are any indication of its popularity. Any diner at Lavagna is treated like a friend. And that's what you'll want to be after you sample the refined and innovative cuisine on the short menu, which is supplemented with a host of daily specials. Dishes such as pizzettes, octopus carpaccio, homemade spinach ricotta ravioli in a porcini cream sauce, roasted baby rack of lamb, and whole wood-oven-roasted fish for two give you a taste of the bill of fare.
A gourmet bargain, the Sunday night prix-fixe menu (served from 5pm to 7pm), comes with an appetizer, main course and dessert for just $29.

Le Tableau

French

019

511 5th St. (bet. Aves. A & B)

Subway: Lower East Side - 2 Av — Dinner daily
Phone: 212-260-1333
Web: www.letableaunyc.com
Prices: $$

This modern bistro, with its vivid orange walls, enjoys a good reputation in the neighborhood—and rightly so. The cuisine here boasts excellent quality at a reasonable price, and the gently lit dining room provides a pleasing setting.
Creative brasserie fare includes seasonal offerings such as pomegranate-glazed duck and Berkshire pork loin with yam and walnut gnocchi gratin. Priced at less than $30, the three-course, prix-fixe menu is the best deal (offered before 7pm Tuesday to Saturday, and all night Sunday and Monday); there's also a five-course chef's tasting menu, which includes wines if you so desire. If you order à la carte, save your appetite for the likes of almond cake with apricot coulis and Valrhona chocolate truffle cake.

Lil' Frankie's Pizza

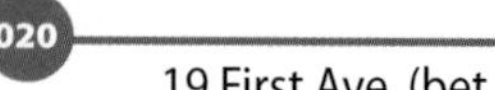

Italian

19 First Ave. (bet. 1st & 2nd Sts.)

Subway: Lower East Side - 2 Av — Lunch & dinner daily
Phone: 212-420-4900
Web: www.lilfrankies.com
Prices: $$

Come with a crowd or expect to wait (reservations are accepted only for parties of six or more), but once you sink your teeth into the pizza at Lil' Frankie's, your grumbling will seem like a distant memory.

As the "it" pizza place in the East Village and an offshoot of the ever-popular Frank Restaurant *(88 Second Ave.)*, Lil' Frankie's applies owner Frank Prisinzano's principle of turning quality ingredients into simple and tasty dishes. The menu features salads, pastas and sandwiches, but the real reason to come is the Naples-style pizza. Cooked to crispy perfection in a wood-burning oven with real lava from Vesuvio, pizza is religion here, with ten different varieties. Slake your thirst with a selection from the all-Italian wine list.

Luzzo's

Pizza

211-13 First Ave. (bet. 12th & 13th Sts.)

Subway: 1 Av — Tue – Sat lunch & dinner
Phone: 212-473-7447
Web: N/A
Prices: $$

These days, it seems that New Yorkers can't do anything without breaking some sort of code. There's no smoking or dancing in bars, and the city no longer issues permits for coal-burning ovens. Has all the fun, and taste, left the city? Not at Luzzo's, a former-bakery-turned-Italian-restaurant complete with a coal-burning oven that has been grandfathered. Thank heaven for small miracles and head straight for this rustic, tavern-style spot with its lip-smacking-good pizza.

Choose from 18 varieties, all with a light, chewy crust and a pleasingly charred flavor. Luzzo's also features a large selection of antipasti and pasta. Desserts are as delicious as they are whimsical, as in two menu specials: chocolate "salami" and nutella "pizza."

Mamlouk

Middle Eastern

211 E. 4th St. (bet. Aves. A & B)

Subway: Lower East Side - 2 Av — Tue – Sun dinner only
Phone: 212-529-3477
Web: N/A
Prices: $$

Want to go out for an authentic Middle Eastern meal, but not up for making decisions? Call a date or a group of friends and shimmy on over to Mamlouk. Inside, you'll be enveloped in an exotic ambience, furnished with octagonal copper-topped tables and wide cushioned seats. In this cozy den, hosted by the charming Iraqi owner, you have only to settle back and savor the multicourse, prix-fixe meal (there's no à la carte menu). The feast begins with a tasty assortment of pickles, meze and fresh-baked pita; then it continues with a couple of appetizers, several entrées, and ends with a sweet. You'll have plenty of good food for the price, and there are two seatings nightly.
As a fitting end to the feast, try a hookah, filled with flavored smokes.

The Mermaid Inn

Seafood

96 Second Ave. (bet. 5th & 6th Sts.)

Subway: Astor Pl — Dinner daily
Phone: 212-674-5870
Web: www.themermaidnyc.com
Prices: $$

With its rough-hewn wood columns, exposed brick walls and dark wainscoting, The Mermaid Inn recalls a New England seaside restaurant. This is no side-of-the-road joint, though. Owned by Jimmy Bradley, the nautical establishment is run like a tight ship.
Seafood stars on the menu, though they often serve a good pan-roasted chicken to appeal to carnivores. Instead of hot dogs, you might find "cod dogs" on the menu—a terrific version of the fried fishwich. The lobster sandwich is another sure hit. Oysters or littlenecks from the raw bar, grilled fish and seafood pasta round out the selection.
For your sweet tooth, a demitasse of creamy chocolate or butterscotch pudding appears, compliments of the house, to polish off your meal.

Momofuku Noodle Bar 

Asian

024

163 First Ave. (bet. 10th & 11th Sts.)

Subway: 1 Av — Lunch & dinner daily
Phone: 212-475-7899
Web: www.momofuku.com
Prices: ⊜

A consistently popular addition to the East Village dining scene, Momofuku is a peach of a restaurant—which is appropriate since its name means "lucky peach" in Japanese. There are no tables here; diners sit, as they do in noodle bars in Japan, on high stools at long communal counters. It's a great way to make new friends, slurping noodles elbow-to-elbow and watching the chefs' sleight of hand behind the blond-wood bar.

Owner and chef David Chang, a former line cook at Craft, fashioned Momofuku's menu with Asian street food in mind. Ramen noodles share the menu with small dishes; try the steamed pork dumplings filled with Iowa Berkshire black pork, an ingredient that figures prominently.

Momofuku Ssäm Bar

Asian

025

207 Second Ave. (at 13th St.)

Subway: 3 Av — Lunch & dinner daily
Phone: 212-254-3500
Web: www.momofuku.com
Prices: $$

Take one thing and do it well is a mantra often overlooked by chefs. David Chang, chef/owner of Momofuku Ssäm Bar takes this saying to heart. His new venture focuses on burrito-like Korean *ssäm*, and raises the bar with its good value, high style, and super-organized open kitchen.

To accommodate diners, the chef builds each ssäm to individual taste, but don't miss the original, with its flavorful, shredded roast Berkshire pork, onions, steamed edamame, pickled shiitakes and red kimchi purée. For lunch, you order ssäm cafeteria-style from the counter. In the evening, it's a different story: the place (full-service at dinner) is jammed with fans of Chang's extensive and ambitious menu of sophisticated fare. The difference is, well, day and night.

Prune

Contemporary

54 E. 1st St. (bet. First & Second Aves.)

Subway: Lower East Side - 2 Av — Lunch & dinner daily
Phone: 212-677-6221
Web: www.prunerestaurant.com
Prices: $$

This shoe-box-size bistro began in 1999 as Gabrielle Hamilton's modest vision of a neighborhood restaurant. While it hasn't grown in size since, it has grown well beyond the East Village in popularity. Despite its cramped quarters, Hamilton's recipe for a home-style eatery has been wildly successful. At Prune she combines vintage bistro décor with a small menu of comfort food—the kind of meals you'd cook for friends in your home.

Loyal fans come here for the chef's unpretentious and irreverent cooking style. Whole grilled fish, fried sweetbreads, and the fluffy Dutch-style pancake served at the weekend brunch are a few of the signature dishes. The menu is not broken down by courses, so if you just want a plate of veggies, that's no problem.

Sigiri

Sri Lankan 

91 First Ave. (bet. 5th & 6th Sts.)

Subway: 1 Av — Lunch & dinner daily
Phone: 212-614-9333
Web: www.sigirinyc.com
Prices:

Indian and Bangladeshi cooking reigns on East 6th Street's Curry Row, but for something different in the neighborhood, climb the stairs to the second-floor dining room of Sigiri to discover the unique and flavorful cuisine of Sri Lanka.

Sigiri, with its cinnamon-colored walls, festive table linens, and stylish modern furnishings, is the perfect place to feel worldly on a budget. The well-priced menu features Sri Lankan specialties such as chicken *lamprais* (a baked rice dish studded with chicken, fish and eggplant, and spiced with whole peppercorns, cinnamon bark and cardamom). Fruit-based non-alcoholic drinks—mango cordial, apple iced tea—are refreshing, but bring your own if you prefer wine or beer, since Sigiri doesn't serve liquor.

Soba-Ya 

028 — Japanese

229 E. 9th St. (bet. Second & Third Aves.)

Subway: Astor Pl — Lunch & dinner daily
Phone: 212-533-6966
Web: www.sobaya-nyc.com
Prices: 

Students from nearby NYU frequent this place for its Zen-like minimalist ambience and its hearty and inexpensive noodle dishes. Soba (Japanese buckwheat noodles) are made on the premises each morning by the chef, and then presented along with your hot or cold broth and an array of garnishes and ingredients. You can substitute the chewier udon, or wheat noodles (which some say taste more like traditional pasta), if you prefer. Seasonal sashimi or "country-style" soft tofu with edamame sauce are other options.

There's a good selection of Japanese beer and sake to pair with your meal. Made by the owner's wife, ice cream boasts unusual flavors like honey wasabi. Soba-Ya is open seven days a week, but the restaurant doesn't take reservations.

Financial District

Widely considered the financial center of the world, the southern tip of Manhattan isn't as buttoned-up as you might expect. Its ample, U-shaped waterfront, lined with appealing parks, draws hordes of visitors to enjoy views of New York Harbor and catch ferries to Staten Island and the Statue of Liberty. Cradled within are the narrow, twisting streets laid out by New York's first Dutch settlers in the 17th century; developers left the curvy street plan largely intact when they built their gargantuan office towers. Gaze up and you'll feel as though you're at the bottom of a deep well, with only tiny patches of sky visible among the tight clusters of looming skyscrapers.

A Bit of History

The area now known as the Financial District was the birthplace of New York in 1625. Trade flourished here under the Dutch West India Company, and the settlement of Nieuw Amsterdam grew quickly. In 1653 the colonists built a wall of wooden planks between the Hudson and East rivers to protect the settlers from Indian attack. Later dismantled by the British, who took over the colony in 1664, the wall is remembered today on **Wall Street**, which traces the original length (less than one mile) of the fortress.

Legend has it that in 1792 a group of 24 brokers met beneath a buttonwood tree at the corner of Wall and Williams streets, and founded the stock exchange. The New York Stock Exchange wasn't formally organized, however, until 1817. Inside the classical façade of the Exchange today, you'll find one of the most technically sophisticated financial operations on the globe.

A Neighborhood Reborn

After the tragic events that unfolded here in September 2001, the Financial District—and indeed, the entire city—turned its focus to rebuilding the neighborhood that is New York's hub of commerce. Today revitalization continues in the Financial District with new construction taking many forms—high-rise condominiums, high-end shops, and the redevelopment of the World Trade Center site among them. Camera-wielding tourists, drawn by attractions such as South Street Seaport, the Museum of Jewish Heritage, and the National Museum of the American Indian, now rub shoulders with briefcase-toting bankers on and around Wall Street. Meanwhile, Battery Park, under the watchful eye of Lady Liberty, teems with cyclists, runners, artists and souvenir peddlers. Restaurants in the area cater more to power-lunchers during the day, and to business travelers at dinnertime.

Peter L. Wrenn/MICHELIN

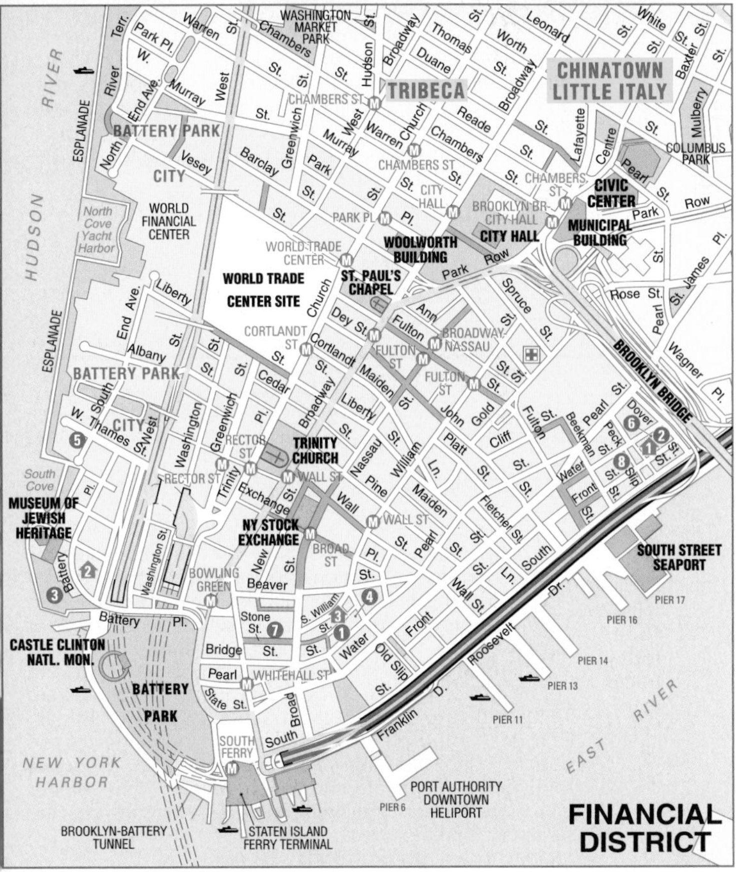

FINANCIAL DISTRICT

Adrienne's Pizzabar

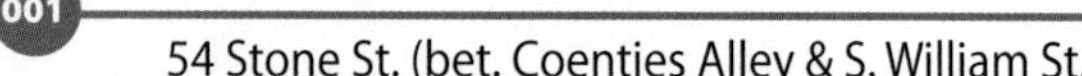

001 Pizza

54 Stone St. (bet. Coenties Alley & S. William St.)

Subway: Bowling Green — Lunch & dinner daily
Phone: 212-248-3838
Web: www.adriennespizzabar.com
Prices: ☺☺

A sleek version of an Italian-American pizza place, Adrienne's bustles day and night. At noon, Wall Streeters crowd the tables or line up at the counter for square pies. In the evening, pizzas change shape from square to round, the lights dim, and the dinner menu adds antipasti as well as entrées like stuffed artichoke, sole oreganata and eggplant rollatini.

The menu is classic Italian-American, but there are no checkered tablecloths here, no straw-covered Chianti bottles, and no shakers of cheese. Pizza purists may quibble over the fact that the pies are baked in a gas oven that's lined with brick, but this is still darn good pizza for a fair price. And though they're constantly on the run, the waitstaff still finds time to be engaging.

Bridge Cafe

002 American

279 Water St. (at Dover St.)

Subway: Fulton St — Sun – Fri lunch & dinner, Sat dinner only
Phone: 212-227-3344
Web: www.bridgecafenyc.com
Prices: $$

Not many establishments in New York City can claim as colorful a history as this one. Billing itself as "New York's oldest drinking establishment," the business opened in 1794 as a grocery in a wooden structure on the bank of the East River. Over the years, the building has housed a restaurant, a brothel, a boardinghouse and a saloon before it became the Bridge Cafe in 1979. The current 1920s structure stands at the foot of the Brooklyn Bridge. In a cozy atmosphere, embellished by paintings of the bridge, you'll find upscale American food. Gourmet sandwiches dominate the lunch menu, while dinner is a more formal affair with creative selections like the signature buffalo steak with lingonberry sauce. Go Sunday for the popular Bridge Brunch.

Gigino at Wagner Park

003 — Italian

20 Battery Pl. (in Wagner Park)

Subway: Bowling Green — Lunch & dinner daily
Phone: 212-528-2228
Web: www.gigino-wagnerpark.com
Prices: $$

Sleek sister to Gigino Trattoria in TriBeCa, this Wagner Park restaurant sits at the tip of Manhattan, between Battery Park's Pier A and the Museum of Jewish Heritage. From its outdoor terrace, you can take in splendid views of Liberty Island, Ellis Island and New York Harbor (be sure to reserve ahead for the terrace in warmer months). If it's not nice enough to sit outside, the small, contemporary dining room offers plenty of large windows for enjoying harbor views.

Chef's specialties include grilled octopus with black beans, homemade chicken sausage and Gigino's gnocchi with chicken, butter and sage. The wine list is an international affair, showcasing wines, champagne and sparkling wines from Italy, France, South Africa and California.

Harry's Cafe

004 — American

1 Hanover Sq. (bet. Pearl & Stone Sts.)

Subway: Wall St (William St.) — Mon – Fri lunch & dinner
Phone: 212-785-9200 — Sat dinner only
Web: www.harrysnyc.com
Prices: $$

Testosterone rules in this hangout for Wall Street movers and shakers. Located in the historic Hanover Bank building facing Hanover Square, Harry's packs in a crowd of power brokers who fill the large, masculine room with animated conversation (listen carefully and maybe you'll pick up a stock tip or two).

The menu indulges lighter appetites with starters (truffled steak tartare; crispy oysters), salads, pastas and sandwiches, while bold fare such as deep-fried "original" crackling pork shank and other manly meat dishes give culinary adventurers a lot to chew on (literally, since portions are tremendous).

An impressive list of whiskies, cognacs and cocktails satisfy Wall Street mavens who stop by after work to belt back a few at the bar.

Liberty View

Chinese 

005

21 South End Ave. (below W. Thames St.)

Subway: Rector St (Greenwich St.) — Open daily 11am - 11pm
Phone: 212-786-1888
Web: N/A
Prices: $$

True to its name, Liberty View looks out over the Statue of Liberty from its perch on the ground floor of an upscale condominium at the southern end of Battery Park City. In warm weather, area denizens and Financial District movers and shakers both clamor to claim the restaurant's prime outdoor tables.

Unlike in Chinatown, the clientele here is predominantly Western, and the service orients itself towards these guests. Chopsticks, tea and traditional accompaniments to dishes must be requested, but even so, contented regulars appreciate the pleasant interactions and attentive service. The tremendous menu features a good selection of dim sum—notably the juicy buns—and Liberty View's strength lies in this and in the Shanghai-style specialties.

MarkJoseph

Steakhouse

006

261 Water St. (bet. Peck Slip & Dover St.)

Subway: Fulton St — Mon – Fri lunch & dinner, Sat dinner only
Phone: 212-277-0020
Web: www.markjosephsteakhouse.com
Prices: $$$

Nestled in the shadow of the Brooklyn Bridge in the South Street Seaport Historic District, MarkJoseph's caters to financiers, Wall Street wunderkinds and tourists with deep pockets. The cozy dining room is a notch above the standard steakhouse design, with art-glass vases and pastoral photographs of the wine country adding sleek notes.

At lunch, regulars devour hefty half-pound burgers (there's even a turkey variety). At dinnertime, prime dry-aged Porterhouse takes center stage, accompanied by salads and favorite sides like creamed spinach, caramelized onions and hash browns, along with less guilt-inducing steamed vegetables. And what better to wash your steak down with than one of the selections on the generous list of red wines?

Nebraska Beef

Steakhouse XX

007

15 Stone St. (bet. Broad & Whitehall Sts.)

Subway: Bowling Green — Mon – Fri lunch & dinner
Phone: 212-952-0620
Web: N/A
Prices: $$$

You could easily walk down Stone Street without noticing the discreet red façade of this little restaurant, three blocks from the New York Stock Exchange. The unpretentious place, with its long bar area opening into a dark, wood-paneled room, is worth seeking out for its comfortable setting and grain-fed Nebraska beef, cooked to your liking. In the evening, the bar can get a bit rowdy with its "boys club" crowd, while at midday the dining room has a pleasant atmosphere dominated by Wall Street traders having business lunches.

As far as beef goes, there are no surprises on the menu here (a whopping 32-ounce prime ribeye that goes by "The Steak!" is the signature dish). The personable and professional waitstaff only adds to the experience.

SUteiShi

Japanese 

24 Peck Slip (at Front St.)

Subway: Fulton St — Mon – Fri lunch & dinner
Phone: 212-766-2344 — Sat – Sun dinner only
Web: www.suteishi.com
Prices: $$

Convenient to South Street Seaport, SUteiShi occupies a corner off the beaten Financial District track. This restaurant makes a good spot for lunch, when a Bento box combination is offered. Aside from that, there are noodles, tapas plates, sushi and sashimi, and inventive special rolls, like the Happy Lobster (sweet chunks of lobster mixed with mayo and wrapped around warm sushi rice crowned with crunchy, red flying-fish roe) or the SUteiShi Pearl (fried oysters with cucumbers and spicy mayo, topped with crab). For dessert, green-tea ice cream tops the list, but why not order outside the box and go for the nutty black-sesame crème brûlée?

Décor is sleek, with lots of windows, red-lacquer accents, and backlit bonsai plants behind the sushi bar.

Gramercy, Flatiron & Union Square

The retail district that stretches from 14th to 30th Streets between the East River and Avenue of the Americas (Sixth Avenue) contains a concentration of fine restaurants with names you'll no doubt recognize. Large 19th-century and early-20th-century buildings line Broadway, and Fifth and Sixth Avenues. Originally built as department stores, many of them now house national chains selling clothing or furniture.

Gramercy Park

New York City's only private park anchors this tranquil neighborhood known for its lovely brownstones and good cafes and restaurants. The area was laid out in 1831 by developer Samuel B. Ruggles, who drained an old marsh (Gramercy is a corruption of a Dutch phrase meaning "little crooked swamp") to build an exclusive residential enclave. Enclosed by an eight-foot-high cast-iron fence, to which only local residents have keys, the green rectangle of **Gramercy Park** consists of formal gardens, paths, benches and trees.

A few blocks northwest of Gramercy Park, the lovely six-acre **Madison Square Park** has been transformed recently into one of downtown's most inviting public spaces. From the 1870s to 1925, a succession of entertainment venues stood on the north end of the square, including the first two (of four) arenas called Madison Square Garden.

Union Square

On the south edge of the district, this pleasant park is crisscrossed with tree-lined paths. The park, so-named because it marked the union of Broadway and the Bowery, was created in 1831; by the mid-19th century it formed the gated focal point of an elegant residential district. In the early 20th century Union Square became a popular place for rallies and demonstrations; today the tiered plaza on the park's southern end still serves as a stage for protesters, who share space with street performers.

Every Monday, Wednesday, Friday and Saturday year-round, **Union Square Greenmarket** hosts farmers, bakers, flower growers, ranchers and artisanal-food makers from all over New York, Pennsylvania and New Jersey. Neighborhood chefs and residents flock here to forage for the freshest meats, cheeses and vegetables to incorporate into their menus.

Flatiron District

This moniker refers to the area around the **Flatiron Building** (Daniel Burnham, 1902). Even if you've never been to New York City, you've likely seen this building before—it's a popular backdrop in television shows and movies. Viewed from the north side (the side that faces Madison Square Park), the structure looks like an iron—hence the name—the acute angle of its façade formed by Broadway and Fifth Avenue. Though it's only 6 feet wide on this sharp corner, the building rises 22 stories straight up from the sidewalk.

Peter L. Wrenn/MICHELIN

GRAMERCY FLATIRON UNION SQUARE

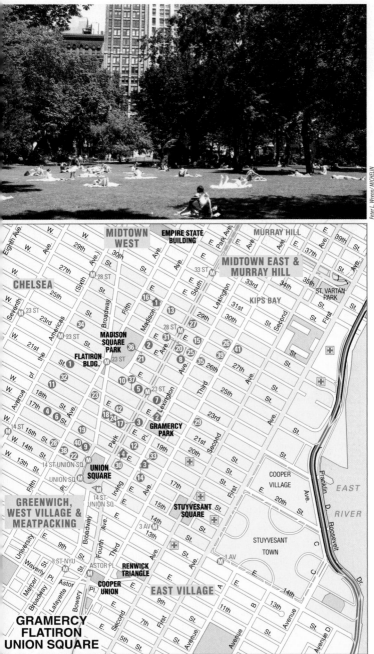

MIDTOWN WEST
EMPIRE STATE BUILDING
MURRAY HILL
MIDTOWN EAST & MURRAY HILL
CHELSEA
KIPS BAY
ST. VARTAN PARK
MADISON SQUARE PARK
FLATIRON BLDG.
GRAMERCY PARK
UNION SQUARE
COOPER VILLAGE
EAST RIVER
GREENWICH, WEST VILLAGE & MEATPACKING
STUYVESANT SQUARE
STUYVESANT TOWN
RENWICK TRIANGLE
COOPER UNION
EAST VILLAGE

Arezzo

Italian XX

46 W. 22nd St. (bet. Fifth & Sixth Aves.)

Subway : 23 St (Fifth Ave.)
Phone : 212-206-0555
Web : www.arezzo-nyc.com
Prices : **$$$**

Mon – Fri lunch & dinner
Sat dinner only

Arezzo benefits from the tutelage of Italian chef/partner Margherita Aloi, who helped make Le Madri a favorite among New Yorkers. Sophisticated and stylish, Arezzo shares the elegance of northern Italy in its design and its menu. Soft lighting lends a golden hue, while dark leather banquettes show off masculine overtones.

The extensive menu is enticing with its wide selection of tempting pasta dishes, grilled meat and seafood entrées, and wood-fired pizzas—so if decision-making is not your forte, go for the prix-fixe option for lunch or dinner. Heavenly cavatelli topped with spicy sausage and tomato-spiked cheese sauce gets raves. No matter your choice, the modern takes on Northern Italian classics will leave you eager to return.

Barbounia

003

Mediterranean X

250 Park Ave. South (at 20th St.)

Subway : 23 St (Park Ave. South)
Phone : 212-995-0242
Web : www.barbounia.com
Prices : **$$**

Lunch & dinner daily

You'll leave the concrete world of New York behind when you step through the door at Barbounia. This gorgeous space, with its whitewashed walls, breezy white fabrics and dark woods, will transport you from Park Avenue South to the serenity of the Greek Islands. Bright and uplifting during the day, Barbounia is sexy and spirited at night. An open kitchen adds to the upbeat vibe, while the small lounge area near the bar is an alluring spot.

The menu is a blend of Greek, Turkish, Mediterranean and American dishes, with the wood oven serving as a central theme. Barbounia's artfully presented cuisine uses top-quality ingredients, and its authentic style, such as strong Turkish coffee served in a copper vessel, adds to the overall experience.

A Voce ✿

Italian XX

002

41 Madison Ave. (enter on 26th St.)

Subway : 28 St (Park Ave. South) — Mon – Fri lunch & dinner
Phone : 212-545-8555
Web : www.avocerestaurant.com
Prices : $$$

©Emilie Baltz

Style and substance triumph at A Voce. Located on the first floor of an office building just off Madison Square Park, A Voce is at once hip and comfortable, with floor-to-ceiling windows fostering terrific people-watching.

This convivial restaurant is jammed day and night with chic patrons who come to sample the skillful dishes from chef Andrew Carmellini. While Carmellini honed his skills for years uptown at the much-lauded Café Boulud, he shines on his own here. Showing off his roots, he prepares rustic and intensely flavorful Italian dishes. Compositions such as Tuscan tripe accompanied by toothsome borlotti beans, a fried egg and crunchy sea salt honor tradition while revealing a contemporary twist.

The decibel level in the dining room provides just one hint that this restaurant will remain on many New Yorkers' short list for quite some time.

Appetizers

- Crostini alla Toscana with Chicken Liver, Foie Gras and Moscato d'Asti
- Grilled Octopus with Pepperonata, Lemon and Chorizo
- Duck Meatball Antipasto with Dried Cherry Mostarda

Entrées

- Black Bass, Shrimp Polpettini, New Potatoes, Ligurian Shellfish Broth
- My Grandmother's Meat Ravioli, Tomato and Parmigiano
- Spaghetti with Local Ramps, Speck and Parmigiano

Desserts

- Bomboloni alla Toscana: Tuscan Doughnuts with Chocolate Sauce
- Chocolate Panna Cotta with Amarena Cherries
- Lemon Rhubarb Yogurt Sorbetti

Basta Pasta

Contemporary XX

004

37 W. 17th St. (bet. Fifth & Sixth Aves.)

Subway: 14 St - Union Sq
Phone: 212-366-0888
Web: www.bastapastanyc.com
Prices: $$

Mon – Fri lunch & dinner
Sat – Sun dinner only

Talk about East meets West—how about an Italian restaurant from Tokyo? Basta Pasta was founded in Tokyo in 1985 and modeled after the TV show *Iron Chef*. The concept here is cooking as theater, and you'll feel like part of the show as you walk through the open kitchen to get to your table.

Enjoy the performance, as a team of Japanese chefs plate up a mix of Asian and Italian courses. Several of the dishes, such as spaghetti with flying-fish roe and shiso, show off an interesting fusion in their ingredients and techniques.

As an additional feast—one for the eyes—changing artwork hangs on the walls of the modern dining room. This is delicious dinner theater—and you don't have to call ahead for tickets (but reservations are recommended).

Beppe

Italian XX

005

45 E. 22nd St. (bet. Broadway & Park Ave. South)

Subway: 23 St (Park Ave. South)
Phone: 212-982-8422
Web: www.beppenyc.com
Prices: $$$

Mon – Fri lunch & dinner
Sat dinner only

Located a half-block from the Flatiron Building, Beppe is a modest place, with an intentionally aged-looking décor made warm and cozy by a working fireplace in winter. Enthusiastic staff members provide knowledgeable, yet informal, service; they are one of the strengths of this welcoming restaurant. From the hospitable waitstaff to the sausage made from pigs raised on the restaurant's own farm, it's the little details that make a big difference here.

Business-lunchers don't seem to mind paying uptown prices for food, like the consistently crowd-pleasing pastas, that reflects the best of each season. The kitchen is committed to offering house-made prosciutto and salami, and Italian varieties of produce organically grown in upstate New York.

BLT Fish

006 **Seafood** XX

21 W. 17th St. (bet. Fifth & Sixth Aves.)

Subway: 14 St - Union Sq
Phone: 212-691-8888
Web: www.bltfish.com
Prices: $$$

Mon – Fri lunch & dinner
Sat – Sun dinner only

After establishing BLT Steak in Midtown, chef Laurent Tourondel turned from turf to surf. His two high-energy seafood restaurants occupy the first and third floors of a Flatiron district town house. Upstairs is the informally elegant dining room; downstairs, New England-style BLT Fish Shack angles in on favorites like lobster rolls and Maryland crab cakes. Both establishments share the same great raw bar.

Available by the pound, exceptionally fresh fish and shellfish are simply brushed with olive oil and grilled; the popular Cantonese red snapper arrives whole in a colorful display. Seasonally inspired sides (Meyer lemon risotto; baby bok choy) are served à la carte. For meat-lovers, Tourondel always includes one or two "Not Fish" dishes.

BLT Prime

007 **Steakhouse** XX

111 E. 22nd St. (bet. Park & Lexington Aves.)

Subway: 23 St (Park Ave. South)
Phone: 212-995-8500
Web: www.bltprime.com
Prices: $$$

Dinner daily

Chef Laurent Tourondel opened BLT Prime, hot on the heels of BLT Fish. Tourondel outfitted the space formerly occupied by Union Pacific in elegant neutral tones, resulting in a cool, classic New York look. Under the vaulted glass ceiling, a large blackboard reiterates the menu, which is divided into sections by product, with an obvious emphasis on meat—beef, veal, lamb and poultry.

Fish lovers are not forgotten, though ; a short selection of fish and shellfish rounds out the list. All dishes are realized by a talented cooking team, and diners are free to choose their own sauces and sides, which include blue-cheese tater tots, barbecue onions and stuffed mushroom caps, among others.

Blue Smoke

American

116 E. 27th St. (bet. Lexington & Park Aves.)

Subway : 28 St (Park Ave. South) — Lunch & dinner daily
Phone : 212-447-7733
Web : www.bluesmoke.com
Prices : $$

Jazz and barbecue make a winning combination, and nowhere more so in the city than at Blue Smoke. One of the few barbecue spots in Manhattan that actually uses smoke (from hickory and applewood) to cook the meat, Blue Smoke replaces traditional canned ingredients with fresh versions. Sharing is encouraged, since platters like Rhapsody in 'Cue, a sampler of St. Louis spareribs, pulled pork, smoked chicken and a hot link are a challenge for one person. With its inclusion of small producers from Europe and North America, the wine list surprises for a barbecue joint. You can enjoy the same food downstairs at Jazz Standard while you listen to live jazz and blues.
Owner Danny Meyer stamps the restaurant with his signature family-friendly service.

Blue Water Grill

Contemporary

009

31 Union Sq. West (at 16th St.)

Subway : 14 St - Union Sq — Lunch & dinner daily
Phone : 212-675-9500
Web : www.brguestrestaurants.com
Prices : $$

Overlooking Union Square, the 1903 Bank of the Metropolis building still welcomes moneyed clients, only now they must be hungry too. Today, the building's soaring ceilings, decorative moldings, floor-to-ceiling windows and white-marble walls enclose the main dining room of the Blue Water Grill. The outdoor terrace functions as a "museum" of Beautiful People, who frequently lunch here on sunny days.
In addition to seeing the lovely interior of the former bank, you'll catch fresh seafood, from Maryland crab cakes to live Maine lobster. And don't ignore the sushi and maki rolls, or the raw-bar offerings, which include a good selection of oysters. Live jazz entertains nightly in the downstairs lounge, and there's a jazz brunch on Sunday.

Bolo

010 Spanish XX

23 E. 22nd St. (bet. Broadway & Park Ave. South)

Subway: 23 St (Park Ave. South) — Mon – Fri lunch & dinner
Phone: 212-228-2200 — Sat – Sun dinner only
Web: www.bolorestaurant.com
Prices: $$$

From the cranberry-red walls to the friendly service, Spain's sunny personality is perfectly captured at Bolo. This restaurant is brought to you by chef Bobby Flay ("Bo") and restaurateur Lawrence Kretchmer ("Lo") of Mesa Grill fame. Although the spirit is Spanish, it's not traditional; the cooking reflects Flay's modernized version of Spanish food.

At dinner, meat and fish are often oven-roasted or grilled, and a selection of rice dishes might run from paella to risotto. Lunch offers mains like the pressed Bolo burger with Manchego cheese, Serrano ham, and smoked-paprika fries.

You'll find that the food is not inexpensive here. Portions are copious, though, so you won't likely go away lighter, even though your wallet may.

Boqueria

011 Spanish XX

53 W. 19th St. (at Sixth Ave.)

Subway: 18 St (Seventh Ave.) — Lunch & dinner daily
Phone: 212-255-4160
Web: www.boquerianyc.com
Prices: $$

New York's craze for small plates rages on at this sociable Flatiron tapas bar. Occupying the space held for years by L'Acajou, Boqueria takes its name from the famous Barcelona market. Like the Catalonian *Boqueria*, the restaurant dishes up a dizzying array of offerings, sized from tiny *(pinxto)* and small *(tapas)* to entrée portions *(racion)* and plates for sharing *(compartir)*. You can get an idea of the variety—smoky squid on a bed of deep-fried chickpeas; potato croquettes with Serrano ham; boar terrine with candied almonds—by eyeing the bar, where examples are set out to tempt you.

To quench your thirst, choose from the all-Spanish wine list, or try a glass of white sangria. You'll find the staff well-versed in all aspects of the menu.

Butai

012 — Japanese

115 E. 18th St. (bet. Irving Pl. & Park Ave.)

Subway: 14 St - Union Sq
Phone: 212-228-5716
Web: www.butai.us
Prices: $$

Mon – Fri lunch & dinner
Sat – Sun dinner only

Butai is an ideal place to enjoy contemporary Japanese cuisine in a sleek setting. Quietly restrained at lunch, the scene turns hip when the sun sets and young professionals depart the nearby offices. The modern interior is accented with gorgeous marble and dark wood, and lively lounge music adds to the cool ambience.

Attractive presentations of sushi are available throughout the day, but Butai is best known for its robata grill offerings, which are only available in the evening. One of the few Japanese restaurants in the city to offer robata-style cuisine, Butai also impresses with its visually appealing presentations. Japanese classic starters, such as Agedashi tofu or various *sunomono* are standouts to begin your robata feast.

Campanile

013 — Italian

30 E. 29th St. (bet. Madison & Park Aves.)

Subway: 28 St (Park Ave.)
Phone: 212-684-4344
Web: www.campanilenyc.com
Prices: $$

Mon – Fri lunch & dinner
Sat dinner only

New York's Campanile (no relation to the noted Los Angeles restaurant of the same name) sprang to life in 1997, the culinary brainchild of Slavko and Linda Dunic. Tradition reigns at this family-owned establishment, from the pale golden walls and blond wood paneling that paint the dining area with a warm glow to the bounteous portions of regional Italian cuisine.

Dishes such as linguini with clam sauce, veal parmigiana, tortellini bolognese and chicken Marsala spell classic Italian-American favorites, in addition to a long list of daily changing specials. The latter will be recited by your waiter, whom you can count on for professional and attentive service.

Up front, the bar offers a more casual setting for an informal meal.

Casa Mono

Spanish

52 Irving Pl. (at 17th St.)

Subway : 14 St - Union Sq — Lunch & dinner daily
Phone : 212-253-2773
Web : www.casamononyc.com
Prices : $$

Brought to you by the winning duo of Joseph Bastianich and Mario Batali, Casa Mono opened in fall 2003. A lively crowd has been filling up the tiny dining room ever since. They come to sample Spanish wines and sherries and to nibble small plates of mussels with chorizo, Serrano ham, tripe with chickpeas, and *crema catalona*. All these Spanish dishes are created by chef/owner Andy Nusser, an alumnus of Batali's venture Babbo.
Slightly cramped, the small quarters do make for a festive atmosphere, and the upbeat servers add to the restaurant's lively personality. If you can't get into Casa Mono, try baby sister, Bar Jamón (Spanish for "ham bar"), next door. There you can nosh on *bocadillos* (Spanish sandwiches) washed down with a glass of Rioja.

Copper Chimney

015

Indian

126 E. 28th St. (bet. Lexington & Park Aves.)

Subway : 28 St (Park Ave. South) — Lunch & dinner daily
Phone : 212-213-5742
Web : www.copperchimney.com
Prices :

Opened in summer 2005 by the folks who founded Pongal, Copper Chimney exudes a trendy ambience that appeals to a young crowd with its candlelit room, loud music, close seating and bare wood tables.
A meal here begins with a small plate of mini-pappadums drizzled with mint and tamarind chutney and served with a neat mound of minced tomato, onion and pepper in the center. Main courses incorporate a wide range of traditional ingredients while emphasizing refined preparation and elegant presentation. All the standards are here, along with more sophisticated offerings, and a good mix of vegetarian dishes. Celebrity mixologist Jerry Banks has tailored cocktails specifically to complement the restaurant's cuisine.

Country ✿

016 **Contemporary** XXXX

90 Madison Ave. (at 29th St.)

Subway: 28 St (Park Ave South)
Phone: 212-889-7100
Web: www.countryinnewyork.com
Prices: $$$$

Tue – Sat dinner only

Eric Laignel

Chef/owner Geoffrey Zakarian offers something for everyone at Country with two eateries in one. Located within the recently renovated Carlton Hotel *(see hotel listing)*, Country's downstairs cafe is a handsome room with wood-paneled walls and plush banquettes. The glamorous upstairs room demands attention with its Art Deco mosaic floors, glittering chandeliers and Tiffany stained-glass dome.

Similarly, the food at Country oozes with urban sophistication. Café at Country features all-day dining, and its cuisine blends French and American influences. In the Dining Room palates are enticed with four- or six-course tasting menus that change daily. In either setting, innovative cuisine is executed with an easy elegance that shows off local ingredients and an elegant French touch. The well-thought-out and organized wine list leans toward French vintages.

Appetizers

- White Gazpacho, Verjus, Caviar, Smoked Almonds
- Grilled Cuttlefish, Riso Venere, Rouille, Chorizo
- Fried Egg, Clam Velouté, Lardons, Black Pepper

Entrées

- Wild Salmon, Dill, Meyer Lemon, Roe
- Berkshire Pork, Piperade, Garlic Cream, Prosciutto
- Grilled Bison, Basil Purée, Olives, Sauce Charon

Desserts

- Pavlova, Strawberry Jam, Meringue, Vanilla Mousse
- Coconut, Black Sesame, Mango, Sticky Rice
- Gianduja, Celery Cream, Crémeux, Milk Chocolate, Lime Ice Cream

Craft

American 

017

43 E. 19th St. (bet. Broadway & Park Ave. South)

Subway : 14 St - Union Sq — Dinner daily
Phone : 212-780-0880
Web : www.craftrestaurant.com
Prices : **$$$$**

Ever go out to eat with one of those people who wants to change everything about his or her order ("I'd like the salad, but hold the tomatoes and put the dressing on the side")? Now you can take your pickiest friends to this contemporary restaurant and they can tailor their meals to their own tastes.

At Craft, chef/owner Tom Colicchio offers a choice of basic products—fish and shellfish, charcuterie, roasted meat, salad, vegetables—that may be combined however you desire. This mix-and-match style has made a star of Colicchio, who is famed for presenting ultra-fresh ingredients (wild arugula, Kumumoto oysters, Berkshire pork, local ramps), preparing them simply, and letting the unadulterated taste of each do its own talking.

Craftbar

Contemporary XX

018

900 Broadway (bet. 19th & 20th Sts.)

Subway : 14 St - Union Sq — Lunch & dinner daily
Phone : 212-461-4300
Web : www.craftrestaurant.com
Prices : **$$**

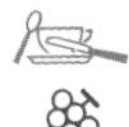

In April 2005, Craftbar, the seductive and always crowded annex to Tom Colicchio's Craft restaurant, moved to bigger digs around the corner to accommodate its burgeoning guest list. Here, at Craft's casual cousin, you can sample Craft-like, top-quality ingredients at a lower price point.

The cuisine successfully blends modern American style with Mediterranean flair. Many of the small plates that made Craftbar famous may be gone now, but sharing items on the extensive new menu is still welcomed. Although the dishes change frequently so customers can enjoy the fresh flavors of select seasonal products, the famous veal ricotta meatballs remain.

Here, as at Craft, you'll revel in a large wine list, with a host of selections by the glass.

Dévi 

019 **Indian**

8 E. 18th St. (bet. Broadway & Fifth Ave.)

Subway: 14 St - Union Sq
Phone: 212-691-1300
Web: www.devinyc.com
Prices: $$$

Mon – Sat lunch & dinner daily
Sun dinner only

Dévi/Ben Fink

It's no wonder that the dining-room décor of Dévi seems fit for a goddess, since the Hindu mother goddess inspired the restaurant's name. In this sumptuous and lively setting, gauzy jewel-tone fabrics swathe the walls; banquettes covered in a patchwork of brown, yellow and orange provide cozy seating; and clusters of colored-glass lanterns hang from the red ceiling.
Cookbook author Suvir Saran and tandoori master Hemant Mathur, who opened the 75-seat restaurant in 2004, put a new spin on traditional Southern Indian specialties. One favorite, samosas, are ramped up here with goat cheese and spinach or lamb and pecorino. In addition to the à la carte selection, encompassing the likes of terrific tandoori prawns and turkey *ka keema*, two seven-course tasting menus (one of which is vegetarian) offer a great way to discover the chefs' talents for modern Indian cuisine.

Appetizers

- Bombay Bhel Puri, Rice Puffs, Tamarind, Mint, Tomatoes and Onions
- Goan Spicy Scallops, Spiced Radish Rice, Balchao Sauce
- Lamb-stuffed Tandoori Chicken, Pickling Spices

Entrées

- Tandoor-grilled Lamb Chops, Pear Chutney, Curry Leaf Potatoes
- Tandoori Prawns with Eggplant Pickle
- Kararee Bhindi, Crispy Tangy Okra Salad, Tomatoes and Red Onions

Desserts

- Emperor's Morsel Saffron Bread Pudding, Cardamom Cream, Candied Almonds
- Pistachio Kulfi, Candied Pistachio, Citrus Soup
- Tasting of Crèmes, Seasonal Fruit and Spice Flavors

Dos Caminos

Mexican

020

373 Park Ave. South (bet. 26th & 27th Sts.)

Subway : 28 St (Park Ave. South) — Lunch & dinner daily
Phone : 212-294-1000
Web : www.brguestrestaurants.com
Prices : $$

If you've never tasted good tequila, here's your chance. The bar at Dos Caminos offers 100 different types of the alcohol made by distilling the fermented juice of the agave plant. Don't taste too many, though, or you won't be able to appreciate the 250-seat dining space, vibrant in pink, orange and brown.

Nor do you want to dull your taste buds before sampling the piquant Mexican cuisine, beginning with excellent guacamole, made to order tableside. Seared-tuna tacos, chorizo-sprinkled Cobb salad, and Oaxacan white- and dark-chocolate fondue bring Mexico to mind while displaying a fusion flair.

Check out Dos Caminos' SoHo location *(475 West Broadway at Houston St.)*, and the newest one, in Midtown *(on the corner of E. 50th St. and Third Ave.)*.

Eleven Madison Park

Contemporary

021

11 Madison Ave. (at 24th St.)

Subway : 23 St (Park Ave South) — Lunch & dinner daily
Phone : 212-889-0905
Web : www.elevenmadisonpark.com
Prices : $$$

An enterprise by Danny Meyer and the Union Square Hospitality Group, this tony establishment is located in the Art Deco MetLife Insurance tower across from Madison Square Park. Inside the splendid 1930s-style setting, 30-foot-high ceilings and marble floors dress the dining room, and huge windows peer out on lovely park views.

Chef Daniel Humm, who hails from San Francisco, now presides over the kitchen at Eleven Madison Park where he focuses his remarkable technical skills on interpreting American dishes with a 21st-century twist. Lunch and dinner feature several menu options; both offer à la carte items, as well as a multicourse Gourmand menu. Efficient, engaging service makes dining here a pleasure.

15 East

Japanese

022

15 E. 15th St. (bet. Fifth Ave. & Union Sq. West)

Subway: 14 St - Union Sq
Phone: 212-647-0015
Web: www.15eastrestaurant.com
Prices: $$$

Mon – Fri lunch & dinner
Sat dinner only

Its name may be non-descript, but 15 East is no plain Jane. In this attractive sushi bar, ivory tiled walls, a polished-concrete floor and dove-gray furnishings complement the warmly lit monochromatic dining room.

Helmed by chef Masato Shimizu, who apprenticed in Japan for seven years, the team at 15 East slices up tender slivers of pristine-quality fish atop warm rice—characteristic of *Edo*-style sushi. First-rate touches like freshly grated wasabi root, house-pickled ginger and handmade ceramic serving pieces accentuate the experience.

In addition to sushi, there's a full menu of contemporary Japanese cuisine. Don't miss the house-made soba noodles, and be sure to consider a sake or a *shochu* from the impressive selection.

I Trulli

Italian

025

122 E. 27th St. (bet. Lexington Ave. & Park Ave. South)

Subway: 28 St (Park Ave. South)
Phone: 212-481-7372
Web: www.itrulli.com
Prices: $$$

Mon – Fri lunch & dinner
Sat – Sun dinner only

Located in the heart of Gramercy, the family of establishments that falls under the I Trulli umbrella includes something for almost everyone. Attached to the restaurant is a wine bar called Enoteca I Trulli, and across the street, you'll find Vino, which sells Italian wines and spirits.

I Trulli features the cuisine of Puglia, the owner's native region ; the restaurant even has its own label of olive oil, harvested and bottled in Italy. Pastas, including the light-as-a-feather *malloreddus* (dumplings filled with sausage) make a wonderful first or second course.

The dining room's rustic fireplace, open kitchen and wood-burning oven evoke the Italian countryside. In the warm seasons, the covered terrace will transport you to the European countryside.

Fleur de Sel ✿

French XX

023

5 E. 20th St. (bet. Broadway & Fifth Ave.)

Subway: 23 St (Broadway) — Lunch & dinner daily
Phone: 212-460-9100
Web: www.fleurdeselnyc.com
Prices: $$$

Fleur de Sel/Xenia B. Buxo

There are many reasons to dine in this delightful French restaurant, whose name ("flower of the salt" in French) refers to a prized type of pure salt hand-harvested on France's Brittany Coast. Foremost among the reasons is the delectable, original cuisine prepared by chef/owner Cyril Renaud. His winning concept at Fleur de Sel distills the essence of seasonal ingredients and highlights dishes of his native Brittany.

In the evening, a three-course prix-fixe menu—with offerings that might range from almond-flour-dusted soft-shell crab with corn, ramps and warm hazelnut vinaigrette to a pork chop marinated in sugarcane and coffee—joins the six-course chef's tasting. Renaud lets his talents loose in the latter, which changes according to the market and his whim.

Weighted toward French varietals, the wine list offers more than 1,000 selections.

Appetizers

- Escargot and Polenta Gâteaux, Parmesan Crisp, Red Wine Sauce
- Pork Belly, Fingerling Potato Purée, American Paddlefish Caviar
- Trio of Foie Gras, Rhubarb Gelée, Brioche

Entrées

- Poussin, Wilted Spinach, Mushrooms, Foie Gras Emulsion
- Halibut, Glazed Endives, Oklahoma Pecans, Bacon, Balsamic Reduction
- Venison Loin, Potato and Venison Sausage Gratin

Desserts

- Gaufrette au Chocolat, Black Mint, Chocolate Ice Cream
- Granny Smith Caramelized Brittany Crêpe
- Red-Wine-Glazed Almond Macaroon, Hazelnut Parfait

Gramercy Tavern ✿

024 **Contemporary** XXX

42 E. 20th St. (bet. Broadway & Park Ave. South)

Subway : 23 St
Phone : 212-477-0777
Web : www.gramercytavern.com
Prices : $$$

Mon – Fri lunch & dinner
Sat – Sun dinner only

Gramercy Tavern/Paul Walsh

The word "tavern" conjures up images of a cozy, wood-paneled room, pints of ale and convivial conversation. That country-inn ambience is what Danny Meyer was going for when he opened Gramercy Tavern in 1994. He did something right; as this place still stands tall on New York's culinary landscape.

Seasonality and market-fresh products light up well-thought-out changing menus. Many dishes, like the braised rabbit, have an old-time appeal, while others remain decidedly modern. Attentive service by pleasant waiters completes the elegant experience.

In the back of the restaurant, the dining rooms kick the tavern concept up a notch with wood-beamed ceilings, velvet draperies and fine artwork. In front, the tavern room and appealing bar capture the essence of hospitality with a casual all-day menu.

Appetizers

- Marinated Calamari with Meyer Lemon and Pine Nuts
- Smoked Brook Trout with Sunchoke Purée and Pickled Onion Vinaigrette
- Sweetbreads and Chanterelles with Chard Ravioli

Entrées

- Smoked Lobster with Celery Root Purée and Ramp Sauce
- Sturgeon with Salsify and Fennel Lemon Sauce
- Flatiron Steak and Short Ribs with Red Cabbage and Puffed Potatoes

Desserts

- Warm Chocolate Bread Pudding with Dried Cherries and Anise Ice Cream
- Blueberry and Corn Ice-Cream Sundae with Toffee Popcorn
- Chocolate Peanut Butter Cake with Frozen Milk

Jaiya

Thai

026

396 Third Ave. (bet. 28th & 29th Sts.)

Subway: 28 St (Park Ave. South)
Phone: 212-889-1330
Web: www.jaiya.com
Prices:

Mon – Sat lunch & dinner
Sun dinner only

Authentic Thai cuisine brings a mixed crowd of couples, families, and groups of friends back to this simple restaurant. There's a reason that groups are drawn to casual Jaiya: generous family-style portions are big enough for sharing, and a group can eat well here for a reasonable price.

Skip the popular pad Thai and satay. A foray into the large number of curries and chef's specialties is bound to delight your palate with authentic tastes of Thailand. The waitstaff is efficient and tries to be helpful by talking diners down from their spice requests. Since the kitchen here does not Americanize the traditional Thai spice levels, ordering a dish "medium spicy" may well yield a more fiery taste than you bargained for.

Les Halles

French 

027

411 Park Ave. South (bet. 28th & 29th Sts.)

Subway: 28 St (Park Ave. South)
Phone: 212-679-4111
Web: www.leshalles.net
Prices: $$

Lunch & dinner daily

This brasserie serves as home base for Anthony Bourdain, culinary bad boy and author of the restaurant exposé, *Kitchen Confidential*. Bourdain presides over the kitchen here, turning out classic bistro fare in typically bustling Belle Époque surroundings. Named for the famous Paris market, Les Halles is designed with a stamped-tin ceiling and antique light fixtures.

The bold personality of this restaurant, which is popular with local business types, turns the typical weekday lunch on its head with tasty French classics. Meat steals the show here with juicy hamburgers and steak *frites* (the fries are to die for) among the most-ordered items.

Visit Les Halles' little sister (it has the same menu) in the Financial District at 15 John Street.

Mesa Grill

028 **Southwestern** XX

102 Fifth Ave. (bet. 15th & 16th Sts.)

Subway: 14 St - Union Sq — Lunch & dinner daily
Phone: 212-807-7400
Web: www.mesagrill.com
Prices: $$$

Between filming TV appearances, writing cookbooks and supervising his empire of restaurants (which includes Bolo and Bar Americain in New York, and Mesa Grill in Las Vegas), Bobby Flay is one busy guy. A graduate of the French Culinary Institute, Flay gravitated not to foie gras and truffles, but to products native to the Americas—corn, chilies, black beans.

While you wouldn't pick Mesa Grill, with its boisterous, brazenly colored dining room, for a quiet evening out, you would come for zesty Southwestern cuisine like yellow-corn-crusted chile relleno, goat cheese *"queso fundido,"* and a great margarita list. Salads and sandwiches dominate the lunch menu, popular with business types. Neighborhood denizens have long favored the weekend brunch.

Molly's Pub & Shebeen

029 **Gastropub** 

287 Third Ave. (bet. 22nd & 23rd Sts.)

Subway: 23 St (Park Ave. South) — Lunch & dinner daily
Phone: 212-889-3361
Web: www.mollysshebeen.com
Prices: ⊜

Molly's is as traditional a pub as you're likely to find in New York. Even the exterior screams "Ireland" with its white stucco façade against dark wood beams, and its carved wooden sign. Inside, low ceilings, dark walls and sawdust floors are warmed by the wood-burning fireplace—a great place to defrost any winter chills.

The pub draws patrons of all stripes, from twenty-somethings to seasoned regulars, minus the boisterous happy-hour set. An ideal watering hole for a pint and an awesome burger, Molly's also serves corned beef and cabbage, fish and chips, and Shepherd's pie.

You may have to wait for a table here, but if so, the bar staff will take good care of you, and the friendly regulars usually have a few good stories to share.

Olives

Contemporary

030

201 Park Ave. South (at 17th St.)

Subway : 14 St - Union Sq — Lunch & dinner daily
Phone : 212-353-8345
Web : www.toddenglish.com
Prices : **$$$**

Chef Todd English burst onto New York's dining scene in 2000 when he opened this outpost of his popular Boston restaurant on the first floor of the W Hotel. A link in the chain of English's empire of eateries, Olives on Union Square packs 'em in seven nights a week.

The draw? A trendy setting, a lively crowd in the lounge, and English's innovative Mediterranean cuisine. Handmade butternut squash tortelli, oven-roasted branzino with curried lobster vinaigrette, and pistachio-crusted lamb loin are seasonal highlights. You might even find the likes of brick-oven-baked flatbread topped with fig and prosciutto, which leaves standard pizza in the dust.

You can purchase a copy of English's cookbook, *The Olives Table*, at the reception desk.

Park Bistro

French

031

377 Park Ave South (bet. 26th & 27th Sts.)

Subway : 28 St (Park Ave. South) — Lunch & dinner daily
Phone : 212-689-1360
Web : www.parkbistrorestaurant.com
Prices : **$$**

This charming little French bistro, opened in 1989 on Park Avenue, recently moved a few doors down from its original location.

Park Bistro, as its name suggests, serves the real thing, not gussied-up nouveau cuisine. For lunch and dinner, the prix-fixe menu (served before 7pm) is a bargain. À la carte selections showcase French classics (escargots, duck foie gras, loup de mer, coq au vin), and the wine list offers a cohesive and affordable selection of Gallic wines.

Periyali

032 Greek

35 W. 20th St. (bet. Fifth & Sixth Aves.)

Subway: 23 St (Sixth Ave.)
Phone: 212-463-7890
Web: www.periyali.com
Prices: $$$

Mon – Fri lunch & dinner
Sat dinner only

If it's a break from the city's hustle and bustle you're after, you'll find it here. With its white-plaster walls and wood-beamed ceiling—draped, sail-like, with white fabric—Periyali suggests the airy ambience of islands in the Aegean. As you'd expect of a restaurant whose name means "seashore" in Greek, the cuisine angles in on the sunny cuisine of the Greek islands. Fantastic bread and olive oil for dipping begin a wonderful meal here. Entrées encompass rustic fare from traditional moussaka to souvlaki.
The dining space, divided into four small rooms, makes a great place to have an intimate rendezvous or to discuss business over a bottle of Greek wine. At midday the crowd comprises stylish and well-spoken Flatiron business lunchers.

Pure Food and Wine

033 Vegetarian

54 Irving Pl. (bet. 17th & 18th Sts.)

Subway: 14 St - Union Sq
Phone: 212-477-1010
Web: www.purefoodandwine.com
Prices: $$$

Dinner daily

Carnivores beware: this restaurant's name means what it says. A disciple of the raw-food movement, Pure Food and Wine serves only raw vegetarian dishes. If you're a first-timer here, the waiters will explain that to preserve vitamins, enzymes, minerals and flavors in the food, nothing is heated above 118°F.
Spicy Thai lettuce wraps with tamarind chile sauce, and zucchini and golden-tomato lasagna with basil pistachio pesto don't just taste good, they're good for you—especially if you buy into the purported health benefits of raw cuisine. Either way, the kitchen uses only the freshest organic produce available, and the results are surprisingly flavorful. The juice bar and take-away counter foster healthy eating on the go.

Sapa

Vietnamese XX

034

43 W. 24th St. (bet. Fifth & Sixth Aves.)

Subway: 23 St (Sixth Ave)
Phone: 212-929-1800
Web: www.sapanyc.com
Prices: $$$

Sun – Fri lunch & dinner
Sat dinner only

Since Sapa opened, throngs of Beautiful People clad in the latest prêt-à-porter designs have filled this restaurant on the border of Chelsea and Gramercy. Why all the buzz? A festive atmosphere; a seductive contemporary setting designed by AvroKo with Asian wire lanterns, French garden urns and exotic woods; and a culinary alchemy that expertly marries Vietnamese and French cuisine.

If it sounds schizophrenic, it doesn't taste that way. Named for a North Vietnamese village built by the French in the 1920s, Sapa surprises with the freshest of ingredients prepared to highlight their delicate, subtle flavors. A light happy-hour menu is offered in addition to lunch, brunch and dinner. At midday, go for the bargain Bento box combos.

Saravanaas 

Indian X

035

81 Lexington Ave. (at 26th St.)

Subway: 28 St (Park Ave. South)
Phone: 212-679-0204
Web: www.saravanaas.com
Prices: 

Lunch & dinner daily

Set smack in the midst of Curry Row, Saravanaas stands out with its simple, clean contemporary décor. Pastel-hued walls, colorful votives and gleaming aluminum serving pieces brighten the dining room.

The menu embraces a contemporary reflection of time-honored Southern Indian dishes. Thalis, a selection of different foods served with appropriate condiments, come in small or large sizes for a set price. Dosas, made with rice and lentils, are a specialty here. You can order these wonderfully thin pancakes plain or with your choice of vegetarian fillings. The dosas are so enormous, it's easy to make a meal of just one—for less than $10. And the veggie fillings are so tasty and satisfying, you'll never miss the protein.

Tabla

036 Contemporary XXX

11 Madison Ave. (at 25th St.)

Subway: 23 St (Park Ave. South)
Phone: 212-889-0667
Web: www.tablany.com
Prices: $$$

Mon – Fri lunch & dinner
Sat – Sun dinner only

A member of Union Square Hospitality Group, Tabla faces Madison Square Park, next door to Eleven Madison Park (another of Danny Meyer's restaurants). At Tabla you have two dining options. On the first floor, the boisterous Bread Bar features a short menu of home-style regional Indian fare at reasonable prices. If you're in the mood for a more upscale dining experience with great people-watching, climb the suspended staircase to the second floor and have a seat in Tabla's sensuous, Art Deco dining room.
There, chef Floyd Cardoz, a native of Bombay, skillfully fuses contemporary American cuisine with spicy Indian accents (as in baby lamb with garam masala jus, or crab cakes with avocado salad and tamarind chutney) on his three-course, prix-fixe menu.

Tamarind

037 Indian XXX

41-43 E. 22nd St. (bet. Broadway & Park Ave. South)

Subway: 23 St (Park Ave. South)
Phone: 212-674-7400
Web: www.tamarinde22.com
Prices: $$$

Lunch & dinner daily

Unlike the sweet-and-sour tropical fruit for which it's named, Tamarind hits no sour notes. Instead, the restaurant achieves a pleasing harmony between its sophisticated décor (no wild colors here) and its regional Indian cuisine.
A floor-to-ceiling wrought-iron "wall" from a maharajah's palace lends a royal air to the dining room, and the back wall holds mirrored niches for a collection of stylized Indian wooden puppets. Inside the glassed-in kitchen, a serious brigade of cooks prepares piquant dishes from Goa, Punjab, Madras and Calcutta. The large range of regional cuisine includes masala, curries and tandoori dishes; goat meat here is a tender delight. A broad selection of international wines puts the icing on the cake.

Tocqueville

Contemporary XX

038

1 E. 15th St. (bet. Fifth Ave. & Union Sq. West)

Subway: 14 St - Union Sq — Lunch & dinner daily
Phone: 212-647-1515
Web: www.tocquevillerestaurant.com
Prices: $$

Named for 19th-century French writer Alexis de Tocqueville, this restaurant puts an American spin on its dishes. Although the chef occasionally spikes the contemporary French-accented cuisine with non-sequiturs (as in a tartare of Japanese yellowtail and tuna) the menu consists mainly of classics. The 200-label wine list features selections from little-known wine regions around the world.

Toqueville's new space, just up the street from the original, is still as intimate as before. Tables snuggle close together in the single dining room, but devotees don't mind the lack of privacy. Service is just as quirky, too, but the space is so elegant that it helps distract diners from any flaws. Lockers in the front hallway offer self-serve coat check.

Turkish Kitchen

Turkish XX

039

386 Third Ave. (bet. 27th & 28th Sts.)

Subway: 28 St (Park Ave. South) — Sun – Fri lunch & dinner
Phone: 212-679-6633 — Sat dinner only
Web: www.turkishkitchenny.com
Prices:

You'll see red when you step inside the Turkish Kitchen's windowed façade—red walls, that is. The inside of the first-floor dining room is painted bright red, with red fabric-covered chairs. Casual enough for jeans, the place feels exotic with copper urns filling shelves and wall alcoves, and colorful martini glasses lining the glowing blue-glass bar. At night, blue-glass votives mounted on the walls cast a romantic light.

Many of the best dishes here are uniquely Turkish, such as the *boregi* (feta-filled phyllo rolls baked to a crisp), or the lamb, grilled and served in a variety of preparations. Try a glass of Turkish wine or beer to round out your experience. For both lunch and dinner, the three-course menu is a terrific deal.

Union Square Cafe

American XX

21 E. 16th St. (bet. Fifth Ave. & Union Sq. West)

Subway: 14 St - Union Sq — Lunch & dinner daily
Phone: 212-243-4020
Web: www.unionsquarecafe.com
Prices: $$$

Quintessentially New York City, Union Square Cafe is a special place. It was founded by a young entrepreneur named Danny Meyer in 1985, and business has been booming ever since. Given the restaurant's comfortable bistro décor, winning service and excellent modern American cooking, it's easy to see why.

Do as the regulars do, get there early and grab a seat at the bar for a great burger or a three-course meal and a sampling of the cafe's wines by the glass. Chef/partner Michael Romano supplements his entrée selection with daily and weekly specials, and the Union Square Greenmarket next door figures largely in the planning. Worth a special mention is the tremendous wine list, which is diverse, well selected and reasonably priced.

Vatan

041

Indian X

409 Third Ave. (bet. 28th & 29th Sts.)

Subway: 28 St (Park Ave. South) — Tue – Sun dinner only
Phone: 212-689-5666
Web: www.vatanny.com
Prices: $$

When you step inside Vatan, you'll instantly be transported to a Gujarati village on the Arabian Sea in western India. Portraits of Ganesh, the god of wisdom, and of Annapurnadevi, the goddess of prosperity, welcome you at the end of a bamboo-lined corridor. Keep going, and you'll find yourself amid a setting of huts, banyan trees, wisteria vines and a whimsical mural of the Indian countryside.

Take your shoes off and have a seat at one of the low tables. There's no need for decision-making here. The fixed-price, all-you-can-eat menu comprises a 20-course repast of regional Indian specialties—all strictly vegetarian—served by waitresses dressed in bright *ghagra choli*. Vatan's flavorful menu proves that avoiding meat isn't a sacrifice.

Veritas ✿

042 — Contemporary XX

43 E. 20th St. (bet. Broadway & Park Ave. South)

Subway: 23 St (Park Ave South) — Dinner daily
Phone: 212-353-3700
Web: www.veritas-nyc.com
Prices: $$$$

Veritas/©Emily Cantrell

In vino veritas. There *is* truth in wine, and the truth is that Veritas spells paradise for oenophiles. Some 100,000 bottles of wine cool their heels in the restaurant's temperature-controlled cellar. It may take you a while to read through the wine list—more of a tome—of 3,000 labels from around the globe. No need to feel overwhelmed, though ; the sommelier is always on hand in the stylish dining room to help you choose.

Wine may vie for the spotlight, but the creative, perfectly prepared American dishes compete for top billing. Scott Bryan crafts a fixed-price menu selection that provides the ideal balance of red meat, fowl and fish. Of course, he designs his dishes to complement the wine, and the combinations mesh wonderfully together. To finish, a silky bamboo-honey panna cotta or a chocolate soufflé will give you a perfect excuse to sample a dessert wine.

Appetizers

- Lobster Salad, Fava Purée, Peppercorns, Sherry Vinegar
- Wild Mushroom Ravioli, Mascarpone, Tarragon, Hon-Shimeji
- Crispy Pork Belly, Balsamic Glaze, Cipollini, Apple Salad

Entrées

- Short Ribs, Parsnip Purée, Porcini, Glazed Carrots
- Monkfish, Melted Cabbage, Bacon, Red Wine Emulsion
- Scallops, Celery Root Purée, Braised Endive, Truffle Vinaigrette

Desserts

- Chocolate Soufflé, Caramel Ice Cream, Chocolate Sauce
- Maple Crème Caramel, Candied Pecans, Sour Cherry Sauce
- Tarte Tatin, Macadamia Nut Brittle, Butter Rum Sauce

Greenwich, West Village & Meatpacking District

Centering on Washington Square, New York's historic bohemia lies between Houston and 14th streets, and contains within it several distinct areas. From Avenue of the Americas (Sixth Avenue) east to the Bowery, the **West Village** keeps itself young with New York University's student population. **Greenwich Village,** bounded on the east by Avenue of the Americas and on the west by the Hudson River, is the prettiest and most historic of the West Village neighborhoods. The gritty northwest corner of the West Village has been transformed in recent years into an über-hip shopping, dining and clubbing destination known as the **Meatpacking District.** Within these three adjoining areas you'll find a high concentration of eateries, offering cuisines from around the globe.

Greenwich Village

Lined with trees and Federal and Greek Revival row houses, this beguiling tangle of narrow streets is ideal for wandering. The heart of historic **Greenwich Village** is bounded by *(clockwise from north)* Christopher Street, Seventh Avenue South, St. Luke's Place and Hudson Street, inside of which is a skewed layout of crooked streets lined with town houses and old trees. The commercial spine of Greenwich Village, **Bleecker Street** grows increasingly upscale as it nears the Meatpacking District. The stretch of **Hudson Street** between Christopher and Bank streets is lined with restaurants and cafes.

West Village

The area anchored by **Washington Square** is largely defined by the presence of **New York University**, founded in 1831 by Albert Gallatin, secretary of the Treasury under Thomas Jefferson. One of the largest private universities in the country, NYU has an undergraduate population of 40,000 and a steadily rising reputation. The blocks south of the square are filled with student hangouts.

Meatpacking District

Not so long ago, "trendy" was the last word anyone would ever use to describe the section of the West Village bounded by West 15th, Hudson and Gansevoort streets, and the Hudson River. The Meatpacking District was a rather dangerous place until the 1990s; after meat wholesalers would close for the day, drug dealers and prostitutes prowled its moody, cobblestone streets. The booming economy, along with Mayor Rudy Giuliani's heavy-handed crime policy in the early 90s, cleaned up the neighborhood. Although some meat companies remain, the neighborhood's grit is, for the most part, a fashion accessory. Big-name chefs have made inroads into the district, opening hot and hard-to-get-into restaurants. All these places are packed to the rafters at night, so reserve well in advance.

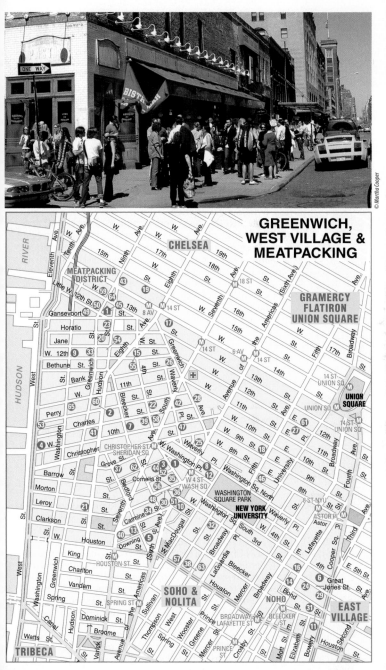

GREENWICH, WEST VILLAGE & MEATPACKING

CHELSEA
MEATPACKING DISTRICT
GRAMERCY FLATIRON UNION SQUARE
UNION SQUARE
WASHINGTON SQUARE PARK
NEW YORK UNIVERSITY
SOHO & NOLITA
NOHO
EAST VILLAGE
TRIBECA
HUDSON RIVER

14 ST
8 AV
18 ST
6 AV
14 ST-UNION SQ
UNION SQ
CHRISTOPHER ST-SHERIDAN SQ
W 4 ST-WASH SQ
8 ST-NYU
ASTOR PL
HOUSTON ST
SPRING ST
BROADWAY-LAFAYETTE ST
BLEECKER ST
PRINCE ST

Eleventh Ave.
Tenth Ave.
Ninth Ave.
Eighth Ave.
Seventh Ave.
Avenue of the Americas (Sixth Ave.)
Fifth Ave.
Broadway
Fourth Ave.
Third Ave.
Second Ave.
West St.
Washington St.
Greenwich St.
Hudson St.
Bleecker St.
W. 4th St.
Greenwich Ave.
Waverly Pl.
Seventh Ave. South
Bedford St.
Varick St.
Sullivan St.
Thompson St.
West Broadway
Wooster St.
Greene St.
Mercer St.
Crosby St.
LaGuardia Pl.
MacDougal St.
University Pl.
Lafayette St.
Cooper Sq.
Bowery
Elizabeth St.
Mott St.
W. 19th St.
W. 18th St.
W. 17th St.
W. 16th St.
W. 15th St.
W. 14th St.
W. 13th St.
W. 12th St.
W. 11th St.
W. 10th St.
W. 9th St.
W. 8th St.
E. 12th St.
E. 11th St.
E. 10th St.
E. 9th St.
E. 8th St.
E. 5th St.
E. 4th St.
Little W. 12th St.
Gansevoort St.
Horatio St.
Jane St.
Bethune St.
Bank St.
Perry St.
Charles St.
Christopher St.
Grove St.
Barrow St.
Cornelia St.
Morton St.
Leroy St.
Clarkson St.
Carmine St.
Downing St.
W. Houston St.
King St.
Charlton St.
Vandam St.
Spring St.
Dominick St.
Broome St.
Watts St.
Canal St.
Prince St.
Houston St.
Bond St.
Great Jones St.
Astor Pl.
Washington Sq. North
Washington Sq. South
W. Washington Pl.
Washington Pl.
Waverly Pl.

aki on west 4

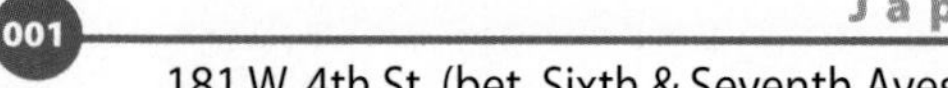

001 — Japanese

181 W. 4th St. (bet. Sixth & Seventh Aves.)

Subway: W 4 St - Wash Sq — Tue – Sun dinner only
Phone: 212-989-5440
Web: www.members.aol.com/akiw4
Prices: $$

At aki, chef/owner Shigeaki "Siggy" Nakanishi goes well beyond the traditional Japanese dishes. Nakanishi did a stint as a private chef to the Japanese ambassador to the West Indies in Kingston, Jamaica, and his cuisine hints at his Caribbean experience.
In addition to the sushi and sashimi standards, Jamaican jerk chicken is rolled with spicy shrimp paste and veggies in mango teriyaki sauce and served with banana tempura. Even the sushi celebrates the flavors of the islands, with the banana-boat roll featuring spicy tuna wrapped with fried banana and the Caribbean roll mixing mango, avocado and yellowtail. For dessert, green-tea tiramisu is topped with passionfruit sauce.
If you want good value, go before 7pm for the four-course prix-fixe menu.

Alfama

002 — Portuguese

551 Hudson St. (at Perry St.)

Subway: 14 St - 8 Av — Mon – Fri dinner only
Phone: 212-645-2500 — Sat – Sun lunch & dinner
Web: www.alfamarestaurant.com
Prices: $$$

Energy surges from every table at Alfama, starting with the vibrant tastes of the Portuguese cuisine and echoed in the cacophony of voices that rises in a room that still packs 'em in (even though it has been open since 1999). The draw? Classic Portuguese fare (codfish cakes, marinated fresh sardines, and *mariscada Alfama*—a traditional fish stew) and theatrical service, from the flaming Portuguese sausages to the *Bife na Pedra*, a filet mignon that's brought to the table on its own sizzling stone grill. Fuel the party further with a bottle from the all-Portuguese wine list or a glass of vintage Port or Madeira.
The decorative handmade tile panel and the Moorish lanterns recall the restaurant's namesake, a historic neighborhood in seaside Lisbon.

Annisa ✿

003 — Contemporary XX

13 Barrow St. (bet. Seventh Ave. South & W. 4th St.)

Subway: Christopher St - Sheridan Sq — Dinner daily
Phone: 212-741-6699
Web: www.annisarestaurant.com
Prices: $$$

Annisa

A serene vibe enfolds you inside this West Village restaurant, whose name is Arabic for "women." Indeed, there is much that is feminine about Annisa, starting with the two owners, chef Anita Lo and sommelier Jennifer Scism. Then there's the minimalist décor, softened by a flowing white curtain that lines one wall. Another tribute to the feminine is the wine list; most of its labels are either made by female vintners and/or made at vineyards with female proprietors.

The chef's inventive, seasonal menu is American at heart, but Lo's Asian roots reveal themselves regularly in lovely dishes such as miso-marinated sable with crispy silken tofu in a bonito broth. In addition to the à la carte selections, guests are invited to try the chef's five- and seven-course tasting menus. Feel free to ask the knowledgeable staff any questions you have about the menu or the wines.

Appetizers

- Seared Foie Gras with Soup Dumplings and Jicama
- Kanpachi Sashimi with Lilies
- Salad of Feta and Grapes with Pine Nuts and Dill

Entrées

- Miso-Marinated Sable with Crispy Silken Tofu in Bonito Broth
- Skate with Avocado and Radishes, Korean Flavors
- Pan-Roasted Chicken with Sherry, White Truffle and Pig's Feet

Desserts

- Poppyseed Bread and Butter Pudding with Meyer Lemon Curd
- Vermont Goat Cheese Cheesecake with Candied Beets and Citrus
- White Chocolate and Peppermint Parfait

Antica Venezia

Italian XX

004

396 West St. (at W. 10th St.)

Subway: Christopher St - Sheridan Sq — Dinner daily
Phone: 212-229-0606
Web: www.avnyc.com
Prices: $$

The romance of Old Venice comes to Greenwich Village at the bottom of a two-story brick building on this busy avenue bordering the Hudson River. Outside, canopies cover the windows all along the façade, and strings of twinkling white lights festoon the small trees by the entrance. The rustic interior is equally engaging, with its two cozy brick-walled rooms, one with an open fireplace, and the other with a wall of cascading water.

On the menu you'll find a large selection of well-prepared, homestyle Italian pastas, gnocchi, fish, chicken and veal, augmented by a list of daily specials. A meal at Antica Venezia begins with an amuse-bouche offered by the chef, and ends with a complimentary glass of limoncello.

AOC Bedford

Mediterranean XX

005

14 Bedford St. (bet. Downing & Houston Sts.)

Subway: Houston St — Dinner daily
Phone: 212-414-4764
Web: www.aocbedford.com
Prices: $$$

The acronym for the French phrase *appellation d'origine controlée* may seem like a high-falutin' name for a restaurant, but in this case it fits perfectly with the quirky Village neighborhood. AOC refers to the French system of designating regional foods and wines, and it symbolizes the restaurant's commitment to using the finest imported and domestic ingredients.

Cuisine centers on French, Spanish and Italian dishes, using items such as *fleur de sel* from France, vinegar from Modena, Italy, and Manchego cheese from Spain. The three-course prix-fixe menu (offered from 5:30pm to 7pm) is a treat for early diners. If you want to impress your date, order one of the tableside preparations for two, such as the suckling pig or the *crêpes Suzette*.

Aroma Kitchen and Wine Bar

Italian

36 E. 4th St. (bet. Bowery & Lafayette St.)

Subway: Bleecker St
Phone: 212-375-0100
Web: www.aromanyc.com
Prices: $$

Mon – Fri lunch & dinner
Sat – Sun dinner only

This sliver of a spot in Greenwich Village has become a festive local hangout, where in warm weather, doors open into the street and the party spills out onto the sidewalk. Aroma's positive energy keeps customers coming back for more fun and food. Luckily, the restaurant's appearance on the Food Network didn't result in diners overwhelming the tiny space. Owners Alexandra Degiorgio and Vito Polosa are passionate about good food and wine, and it shows in the house-made pastas, marinated olives and other fine ingredients, which are a step up from the usual wine-bar fare. All Italian, the unique and fairly priced wine list contains many varietals rarely found outside Italy.
Go Sunday for the prix-fixe family dinner menu and live guitar music.

August

European 

359 Bleecker St. (bet. Charles & W. 10th Sts.)

Subway: Christopher St - Sheridan Sq
Phone: 212-929-8727
Web: www.augustny.com
Prices: $$

Lunch & dinner daily

From the moment you enter this cozy, neighborhood place, your mouth will water at the enticing scents wafting through the room from the wood-burning oven. Billed as "regional European," the honest cuisine here roams the continent from France to Italy to Portugal to Greece. A salad of escarole and pompano or a grilled bavette with nasturtium butter exemplify the changing offerings; of course, if you want a dish that's closer to home, the August burger (jazzed up with house-made mayonnaise) is available at lunch and brunch.
August radiates warmth from its exposed brick walls to its amiable waitstaff. This charming town house on a bustling street in Greenwich Village offers a small dining room up front and a bright glassed-in patio in the back.

Babbo 

008 — Italian XX

110 Waverly Pl. (bet. MacDougal St. & Sixth Ave.)

Subway: W 4 St - Wash Sq — Dinner daily
Phone: 212-777-0303
Web: www.babbonyc.com
Prices: $$$

Babbo/Christopher Hirscheimer

With an empire of New York City restaurants, including Lupa, Esca and Otto, and an armful of cookbooks to his credit, Mario Batali is indeed *"molto"* Mario. It's amazing that this peripatetic ponytailed chef finds time to man the kitchen at his flagship, but luckily for diners, he does.

Local seasonal ingredients fresh from the Union Square Greenmarket team up with products imported from Italy to make memorable meals at this boisterous, always-packed osteria (the second-floor room is quieter). Mario is a disciple of the slow-food style of cooking, and the proof is in his rustic, authentic preparations. Homemade mint "Love letters" with spicy lamb sausage make an excellent beginning, or, if you're a pasta fanatic, the pasta tasting menu offers a small portion of all the highlights.

The exclusively Italian wine list is one of the most exhaustive selections in New York.

Appetizers

- Warm Tripe "alla Parmigiana"
- Asparagus "Milanese" with Duck Egg and Parmigiano
- Pig Foot "Milanese" with Rice, Beans and Arugula

Entrées

- Mint Love Letters with Spicy Lamb Sausage
- Duck with "Scafata", House-made Pancetta and Brovada
- Spicy Two Minute Calamari Sicilian Lifeguard Style

Desserts

- Saffron Panna Cotta with "Agrumi Misti" and Blood Orange Sorbetto
- Meyer Lemon Semifreddo
- Ricotta Cheesecake with Rhubarb and Sweet Vanilla Cream

Barbuto

American 

775 Washington St. (at W. 12th St.)

Subway: 14 St - 8 Av — Lunch & dinner daily
Phone: 212-924-9700
Web: www.barbutonyc.com
Prices: $$

When the weather is warm, the garage-style doors are open, and tables spill out onto the front sidewalk, there's nothing like the ambience at Barbuto. You'll enjoy prime West Village people-watching here on the ground floor of the building that houses Industria Superstudios.

Chef Jonathan Waxman's flavorful, market-based cuisine plays up the best qualities of pristine ingredients. Simple is a good thing here, where fettucine may be bathed in a bright and briny sauce made with cockles, chilies and mint, and shaved Brussel sprouts served as a salad accented with pecorino and walnuts.

The long bar is usually packed by 5pm, and no wonder. From the celebrity-studded crowd to the fresh, tasty fare, Barbuto rules as a neighborhood favorite.

Bellavitae

Italian

24 Minetta Ln. (bet. MacDougal St. & Sixth Ave.)

Subway: W 4 St - Wash Sq — Dinner daily
Phone: 212-473-5121
Web: www.bellavitae.com
Prices: $$

Start your diet tomorrow and visit Bellavitae tonight for a delicious, blow-out of a meal. Staffed by chattering and bustling Italian servers, this charming West Village Italian restaurant takes its wining and dining very seriously. The comprehensive wine list offers a veritable education and includes many hard-to-find and undiscovered wines. Additionally, many of the wines are available by the quartino, or small carafe, which allows diners to explore the wealth of choices.

Sophisticated comfort food is the mantra here. You could make a meal from the appetizers alone, unless you decide to tuck into a bowl of steaming pasta. Before you leave, do as many of the city's renowned chefs do, and pick up a bottle of olive oil from the Bellavitae Pantry.

Bianca

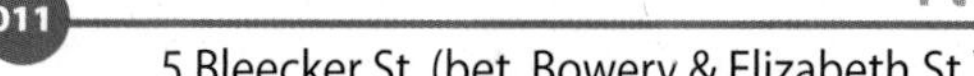

011 **Italian**

5 Bleecker St. (bet. Bowery & Elizabeth St.)

Subway: Bleecker St — Dinner daily
Phone: 212-260-4666
Web: www.biancarestaurantnyc.com
Prices: $$

From its charming owners (Teodora and Celeste) to its intimate seating, Bianca simply radiates warmth. This fetching Italian in the heart of Nolita is perfect for a date or a get-together with friends. Tables are close together, making diners feel like part of the family, and soft lighting adds to the atmosphere.

Bianca's casual personality extends to its cuisine; genuine Italian food with simple, rustic presentations. Rarely found in the U.S., the *cotechino* (a rustic sausage) is a winner. Generous portions of tasty food and a moderately priced Italian-focused wine list make for a very good value in a city often dominated by overpriced meals.

The restaurant does not take reservations so you may expect a short wait outside when things are busy.

Blue Ribbon Bakery

013 **Contemporary**

35 Downing St. (at Bedford St.)

Subway: Houston St — Lunch & dinner daily
Phone: 212-337-0404
Web: www.blueribbonrestaurants.com
Prices: $$

The story of Blue Ribbon Bakery begins with an oven—an abandoned 140-year-old brick oven that brothers Eric and Bruce Bromberg found in the basement of an old bodega. Their discovery sparked an idea for a bakery, and they hired a master craftsman from Italy to rebuild the oven. That same appliance now forms the centerpiece of Blue Ribbon Bakery, opened in 1998.

Bread, from challah to country white, is baked on-site and stars on sandwiches at lunch and appears in a basket at dinner. On the divine menu you'll find everything from terrine of foie gras to a turkey burger, each dish prepared with outstanding ingredients, rich flavor and impressive skill. Those in the know frequent the expertly staffed bar when they want a quick meal.

Blue Hill ✿

American XX

012

75 Washington Pl. (bet. Sixth Ave. & Washington Sq. Park)

Subway: W 4 St - Wash Sq — Dinner daily
Phone: 212-539-1776
Web: www.bluehillnyc.com
Prices: $$$

Blue Hill Farm/Carla Roley

It's not every restaurant that can draw on its own farm for meat and organic vegetables, but luckily for Greenwich Villagers, Blue Hill is one of them. Opened in 2000 by Dan, David and Laureen Barber, Blue Hill occupies a lovely town house near Washington Square Park.

Clean flavors mark the cuisine, which incorporates pristine products like Stone Barns Berkshire pork, Hudson Valley pastured beef, and produce grown at the family's Massachusetts farm. Thus half-moon-shaped ravioli may be stuffed with chestnuts and Delicata squash and arranged atop arugula purée, or poached Chatham cod paired with a briny caviar sauce. A well-chosen list of international boutique wines complements the food.

If you're up that way, stop by Blue Hill at Stone Barns Pocantico Hills, New York. This working farm, with its restaurant and educational center, is a must-see for any serious foodie.

Appetizers

- Stone Barns Raw and Marinated Vegetable Salad
- Fennel and Calville Blanc Apple Salad
- This Morning's Farm Egg, Foraged Mushrooms, Stone Barns Mustard Greens and Herb Broth

Entrées

- Wild Striped Bass, Pistou of Soybeans and Broccoli
- Grass-fed Lamb, Cracked Wheat, Parsnips, Ramps and Squash
- Hudson Valley Venison, Foraged Mushrooms and Stone Barns Greens

Desserts

- Apples, Almond and Oatmeal Crumble with Cinnamon Ice Cream
- Fromage Blanc Soufflé with Ginger Ice Cream
- Pear and Almond Cake, Red Wine Granité and Cream Cheese Ice Cream

Bond Street

014 **Japanese** XX

6 Bond St. (bet. Broadway & Lafayette St.)

Subway: Bleecker St — Dinner daily
Phone: 212-777-2500
Web: N/A
Prices: $$$

You'll want to dress to impress at this stylish, always hopping sushi bar—can New Yorkers ever have enough of these?—where the trendy crowd doesn't seem at all concerned about the prices. Sure, they're high—the prices, that is—but the quality of the food stands up to them. Bond Street's ambitious menu lists a wide array of sophisticated sushi, sashimi, rolls and tempura, all well executed and elegantly presented. The chef, who formerly worked at Nobu, is known for his elaborate creations, like gold-leaf-topped sushi.

Set in a historic brownstone, the restaurant stretches over three levels: the ground-floor lounge, the main dining room and its lively sushi bar on the second floor, and a third-floor space, which includes two tatami rooms.

Café Cluny

015 **American** X

284 W. 12th St. (at W. 4th St.)

Subway: 14 St - 8 Av — Lunch & dinner daily
Phone: 212-255-6900
Web: N/A
Prices: $$

Café Cluny just might be the quintessential West Village restaurant. Set amid the cobblestone streets and charming brick town homes that make the area so well loved, this neighborhood newbie lures patrons with its lineage (its owners are the same winning team responsible for the wildly successful Odeon) and its sweet style. Breezy, with cream-colored chairs, settees and screen doors, the place feels like a beachside bungalow—minus the salty air.

The bistro-style menu focuses on the familiar. Baby beet salad with figs and goat cheese, and a yellowfin tuna sandwich slathered with tapenade may seem commonplace, but whimsical takes on stand-bys (a Concord grape tart with peanut-butter ice cream) will put a smile on your face.

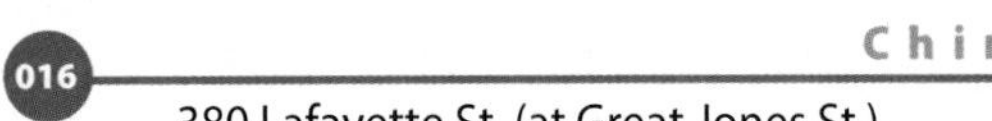

Chinatown Brasserie

Chinese XX

016

380 Lafayette St. (at Great Jones St.)

Subway: Bleecker St — Lunch & dinner daily
Phone: 212-533-7000
Web: www.chinatownbrasserie.com
Prices: $$

Despite a vague feeling of déjà vu, nothing in this restaurant will seem familiar to New Yorkers who remember the space as home to the former Time Café (and Fez downstairs). From the stylish folks behind Lure Fishbar and Lever House comes a China-chic brasserie with dim sum and then some.

The mammoth place promotes sharing, from the size of the tables to the generous menu. Dim sum is impressive—not quite as authentic as in Chinatown, but approachable for the novice, and served by a friendly staff. In addition, the menu includes a mix of Cantonese-American and fusion favorites like General Tso's chicken, and Chinese chicken salad. Downstairs, the mod lounge—complete with a koi pond—sets the mood for canoodling over creative cocktails.

Crispo

Italian XX

017

240 W. 14th St. (bet. Seventh & Eighth Aves.)

Subway: 14 St (Seventh Ave.) — Dinner daily
Phone: 212-229-1818
Web: www.crisporestaurant.com
Prices: $$

Frank Crispo reigns over the kitchen in his West Village eatery, recognizable by the black wrought-iron fence that encloses its entrance below street level. Crispo, who cut his teeth in La Côte Basque and Zeppole, presents his culinary artwork against a cozy canvas of rough-hewn brick walls, soft lighting and closely spaced tables.

A do-not-miss starter is the fragrant, air-cured prosciutto di San Daniele, from the Friuli region of northeastern Italy. If you're in the mood for pasta, order the spaghetti carbonara, the restaurant's signature dish and one of the best of its kind. If you can't make up your mind from mouthwatering menu, the accommodating kitchen will gladly do a tasting for your table and share the best they have to offer.

Cru ✿

018 **Contemporary**

24 Fifth Ave. (at 9th St.)

Subway: 8 St - NYU — Mon – Sat dinner only
Phone: 212-529-1700
Web: www.cru-nyc.com
Prices: $$$$

Cru

As its name suggests, Cru spotlights fine wines. The wine "list" here comes in two separate leather-bound tomes and ranks as one of the best in the city. Some 3,500 selections span the globe and include a number of truly exceptional premier cru bottles; nearly a third of the roster is devoted to burgundies.

To complement your wine, chef Shea Gallante's innovative seasonal tasting menus often include his signature homemade pastas. In addition to the seasonal tasting, guests may choose from the three-course prix-fixe menu. Prune-glazed loin of venison with chestnut-studded wild rice satisfies in winter, while Maine diver scallops with roasted baby artichokes sings the praises of spring.

All this wonderful food and wine is served by an attentive waitstaff in a smart Art Deco setting. Sit at the casual bar if you prefer an à la carte menu and no reservation requirements.

Appetizers

- Yellow Basinga Tomato Gazpacho, Langoustine, Avocado and Wasabi Crème Fraîche
- Nantucket Bay Scallops, Saffron Hubbard Squash, Mutsu Apple and Endive Pumpkin-seed Salad

Entrées

- Sweet Potato Gnocchi, Braised Cinghiale, Thyme Croutons and Raschera Crema
- Chatham Cod, Cabbage Lasagna with Brandade, Sausage, Oven-dried Tomato, Roasted Garlic Emulsion

Desserts

- Cherry "Shortcake", Frog Hollow Cherries, Almond Pound Cake, Amaretto Semifreddo
- Valrhona Chocolate Tart, Chai-Caramel Ice Cream with Butter Pecan, Bourbon-Vanilla Shake

El Cid

Spanish

322 W. 15th St. (bet. Eighth & Ninth Aves.)

Subway: 14 St - 8 Av — Tue – Sun dinner only
Phone: 212-929-9332
Web: N/A
Prices: $$

This unpretentious little neighborhood eatery may seem out of place in the hip Meatpacking District, but the truth is, El Cid was here long before the designer boutiques moved in. Hot and cold tapas provide the food focus in the cramped and anything-but-trendy setting. Count on the proud staff to offer careful, kind service to eager crowds. And count on the tapas, from baby eels to chicken, to be flavorful and redolent with garlic. Tender, smoky *calamari al ajillo, chorizo al vino,* and *croquetas* particularly shine. Sangria makes the perfect accompaniment; it comes in red or white versions with enough fruit to liven up the mix, but not so much to clutter your glass.
Save room for the signature *torrejas,* a wine-dipped version of French toast.

El Faro

Spanish 

020

823 Greenwich St. (at Horatio St.)

Subway: 14 St - 8 Av — Tue – Sun lunch & dinner
Phone: 212-929-8210
Web: www.elfaronyc.com
Prices: $$

Located in a part of the West Village once known as "Little Spain" for the influx of Spanish immigrants that flocked here in the 1940s after the Spanish Civil War, El Faro began as a bar and grill in 1927. Its current owners, the Lugris and Perez families, purchased the restaurant in 1959 and have run it ever since.
Never mind the aging 1960s-era décor, highlighted by a mural of flamenco dancers in the main dining room; it's the food that stands out here. Paella is a favorite, teeming with seafood and sausages and brought to the table in a traditional double-handled dish. If you crave something light, check out the extensive tapas menu; whatever you order, be sure ask for a pitcher of the house sangria to quench your thirst.

EN Japanese Brasserie

021 Japanese XX

435 Hudson St. (at Leroy St.)

Subway: Houston St — Dinner daily
Phone: 212-647-9196
Web: www.enjb.com
Prices: $$$

Brainchild of Japanese restaurateurs and siblings Reika and Bunkei Yo, EN centers on an open kitchen, where the chef and his team craft their own tofu and yuba (the delicate skin that forms when soy milk is heated). A house specialty, yuba appears in dishes such as yuba sashimi and crispy yuba cheese roll stuffed with eel. Tofu, made fresh each night, is available at 90-minute intervals throughout the evening. Signature dishes include black cod in miso, Kakuni-braised Berkshire pork belly in shanso miso, and duck-filled croquettes.
True to its name, EN styles itself as a Japanese brasserie. Its industrial-chic, high-ceilinged dining space is decked out in dark woods, glass and stone and embellished with an eye-catching carved-wood screen.

Extra Virgin

022 Mediterranean X

259 W. 4th St. (at Perry St.)

Subway: Christopher St - Sheridan Sq — Tue – Sun lunch & dinner
Phone: 212-691-9359 — Mon dinner only
Web: www.extravirginrestaurant.com
Prices: $$

Extra Virgin's name, of course, refers to olive oil, used liberally in the Mediterranean-inspired dishes served in this West Village brownstone. Mirrors in the bistro-style dining room create a sense of space, and fresh flowers bring the outdoors in. To add to the aesthetics, the young waitresses are as attractive as they are attentive.
Moderate prices mark the menu of simple dishes, where Classics for Two, the restaurant's equivalent of *plats du jour,* change regularly. The specialty cocktails list includes breezy summer specials like blueberry and watermelon margaritas and kiwi caipirinhas. Be sure to save room for dessert, like the warm chocolate cake topped with caramel ice cream. The place is always packed on Sunday for the popular brunch.

Fatty Crab 

Malaysian

023

643 Hudson St. (bet. Gansevoort & Horatio Sts.)

Subway: 14 St - 8 Av — Lunch & dinner daily
Phone: 212-352-3590
Web: www.fattycrab.com
Prices: $$

Fatty Crab delivers bold Malaysian cooking just out of earshot of the Meatpacking district. The diminutive dining room is China-chic, with dark wood tables and antique Chinese chairs, red lacquer accents and vases of chopsticks.
Chef Zak Pellacio spent time in Malaysia, and the menu pays tribute to his experience. Go for any of the house specialties, especially the chili crab, a messy bowl of fun with large pieces of Dungeness crab in a spicy-sweet, tomato chili sauce; or the Fatty Duck, brined, steamed, fried and brushed with a sticky soy-chile glaze. (If you plan to share several dishes, expect an onslaught of food to arrive at your tiny table.)
Fatty Crab doesn't accept reservations, but this food is worth the wait—even in prime time.

Five Points

Contemporary

024

31 Great Jones St. (bet. Bowery & Lafayette St.)

Subway: Bleecker St — Lunch & dinner daily
Phone: 212-253-5700
Web: www.fivepointsrestaurant.com
Prices: $$

At Five Points, chef Marc Meyer creates consistently good seasonal American cuisine with Mediterranean flair (such as fava-bean hummus and cornmeal-crusted skate with Sardinian couscous). Many of the dishes—Arctic char, pizzettes, wild salmon—are roasted in the wood oven in the open kitchen.
Lunch is a good time to enjoy updated favorites, like chicken salad dressed with jicama, pineapple and avocado. Locals love the Sunday brunch, which features the likes of lemon-ricotta pancakes, dulce de leche French toast, and a spinach and goat-cheese frittata. Enhancing the atmosphere, a little stream courses through a hollowed-out oak log that runs the length of the dining room.
Drop by during the week from 5pm to 6pm, for $2 oysters and $5 martinis.

Gobo

Vegetarian

401 Sixth Ave. (bet. Waverly Pl. & W. 8th St.)

Subway: W 4 St - Wash Sq — Lunch & dinner daily
Phone: 212-255-3902
Web: www.goborestaurant.com
Prices:

Taste, touch, sight, hear, smell. Gobo (and its Upper East Side sister) caters to the five senses with its refined contemporary décor and innovative vegetarian cuisine. Soft neutrals and honey-colored woods highlight the dining area, adorned by wooden bowls and glass containers filled with fresh fruit and vegetables.

From quick bites (tea-smoked yuba with sautéed mushrooms) to small plates (white bean and cremini casserole) to large plates (green-tea noodles with vegan bolognese sauce), the menu spans the globe for inspiration. An organic juice bar is a perfect alternative to the local coffee shop, and the restaurant even serves organic wines.

The name? It's Japanese for burdock root, long used by herbalists to detoxify the body.

Good

American

89 Greenwich Ave. (bet. Bank & W. 12th Sts.)

Subway: 14 St - 8 Av — Tue – Sun lunch & dinner
Phone: 212-691-8008
Web: www.goodrestaurantnyc.com
Prices: $$

Set in the heart of the West Village, this attractive establishment lives up to its name in more ways than one. Slices of Americana (a wooden pig, potted cacti, and a large painting of an ear of corn) spiff up the dining room, while the food finds its roots in rustic dishes and adds a contemporary twist.

Take the signature green-chile macaroni and cheese, for instance. Chef/owner Steven Picker kicks up this American comfort food with spicy chilies and cilantro. Even the hamburger goes uptown as a grilled goodBurger, filled with pulled pork and smoked mozzarella, and served with barbecue sauce.

At just under $10, the weekday lunch includes your choice of entrée with a beverage and a small salad or a cup of soup—mmm, mmm good.

Gotham Bar and Grill ✿

Contemporary XXX

12 E. 12th St. (bet. Fifth Ave. & University Pl.)

Subway: 14 St - Union Sq
Phone: 212-620-4020
Web: www.gothambarandgrill.com
Prices: $$$

Mon – Fri lunch & dinner
Sat – Sun dinner only

Gotham Bar & Grill

French-trained chef Alfred Portale, who has headed Gotham Bar and Grill's kitchen since the restaurant opened in 1984, is well known for being a defining force in New American cuisine. In the restaurant's chic high-ceilinged room, the chef offers a monthly changing list of dishes prized for their clean, intense flavors and top-quality ingredients.

Gotham eschews rich dishes for fresh vegetables and herbs. Pan-seared miso-marinated black cod and yellowfin tuna tartare are just a couple of the longstanding favorites that show off the kitchen's skill. Even desserts, like the Gotham chocolate cake that started the molten-chocolate craze, elevate the mundane to the sublime.

The three-course lunch, served weekdays all year long, is accompanied by a special wine menu that gives you the option of a wine flight, a half bottle or a full bottle, all for the same set price.

Appetizers

- Tuna Tartare with Japanese Cucumber, Shiso, Sweet Miso and Ginger Dressing
- Duck and Foie Gras Terrine with Haricots Vert, Green Lentils, Pickled Onion and Port Glaze

Entrées

- Nova Scotia Halibut with Morels, Ramps, English Peas and Fingerling Potatoes
- Tandoori-spiced Duck with Basmati Rice, Curried Cauliflower, Sambal and Mango Chutney

Desserts

- Gotham Warm Chocolate Cake with Espresso Walnut Ice Cream
- Banana Split with Vanilla and Chocolate Ice Cream, Strawberry Compote and Peanut Truffles

Gusto

Italian XX

60 Greenwich Ave. (at Perry St.)

Subway: 14 St (Seventh Ave.) — Lunch & dinner daily
Phone: 212-924-8000
Web: www.gustonyc.com
Prices: $$

From the street-level room with its sleek bistro feel to the dark and sultry lower level, Gusto just oozes style. Between the white marble bar and the black velvet banquettes, you might think you're on the set of a black-and-white film.

After the departure of chef Jody Williams, Amanda Freitag took the reins and set the pace for the kitchen. Her food continues to please with its layered flavors, simple combinations and utmost freshness—a mantra in Italian cooking. The appealing menu hones in on the Mediterranean with superlative preparations (think moist grilled octopus dressed with olive oil and lemon juice) executed with passion and commitment.

Specialty liquors marinate behind the bar, and cocktails infused with fresh fruit juices sing with flavor.

Hedeh

Japanese X

57 Great Jones St. (bet. Bowery & Lafayette St.)

Subway: Bleecker St — Mon – Sat dinner only
Phone: 212-473-8458
Web: www.hedeh.com
Prices: $$

On a stylish little block, Hedeh takes the nickname of its chef, Hideyuki Nakajima, formerly of Nobu. Nakajima dreams up an inventive selection of top-quality sushi, maki and sashimi, prepared according to his whim. You'll also find a few crossover dishes with French inspiration (foie gras with balsamic ginger sauce, green-tea crème brûlée), along with the chef's *omakase*.

Located at the border of the East Village, Hedeh is a modest place, its contemporary décor limited to neutral colors, soft lighting and a bamboo screen separating the dining room from the sake bar in front. The bar is worth a stop for its impressive list of cold, hot and unfiltered sakes—not to mention Japanese beers. In summer, sake sangria is a popular choice at happy hour.

Home 

030 **American**

20 Cornelia St. (bet. Bleecker & W. 4th Sts.)

Subway: W 4 St - Wash Sq — Lunch & dinner daily
Phone: 212-243-9579
Web: www.recipesfromhome.com
Prices: $$

Domain of husband-and-wife team Barbara Shinn and chef David Page, Home serves three squares a day, beginning with baked eggs with New York cheddar and homemade salami for breakfast. Bead-board paneling, pine-plank floors and family photographs create a homey atmosphere where you almost expect your mother to walk out of the kitchen.
Supporters of sustainable agriculture, the owners rely on nearby markets and local family farms for their kicked-up comfort food; fried chicken, macaroni and cheese with slow-roasted tomatoes, and butterscotch pudding represent a sampling of the American fare here. Labels from Long Island—including their own vineyard—form the core of the wine list. It seems Dorothy was right all along: there's no place like Home.

Il Buco

031 **Italian**

47 Bond St. (bet. Bowery & Lafayette St.)

Subway: Bleecker St — Tue – Sat lunch & dinner
Phone: 212-533-1932 — Sun – Mon dinner only
Web: www.ilbuco.com
Prices: $$

When independent filmmaker Donna Lennard and her partner Alberto Avalle opened their antique shop in the Village in 1994, little did they guess that they'd be running a restaurant in that same space several years later. Set on cobblestone Bond Street, Il Buco features the aromatic cuisine of Italy and the Iberian Peninsula in a charming dining room that's perfect for a romantic tête-à-tête. Vintage pine pieces and bare wood tables with painted chairs furnish the room, which is decorated with antique kitchen utensils and plenty of fresh flowers.
The market-based menu changes daily, and constantly looks to the seasons for inspiration. A Mediterranean theme applies to satisfying pasta and risotto dishes, highlights of the tempting selection.

Il Mulino

Italian XX

86 W. 3rd St. (bet. Sullivan & Thompson Sts.)

Subway: W 4 St - Wash Sq
Phone: 212-673-3783
Web: www.ilmulinonewyork.com
Prices: $$$$

Mon – Fri lunch & dinner
Sat dinner only

Mouth-watering displays of Italian wines, olive oils, fruits and vegetables tantalize you as you enter the small, flatteringly lit dining room at this Italian institution (opened in 1981) in the heart of Greenwich Village. Reservations are hard to come by; a cadre of regulars packs the place night after night (lunch reservations are easier to get).

Cuisine here centers on the bold, garlicky flavors of the Abruzzi region, where the owners, Fernando and Gino Masci, were born. Everything here is abbondanza-size, from the gorgeous antipasti to the signature veal dishes. Expect larger-than-life black-tie service and hefty prices to match.

Il Mulino also packages its marinara sauce, along with coffee, olive oil and balsamic vinegar, for purchase.

Jarnac

033

French XX

328 W. 12th St. (at Greenwich St.)

Subway: 14 St - 8 Av
Phone: 212-924-3413
Web: www.jarnacny.com
Prices: $$

Tue – Sat dinner only
Sun lunch & dinner

Expect to find a good selection of Cognac on Jarnac's menu, since the restaurant is named for the city in the Poitou-Charentes region of France that is home to the famed cognac producer Courvoisier. Indeed, owner Tony Powe honors the town where he grew up by offering a host of Cognacs from a handful of producers.

Contemporary French fare is interpreted with an American flair, and the menu changes daily to reflect the season (in spring the menu incorporates products like wild ramps, fava beans and soft-shell crabs, while in winter the cassoulet wins raves). All appetizers and salads can be ordered as entrée-size plates.

Fans of Jarnac may want to join the restaurant's club, which offers special dinners, tastings and cooking courses.

Kirara

Japanese

033 Carmine St. (bet. Bedford & Bleecker Sts.)

Subway: W 4 St - Wash Sq — Mon – Fri lunch & dinner
Phone: 212-741-2123 — Sat – Sun dinner only
Web: N/A
Prices: $$

If you're feeling adventurous at this family-run restaurant, ask about the *omakase*, or tasting menu. In Japanese, *omakase* means "to put yourself in the chef's hands," so go ahead and trust his judgment regarding your meal. You'll be treated to an assortment of the chef's choice of appetizers, followed by a generous platter of sushi and sashimi; it's a great idea for sharing. Of course, you can always order off the à la carte menu if you prefer. Gentle pricing ensures that Kirara is a local favorite, and takeout is a popular option for those who live nearby.
Whatever you order, you'll be treated to artfully presented dishes, since chef/owner John Hur is an artist himself. Admire his Japanese-style paintings on the walls of the restaurant.

Las Ramblas

035 Spanish

170 W. 4th St. (bet. Cornelia & Jones Sts.)

Subway: Christopher St - Sheridan Sq — Dinner daily
Phone: 646-415-7924
Web: www.lasramblasnyc.com
Prices: $$

Attention to detail marks this tiny tapas bar in Greenwich Village: artful flower arrangements balance on the sliver of a shelf, a water fountain is embedded in a brick wall, and a banquette backed with colorful silk pillows cozies up against the front windows.
This diminutive stage sets the scene for small plates that pack a big flavor punch. Round up a few friends and spend an evening noshing on the likes of broiled octopus served cold with purple potatoes, savory fried *croquetas de jamón*, and warm, buttery *pintxos de caracoles* (snails and mushroom caps on toast points).
Named for Barcelona's central commercial thoroughfare, Las Ramblas impresses with its service, which is smooth, well informed and well timed.

Le Gigot

French

18 Cornelia St. (bet. Bleecker & W. 4th Sts.)

Subway: W 4 St - Wash Sq — Tue – Sun lunch & dinner
Phone: 212-627-3737
Web: N/A
Prices: $$

"A great place to take a date" is how many regulars describe this cozy little bistro, located on the same block as Pó and Home. Of course, you'd expect to find leg of lamb on the menu (since that's what *le gigot* means in French), and so you will; Senegalese chef Alioune Ndiaye's version is an uncomplicated preparation, served with flageolet beans. Other country French dishes include *coquilles St. Jacques* and lamb stew. Fresh, healthy bistro food here avoids heavy cream sauces in favor of lighter fare, including several vegetarian selections.

The handful of tables may cluster elbow to elbow, but the service is eager and smiling, and the Gallic ambience, complete with French posters, oversized mirrors and varnished woods, invites romance.

The Little Owl

Contemporary

037

90 Bedford St. (at Grove St.)

Subway: Christopher St - Sheridan Sq — Mon – Fri dinner only, Sat – Sun lunch & dinner
Phone: 212-741-4695
Web: www.thelittleowlnyc.com
Prices: $$

Nesting on the corner of Bedford and Grove streets, The Little Owl is a homey roost, one that puts the pleasure back into dining out. Partners Joey Campanaro and Gabriel Stulman, who opened this place in May 2006, work hard at hospitality—a theme that carries through to the staff and even the diners, all of whom seem to leave any attitude at the door.

Inside, natural light floods in through the two large windows that frame the corner of the small room. The menu is limited, but in this case that's a good thing. By focusing on what it does well, the kitchen crew creates earthy and intensely flavorful dishes. The meatball "sliders" appetizer and the utterly satisfying ricotta cavatelli both elicit hoots of delight from the regulars.

Lupa

Italian

038

170 Thompson St. (bet. Bleecker & Houston Sts.)

Subway: W 4 St - Wash Sq — Lunch & dinner daily
Phone: 212-982-5089
Web: www.luparestaurant.com
Prices: $$

Brought to you by the team of Mario Batali, Joseph Bastianich, Jason Denton and Mark Ladner (the group behind Babbo and Esca), Lupa stands out as a pearl among a string of Italian establishments that line Thompson Street. The restaurant is Roman from its trattoria menu to its name, a reference to the she-wolf in Roman mythology.
Offering the best authentic seasonal ingredients at reasonable prices is the philosophy here. Lupa achieves that goal with its own *salumeria* that features Italian artisan meats and cheeses, and by making fresh pastas and products like tuna cured in-house. Creative and traditional dishes—including an exemplary spaghetti alla carbonara—always please, along with a list of wines spotlighting the regions of Italy.

Mary's Fish Camp

Seafood

039

64 Charles St. (at W. 4th St.)

Subway: Christopher St - Sheridan Sq — Mon – Sat lunch & dinner
Phone: 646-486-2185
Web: www.marysfishcamp.com
Prices: $$

Mary Redding opened this tiny Florida-style seafood joint in a West Village brownstone in 2000 and has been enjoying wild success ever since. Her lobster rolls overflow with succulent chunks of meat, slathered in mayonnaise and piled on a buttered hotdog bun—they might be messy, but they sure are good! Other selections such as conch chowder and conch fritters recall Key West cuisine, while lobster potpie and pan-seared diver scallops pay homage to the bounty of New England waters. Old Bay French fries, steamed spinach and grilled corn on the cob accompany the delicious, fresh preparations.
Bear in mind that Mary's only serves seafood and the restaurant doesn't accept reservations, but the counter couldn't be better for dining on your own.

Mas

Contemporary

040

39 Downing St. (bet. Bedford & Varick Sts.)

Subway: Houston St — Mon – Sat dinner only
Phone: 212-255-1790
Web: www.masfarmhouse.com
Prices: $$$

Think French country farmhouse, and you've got Mas, literally (*mas* refers to the farmhouses of Provence) and figuratively. Amid barn wood and aged beams, a long leather banquette, Prouvé chairs and antique flatware, you'll find yourself ensconced in a rustic-chic ambience. This little slice of old Provence in the heart of the Village draws an equally laid-back, yet hip crowd.

Swiss-born chef Galen Zamarra (who formerly worked at Bouley) revels in putting new spins on classic preparations, as in rainbow trout stuffed with wild ramps. Add to this an intriguing wine list and wonderful service and you have a sure recipe for success. Partyers looking for a place to have a late—as in really late—bite, will appreciate that Mas stays open until 4am.

Mexicana Mama

Mexican

041

525 Hudson St. (bet. Charles & W. 10th Sts.)

Subway: Christopher St - Sheridan Sq — Tue – Sun lunch & dinner
Phone: 212-924-4119
Web: N/A
Prices: ⊜

A little restaurant with a big heart, Mexicana Mama raises south-of-the-border cuisine to new heights with food as bright as its décor (purple walls, tables painted in primary colors). Flavors shine in dishes like chicken with mole, and roasted chile relleno served with aromatic green rice that gets its color from the addition of cilantro and poblano chile. Delicious vegetables serve as the inspiration behind quesadillas and burritos, and the pork tacos are always a hit. Save room for the rich *pastel tres leches* (otherwise known as cake with three milks).

This unpretentious and popular place features good food for a good price—and if you're lucky enough to live in the neighborhood, they offer takeout and local delivery.

Morandi

Italian

15 Charles St. (bet. Greenwich Ave. & Waverly Pl.)

Subway: 14 St (Seventh Ave.) — Lunch & dinner daily
Phone: 212-627-7575
Web: www.morandiny.com
Prices: $$$

Everything restaurateur Keith McNally touches seems to turn to gold. Balthazar, Pastis and Pravda have established his empire, and they've been packed to the gills for years. His latest venture, Morandi, is no exception. Run by talented chef Jody Williams, formerly of Gusto, Morandi shows that McNally can stray from his signature sexy French bistro and venture into the Italian countryside. Its antique-tile floor, weather-beaten wood, and shelves displaying straw-covered Chianti bottles is Tuscany with all its cliches.

Those who know Gucci better than gnocchi have been filling the place since it opened, but the Italian comfort food—lemon risotto, fried artichokes, marinated octopus—doesn't miss a stiletto-heeled step.

Old Homestead

Steakhouse 

56 Ninth Ave. (bet. 14th & 15th Sts.)

Subway: 14 St - 8 Av — Lunch & dinner daily
Phone: 212-242-9040
Web: www.theoldhomesteadsteakhouse.com
Prices: $$$$

This classic steakhouse has stood in the Meatpacking District since 1868, way before the neighborhood ever became trendy. Old Homestead is a wealthy-guy's-night-out kind of place, with its gentleman's-club-meets-French-bistro décor.

Remember that old saying about never eating anything bigger than your head? You'll have to ignore it here, where the "Empire Cut" of prime rib weighs in at two pounds, and the four-and-a-half-pound lobsters are fittingly billed as "whale-size." Signatures include the domestically raised Kobe-style beef and the legendary $41 hamburger.

Prices may be high, but the meat is top quality, the service is professional, and the elegant dining rooms are papered with photographs of the district in the early 20th century.

One if by Land, Two if by Sea

Contemporary

044

17 Barrow St. (bet. Seventh Ave. South & W. 4th St.)

Subway: Christopher St - Sheridan Sq — Mon – Sat dinner only
Phone: 212-255-8649 — Sun lunch & dinner
Web: www.oneifbyland.com
Prices: $$$

Despite the name (a reference to the lantern hung in Boston's Old North Church in 1775 to warn the colonists of approaching British troops), Paul Revere did not sleep here. This 18th-century carriage house originally formed part of the Richmond Hill estate. It was later restored as a restaurant and opened in 1972.

Well-executed American fare (spice-marinated Maine lobster; smoked duck breast) stars on both the prix-fixe menu and the chef's multicourse tasting. Beef Wellington is the specialty of the house. The lovely brick building, with its four fireplaces, candlelit tables and live piano music, is justly touted as one of the most romantic restaurants in the city. If you have any important proposals to make, this is the place to do it.

Ono

Japanese

045

18 Ninth Ave. (at 13th St.)

Subway: 14 St - 8 Av — Lunch & dinner daily
Phone: 212-660-6766
Web: www.chinagrillmgt.com
Prices: $$$

Housed in the Gansevoort Hotel *(see hotel listing)*, Ono is all about style. "O-no" is also the reaction Jeffrey Chodorow's wife had when he told her he'd be adding another notch to his restaurant-management belt. Beautiful People flock to the bamboo-filled outdoor garden, topped by a retractable roof.

The action begins at the bar, where silk-tunic-clad bartenders mix drinks with names like Blushing Geisha and Blue Yuzu. But the real show centers on the open kitchen, where you can watch the chefs prepare robatayaki, meats grilled over an open flame. The large menu focuses on traditional Japanese fare along with creative sushi combinations. And how cool is the edamame "alphabet soup," poured over cubes of tofu carved to form the letters O-N-O?

Otto

Italian

1 Fifth Ave. (at 8th St.)

Subway: W 4 St - Wash Sq — Lunch & dinner daily
Phone: 212-995-9559
Web: www.ottopizzeria.com
Prices: **$$**

Fans of chef Mario Batali flock to Otto, among the more modest of his establishments, which bills itself as an enoteca/pizzeria. The enoteca part refers to the restaurant's remarkable number (700) of unique Italian wines. For the pizzeria part, thin-crust pies are cooked on a flat-iron griddle, and are complemented by a menu of pasta, seafood, cured meats and more. The variety makes dishes ideal for sharing, and easily accommodates groups and families, who jam the place even at off hours.
The lively bar area is a great place to wait for a table and sample some of the excellent wines poured by the glass. For impatient types, Otto also delivers—or you can get your pizza to go, along with a pint or two of the yummy house-made gelato.

P*Ong

Fusion 

150 W. 10th St. (at Waverly Pl.)

Subway: 14 St (Seventh Ave.) — Tue – Thu dinner only
Phone: 212-929-0898 — Fri – Sun lunch & dinner
Web: www.p-ong.com
Prices: **$$$**

You'll find P*Ong in the West Village, tucked amid apartment buildings and quiet, narrow streets. If you're dining alone, claim a seat at the bar where you can chat with chef Pichet Ong, who puts the finishing touches on every dish. If you're dining with friends, don't expect privacy; tables in this little space snuggle close together.
A spirited focus pervades the chef's cuisine, which takes the form of small plates. Intriguing tapas-like dishes here don't stick to Spain. They hop from the Mediterranean to Asia, borrowing influences from afar to flavor the likes of woodsy organic mushrooms with mint-infused, black "forbidden rice." Fabulous sweets (think Kaffir lime and lemon Pavlova) further illustrate the chef's serious pedigree.

Palma

Italian

048

28 Cornelia St. (bet. Bleecker & W. 4th Sts.)

Subway: W 4 St - Wash Sq
Phone: 212-691-2223
Web: www.palmanyc.com
Prices: $$

Tue – Sun lunch & dinner
Mon dinner only

Set on a lively Greenwich Village restaurant row, Palma exudes a Mediterranean vibe with its sunflower-yellow façade, rustic wood beams and candlelit dining area. The menu leans toward Sicilian dishes, with an emphasis on fresh, simply prepared seafood (whole roasted lobster; sautéed swordfish with fresh mint and capers; sea bass grilled with herbs and lemon), including the house specialty, *frutti di mare al cartoccio*. If you're not up for a big meal, half-portions are available.

Service is casual and efficient, and moderate prices give this place wide appeal. Weekend brunch offers a bargain set-price option that includes baked goods, your choice of entrée (Palermo omelet, Benedict bruschetta) and side item, plus a cocktail.

Paradou

French

049

8 Little W. 12th St. (bet. Greenwich & Washington Sts.)

Subway: 14 St - 8 Av
Phone: 212-463-8345
Web: www.paradounyc.com
Prices: $$

Mon – Fri dinner only
Sat – Sun lunch & dinner

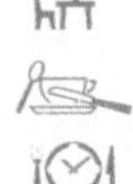

Step into Provence through the weathered French-blue doors of Paradou, which recalls a town in the South of France whose name means "paradise." White-washed walls, high ceilings and tables fashioned out of vintage French wine crates create an airy, country ambience.

Like the atmosphere, the food is Mediterranean in spirit; dishes from that sun-washed region share the menu with the likes of chicken *grand-mère* and Provençal thick-cut pork chops. For dessert, go for the plate of four truffles, handmade by chocolatier Joel Durand in 32 different flavors. Brunch is an entirely French affair, offering items like crab Napoleon, tarte Tatin and seafood aïoli.

In summer, the verdant garden out back makes a hidden oasis for dining. Ah, paradise.

Pastis

French

050

9 Ninth Ave. (at Little W. 12th St.)

Subway: 14 St - 8 Av

Lunch & dinner daily

Phone: 212-929-4844

Web: www.pastisny.com

Prices: $$

A classic New York success story, Pastis was one of the first hotspots here, back when the now-booming Meatpacking District was still a bit sleepy. Today this ever-popular place still packs in a fashionable flock from breakfast through dinner, and celebs sightings are a given.

Brought to you by Keith McNally, Pastis transports diners back to the south of France circa 1960 with its decorative mirrors, long zinc bar, bistro tables and walls lined with vintage Pastis ads. The menu includes all the French classics that locals love (skate, onion soup *gratinée, steak frites, moules frites*—it's all about the *frites* here). As you'd expect, the cocktail list leans heavily on the namesake anise-flavored aperitif, which originally hails from Marseille.

Pearl Oyster Bar

Seafood

051

18 Cornelia St. (bet. Bleecker & W. 4th Sts.)

Subway: W 4 St - Wash Sq

Mon – Fri lunch & dinner
Sat dinner only

Phone: 212-691-8211

Web: www.pearloysterbar.com

Prices: $$

Pearl Oyster Bar is like a sliver of New England in the heart of Manhattan. This beloved eatery—once just a 12-seat counter—has expanded with a small dining room in order to handle a brisk business of shellfish aficionados, but its no-reservations policy often means long waits.

Rebecca Charles named her restaurant for her grandmother, in memory of childhood summers she spent in Maine. The food is New England through and through: wonderful oysters, creamy clam chowder, and the huge lobster roll—chunks of fresh lobster moistened with seasoned mayonnaise, tossed with a hint of celery and parsley and piled on a toasted bun alongside a mound of shoestring fries. Don't forget the blueberry crumble pie, another Down East staple, for dessert.

Perilla

052 **Contemporary**

9 Jones St. (bet. Bleecker & W. 4th Sts.)

Subway: W 4 St - Wash Sq — Dinner daily
Phone: 212-929-6868
Web: www.perillanyc.com
Prices: $$$

Chef Harold Dieterle won a mint of money on the cable-television series, *Top Chef*, so it's only fitting that he named his new restaurant after a member of the mint family (also known as *shiso*). Perilla is simply outfitted with warm woods, swirling ceiling fans and pale walls. The inviting bar area has windows that open to the tree-lined street, and despite Perilla's unassuming style, the boisterous crowds that fill the narrow space speak of celebrity chefdom.

The eager-to-please staff is forthcoming with suggestions from the concise, seasonally inspired menu that features a world of influences from spicy duck meatballs to pan-roasted langoustines. Created by the chef's managing partner, the wine list matches the menu in its global stature.

Piccolo Angolo

054 **Italian**

621 Hudson St. (at Jane St.)

Subway: 14 St - 8 Av — Tue – Sun dinner daily
Phone: 212-229-9177
Web: www.piccoloangolo.com
Prices: $$

Sited at the "little corner" (*piccolo angolo* in Italian) of Hudson and Jane streets, this family-run Italian place is constantly packed with a throng of diners willing to wait in line for chef Mario Migliorini's wonderful food. If you're looking for a quiet place, you'd best go elsewhere; Piccolo Angolo is noisy, crowded and the tables are squeezed together like sardines in a can. It may be a tight fit, but the vibe is friendly and welcoming. Mario's brother, Renato Migliorini, runs the front of the house with aplomb.

That said, the house-made pastas are superior, the fresh tomato sauce is redolent with garlic and fragrant with basil, and the toasted garlic bread is even more terrific if you dip it in a bit of fruity olive oil.

Perry Street 

053 **Contemporary** XXX

176 Perry St. (at West St.)

Subway: Christopher St - Sheridan Sq — Lunch & dinner daily
Phone: 212-352-1900
Web: www.jean-georges.com
Prices: $$$

Jean-Georges Management

Jean-Georges Vongerichten's Village venture occupies the ground floor of the southernmost building in a group of glass-tower condominiums designed by Richard Meier. A healthy walk from the subway station, this relatively remote address is located on the corner of the West Side Highway, overlooking the Hudson River. The glamorous, modern dining room is entirely walled in glass covered by sheer white-fabric panels, creating an ambience that is at once downtown and upscale.

At Perry Street, the food—a fusion of European, American and Asian cuisines—is as up-to-date as the décor. Cutting-edge à la carte preparations are flawlessly executed by a passionate staff of chefs, who orchestrate an ever-changing menu of exquisite global dishes in which the vibrant flavors harmonize perfectly.

The short but well-selected wine list finds its strength in French varietals.

Appetizers

- King Oyster Mushroom and Avocado Carpaccio, Charred Jalapeño Oil and Lime
- Rice Cracker-crusted Tuna, Sriracha Citrus Emulsion
- Crispy Poached Eggs with Caviar and Brioche

Entrées

- Arctic Char, Maitake, Smoked Sea Salt and Basil
- Steamed Skate, Julienne Vegetables, Fennel Purée and Basil Vinaigrette
- Rack of Lamb, Chile Crumbs, Braised Artichokes

Desserts

- Chocolate Pudding, Crystallized Violets, Fresh Cream
- Angel Food Cake, Grapefruit Segments, Yogurt, Star Anise
- Baked Hazelnut Frangipane, Poached Pear, Amaretto Truffle

The Place

Contemporary XX

310 W. 4th St. (bet. Bank & W. 12th Sts.)

Subway: 14 St - 8 Av — Dinner daily
Phone: 212-924-2711
Web: www.theplaceny.com
Prices: $$

Looking for a restaurant for that intimate tête-à-tête? This is The Place. With its grotto-like dining space carved into a series of cozy, dimly lit rooms with rough stone walls and a beamed ceiling, this is certainly the place for romance. White-linen-clad tables are brightened by candles and fresh flowers, and the service is obliging and efficient.

The food is an ever-evolving roster of carefully prepared American fare, based on fresh market produce. Tender leg of roasted lamb, for example, is accompanied by rosemary potatoes and provençal vegetables; homemade fettucini is tossed with roasted tomatoes, toasted garlic, zucchini, baby eggplant, fresh thyme and shaved parmesan.

Pó

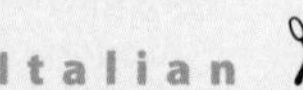

31 Cornelia St. (bet. Bleecker & W. 4th Sts.)

Subway: W 4 St - Wash Sq — Wed – Sun lunch & dinner
Phone: 212-645-2189 — Mon – Tue dinner only
Web: www.porestaurant.com
Prices: $$

Tables aren't easy to come by at this Greenwich Village favorite. Housed in a former coffeehouse/theater (its founder was an out-of-work dancer who staged plays and served cake and coffee here), Pó was the starting point for chef Mario Batali. He has since moved on from his original kitchen, but the restaurant remains popular for its contemporary Italian fare. The waitstaff buoys up the convivial mood in the tiny dining room with cheerful service.

High-quality food at reasonable prices rules here; the four- and six-course tasting menus are the best deals. Fresh pastas are delectable, and entrées are rustic works of art, with choices like beer-braised short ribs and grilled guinea hen. The short wine list includes a nice selection by the glass.

Prem-on Thai

057 **Thai** XX

138 Houston St. (bet. MacDougal & Sullivan Sts.)

Subway: Spring St (Sixth Ave.)
Phone: 212-353-2338
Web: www.prem-on.com
Prices: $$

Mon – Fri lunch & dinner
Sat – Sun dinner only

Perfectly positioned on Houston Street, Prem-on Thai pleases with its modern décor, hip ambience and refined Thai cuisine. The dining space is broken up into several small rooms with a garden in back. Dark wood tables are left without cloths, and Buddhas, bamboo, and Asian flower decals adorn the rooms (consistently trendy, men's and women's bathroom stalls are adjacent to each other with a shared sink).

On the menu, spring rolls and pad Thai pay homage to the familiar, while crisp and soft noodle curry represents regional dishes rarely found in the city. With every dish, the kitchen pays great attention to presentation. The bargain lunch special, a choice of appetizer and entrée arranged on the same plate, will set you back less than $10.

Sevilla

058 **Spanish** X

62 Charles St. (at W. 4th St.)

Subway: Christopher St - Sheridan Sq
Phone: 212-929-3189
Web: www.sevillarestaurantandbar.com
Prices: $$

Lunch & dinner daily

There's something to be said for age. Although Sevilla has been around since 1941, it retains a warm patina in its *taberna*-style interior. José Lloves, who hails from northern Spain, acquired the restaurant in 1962 and has been running it ever since. Tradition reigns here, starting with the attentive waiters, and continuing with the menu, which offers a slice of Spain in its delightful paellas, seafood and meat dishes. Refreshing sangria makes the perfect accompaniment to heaping portions of Spanish favorites, all authentically fragrant and garlicky.

Sevilla doesn't take reservations, but if you go during the week when it's a bit quieter, ask for a table by the windows, which look out on one of the most charming blocks in the West Village.

Spice Market

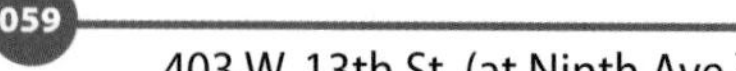

059 — Asian XX

403 W. 13th St. (at Ninth Ave.)

Subway: 14 St - 8 Av — Lunch & dinner daily
Phone: 212-675-2322
Web: www.jean-georges.com
Prices: $$$

Another venture by Jean-Georges Vongerichten, Spice Market is a Meatpacking District hotspot. The cuisine concept is inspired by Southeast Asian food—what you might nosh on while roaming marketplace stalls in Thailand or Malaysia. Subtly seasoned dishes (chicken samosas, red curried duck, pork vindaloo) are placed in the middle of the table, for all to enjoy.
Realized by Jacques Garcia, the design transforms the mood inside this former warehouse from industrial to brooding and sexy, in deep shades of red, violet and gold. A large teak pagoda takes center stage, while wooden arches divide the seating areas. The crowd is strictly A-list, especially in the evenings. For those who want to party VIP-style, there are private rooms downstairs.

Strip House

061 — Steakhouse XX

13 E. 12th St. (bet. Fifth Ave. & University Pl.)

Subway: 14 St - Union Sq — Dinner daily
Phone: 212-328-0000
Web: www.theglaziergroup.com
Prices: $$$

A seductive name, yes—but don't go peeling your clothes off just yet. The "strip" here refers to steak, although the suggestive logo and the alluring décor, in deep bordello-red with photos of semi-nude pinup girls on the walls, might lead you to think otherwise.
Broiled New York strip is the signature dish, available in single or double cut. Then there are the standard steakhouse offerings: filet mignon, veal chops and rack of Colorado lamb (and a few seafood entrées). Sides (all à la carte) such as potatoes crisped in goose fat, and rich black-truffle creamed spinach are not for the faint of arteries, nor are the huge dessert portions.
Additional locations take the Strip House's recipe for success to New Jersey, Florida and Texas.

Spotted Pig 

Gastropub

060

314 W. 11th St. (at Greenwich St.)

Subway: Christopher St - Sheridan Sq
Lunch & dinner daily
Phone: 212-620-0393
Web: www.thespottedpig.com
Prices: $$

The Spotted Pig

The gastropub craze has hit Greenwich Village in the form of the Spotted Pig. This casual place has become a dining destination, and for good reason. With its brown butcher-paper table coverings, farm-animal design motif, and young, friendly staff, the little pub oozes character. Although an upstairs seating area has been added to handle the crowds, expect a wait since this tiny restaurant doesn't take reservations.

Chef/partner April Bloomfield, an alum of London's River Café and Chez Panisse in Berkeley, California, interprets top-quality pub food with an Italian flair. Not intended to be fussy, the seemingly simple dishes exhibit a spot-on depth of flavor and stunning contrasts. Sautéed calf's liver, smoked-haddock chowder, and rich sheep's-milk-ricotta gnudi represent the upscale "pub grub" that is regularly featured on the daily changing bill of fare.

Appetizers

- Smoked Haddock Chowder with Homemade Crackers
- Sheep's Ricotta Gnudi with Brown Butter and Sage
- Roasted Carrot Salad with Cumin

Entrées

- Chargrilled Burger with Roquefort and Shoestrings
- Pan-Fried Calf's Liver with Crispy Pancetta
- Pot Roast Rabbit with Fiddlehead Ferns and Ramps

Desserts

- Crème Catalan
- Flourless Chocolate Cake
- Prune and Armagnac Tart

Surya

062 Indian

302 Bleecker St. (bet. Grove St. & Seventh Ave. South)

Subway: Christopher St - Sheridan Sq — Lunch & dinner daily
Phone: 212-807-7770
Web: www.suryany.com
Prices: $$

There is much that is sunny about this unassuming little Indian restaurant in the West Village. First, there's the name, which means "sun" in Tamil. Then there's the sleek décor, done in blazing tones of orange and red; and the service, which is delivered with a warmth that's rare to find.
Last, but not least, there's a host of meat and vegetable dishes, influenced by the aromatic cuisine of Southern India. Lamb, chicken and shrimp are all prepared tandoori-style, cooked over high heat in a traditional Indian clay oven. The sauces that bathe the dishes—aside from the tandoori items—are especially rich, flavorful and well balanced with a desirable elegance.
No time to sit down for lunch? From noon until 3pm, you can pick up a box lunch to go.

Tomoe Sushi

063 Japanese

172 Thompson St. (bet. Bleecker & Houston Sts.)

Subway: Spring St (Sixth Ave.) — Tue – Sat lunch & dinner
Phone: 212-777-9346 — Sun – Mon dinner only
Web: N/A
Prices:

Patience is clearly the virtue to have if you're planning dinner at Tomoe Sushi, where the wait in the evening can range up to an hour or more. Why all the buzz? Diners don't come for the spartan décor, which consists of a small sushi bar, bare pine tables and specials scrawled on pieces of paper.
They do come, though, for the high-quality sushi and sashimi, which is cut in large pieces for those who don't relish bite-size morsels. Of course, if you're squeamish about sushi, there's cooked seafood, too. You might want to give a second thought to Japanese desserts here. Tomoe's creamy version of cheesecake is scented with green tea and served with a coulis of red fruits.
The only downside? Long waits followed by rushed service can be a drag.

Vento

Italian XX

675 Hudson St. (at 14th St.)

Subway: 14 St - 8 Av — Lunch & dinner daily
Phone: 212-699-2400
Web: www.brguestrestaurants.com
Prices: $$

When the weather is warm and the breeze is coming off the Hudson river, there's no place like Vento's prime corner spot in the Meatpacking District to see and be seen. The menu is ideal for sharing, and a convivial meal materializes effortlessly from the small plates of cheeses, olives, and other Mediterranean starters. Wood-fired pizzas, house-made pastas, whole-roasted fish, and meats round out your family-style feast. If you run out of room for dessert, house-made gelati and sorbetti are available to go.
Brunch brings a chic crowd to the pie-shaped dining space, which is lined on two sides with full-length windows, and a bar in the back. Stick around to check out the late-night scene in the hip downstairs bar, called Level V.

Wallsé ✿

065 **Austrian** XX

344 W. 11th St. (at Washington St.)

Subway: Christopher St - Sheridan Sq
Phone: 212-352-2300
Web: www.wallse.com
Prices: $$$

Mon – Fri dinner only
Sat – Sun lunch & dinner

Wallsé

You don't see many Austrian restaurants in New York, and this one is a keeper. Residents rejoice that chef Kurt Gutenbrunner, who was born in the 16th-century Austrian town of Wallsé, brought his talents to the West Village. His sophisticated Austrian cuisine is served in one of two charming dining rooms, decorated with original 20th-century German and Austrian art.

The ambitious menu showcases traditional dishes (Wiener Schnitzel, Spätzle with braised rabbit, *Palatschinken* with smoked trout, apples and horseradish) as well as more updated fare (thyme-roasted red snapper with Reisling sauerkraut and black truffle sauce), all of which rely on market-fresh produce. Of course, Wallsé brings a taste of the Old World to New York with its delightful desserts.

While there's a refined list of Austrian wines, the specialty cocktails are worth a taste for their delicate flavors.

Appetizers

- Spätzle, Braised Rabbit, Sweet Peas, Corn, Mushrooms
- Palatschinken, Smoked Trout, Apples, Horseradish, Crème Fraîche
- Chestnut Soup, Viennese Mélange, Armagnac Prunes

Entrées

- Brook Trout, Creamed Spinach, Caperberry Sauce
- Wiener Schnitzel, Potato-Cucumber Salad, Lingonberries
- Kavalierspitz, Root Vegetables, Rösti, Apple Horseradish

Desserts

- Apple Walnut Strudel with Roasted Apple Sorbet and Schlag
- Salzburger Nockerl with Huckleberries
- Green Apple and Celery Sorbet, Horseradish, Sea Salt, and Olive Oil

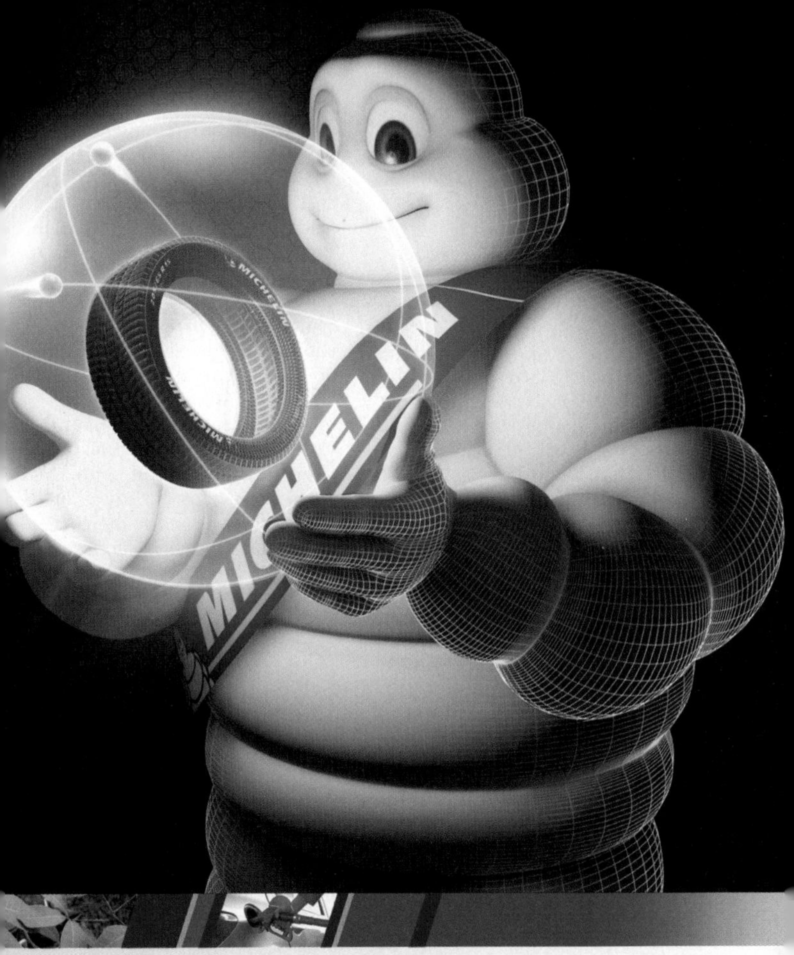

Harlem & Washington Heights

The northernmost reaches of Manhattan, these two neighborhoods stand shoulder to shoulder. Harlem is known for its soul food and rich history, while Washington Heights boasts a storied collection of medieval artifacts housed at The Cloisters.

HARLEM

This diverse neighborhood has a split personality. East of Fifth Avenue and north of East 97th Street lies Spanish and East Harlem, with its distinctive Puerto Rican flavor. Northwest of Fifth Avenue, central Harlem ranks as the most famous African-American community in America.

Railroads to Renaissance

Dutch governor Peter Stuyvesant established Nieuw Haarlem in northern Manhattan in 1658. The hamlet remained largely rural until the railroad and the elevated trains linked it to the rest of the city in the first half of the 19th century. By the 1890s, Harlem was an affluent residential area. As a result of a slumping real-estate market early in the 20th century, landlords rented to the increasing numbers of working-class black families who were moving into the area at that time.

Harlem's golden era, the **Harlem Renaissance**, lasted from 1919 to 1929. During this period, writers Langston Hughes and Zora Neale Thurston electrified the world with their originality. Nightclubs—including the original Cotton Club—hosted performances by jazz greats Duke Ellington, Count Basie, and Cab Calloway. Everything changed with the Depression. Jobs became scarce and poverty set in. By the 1960s, a climate of violence and crime overran Harlem, forcing many middle-class families to leave.

21st-Century Renaissance

Today, a renaissance of another sort is taking place. Investors

Brigitta L. House/MICHELIN

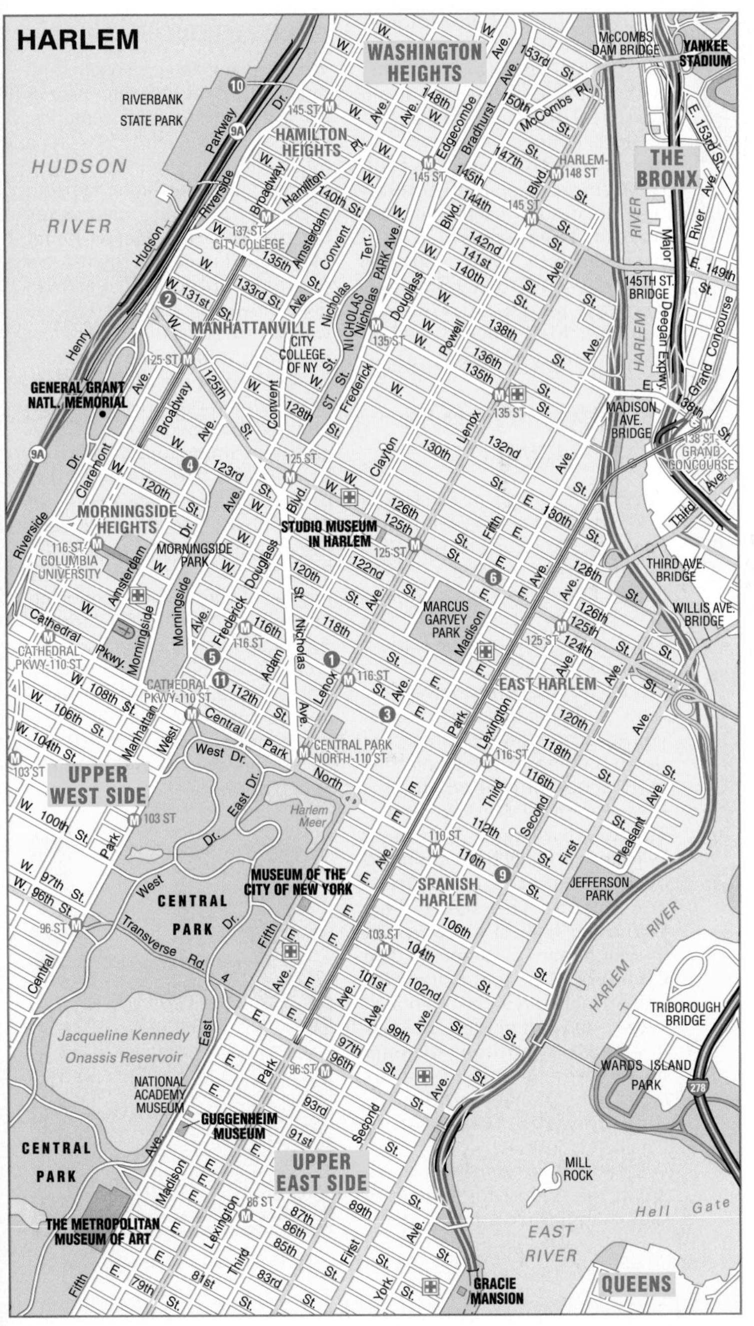
HARLEM
WASHINGTON HEIGHTS
McCOMBS DAM BRIDGE
YANKEE STADIUM
RIVERBANK STATE PARK
HUDSON RIVER
HAMILTON HEIGHTS
THE BRONX
HARLEM-148 ST
145 ST
137 ST-CITY COLLEGE
145TH ST. BRIDGE
MANHATTANVILLE
CITY COLLEGE OF NY
ST. NICHOLAS PARK
HARLEM RIVER
GENERAL GRANT NATL. MEMORIAL
MADISON AVE. BRIDGE
138 ST-GRAND CONCOURSE
135 ST
125 ST
MORNINGSIDE HEIGHTS
STUDIO MUSEUM IN HARLEM
116 ST-COLUMBIA UNIVERSITY
MORNINGSIDE PARK
THIRD AVE. BRIDGE
WILLIS AVE. BRIDGE
MARCUS GARVEY PARK
CATHEDRAL PKWY-110 ST
116 ST
EAST HARLEM
CENTRAL PARK NORTH-110 ST
103 ST
UPPER WEST SIDE
Harlem Meer
110 ST
MUSEUM OF THE CITY OF NEW YORK
SPANISH HARLEM
JEFFERSON PARK
CENTRAL PARK
96 ST
TRIBOROUGH BRIDGE
Jacqueline Kennedy Onassis Reservoir
WARDS ISLAND PARK
NATIONAL ACADEMY MUSEUM
GUGGENHEIM MUSEUM
UPPER EAST SIDE
MILL ROCK
86 ST
Hell Gate
THE METROPOLITAN MUSEUM OF ART
EAST RIVER
GRACIE MANSION
QUEENS

are renovating old brownstones, and West 125th Street—the main thoroughfare—teems with fast-food joints and chain stores. Tour buses fill with visitors, who come to marvel at the neighborhood's wealth of architectural and cultural treasures, such as the historic **Apollo Theater**, which still packs in the crowds. Today as yesterday, soul-food restaurants dish up hearty servings of Southern fried chicken, collard greens, and black-eyed peas.

WASHINGTON HEIGHTS

Keep going north from Harlem and you'll reach Washington Heights. Reaching from West 145th Street to West 218th Street, this narrow neck of land is rimmed by water: the Hudson River on the west and the Harlem River on the east.

Attracted by the comparatively low rents and spacious apartments, young urban professionals are slowly adding to the ethnic mix in this neighborhood, thanks to a recent real-estate boom. The northwestern section of Washington Heights is dominated by the green spaces of Fort Tryon and Inwood Hill parks. Fort Tryon, the highest natural point in Manhattan, is home to **The Cloisters.** The main draw for visitors to this area, the re-created 12th-century monastery belongs to the **Metropolitan Museum of Art** and is fabled for its collection of medieval artifacts, including the 16th-century Unicorn tapestries.

While you're visiting, there are several good restaurants to sample in this pleasant quarter.

An Illustrious Past

Wealthy New Yorkers sought rural sanctuaries near the water here in the late 18th and 19th centuries. One of these, the 130-acre estate where George Washington planned the battle of Harlem Heights in 1776, welcomes the public as the **Morris-Jumel Mansion.** Lining the mansion's original cobblestone carriage drive, now called Sylvan Terrace, you can see some of the city's few remaining wood-frame houses.

By the turn of the 20th century, the neighborhood was populated primarily by working-class Greek and Irish immigrants, followed by German Jews fleeing Nazi persecution in the late 1930s and 40s. Cubans and Puerto Ricans began to move to the area in the 50s, and a large influx of residents immigrated from the Dominican Republic in the late 70s. African-American luminaries such as jazz great Duke Ellington, Supreme Court Justice Thurgood Marshall, and historian W.E.B. Dubois, co-founder of the NAACP, all called this neighborhood home at one time.

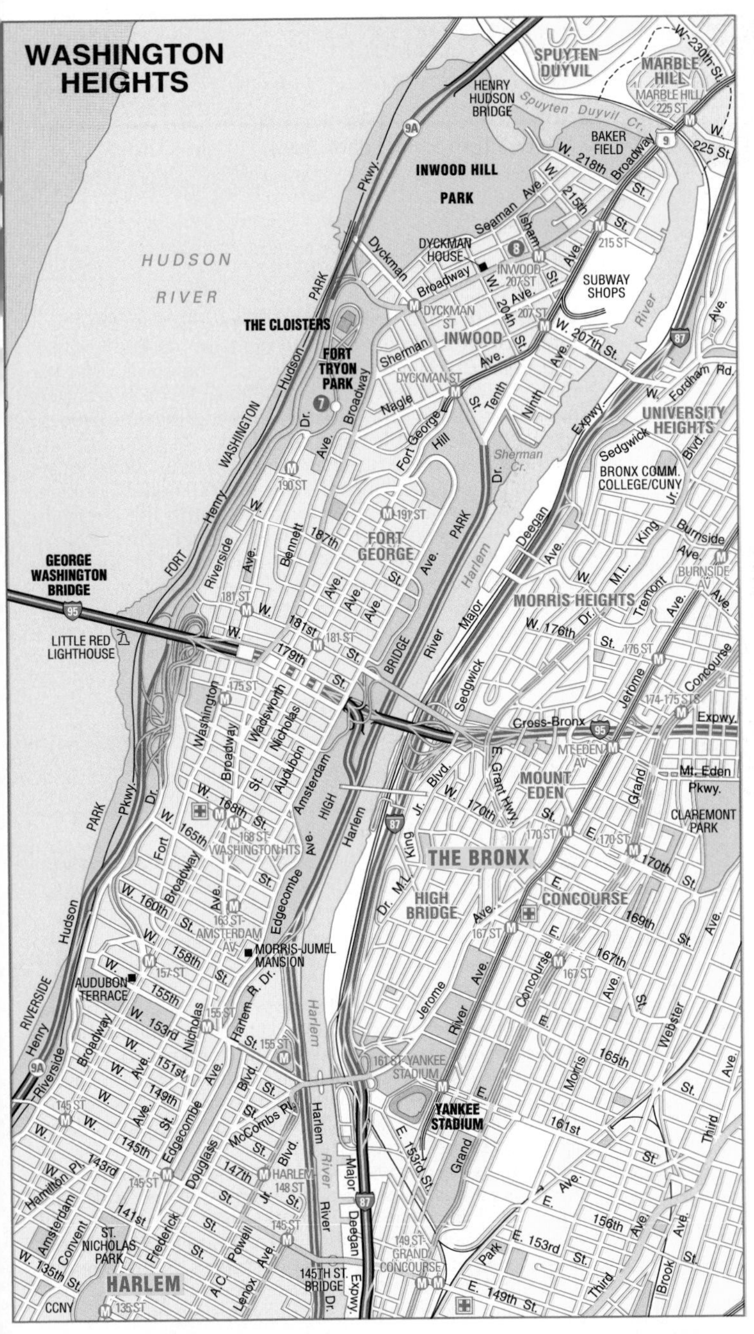
WASHINGTON HEIGHTS
HUDSON RIVER
THE CLOISTERS
FORT TRYON PARK
INWOOD HILL PARK
DYCKMAN HOUSE
INWOOD
SPUYTEN DUYVIL
MARBLE HILL
HENRY HUDSON BRIDGE
BAKER FIELD
SUBWAY SHOPS
UNIVERSITY HEIGHTS
BRONX COMM. COLLEGE/CUNY
FORT GEORGE
GEORGE WASHINGTON BRIDGE
LITTLE RED LIGHTHOUSE
MORRIS HEIGHTS
MOUNT EDEN
CLAREMONT PARK
THE BRONX
HIGH BRIDGE
CONCOURSE
MORRIS-JUMEL MANSION
AUDUBON TERRACE
YANKEE STADIUM
ST. NICHOLAS PARK
HARLEM
145TH ST. BRIDGE
CCNY

Amy Ruth's

001 **Southern**

113 W. 116th St. (at Lenox Ave.)

Subway: 116 St (Lenox Ave.) — Lunch & dinner daily
Phone: 212-280-8779
Web: www.amyruthsharlem.com
Prices: ⊜

When you get a hankering for down-home Southern food, forget that you're in the heart of Yankee country and head uptown to Amy Ruth's. If you spot a smoker parked out front, rest assured that it's not a prop—barrels nearby are filled with wood for fueling the fire used to smoke the delectable barbecue ribs.
The place is perpetually crowded, mainly with locals who have caught wind of Amy Ruth's soulful cooking. From chicken and waffles for breakfast to the excellent cornmeal-crusted fried catfish for dinner, the carefully prepared food here will satisfy the heartiest of appetites. Be sure to order a side of the sweet, smoky collard greens, and to complete your comfort-food feast, don't pass up the luscious peach cobbler for dessert.

Dinosaur Bar-B-Que

002 **Barbecue**

646 W. 131st St. (at Twelfth Ave.)

Subway: 125 St (Broadway) — Tue – Sun lunch & dinner
Phone: 212-694-1777
Web: www.dinosaurbarbque.com
Prices: $$

Dinosaur Bar-B-Que has become a destination. Though it's off the beaten path in a Harlem neighborhood, Dinosaur lures a spirited crowd from bikers to yuppies who flock here by car (parking is nearby) or subway (a few blocks away) for finger-licking-good barbecue and down-home décor (walls lined with license plates, beer signs and sports paraphernalia).
Dinosaur is an outpost of the Syracuse original, and the menu is almost identical. Unlike most New York City barbecue joints, Dinosaur smokes their own meat, and everything (pulled pork, ribs, brisket, sausage and chicken) is drenched in the restaurant's own sauces. Sides of honey hush cornbread, mac and cheese, deviled eggs and fried green tomatoes round out the belly-busting meals.

Ginger

Chinese XX

003

1400 Fifth Ave. (at 116th St.)

Subway: 116 St (Lenox Ave.) — Dinner daily
Phone: 212-423-1111
Web: www.gingerexpress.com
Prices: $$

Ginger is an eye-popping sign of the times. Poised between East and West Harlem, which has been experiencing an exciting renaissance after years of neglect, Ginger brings an audacious concept to this bustling neighborhood's culinary scene. This restaurant delivers healthy, fresh and low-fat Chinese food. Avoiding oils, MSG and frying, Ginger's organic-based cuisine is delicious and portions are large. Marinated spicy tofu is a vegetarian's dream; stir-fry dishes are available with meat, chicken or seafood; and a delightful selection of healthy sides proves a perfect complement to any meal.
The dramatic space is sleek and gorgeous, with warm rosy-toned lighting, sexy dark woods and unique decorative accents showing off an Asian-chic style.

Max SoHa

Italian 

004

1274 Amsterdam Ave. (at 123rd St.)

Subway: 125 St (Broadway) — Lunch & dinner daily
Phone: 212-531-2221
Web: www.maxsoha.com
Prices: $$

Set in the shadow of prestigious Columbia University in the ever-evolving neighborhood of Morningside Heights, Max SoHa is a sweet little place. In the dining room, mirrors double as menu boards, and the staff in the semi-open kitchen turns out a small list of dishes that stays the same through lunch and dinner (in the evening, portions and price tags are a bit bigger). Pastas include a ravioli of the day, while the handful of entrées meanders from *filetto di baccala al forno* to *osso buco di Mamma Bora* (a recipe of the owner's mother-in-law).
Down the street at no. 1262, little sister, Max Caffé, pampers the locals with breakfast and lunch. The original restaurant, Max, is at 51 Avenue B in the East Village. None of the three locations accepts reservations.

Melba's 

005 **Southern**

300 W. 114th St. (at Frederick Douglass Blvd.)

Subway: 116th (Frederick Douglass Blvd.)
Phone: 212-864-7777
Web: www.melbasrestaurant.com
Prices: $$

Tue – Sat dinner
Sun lunch & dinner

Morningside Heights is richer for having restaurants like Melba's. The well-appointed eatery sits on a corner in this rapidly gentrifying area of West Harlem. Owned by a longtime employee of Sylvia's, Harlem's legendary soul-food spot, Melba's dishes up "American comfort food" along with engaging service.

Begin a meal here with "comfortizers" like the spring roll (filled with black-eye peas, yellow rice and collard greens) or the catfish strips (fried, of course). Then on to thick slices of barbecue turkey meatloaf topped with smoky, vinegar-spiked sauce; wine-braised short ribs on a cake of cheddar grits; or satisfying buttermilk chicken and waffles.

To further entice you, Tuesday is open-mike night, and Wednesday night brings live music.

MoBay Uptown

006 **Caribbean**

17 W. 125th St. (bet. Fifth & Lenox Aves.)

Subway: 125 St (Lenox Ave.)
Phone: 212-828-3400
Web: www.mobayrestaurant.com
Prices: $$

Lunch & dinner daily

A sparkling oasis amid the flurry of activity in this frenetic part of Harlem, MoBay Uptown fosters an upscale ambience with its fresh flowers, sultry colors, and embroidered silk panels.

A diverse clientele comes for baby back ribs and Maryland crab cakes, as well as Caribbean specialties such as piquant jerk chicken, fried green plantains, and tender, spicy curried goat. A Jamaican treat, the signature rummy rum cake is soaked in a blend of three rums; it's sure to satisfy your craving for sweets and an after-dinner drink—all in one luscious treat.

Live music keeps toes tapping Tuesday through Saturday nights, and on Sunday the party rocks on with a Gospel brunch. The long communal table helps maximize seating space during performances.

New Leaf Café

American

007

1 Margaret Corbin Dr. (Fort Tryon Park)

Subway: 190 St — Tue – Sun lunch & dinner
Phone: 212-568-5323
Web: www.nyrp.org/newleaf
Prices: $$

There are few better places to be on a summer's day than on the sunny terrace of this adorable little place in Fort Tryon Park. Housed in a 1930s-era stone building a few minutes walk from The Cloisters, the cafe offers a cozy getaway with arched windows overlooking the park. If the sun is shining, this place fills up fast at lunch, so be sure to make reservations. Otherwise, go for dinner and enjoy the luxury of on-site parking.

At lunch the menu offers salads and sandwiches, while at dinner the kitchen shows off its more creative instincts, offering everything from fried rock shrimp and beef carpaccio to pan-roasted salmon and handmade pappardelle. Order freely, as all proceeds from the cafe go toward the upkeep of the historic park.

Park Terrace Bistro

Moroccan 

008

4959 Broadway (bet. W. 207th & Isham Sts.)

Subway: Inwood - 207 St — Dinner daily
Phone: 212-567-2828
Web: www.parkterracebistro.com
Prices: $$

A slice of Morocco in Inwood, this sweet bistro sits a couple of blocks east of Inwood Hill Park, just steps from the last stop on the A-train line. Inside they've captured the essence of the Casbah with deep colors, sultry lighting and soft Moroccan music.

The cuisine of North Africa is celebrated here; traditional tagines are served with your choice of fish, chicken or lamb, or opt for a taste of history with the "Fifteenth-Century couscous," a combination of seafood, almonds and stewed fruits in a light saffron cream sauce. French-influenced dishes include filet mignon and grilled pork chops. Casablanca-born owner, Karim Bouskou, and his wife, Natalie Weiss, promote a convivial atmosphere, aided by the delightful waitstaff.

Ricardo Steakhouse

Steakhouse

2145 Second Ave. (bet. 110th & 111th Sts.)

Subway: 110 St

Dinner daily

Phone: 212-289-5895

Web: www.ricardosteakhouse.com

Prices: $$

If the Mambo Kings were still around, Ricardo Steakhouse would be their haunt. This top-notch steakhouse delivers quality dishes with a Latin beat. Classics such as NY strip steak and filet mignon share space with Angus beef-filled empanadas and other Latin favorites.

While East Harlem has yet to benefit from the gentrification seen in other neighborhoods, Ricardo Steakhouse remains a true destination restaurant, drawing a mix of diners from all over the city lured by the promise of a good, reasonably priced meal. From the brightly colored walls to the distinctive artwork, the mood is decidedly upbeat. An open kitchen and exposed brick add warmth to the dining room, which is serviced by an extremely engaging and professional staff.

The River Room

Southern 

750 W. 145th St. (at Riverside Dr.)

Subway: 145 (Broadway)

Wed – Sat dinner only
Sun lunch only

Phone: 212-491-1500

Web: www.theriverroomofharlem.com

Prices: $$

Despite its location in Riverbank State Park (the site of a filtration plant that encompasses a lovely recreation area), The River Room boasts great views of the Hudson and the twinkling lights of the George Washington Bridge from its floor-to-ceiling windows.

Sophisticated, stick-to-your-ribs Southern cooking here includes everything from open-faced oyster po' boy sandwiches and shrimp 'n grits (made with South Carolina's organic Anson Mill grits) with red-eye gravy to red velvet cake. There's live jazz on weekends ($5 cover), but the upbeat scene is entertainment enough.

Though service is far from formal, the sweet waitstaff will see to it that your meal makes you as happy as a clam. Come by car, since only a few buses enter the park.

Zoma

Ethiopian

011

2084 Frederick Douglas Blvd. (at 113th St.)

Subway: Cathedral Pkwy - 110 St

Phone: 212-662-0620

Web: www.zomanyc.com

Prices: $$

Mon – Fri dinner only
Sat – Sun lunch & dinner

Morningside Heights is more multicultural than ever now, between the influx of young residents and the expansion of Columbia University. So, it's not surprising to find a restaurant that highlights the cuisine of Abyssinia in this lively area. Zoma joins the melting pot as one of many more to come.

Traditional textiles and other Ethiopian artifacts decorate the welcoming room, where a serious team goes about their business. Intriguing food here is placed on a communal platter in the middle of the table, and served with *injera* (a pancake-like, fermented bread) used to pick up bits of *Tibs Wett* (beef sirloin simmered with cardamom, coriander, garlic, clarified butter, and spicy berbere sauce) or *Doro Alitcha* (chicken stewed in a mild herb sauce).

Lower East Side

Despite being one of New York's hippest neighborhoods, the Lower East Side has, for the most part, a refreshing lack of attitude and an astounding amount of local pride. "Come one, come all" has been its message to visitors since the 1880s, when it became the quintessential American melting pot. Though today's immigrants tend to be young artists, musicians and designers, artsy types aren't the only ones working on their craft on the Lower East Side. In recent years the neighborhood has become a breeding ground for new culinary talent, while history lives on in the district's many famous ethnic eateries.

The Governor's Farm

The area now known as the Lower East Side—clockwise from north, is bounded by Houston Street, the East River, Pike Street, and the Bowery—was rural long after the southern tip of Manhattan was developed. Peter Stuyvesant, the last Dutch governor of Nieuw Amsterdam, bought much of this land in 1651 from the Indians. To facilitate transport between his farm, or *bouwerie*, and the urban market, he laid out a straight road now known as the **Bowery**.

Gateway to America

The first mass migration to the Lower East Side occurred with the arrival of Irish immigrants fleeing the Great Hunger of 1845 to 1852. From the 1880s until World War I, millions of southern and eastern Europeans arrived via Ellis Island and settled in the Lower East Side, where they could meet other recently arrived immigrants. The neighborhood swiftly became the most densely populated in the country.

Eastern European Jews set down some of the strongest roots here, building synagogues and schools, publishing Yiddish newspapers, and opening Kosher delis. The Lower East Side was the original nosher's paradise, and for those in the know, it remains just that.

The Lower East Side Today

Today only 10 percent of Lower East Side residents are Jewish. The southern edge of the district is largely Chinese. Latinos still have a presence, but more prevalent—or at least visible—are the hordes of young Anglos who have transformed the once-gritty neighborhood into a free-spirited urban village.

Orchard Street between Canal and Houston streets is the district's spine; to the south it's lined with bargain stores; farther north (around Broome Street) trendy boutiques begin. Stanton and Rivington streets all the way east to Clinton Street are good for galleries, shops and cafes. A carnival atmosphere prevails at night on and around Ludlow Street between Houston and Delancey, where restaurants, bars and clubs stay full until the wee hours.

© Martha Cooper

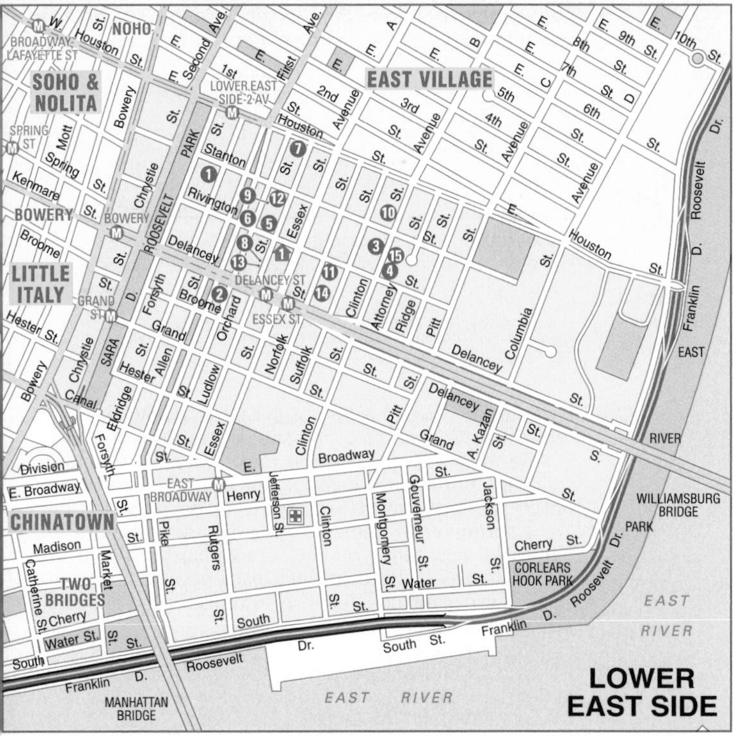

LOWER EAST SIDE

Ápizz

001

217 Eldridge St. (bet. Rivington & Stanton Sts.)

Subway: Lower East Side - 2 Av — Mon – Sat dinner only
Phone: 212-253-9199
Web: www.apizz.com
Prices: $$$

A huge brick oven forms the focal point of Ápizz (say ah-BEETS), whose name derives from the Neapolitan word for pizza. The restaurant's concept, brought to you by the same duo—John LaFemina and Frank DeCarlo—who run Peasant in SoHo, is simple: "one room, one oven." This means that nearly all the dishes, from baked pastas to whole roasted fish, are fired in the wood-burning oven.
While the thin-crust pizzas go without saying, almost every dish that comes out of the wood-burning oven is worth attention, and pastas sing with flavor. A meal in the dining room, which blends old and new between the rustic oven, the wood-beamed ceiling and the contemporary table settings, begins with fresh ricotta and warm tomato sauce with crusty country bread.

Congee Village

Chinese

002

100 Allen St. (at Delancy St.)

Subway: Delancey St — Lunch & dinner daily
Phone: 212-941-1818
Web: www.sunsungroup.com/congeevillage
Prices:

Porridge for dinner may not sound tempting, but with more than 25 varieties of *congee*, this attractive place is sure to win over even the most wary. This soothing specialty, popular throughout China, is served bubbling hot in an earthenware pot, ready to be seasoned with an assortment of tableside condiments. Besides the namesake signature, you can sample hard-to-find dishes like the sautéed short rib with black-pepper sauce on a sizzling hot plate, cold jellyfish, and rice baked with meat and vegetables in a bamboo vessel.
Located on the fringe of Chinatown, the multilevel space covered in bamboo and stone has a warm ambience. Large tables, a buzzing bar area and a host of private rooms fill the space with all the revelry of a town square.

Cube 63

003 **Japanese**

63 Clinton St. (bet. Rivington & Stanton Sts.)

Subway: Delancey St — Sun – Sat dinner only
Phone: 212-228-6751
Web: www.cube63.com
Prices: $$

Eclectic sushi is the name of the game at Cube 63, where the chef certainly thinks outside the box. He comes up with some pretty far-out combinations, such as the Mexican roll (white fish with jalapeño and spicy sauce) and the Puerto Rico roll (eel tempura and lobster salad with cucumber). Additionally, a wide selection of cooked items, from tempura to teriyaki, is available.

Bring your own bottle if you want an alcoholic beverage at this little sushi joint; they don't have a liquor license. Not to worry, though, there's a liquor store just down the street, and the restaurant doesn't charge a corkage fee.

The crowd is trendy and the design is sparse and ultra-modern—check out the lime-green spotlights that illuminate the sushi bar.

Falai

004 **Italian**

68 Clinton St. (bet. Rivington & Stanton Sts.)

Subway: Lower East Side - 2 Av — Tue – Sun dinner only
Phone: 212-253-1960
Web: www.falainyc.com
Prices: $$

With its concentration of good restaurants, Clinton Street is already a destination for foodies. Falai and its bakery just makes it more so. This sliver of a spot, with its hip lounge ambience, has an airy feel, even though the only window is at the front. During warm months, diners clamor for a table in the garden out back.

The Italian staff is welcoming and genuinely enthusiastic about the food—and for good reason. Trained as a pastry chef, Ioacopo Falai peppers his menu with sweet notes (cocoa, dates, raisins, apricots) that accent and enhance each dish. It may be a challenge to select between the many *dolci* on a full stomach, but it's worth saving room for the likes of *millefoglie* or an unexpected savory celery cake with milk gelato.

'inoteca 

005 — **Italian**

98 Rivington St. (at Ludlow St.)

Subway: Delancey St — Lunch & dinner daily
Phone: 212-614-0473
Web: www.inotecanyc.com
Prices: 

Big Sister to 'ino in the West Village, 'inoteca caters to the chic, young Lower East Side set. This spot owes its popularity in part to co-owner Jason Denton, who also has a hand in Otto. True to its name (an *enoteca* is an Italian wine bar), the restaurant offers a superb selection of well-priced Italian wines from every region of Italy. Of these, 25 are available by the glass.

The menu emphasizes small plates and panini (perhaps stuffed with bresaola, fontina and arugula, or roasted vegetables and fresh ricotta); pick up a copy of the 'inoteca's cookbook to learn how to perfect the art of this Italian sandwich. If wine and cheese is your thing, you can choose assortments of 3, 5 or 7 different types of Italian cheeses to sample with your *vino*.

Kampuchea Noodle Bar

006 — **Asian**

78 Rivington St. (at Allen St.)

Subway: Lower East Side - 2 Av — Mon – Thu dinner only
Phone: 212-529-3901 — Fri – Sun lunch & dinner
Web: www.kampucheanyc.com
Prices: $$

It may not be priced like it came from a vendor's cart, but the cuisine at Kampuchea Noodle Bar nonetheless celebrates Cambodian street food. Divided among sandwiches *(num pang)*, Cambodian savory crêpes, soups and noodle dishes, the menu offers a comprehensive look at this satisfying fare. Best way to dine here? Order a little bit of everything. *Katiev,* or noodle soups, are the house specialty, and are brimming with everything from filet mignon to tofu to prawns.

The décor is part downtown New York, part kindergarten classroom, with its wooden counters complete with cubbyholes and hooks for storage, backless stools, and Mason jars filling in for water glasses. If you're looking to lunch, Kampuchea Noodle Bar serves it only on weekends.

Katz's 

007 — Deli

205 E. Houston St. (at Ludlow St.)

Subway: Lower East Side - 2 Av — Lunch & dinner daily
Phone: 212-254-2246
Web: www.katzdeli.com
Prices:

Established in 1888, Katz's is as much a New York institution as the Statue of Liberty. One of the few original Eastern European establishments remaining in the Lower East Side, Katz's attracts out-of-towners, residents and celebrities. In the never-ending debate over who serves the best pastrami in the city, Katz's often tops the list.
For an authentic experience, queue up in front of the salty countermen, collect your meal, and head to a table. What to order? Matzo ball soup and a pastrami sandwich—on rye, 'natch, and not toasted, please—with a side of fries. Just be sure not to lose the ticket you get upon entering. It's your ticket out, and if you don't have it, they make such a fuss that you'll want to crawl under a table and hide.

Kuma Inn

008 — Asian

113 Ludlow St. (bet. Delancey & Rivington Sts.)

Subway: Delancey St — Tue – Sun dinner only
Phone: 212-353-8866
Web: www.kumainn.com
Prices:

Grit meets glam in the Lower East Side as gentrification continues to take hold. At Kuma Inn, chef King Phojanakong, a veteran of Daniel and Jean-Georges, brings a touch of culinary polish to the 'hood. The second-floor dining room has a compact open kitchen and walls accented with bamboo and rice-paper sconces.
The décor is spare, allowing diners to focus on the food. Tapas-size portions are infused with the multicultural influences of Southeast Asia, reflecting the chef's own Thai-Filipino background. Order several items and share with some friends; just be sure to try the sautéed Chinese sausage with chile-lime sauce and the drunken shrimp. Genteel service and a background soundtrack of the chef's favorite hits add to the ambience.

The Orchard

009 Contemporary XX

162 Orchard St. (bet. Rivington & Stanton Sts.)

Subway: Delancey St — Mon – Sat dinner only
Phone: 212-353-3570
Web: www.theorchardny.com
Prices: $$

Creative and funky, modern and cool, The Orchard sparkles as a star on the Lower East Side. This delightful place celebrates contemporary style with its light woods and warm beige walls covered by strips of mirrors. From the young waitstaff to the diverse crowd of diners, The Orchard gives off a hip, unpretentious vibe. Great food and a small room make reservations hard to come by.

The menu is Italian-inspired and upmarket, with an entire section devoted to crispy flatbreads (topped with steak tartare, royal trumpet mushrooms, or house-made hummus), a specialty here and great for groups—that is, if you can bring yourself to share. Entrées focus on inventive pastas like spaghettini with black tiger shrimp, crispy chorizo and panko oreganata.

Sachiko's On Clinton

010 Japanese X

25 Clinton St. (bet. Houston & Stanton Sts.)

Subway: Delancey St — Tue – Sun dinner only
Phone: 212-253-2900
Web: www.sachikosonclinton.com
Prices: $$

Sachiko's is a survivor of the ever-changing landscape of the Lower East Side restaurant scene. This sushi and sake bar comes alive with bright orange walls, blond woods and an intimate sushi counter where fresh raw fish are displayed.

The restaurant draws an international clientele who clamor for creative sushi, including some made with luxe ingredients such as caviar and lobster. *Kushiage* is the specialty: beef, chicken or vegetables are threaded on bamboo sticks (*kushi* in Japanese), breaded and deep-fried. Think of kushiage as Japanese kebabs—and know that they have way more fat calories than sushi. Even the cocktail menu has a Japanese focus, with sake making its way into cosmopolitans, margaritas and mojitos.

Schiller's Liquor Bar

European

131 Rivington St. (at Norfolk St.)

Subway: Delancey St — Lunch & dinner daily
Phone: 212-260-4555
Web: www.schillersny.com
Prices: $$

Founded by restaurateur Keith McNally, Schiller's fancies itself as a "low life" bar, but if this is how that other half lives, then lowbrow never looked so good. It's a lively, happening scene, decked out with subway tiles, antique mirrors and bare bistro tables; the noise level ratchets up higher and higher as the night goes on.
On the eclectic menu you'll find everything from steak *frites* to fish and chips to eggplant parmesan. For dessert, don't miss the sticky toffee pudding, a wonderful, creamy confection topped with vanilla ice cream. Schiller's serves a light supper menu until 3am on Friday and Saturday.
The wine list is divided into three sections: cheap, decent and good; according to the restaurant, "cheap" is the best.

The Stanton Social

012

Fusion

99 Stanton St. (bet. Ludlow & Orchard Sts.)

Subway: Lower East Side - 2 Av — Mon – Fri dinner only
Phone: 212-995-0099 — Sat – Sun lunch & dinner
Web: www.thestantonsocial.com
Prices: $$

Designed by the hip firm of AvroKO, Stanton Social fills a duplex with two floors of fun. The décor here honors the erstwhile haberdashers and seamstress shops of the Lower East Side with elements such as a wall of woven leather, vintage hand mirrors displayed in the upstairs bar, and wine shelves laid out in a herringbone pattern, inspired by a man's jacket.
Chef/owner Chris Santos' wildly eclectic menu of small plates zigzags all over the globe, from Europe to China. Adorable little "sliders," filled with lobster, Kobe-style beef or pulled pork, are served on brioche buns. Don't forget to bring some friends; sharing is part of the deal. Weekend brunch is equal parts sweet and savory, and the Bloody Mary bar offers several thirst quenchers.

Suba

013 **Spanish** XX

109 Ludlow St. (bet. Delancey & Rivington Sts.)

Subway: Delancey St — Dinner daily
Phone: 212-982-5714
Web: www.subanyc.com
Prices: $$

Hot, hot, hot. Spruced up in 2007, Suba's three sleek levels fill a former 1909 tenement from the ground-floor tapas lounge down the twisting steel staircase to the sexy Grotto; there, a polished-concrete dining island floats in an illuminated pool of water, and farther down still to the bright Skylight Room that does dual duty as a private dining space and a late-night weekend lounge.

The menu's been revamped too, offering a selection of small plates designed for sharing. Tempting creations like *gambas a la plancha* with chorizo and garbanzo purée reflect chef Seamus Mullen's experience in some of Spain's top kitchens. You'll likely have trouble deciding between the wine selections on the Spanish-focused list and the creative sangrias.

Tides

014 **Seafood** X

102 Norfolk St. (bet. Delancey & Rivington Sts.)

Subway: Delancey St — Tue – Fri lunch & dinner
Phone: 212-254-8855 — Sat – Sun dinner only
Web: www.tidesseafood.com
Prices: $$

From anywhere in Tides' tiny 450-square-foot dining room, you can see the kitchen with its small staff hard at work. Above your head, tens of thousands of bamboo skewers are embedded in the backlit ceiling, forming wavy patterns that suggest a grassy dune.

Lunch is an ultra-casual affair, with a limited menu (no dessert), plastic plates and cutlery, and a mix of table service and serve-yourself. At dinner, Tides displays a more stylish veneer, switching to contemporary serving pieces, all with an Asian flair. No matter when you dine here, you'll catch fabulously fresh seafood. The enthusiastic owners—who alternately play the role of waiter, sommelier and manager—refuse to skimp on quality, and the kitchen prepares seafood with a talented hand.

wd~50 ✿

015 Contemporary XX

50 Clinton St. (bet. Rivington & Stanton Sts.)

Subway: Delancey St
Dinner daily
Phone: 212-477-2900
Web: www.wd-50.com
Prices: $$$

wd~50/Robert Polidori

At wd~50, life, or at least the food part of it, most certainly imitates art. Award-winning chef Wylie Dufresne transforms simple plates into works of art by devising avant-garde, meticulously arranged compositions that taste as good as they look. At times it's debatable whether Dufresne, who trained under Jean-Georges Vongerichten, is a chef or a mad scientist.

Foie gras with mole lentils and quince yogurt, or pork belly with smoked yucca, romaine and papaya typify the eyebrow-raising and excellently prepared dishes you'll enjoy here. The experimental style continues to the final course, where ingredients not normally associated with dessert—parsnips for cake, chicory for ice cream, olives for clafouti—boldly go where no sweets have gone before.

With its custom-designed furnishings and style-conscious crowd, the dining room comes alive at night with a carnival vibe.

Appetizers

- Slow Poached Egg, Chorizo, Pickled Beets, Dried Black Olives
- Foie Gras, Mole "Lentils," Quince Yogurt
- Corned Duck, Rye Crisp, Purple Mustard, Horseradish Cream

Entrées

- Cod, Baby Fennel, Black Eyed Peas, Espelette Yogurt
- Parsnip Tart, Quinoa, Hazelnuts, Bok Choy
- Lamb Loin, Potato Noodles, Mustard Crumbs, Pretzel Consommé

Desserts

- Yogurt Parfait, Pine, Apple, Pineapple
- Yuzu Curd, Shortbread, Spruce Yogurt, Pistachio
- Soft Chocolate, Avocado, Licorice, Lime

Midtown East & Murray Hill

A bustling business district, the swatch of land east of Fifth Avenue – contains some of the city's finest office buildings, from the Art Deco **Chrysler Building** to the modernist **Lever House**, as well as the spectacular Beaux-Arts **Grand Central Terminal**. All the way east, at the river, you'll find the headquarters of the United Nations. Tucked among these landmarks are historic hotels, posh shops lining Madison and Fifth avenues, and, last—but far from least—a plethora of restaurants to suit every taste.

A Bit of History

The area bounded by Fifth Avenue and the East River, between East 30th and 60th streets, was not always the tony place it is today. In the early 19th century, steam-powered locomotives chugged down Park Avenue all the way to a depot on 23rd Street, bringing with them noise and dirt. Residents complained, and in 1854 an ordinance was passed banning trains south of 42nd Street. That helped pave the way for downtown development, but did nothing to improve the lot of those in Midtown East, whose tenements surrounded a sooty railyard that spread from 42nd to 56th Street.

Underground Railroad

Enter railroad magnate "Commodore" **Cornelius Vanderbilt** (1794–1877), who opened the first Grand Central depot in 1871 on the present site of the Grand Central Terminal. Shortly thereafter, he began lowering the tracks feeding into it below street level, reducing some of the noise pollution. But smoke was still a big problem, and in 1889 the city demanded that the railroad electrify the trains or leave the city. To finance the electrification process, the Vanderbilts sunk the entire railyard fronting the depot below ground and sold the land above it to developers, who soon lined Madison and Park avenues with exclusive apartment buildings. The Grand Central Terminal you see today, which now houses a gourmet market and a sprawling dining concourse, was completed in 1913.

Onward and Upward

After World War II, many of the apartment houses along Madison, Park and Lexington Avenues in Midtown were replaced by high-rise office towers. Today the area claims an eclectic mix of old and new, including the residential enclave of opulent mansions, elegant brownstones and converted 19th-century carriage houses known as **Murray Hill** *(between 40th & 30th Sts.)*. In quiet Murray Hill, foodies will discover a world of cuisines, from sophisticated sushi and Indian curries to hearty steak.

Brigitta L. House/ MICHELIN

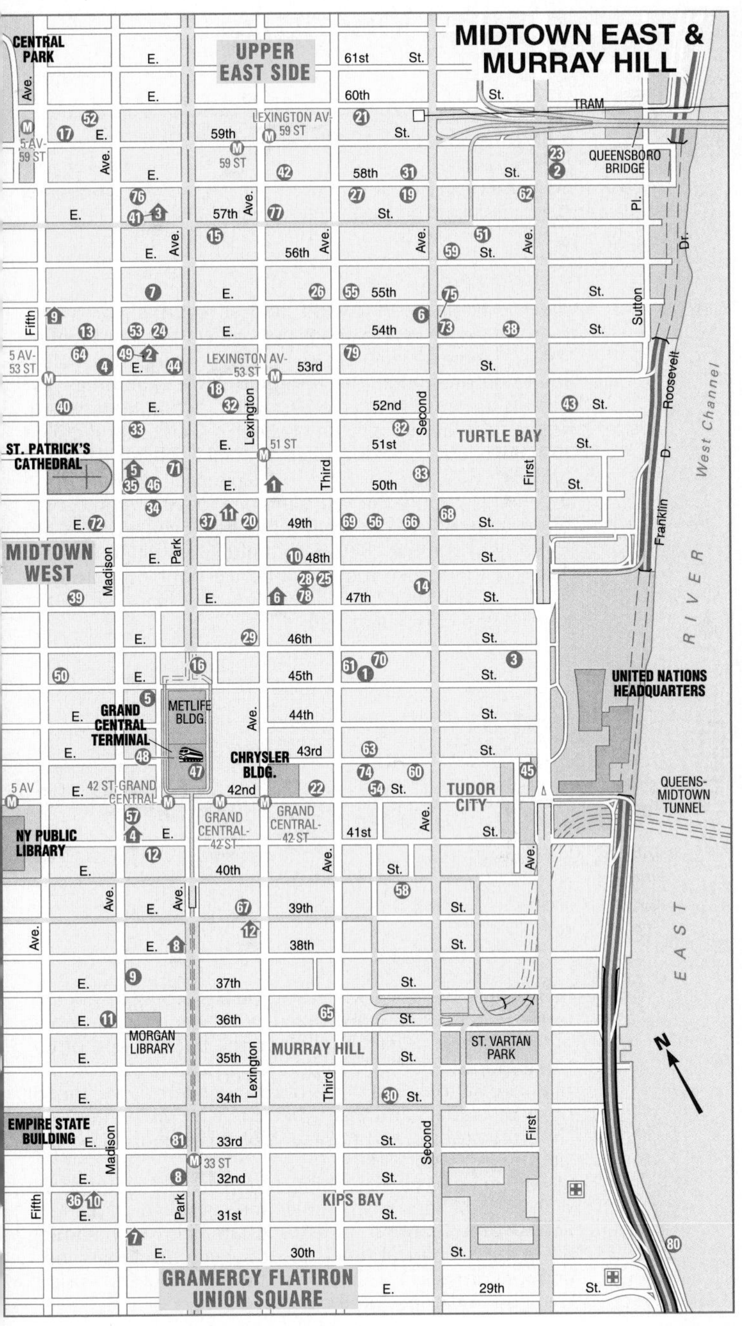
MIDTOWN EAST &
MURRAY HILL
CENTRAL PARK
UPPER EAST SIDE
MIDTOWN WEST
GRAMERCY FLATIRON UNION SQUARE
ST. PATRICK'S CATHEDRAL
GRAND CENTRAL TERMINAL
METLIFE BLDG.
CHRYSLER BLDG.
NY PUBLIC LIBRARY
MORGAN LIBRARY
EMPIRE STATE BUILDING
UNITED NATIONS HEADQUARTERS
QUEENSBORO BRIDGE
QUEENS-MIDTOWN TUNNEL
TURTLE BAY
TUDOR CITY
MURRAY HILL
KIPS BAY
ST. VARTAN PARK
TRAM
LEXINGTON AV-59 ST
59 ST
5 AV-59 ST
LEXINGTON AV-53 ST
5 AV-53 ST
51 ST
42 ST-GRAND CENTRAL
GRAND CENTRAL-42 ST
5 AV
33 ST
EAST RIVER
West Channel
Franklin D. Roosevelt Dr.
Sutton Pl.
Fifth Ave.
Madison Ave.
Park Ave.
Lexington Ave.
Third Ave.
Second Ave.
First Ave.
E. 61st St.
E. 60th St.
E. 59th St.
E. 58th St.
E. 57th St.
E. 56th St.
E. 55th St.
E. 54th St.
E. 53rd St.
E. 52nd St.
E. 51st St.
E. 50th St.
E. 49th St.
E. 48th St.
E. 47th St.
E. 46th St.
E. 45th St.
E. 44th St.
E. 43rd St.
E. 42nd St.
E. 41st St.
E. 40th St.
E. 39th St.
E. 38th St.
E. 37th St.
E. 36th St.
E. 35th St.
E. 34th St.
E. 33rd St.
E. 32nd St.
E. 31st St.
E. 30th St.
E. 29th St.
N

Aburiya Kinnosuke

001 — Japanese XX

213 E. 45th St. (bet. Second & Third Aves.)

Subway: Grand Central - 42 St — Mon – Fri lunch & dinner
Phone: 212-867-5454 — Sat – Sun dinner only
Web: www.torysnyc.com
Prices: $$

New York offers the world, and at Aburiya Kinnosuke, patrons are treated to an insider's view of Japan. From its mostly Japanese clientele to the extensive menu not often found outside Japan, this restaurant is the real thing.

Guests are invited to take part in the action here, where *sochu* cocktails involve hand-squeezed citrus, and grilled dishes require cooking over a small tabletop charcoal grill. *Yawarakani,* a kind of Japanese comfort food involving ground-chicken mini-meatloaves cooked over open charcoal is one of the highlights. Ingredients are top-notch, and the chefs pay careful attention to detail.

Aburiya Kinnosuke requires advance booking, but once you're in, you won't be rushed through your meal by the cordial and competent staff.

Aja

002 — Asian XX

1068 First Ave. (at 58th St.)

Subway: 59 St — Dinner daily
Phone: 212-888-8008
Web: N/A
Prices: $$$

Inside Aja's windowless façade you'll discover a dark and temple-like décor constructed with stone walls, water elements, and a giant Buddha at the back of one of the small rooms. Loud contemporary music raises the volume of conversations, but this is of little concern to the mix of posh East Siders and young bankers with their dates who shun the sushi bar in favor of tables by the Buddha and side-by-side banquettes.

Strikingly fresh sushi, sashimi and maki split menu space with original Pan-Asian entrées and combination platters. Flashy presentations have an Asian flair, with flaming rocks and colorful cocktails traveling to tables past admiring guests. You'll pay for the show, but high prices don't put a damper on the party.

Alcala

Spanish

342 E. 46th St. (bet. First & Second Aves.)

Subway: Grand Central - 42 St
Phone: 212-370-1866
Web: www.alcalarestaurant.com
Prices: $$

Mon – Fri lunch & dinner
Sat – Sun dinner only

A pan of rustic paella, a friend to share it with, and a seat in Alcala's covered garden on a clear summer day will capture the spirit of Spain's sun-drenched coast. Located just across from the United Nations, this neighborhood favorite serves Basque and other regional Spanish specialties to an international crowd in its cozy, brick-walled dining room.

At Alcala, the attentive staff caters to regulars as well as newbies with warm, old-school-style service. Begin with one of the authentic appetizers, then move on to hearty main dishes like roast baby pig or red piquillo peppers stuffed with codfish. Tempranillo, Garnacha and Albariño number among the noteworthy Spanish varietals available to complement your meal.

Alto

Contemporary

11 E. 53rd St. (bet. Fifth & Madison Aves.)

Subway: 5 Av - 53 St
Phone: 212-308-1099
Web: www.altorestaurant.com
Prices: $$$

Mon – Fri lunch & dinner
Sat dinner only

Opened in April 2005, Alto takes its name from the Alto Adige region of northeastern Italy, an area that inspires the restaurant's cuisine (the name also refers to *alta cucina,* the term for refined Italian cuisine). This region's proximity to Austria influences many of the menu items, including smoked ocean trout with horseradish and trout roe, herbed Spätzle with slow-braised rabbit, and house-made pastas.

A large piece of the Berlin Wall serves as an impressive entrance to the restaurant. The dining space is swanky, with red-velvet chairs and huge windows. Though the floor-to-ceiling wall of wine bottles is for display purposes only, oenophiles will certainly find something to suit their palates in a cellar stocked with 12,000 bottles.

Ammos Estiatorio

Greek XX

005

52 Vanderbilt Ave. (at 45th St.)

Subway: Grand Central - 42 St — Mon – Fri lunch & dinner
Phone: 212-922-9999 — Sat – Sun dinner only
Web: www.ammosnewyork.com
Prices: $$$

Set in the shadow of Grand Central Terminal, Ammos Estiatorio opened its Manhattan branch (the original is in Astoria) in November 2005. True to its name ("sand" in Greek), the open, airy restaurant sports a modern décor that adheres to a Greek island theme. Hand-blown glass fishing buoys and canvas market umbrellas add to the décor, while weathered stone and wood beams provide rustic touches.

You could easily make a meal out of the terrific meze alone (be sure to share!), but the kitchen is skilled with grilled dishes and it would be a shame to miss the likes of *arni souvlaki* (skewers of lamb loin with red and yellow bell peppers and pearl onions). The menu also offers a good selection of whole grilled fish, priced by the pound.

Angelo's

Pizza X

006

1043 Second Ave. (at 55th St.)

Subway: 51 St — Lunch & dinner daily
Phone: 212-521-3600
Web: www.angelospizzany.com
Prices: ⓢⓢ

Angelo's is the kind of place you'd love to have as your neighborhood haunt. A cut above the rest in terms of service, presentation, and quality of the food, this family-friendly Midtown pizzeria draws a loyal coterie of locals. No wonder. The thin-crust pies here are fantastic, topped with great ingredients and delivered to your table hot from the wood-burning oven. Fresh salads and pastas (think homemade spinach and cheese ravioli) equally accommodate small or large appetites in individual or family portions, and the price is definitely right. Not to mention the welcoming Eastern European servers, who win newcomers over with their upbeat attitude and spot-on timing.

There's even a second Angelo's on the West Side at 117 West 57th Street.

Aquavit

Scandinavian XX

65 E. 55th St. (bet. Madison & Park Aves.)

Subway: 5 Av - 53 St — Lunch & dinner daily
Phone: 212-307-7311
Web: www.aquavit.org
Prices: **$$$**

Everything about Aquavit is Scandinavian; its design, its cuisine, its chef. Named for the Scandinavian spirit that figures prominently on its beverage menu, Aquavit occupies the ground floor of the Park Avenue Tower. There's a casual cafe and bar area up front; the more refined contemporary dining room, softened by beige tones and varnished woods, lies beyond.

Born in Ethiopia and raised in Sweden, chef/owner Marcus Samuelsson excels at pairing unexpected textures and flavors, and fish dominates his à la carte menu. For dessert, go for the Arctic Circle, a luscious goat-cheese parfait filled with passionfruit curd and topped with tart blueberry sorbet. The restaurant even makes its own Aquavit, infused with everything from pineapple to pumpkin.

Artisanal

French XX

2 Park Ave. (enter on 32nd St. bet. Madison & Park Aves.)

Subway: 33 St — Lunch & dinner daily
Phone: 212-725-8585
Web: www.artisanalcheese.com
Prices: **$$**

Say cheese. That's the focus of Terrance Brennan's Artisanal restaurant, which celebrates cheese from around the world. Brennan's Murray Hill brasserie, with its high ceilings, burgundy-colored walls and velour banquettes, serves cheese in many forms: fondue, mac and cheese, puffy gougères and cheese ravioli, to name a few. There's even a separate cheese menu, offering tastings of some 250 types of artisan cheese. Choose your beverage from the equally dizzying list of more than 150 wines by the glass. Don't like cheese? Never fear, Artisanal offers a wide array of classic French fare, as in escargots, trout amandine, and lamb cassoulet.

Check out the tempting cheese display in the back of the dining room, and perhaps buy some to take home.

Asia de Cuba

Fusion XX

237 Madison Ave. (bet. 37th & 38th Sts.)

Subway: Grand Central - 42 St — Mon – Fri lunch & dinner
Phone: 212-726-7755 — Sat – Sun dinner only
Web: www.chinagrillmgt.com
Prices: $$$

A trendy venue in the Morgans Hotel in residential Murray Hill, Asia de Cuba still packs in a chic crowd, despite the fact that it's no longer new. Designer Philippe Starck fitted the striking bi-level interior with gauzy drapes lining the soaring walls, a 25-foot-high hologram of a flowing waterfall and a 50-foot-long, alabaster communal table running the length of the downstairs room.
Generously sized dishes marry elements of Asian and Latin cuisines in signatures such as tunapica (tuna tartare picadillo style), calamari salad, and *ropa vieja* of duck. Round up a few gorgeous friends who like to share, and order from the family-style menu. Don't overlook sides like panko-crusted crispy plantains or Thai coconut sticky rice.

Avra Estiatorio

010

Greek XX

141 E. 48th St. (bet. Lexington & Third Aves.)

Subway: 51 St — Lunch & dinner daily
Phone: 212-759-8550
Web: www.avrany.com
Prices: $$$

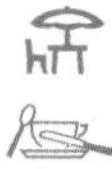

Fresh fish nets the most attention here, and you can view a display of the day's catch on ice in the front dining room. Flown in from Europe or purchased from New York's new Fulton Fish Market, fish and shellfish are brushed with olive oil and grilled whole over charcoal. Your choice will be priced per pound, so be forewarned if your eyes tend to be bigger than your wallet. Avra's "spread *pikilia*" (your choice of three) make an authentic and delicious way to start your meal.
This boisterous and always busy taverna-style eatery recalls the Mediterranean with its limestone floors, faux-stone walls and arched doorways. In warm weather, you can sit inside or out, or compromise with a table near the doors that open onto the terrace.

Barbès

Mediterranean XX

011

21 E. 36th St. (bet. Fifth & Madison Aves.)

Subway: 33 St — Lunch & dinner daily
Phone: 212-684-0215
Web: www.barbesrestaurantnyc.com
Prices: $$

A sparkling diamond in an otherwise unpolished neighborhood rife with generic delis and overpriced Italian restaurants, Barbès glows with its friendly staff and traditional French-Moroccan fare. Brick walls and a beamed ceiling create a rustic mood in the cozy dining room, while the infectious Moroccan music lends an exotic note.

Here, the menu presents diners with a wide choice of items; dishes have a decidedly North African bent but with heavy Mediterranean influences (the names of the dishes—*moules à la Marocaine, crevettes aux pistou,* traditional *couscous Marocaine*—are all in French). The manager's presence ensures the warm quality of the service; he employs the requisite flourish when pouring mint tea into small Moroccan-style glasses.

Benjamin Steak House

Steakhouse XX

012

52 E. 41st St. (bet. Madison & Park Aves.)

Subway: Grand Central - 42 St — Lunch & dinner daily
Phone: 212-297-9177
Web: www.benjaminsteakhouse.com
Prices: $$

After manning the grill at Brooklyn's famous Peter Luger for twenty years, chef Arturo McLeod brings his culinary prowess to Midtown at Benjamin Steak House. His passionate project, set within the 1903 Dylan Hotel, defines the classic steakhouse in a luscious Beaux-Arts setting rendered elegant and clubby by oak-paneled walls, a vaulted ceiling, and a 10-foot-high roaring fireplace.

The professional staff will guide you through the menu, which includes meat-lovers favorites from prime sirloin to extra-thick lamb loin chops, all dry-aged on the premises. Of course, there are lobster tails, along with several other nice seafood options. Make sure to save room for dessert; 13 different sweets are all available with a dollop of homemade Schlag.

Bice

013 **Italian** XXX

7 E. 54th St. (bet. Fifth & Madison Aves.)

Subway: 5 Av - 53 St — Lunch & dinner daily
Phone: 212-688-1999
Web: www.bicenewyork.com
Prices: $$$

Opened in 1987, Bice New York forms part of a chain of some 40 Italian restaurants that reaches around the world. Bice was founded in Milan in 1926 by Beatrice ("Bice") Ruggeri. Her sons, Roberto and Remo, later opened additional branches, first in Italy, and in 1987, on East 54th Street in New York City—the first location in North America.
The Manhattan outpost owes its cool yet elegant Art Deco interior to Adam Tihany, who has done work for many big-name chefs. Northern Italian fare makes up the menu (veal Milanese, risotto, hearty homemade pasta), and Midtown's chic set dines at Bice on a regular basis. Even fashionistas save room for dessert here, where the enticing menu includes tiramisu, panna cotta and gelato, among other selections.

Blair Perrone

014 **Steakhouse** XX

885 Second Ave. (bet. 47th & 48th Sts.)

Subway: 51 St — Mon – Fri lunch & dinner
Phone: 212-796-8000 — Sat dinner only
Web: www.blairperrone.com
Prices: $$$

Partners Charlie Blair (a Peter Luger alumnus) and Joe Perrone set up shop in this former Ruth's Chris Steakhouse on the ground floor of an imposing Midtown office building. A wine wall splits the ambitious, contemporary space into two large rooms, both rich in dark woods, marble, and floor-to-ceiling windows. It's an upscale setting that draws casual business types.
USDA prime dry-aged Porterhouse comes in cuts for two, three or four people. Steaks and chops are all perfectly cooked to order, the meat juicy and flavorful. A list of seafood makes non-carnivores feel like they're part of the club. Before you order that Flintstone-sized steak, think about saving room for the New York-style cheesecake, served with a dollop of Schlag.

BLT Steak

015 **Steakhouse** XXX

106 E. 57th St. (bet. Lexington & Park Aves.)

Subway: 59 St — Mon – Fri lunch & dinner
Phone: 212-752-7470 — Sat dinner only
Web: www.bltrestaurants.com
Prices: $$$$

Why would a French chef name his restaurant after an American sandwich? He would, if he fancied his restaurant to be a contemporary bistro (B) and his name was Laurent Tourondel (LT). In fact, Bistro Laurent Tourondel is not a French bistro at all, but a Frenchman's vision of an American steakhouse. Sleek décor smacks of big-city sophistication, and the hip crowd with money to spend loves the noise and loud music.

On the menu, Japanese Kobe and American Wagyu beef complement the steakhouse classics, and many of the sides, like roasted hen-of-the-woods mushrooms or potato gratin, are served with a playful touch in cute cast-iron pans or copper pots. There are few bargains on the wine list, but it does offer a great selection by the glass.

Bobby Van's Steakhouse

016 **Steakhouse** XX

230 Park Ave. (at 46th St.)

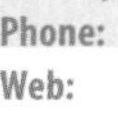

Subway: Grand Central - 42 St — Mon – Fri lunch & dinner
Phone: 212-867-5490 — Sat dinner only
Web: www.bobbyvans.com
Prices: $$$$

Bobby Van's owes its first Manhattan location to Leona Helmsley, who cajoled the owners into opening an outpost here (the original Bobby Van's is in Bridgehampton). This is clearly a carnivores paradise, catering to business people on expense accounts. As you'd imagine, it's a clubby, old-boy kind of place, with lots of wood and mirrors in the spacious dining room.

Expect to pay rather dearly for huge portions of meltingly tender beef and well-cooked seafood (lobster is priced by the pound, and you can order the USDA prime Porterhouse for two, three or four people.)

You'll find other Bobby Van's locations in Midtown East *(131 E. 54th St.)*, in Midtown West *(135 W. 50th St.)*, and in the Financial District *(25 Broad St.)*.

Bottega del Vino

Italian XXX

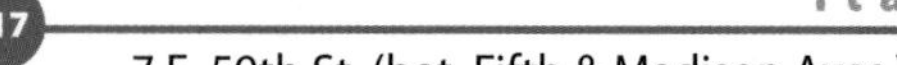

017

7 E. 59th St. (bet. Fifth & Madison Aves.)

Subway: 5 Av - 59 St — Lunch & dinner daily
Phone: 212-223-2724
Web: www.bottegadelvinonyc.com
Prices: $$$

From Verona comes not two, but one gentleman, Severino Barzan, who opened the New York outpost of his Italian wine bar in fall 2004. The words painted on a beam along the restaurant's wall sum up his philosophy: *Dio mi guardi da chi non beve vino* ("may God protect me from those who do not drink wine"). Thus, wine steals the show here, with bottles displayed on shelf after shelf in the dining room, and a cellar that stocks some 2,800 bottles. Barzan even designed a line of hand-blown stemware to highlight the taste of each varietal.

Wine, of course, influences the food, and many of the wonderful dishes are wine-focused or include wine in the preparation. Hailing from the Veneto region, the "antica bottega" creations are the house signatures.

Brasserie

Contemporary XX

018

100 E. 53rd St. (bet. Lexington & Park Aves.)

Subway: Lexington Av - 53 St — Lunch & dinner daily
Phone: 212-751-4840
Web: www.rapatina.com/brasserie
Prices: $$$

The original concept of a brasserie as a brewery that provided food for hungry travelers has come a long way to this modern version; its retro design employs white leather chairs and small plastic-topped tables, with pearwood panels lining the ceiling in a sort of wave.

Features on the short menu are American and French, and many are rendered with a European touch (steak *frites*, whole fish with *herbes de Provence*). For a sweet finish, try the chocolate beignets.

Brasserie is more suited for a group of friends or a business meal than a romantic date. Seating is close, and the appealing menu and attractive space make this a lively and popular spot. The long bar serves tasty snacks and is a sophisticated lair for an adult beverage.

Bruno

Italian XX

019

240 E. 58th St. (bet. Second & Third Aves.)

Subway: 59 St — Mon – Fri lunch & dinner
Phone: 212-688-4190 — Sat dinner only
Web: www.brunosnyc.com
Prices: $$$

Bruno Selimaj must be doing something right; his eponymous eatery has been around since 1978. Italian dishes fill the menu with the likes of bruschetta with prosciutto di Parma and fig jam, and ravioli made in-house with a different filling every day. Meat is also well represented here, with selections such as porcini-rubbed ribeye steak, grilled veal chop and rack of lamb. Daily specials, such as a whole roasted fish *del giorno*, add another dimension to the menu.
Service is casual in the Art Deco-style dining room, where white tablecloths, hand-decorated porcelain and delicate orchids add an air of refinement. Four nights a week (Wednesday to Saturday from 9pm to 1am), a pianist tickles the ivories for patrons' entertainment in the bar area.

Bull and Bear

Steakhouse XX

020

301 Park Ave. (bet. 49th & 50th Sts.)

Subway: 51 St — Mon – Fri lunch & dinner
Phone: 212-872-4900 — Sat – Sun dinner only
Web: www.waldorfastoria.com
Prices: $$$

Picture an elegant English pub set about with mahogany wood, brass and crystal chandeliers, wine cabinets, cushy banquettes and plenty of mirrors, and you've got the Bull and Bear. Located on the ground floor of the legendary Waldorf=Astoria *(see hotel listing)*, this bar/restaurant takes its moniker from the bronze bull and bear statues—representing the rise and fall of the stock market—that stand over the mahogany bar.
The place is popular with brokers and finance types, who come for the signature martinis, the dry-aged prime Angus beef and the classy men's-club ambience. Beef may be the focal point, but seafood is given equal attention. Don't wear jeans and sneakers, though; the Bull and Bear's "elegant casual" dress code forbids them.

Canaletto

Italian

021

208 E. 60th St. (bet. Second & Third Aves.)

Subway: Lexington Av - 59 St — Lunch & dinner daily
Phone: 212-317-9192
Web: N/A
Prices: $$

Attention Bloomingdale's shoppers: this neighborhood Italian spot, a half-block down 60th Street from Bloomie's, makes a great place for a lunch if you want to take a break from riffling through the racks.

A meal at classy Canaletto begins with a plate of Italian salami and aged parmesan. Then move on to a pasta such as *penne all'arabiatta,* cooked perfectly al dente with spicy homemade tomato sauce. As for entrées, head towards the meat dishes, where the best flavors lie. It's easy to get your daily serving of olive oil and greens when you add on a side of the garlicky spinach or broccoli rabe.

You'll feel like part of the family here, where you'll find patient, cheerful service, along with prices that are very reasonable for the neighborhood.

The Capital Grille

Steakhouse

022

155 E. 42nd St. (bet. Lexington & Third Aves.)

Subway: Grand Central - 42 St — Mon – Fri lunch & dinner
Phone: 212-953-2000 — Sat – Sun dinner only
Web: www.thecapitalgrille.com
Prices: $$$$

Here's an address that's well located for Midtown business lunchers. Two blocks east of Grand Central Terminal, the clubby Capital Grille occupies the ground floor of the Trylon Towers, part of the complex that includes the famed Chrysler Building. The Atlanta, Georgia-based chain made its New York debut in summer 2004, and Manhattanites are glad it did.

Here you can dine on juicy dry-aged steaks and chops, hand-cut and grilled precisely to your liking; or, if you prefer, there's broiled lobster and a selection of fresh fish. As far as wine goes, the inventory of 400 labels includes a Captain's List of rare vintages to round out your meal. Highly professional service from an amiable waitstaff completes the enjoyable experience here.

Casa La Femme North

Egyptian

023 1076 First Ave. (bet. 58th & 59th Sts.)

Subway: Lexington Av - 59 St — Dinner daily
Phone: 212-505-0005
Web: N/A
Prices: $$

Here's a place for a romantic interlude. Gauzy tents provide privacy for the tables lining the walls, creating the perfect setting in which to steal a kiss or make a proposal (note that the only dining option available at the tented tables is the prix-fixe menu). Formerly located on Prince Street in SoHo, Casa La Femme North brings its exotic mix to Midtown.

Not in the mood for romance? That's okay, you'll still enjoy the restaurant's foreign feel, with its hanging lanterns, curving banquettes and leafy palm trees. At dinner, a belly dancer shimmies around the room, but don't let that distract you from the tasty North African cuisine such as meaty tagines served with fluffy homemade couscous, or baked whole fish.

Cellini

Italian 

024 65 E. 54th St. (bet. Madison & Park Aves.)

Subway: Lexington Av - 53 St — Mon – Fri lunch & dinner
Phone: 212-751-1555
Web: www.cellinirestaurant.com
Prices: $$$

Rustic and homey, that's Cellini. Indeed, you'll feel like family at this warm and welcoming restaurant, blocks from the south end of Central Park. The dimly lit dining room is simply decorated with wood wainscoting, and wrought-iron chandeliers and wall sconces. Folk art and crockery plates enliven the otherwise plain walls, while the beamed ceiling is draped with cheery red fabric.

Like the décor, the food is not complicated; regional Italian dishes here are interpreted with a careful touch and prepared using high-quality ingredients. Specials might include homemade ravioli filled with grilled beets and sage in a four-cheese reduction, or veal martini, crusted with parmesan and sautéed in Absolut vodka and dry vermouth.

Chiam

025 Chinese XX

160 E. 48th St. (bet. Lexington & Third Aves.)

Subway: 51 St — Lunch & dinner daily
Phone: 212-371-2323
Web: N/A
Prices: $$

Don't confuse Chiam with the neighboring noodle joints. Chiam may not have the neighborhood authenticity of Chinatown, or the star appeal of Mr Chow, but it continues to win diners over with its serious Chinese cuisine and top-notch service. Think of this place, with its elegant dining room, quality wine list, and well-heeled clientele, as a place for a special-occasion feast or for an expense-account business dinner.
Presenting Cantonese-style preparations with flair, the kitchen staff uses excellent products and a refined technique that yields consistently good and well-balanced fare. Dishes, such as the rich Grand Marnier prawns, are intended to be shared, so order some steamed or sautéed vegetables to round out the mix.

Da Antonio

026 Italian XX

157 E. 55th St. (bet. Lexington & Third Aves.)

Subway: Lexington Av - 53 St — Mon – Fri lunch & dinner
Phone: 212-588-1545 — Sat dinner only
Web: www.daantonio.com
Prices: $$

Father-and-son team Antonio and Mario Cerra preside over the dining room at this animated restaurant, which is festooned with fresh flowers and oil paintings, and crowded with white-clothed tables.
From the kitchen come wonderful pastas and well-prepared seafood, poultry and meat dishes, all made with fresh ingredients. The lunch and dinner menu is the same, and a pre-theater menu, with choice of appetizer, entrée and dessert, is offered nightly. Ignore the occasional flaws in the service, which makes up for in sincerity what it might lack in execution.
The bar scene here is a vibrant one, enlivened by nightly entertainment on the piano—you'll hear everything from oldies to jazz to show tunes, depending on who's playing.

Dawat

Indian XX

027

210 E. 58th St. (bet. Second & Third Aves.)

Subway: 59 St
Phone: 212-355-7555
Web: www.restaurant.com/dawat
Prices: $$

Mon – Sat lunch & dinner
Sun dinner only

It's not every restaurant whose chef started out as an actor, but that's what Madhur Jaffrey did. The Delhi native came to Dawat by way of the stage in England, and then to America, where she wrote articles about food to help support her family. Those articles led to a series of cookbooks about Indian cuisine, and the rest, as they say, is history.

With a string of books to her credit, Jaffrey designed the menu at Dawat, where Tandoori dishes, curries and kebabs, as well as a host of vegetarian specialties, are as authentic as they are delicious. Guests can alternately choose to sample Jaffrey's tasting menus, prepared for the entire table. Come on, dig in. How can you go wrong at a restaurant whose name means "invitation to feast?"

Diwan

Indian 

148 E. 48th St. (bet. Lexington & Third Aves.)

Subway: 51 St
Phone: 212-593-5425
Web: www.diwanrestaurant.com
Prices: $$

Lunch & dinner daily

The bounteous, inexpensive lunch buffet draws diners here at midday for a varied selection of traditional dishes. Set out in front of the windows looking into the busy kitchen, the buffet is a good way to sample India's regional fare like biriyani, curries, and vegetables spiced by Diwan's own special blend of masala. At dinner, you can order from the pricier and well-edited à la carte menu, which is careful not to list too many items. Spice levels are toned down for an American palate, while many dishes get a modern, lighter interpretation.

Attractive rich fabrics and low lighting give the room warmth (though the leather chairs sit very low to the table), and a lively mix of locals and tourists lends the place a lived-in feel.

Django

Contemporary

029

480 Lexington Ave. (at 46 St.)

Subway: Grand Central - 42 St — Mon – Fri lunch & dinner, Sat dinner only
Phone: 212-871-6600
Web: www.djangorestaurant.com
Prices: $$$

In the bohemian spirit of jazz guitarist Django Reinhardt, who wowed Paris audiences in the 1930s with his improvisational riffs, this restaurant embraces the carefree soul of a gypsy. Designed by David Rockwell, the eclectic interior exudes an ethnic ambience with a Murano glass chandeliers and bright banquettes backed by cushy pillows. High ceilings and large windows lend an openness rarely found in city dining rooms.

From the kitchen comes sunny "Riviera cuisine," which can include anything from bouillabaisse to spiced Angus beef tagine. Five- and eight-course dinner tasting menus show off inspired combinations. To set the mood, start with the house cocktail—the Djangito—a potent blend of Stoli Ohranj, yuzu juice and a dash of Cointreau.

El Parador

Mexican

030

325 E. 34th St. (bet. First & Second Aves.)

Subway: 33 St — Lunch & dinner daily
Phone: 212-679-6812
Web: www.elparadorcafe.com
Prices: $$

Everything about El Parador is old-fashioned, but in the best possible way. Don't let the windowless façade or the location (near the entrance to the Midtown Tunnel) turn you away; inside, the upbeat Mexican ambience attracts a grown-up crowd who enjoy animated conversation and killer margaritas at the bar.

While the cuisine balances traditional fare with Americanized preparations, all the food bursts with flavor and good-quality ingredients. A line on the bottom of the menu sums up the restaurant's attitude, which is completely focused on the customer: "Please feel free to ask for any old favorite dish that you like." Even if it's not on the menu, they'll make it for you—and that includes special requests for fiery habañero salsa.

Felidia

Italian XX

031

243 E. 58th St. (bet. Second & Third Aves.)

Subway: Lexington Av - 59 St
Phone: 212-758-1479
Web: www.lidiasitaly.com
Prices: $$$

Mon – Fri lunch & dinner
Sat – Sun dinner only

Lidia Bastianich is no stranger to the restaurant business. The empire of this TV personality and cookbook author currently ranges west from New York City, but Felidia remains her flagship. In the bi-level dining room, sunny colors, towering flower arrangements and hardwood wine racks set a refined palette on which to present competent Northern Italian cooking.

Whole-grilled Mediterranean sea bass and bitter chocolate pappardelle with wild boar ragu are just a sampling of what you might find on the seasonal menu. Pastas are expertly prepared and topped with a variety of sauces, and Lidia's famous homemade cheesecake with caramelized pears guarantees a sweet finish. The award-winning wine list cites some 1,400 selections, most of them Italian.

The Four Seasons

American XXXX

032

99 E. 52nd St. (bet. Lexington & Park Aves.)

Subway: 51 St
Phone: 212-754-9494
Web: www.fourseasonsrestaurant.com
Prices: $$$$

Mon – Fri lunch & dinner
Sat – Sun dinner only

The moneyed, the powerful, the chic all frequent the Four Seasons, where they blend right in with the opulent setting designed by Mies van der Rohe and Philip Johnson.

A serene white-marble pool forms the centerpiece of the Pool Room, while the Grill Room, lined with French walnut, sports an appealing bar with an expert staff and a power-lunch scene to match. You know you've really made it in New York when Julian assigns you a regular lunch table in the Grill Room.

The kitchen updates classics (Chateaubriand, Dover sole), while respecting the traditional dishes patrons have been paying sizeable sums for since 1959. Dramatic floral displays add to the ambience—there's nothing like cherry-blossom season by the pool here.

Fresco by Scotto

033 — **Italian** XXX

34 E. 52nd St. (bet. Madison & Park Aves.)

Subway: 5 Av - 53 St — Mon – Fri lunch & dinner
Phone: 212-935-3434 — Sat dinner only
Web: www.frescobyscotto.com
Prices: $$$

You never know what familiar faces you might see here. Known as the "NBC Commissary," this lively Italian place has long attracted media moguls and politicos, whose expense accounts accommodate the upscale prices. The Scotto family established their restaurant in Midtown in 1993, not far from Rockefeller Center. Here, Marion Scotto warmly welcomes customers to the bright dining room, decorated with sunny scenes of the Italian landscape.

Hearty entrées include grilled Italian sausage filled with cheese and parsley, or a plate of fettucine with parmesan and black-truffle cream sauce. For those who don't have time for a sit-down lunch, adjacent Fresco by Scotto On The Go offers Scotto-quality food for home or office.

Giambelli 50th

034 — **Italian** XX

46 E. 50th St. (bet. Madison & Park Aves.)

Subway: 5 Av - 53 St — Lunch & dinner daily
Phone: 212-688-2760
Web: www.giambelli50th.com
Prices: $$$

There's something to be said for consistency, and you can count on the Giambelli family for that. Over the years since the late Frank Giambelli opened his Gotham restaurant in 1960, Giambelli 50th has fed mayors and minions, politicos and pundits—even the Pope. The draw? Consistently good, home-style Italian food, cooked to order; from the rolls to the desserts, everything here is made in-house. The menu presents a dizzying array of homemade pastas, tender meat dishes and fresh seafood. Before you leave, scope out the restaurant's walls (upstairs and downstairs) for the collection of portraits by members of the Bachrach family, which, beginning with Bradford Bachrach, have photographed every American president since Abraham Lincoln.

Gilt ✿

Contemporary XXX

035

455 Madison Ave. (bet. 50th & 51st Sts.)

Subway: 51 St — Tue – Sat dinner only
Phone: 212-891-8100
Web: www.giltnewyork.com
Prices: $$$$

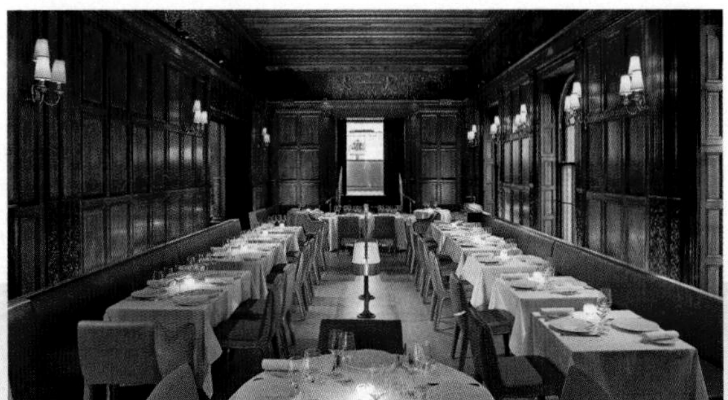

Gilt, New York Palace Hotel

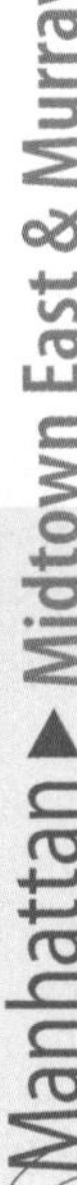

McKim, Mead and White's stunning Villard Mansion, part of the New York Palace Hotel *(see hotel listing)*, makes a stunning setting for a restaurant named Gilt. Patrick Jouin's design juxtaposes past and present, presenting a sleek, contemporary stage set installed against the 1882 mansion's ornate Italian Renaissance backdrop of rich, carved-wood details and a coffered cathedral ceiling.

Acclaimed chef Christopher Lee now presides over Gilt's kitchen. Although seafood was his focus at Striped Bass in Philadelphia, he equally divides entrées here between "Ocean" and "Land." Select ingredients combine in playful combinations, as in farm-raised turbot with a sauce made from Meyer lemon and caviar crème fraîche, or Alaskan spotted prawns atop potato mousseline flavored with smoked ham.

California "cult" Cabernets, and French Burgundy and Bordeaux stand out on the wine list.

Appetizers

- Yellowfin Tartare with Kimchee and Scallion Pancakes
- Maine Diver Sea Scallop Ceviche with Pacific Sea Urchin
- Alaskan Spotted Prawns with Smoked-Ham Potato Hash

Entrées

- Yellowfin "Wellington", Porcini, Foie Gras
- "Haus-Made" Bratwurst, Herb Spätzle, Belgian Beer-Cheese Sauce
- Rack of Lamb, Lamb Shoulder Ragoût, Golden Raisin Falafel

Desserts

- Chocolate "Solar System," Ovaltine Atmosphere
- Rhubarb Crumble, Honey Mousse, Marion Berry Granité
- Meyer Lemon Panna Cotta, Champagne Sabayon, Pixie Mandarin Sponge Cake

HanGawi

036 **Korean** XX

12 E. 32nd St. (bet. Fifth & Madison Aves.)

Subway: 33 St — Lunch & dinner daily
Phone: 212-213-0077
Web: www.hangawirestaurant.com
Prices: $$

Don't worry about wearing your best shoes to HanGawi; you'll have to take them off at the door before settling in at one of the restaurant's low tables. In the serene space, decorated with Korean artifacts and soothed by meditative music, it's easy to forget you're in Manhattan. The menu is all vegetarian, in keeping with the restaurant's philosophy of healthy cooking to balance the yin and yang—or *um* and *yang* in Korean. You can quite literally eat like a king here; the emperor's roll and steamboat soup (on the prix-fixe menu) were once cooked in the royal kitchen. Of course, all good things must end, and eventually you'll have to rejoin the rat race outside. Still, it's nice to get away from the pulsing vibe of the city... now and Zen.

Inagiku

037 **Japanese** XXX

111 E. 49th St. (bet. Lexington & Park Aves.)

Subway: 51 St — Mon – Fri lunch & dinner
Phone: 212-355-0440 — Sat – Sun dinner only
Web: www.inagiku.com
Prices: $$$

Tucked into a corner of the Waldorf=Astoria, Inagiku may look a bit outdated these days, but the knowledgeable and charming service and top-quality Japanese cuisine more than make up for any fading décor.
The sizeable menu is divided between modern fusion dishes using Western ingredients and techniques, and traditional Japanese fare. Stick to the latter and you won't be disappointed. Sushi is expertly prepared, and delicate tempura defines the art. Starters are perfectly done: the thin rice crêpes for the uni canapes are generously topped with vibrant uni; *uzaku*, a classic broiled eel salad, is accompanied by fresh cucumber and tossed in a light vinegar dressing. Everything comes elegantly presented with the appropriate garnishes and condiments.

Jubilee

French

038

347 E. 54th St. (bet. First & Second Aves.)

Subway: Lexington Av - 53 St
Phone: 212-888-3569
Web: www.jubileeny.com
Prices: $$

Mon – Fri, Sun lunch & dinner
Sat dinner only

Your mother was right when she told you never to judge a book by its cover. From the outside, this little restaurant may not look like much, but inside lies a pleasant space with the welcoming feel of a family restaurant that you'd want to frequent regularly for the appealing Belgian cooking.

Prince Edward Island mussels are the signature dish; they're prepared five different ways, and served Belgian-style with *frites*, or with a green salad. Otherwise, the menu highlights such classics as roasted breast of chicken with *pommes purée*, duck leg confit, escargots, and a pavé of roasted salmon served with caramelized cauliflower. Desserts, including molten chocolate mousse cake, profiteroles and crème brûlée, are memorable.

La Grenouille

French

040

3 E. 52nd St. (bet. Fifth & Madison Aves.)

Subway: 5 Av - 53 St
Phone: 212-752-1495
Web: www.la-grenouille.com
Prices: $$$$

Tue – Fri lunch & dinner
Mon & Sat dinner only

Opened in 1962, La Grenouille has managed to remain the Masson family's bastion of traditional high-priced French cuisine in Midtown. Charles and Gisèle Masson founded the establishment; today Charles junior oversees the enterprise. A high coffered ceiling, silk wall coverings and stunning arrangements of fresh flowers—a signature of the late Charles Masson the elder—create an Old World opulence in the lovely dining room, which is worthy of a special occasion for those who still prefer to dress for dinner.

Menu selections might include classically roasted chicken *grande-mère*, oxtails braised in Burgundy, and a divinely flaky warm apple tart. And don't overlook the signature dish: *les cuisses de grenouilles Provençale* (sautéed frogs' legs).

Kurumazushi ✿

039 **Japanese**

7 E. 47th St. (bet. Fifth & Madison Aves.)

Subway: 47-50 Sts - Rockefeller Ctr
Mon – Sat lunch & dinner
Phone: 212-317-2802
Web: N/A
Prices: $$$$

George Boomer III

Located on the second floor of a Midtown office building, Kurumazushi offers some of the best sushi in town. The décor is typically Japanese in its simple, clean design, and the team behind the red- and black-lacquer sushi bar will shout a traditional welcome in Japanese to you as you enter.

Get ready to be wowed by sushi master Toshihiro Uedo and his lovely assistant, in whose hands impeccably fresh sushi and sashimi set the standard. Even the rice here is handled with a fastidious touch. Quality doesn't come cheaply at this restaurant, which is preferred by those on expense accounts. But still, the small place is full every day with a loyal following of regulars.

You could sit at one of the few tables and be coddled by the perfect service, but at the sushi bar you're sure to have the best the chef has to offer and a little friendly banter on the side.

Appetizers

- Russian King Crab Legs Marinated with Special Vinegar Sauce
- Toro Tartare with Russian Beluga or Russian or Iranian Osetra Caviar
- Seared Toro with Special Sauce

Entrées

- Omakase with Master Chef's Selected Sushi and Sashimi

Desserts

- Traditional Japanese Red Bean Cake
- Seasonal Fruit
- Green Tea or Vanilla Ice Cream with or without Red Bean Sauce

L'Atelier de Joël Robuchon ✿

Contemporary XX

041

57 E. 57th St. (bet. Madison & Park Aves.)

Subway: 5 Av - 59 St

Lunch & dinner daily

Phone: 212-350-6658

Web: www.fourseasons.com/newyork

Prices: $$$$

Four Seasons New York

Whether it's the celebrated French chef, the chic space in the Four Seasons Hotel *(see hotel listing)*, or the rich and fabulous clientele, L'Atelier de Joël Robuchon is surely one of New York's hottest spots. Other locations in Paris, Tokyo, and Las Vegas made New Yorkers salivate pre-opening, and it's been a popular spot ever since.

L'Atelier uses crimson decorative accents to give Asian undertones to the sophisticated room, formerly occupied by 57-57. Seats at the pearwood counter, with its coveted view of the talented chefs working their artistry in the open *atelier* (studio), are considered the best.

Robuchon's expertise glows in his series of splendid small plates; langoustine, foie gras (six different ways), and *pommes purée* are among the signature dishes. Flawlessly executed and elegantly presented, Robuchon treats diners to a cavalcade of culinary masterpieces.

Appetizers

- Sea Urchin in Lobster Gelée with Cauliflower Cream
- Crispy Frog Legs with Garlic Purée and Parsley Coulis
- Crispy Langoustine Papillote with Basil Pesto

Entrées

- Venison Medallions, Caramelized Quince, Port Reduction
- Free-Range Caramelized Foie Gras-stuffed Quail with Truffled Potato Purée
- Steak Tartare with French Fries

Desserts

- Golden Sugar Sphere, Vanilla Ice Cream, Saffron Mousse
- Floating Caramel Soufflé, Spiced Chocolate Essence, Orange Ice Cream
- Grapefruit Segments, Wine Gelée, Mint Sorbet

Le Cirque

042 Contemporary 

151 E. 58th St. (bet. Lexington & Third Aves.)

Subway: 59 St
Phone: 212-644-0202
Web: www.lecirque.com
Prices: $$$$

Mon – Fri lunch & dinner
Sat dinner only

Like many of its loyal ladies-who-lunch, the grand dame of New York restaurants, Le Cirque 2000, needed some time off to rest and revamp. After closing its doors in the New York Palace Hotel, the newest Le Cirque reopened in the stylish Bloomberg Building. This incarnation is a masterpiece of design. Huge curving windows add a modern feel, while the distinguished air of the past remains in the canopied ceiling and the burgundy carpets detailed with rich gold patterns.

Sirio Maccioni keeps a tight leash on his latest heir. It still draws one of the best power scenes in the city, with a mix of masters of the universe and socialites, who come here as much to be seen as they do for dishes such as Icelandic cod, Berkshire pork and foie gras ravioli.

Le Périgord

043 French

405 E. 52nd St. (off First Ave.)

Subway: 51 St
Phone: 212-755-6244
Web: www.leperigord.com
Prices: $$$

Mon – Fri lunch & dinner
Sat – Sun dinner only

Just a few blocks from the United Nations in Sutton, Le Périgord wraps diners in luxury under its coffered ceiling amid period chairs covered in willow-green fabric, Limoges china, crystal stemware and fresh flowers. This is a jacket-and-tie kind of place, where waiters in black tuxedos provide formal service, and the lunch crowd consists largely of diplomats from the U.N.

Le Périgord is one of the few remaining old-fashioned French restaurants in New York City, and the classic entrées, from rack of lamb to sole meunière, bear testament to the tried and true. For the pièce de résistance, desserts are rolled to your table on a cart; count on a mouth-watering selection of homemade seasonal fruit tarts being among the choices.

Lever House

Contemporary

044

390 Park Ave. (enter on E. 53rd St. bet. Madison & Park Aves.)

Subway: Lexington Av - 53 St
Phone: 212-888-2700
Web: www.leverhouse.com
Prices: $$$

Mon – Fri lunch & dinner
Sat dinner only

If you fancy retro-modern design, make a beeline for this podlike dining room, where Mark Newson's honeycomb motif, repeated in everything from the carpet and the light fixtures to the hexagonal cubbyholes for wine bottles, grabs the eye. The rounded corners of the dining room complement the angular tower of green-blue glass and steel that is the landmark Lever House building, designed by Gordon Bunshaft in 1952 as Park Avenue's first glass-clad tower. Its Midtown location makes it a natural choice for power lunches.

Dan Silverman, whose culinary resumé includes Chez Panisse in Berkeley, as well as Le Bernardin and Union Square Café, knows how to pick excellent ingredients. Tastes of the seasons illuminate his modernized American cuisine.

L'Impero

Italian

045

45 Tudor City Pl. (bet. 42nd & 43rd Sts.)

Subway: Grand Central - 42 St
Phone: 212-599-5045
Web: www.limpero.com
Prices: $$$

Mon – Fri lunch & dinner
Sat dinner only

You'll find L'Impero on the ground floor of one of the structures of Tudor City, a complex of 12 Tudor-style apartment buildings completed in 1928. The soberly elegant dining space, with its pale gray-green leather chairs and dark fabric banquettes, was fashioned by renowned designer Vicente Wolf.

A recent turnover in the kitchen has resulted in a new chef coming on board. Though the menu still reflects the creative Italian pastas, fish and meat dishes that L'Impero is popular for, there may be some changes ahead as the new chef settles in. Whatever happens, the staff will undoubtedly continue to honor Italian culinary tradition by using the best-quality seasonal products they can find.

Maloney & Porcelli

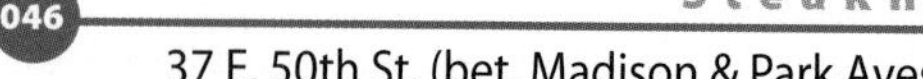

046 Steakhouse XXX

37 E. 50th St. (bet. Madison & Park Aves.)

Subway: 51 St
Phone: 212-750-2233
Web: www.maloneyandporcelli.com
Prices: $$$

Mon – Fri lunch & dinner
Sat – Sun dinner only

No wonder lawyers frequent this restaurant; it's named after the owner's law firm. Torts are no doubt discussed in the attractive, bi-level dining room with its varnished woods and copper accents. Whether you have a law degree or not, you'd best bring a big appetite (and a big wallet) to dine on mammoth portions of grilled rib steaks and veal chops here.

The signature dish, the much-ordered crackling pork shank, is first deep-fried, then slow-roasted to hold in the juices. This hearty chunk of meat comes with jalapeño-pepper-spiked "firecracker" apple sauce. Side dishes (fresh-cut French fries, creamed spinach, whipped potatoes) are sized for sharing.

Métrazur

047 American XX

Grand Central Terminal (42nd St. at Park Ave.)

Subway: Grand Central - 42 St
Phone: 212-687-4600
Web: www.charliepalmer.com
Prices: $$$

Mon – Fri lunch & dinner
Sat dinner only

Métrazur takes advantage of its spectacular location on the east balcony of Grand Central Terminal. The sleek design of the two large dining rooms plays against the opulence of the station's cavernous main concourse. Prime seats here allow guests to view the intricate architectural details.

Owned by famed chef Charlie Palmer, Métrazur is named for a train that once traveled France's Côte d'Azur on its way to Monaco. Indeed, you'll find that flavors of the Mediterranean infuse seasonally changing American dishes like tapenade-brushed halibut and ravioli filled with pulled oxtail meat, served in a heady porcini broth. The large bar that wraps around the dining space provides a prime spot for a pre-train cocktail.

Michael Jordan's

048

Grand Central Terminal (corner of Park Ave. & 42nd St.)

Subway: Grand Central - 42 St — Lunch & dinner daily
Phone: 212-655-2300
Web: www.theglaziergroup.com
Prices: **$$$**

There's no denying that dining in Grand Central Terminal affords one of the best views in the city—indoor views, anyway. From Michael Jordan's on the west balcony, you can gaze up to see the constellations of the zodiac painted on the soaring vaulted ceiling; its 12-story height would dwarf even "His Airness" himself.

At dinner, expect generous servings of prime dry-aged Angus beef. Sides are heavy on the carbs (potatoes come mashed, baked or as fries). Lunch adds lighter salads (Cobb; Maine lobster; breast of chicken) for those who don't want to lapse into a food-induced stupor during an afternoon meeting.

The elliptical mahogany bar is a chic setting for a happy-hour beverage, and the wine salon is a great place for a cocktail party.

Monkey Bar

Asian XX

049

60 E. 54th St. (bet. Madison & Park Aves.)

Subway: 5 Av - 53 St — Mon – Sat dinner only
Phone: 212-838-2600
Web: www.theglaziergroup.com
Prices: **$$$**

If these walls could talk, they'd definitely have a lot to say. Once the former haunt of cultural icons like actor Marlon Brando, baseball great Joe DiMaggio and playwright Tennessee Williams, the Monkey Bar received a well-earned facelift to celebrate her 80th anniversary. The hand-painted simians frolicking on the walls have been restored, adding a nostalgic charm to this Depression-era bar located in the Hotel Elysée *(see hotel listing)*. The multilevel room now radiates a sexy vibe with its dark woods, dim lighting (watch your step) and a "lucky" red mural surrounding the room.

Luckily, chef Patricia Yeo doesn't monkey around. Her pan-Asian menu is sure to please, so loosen up with a cocktail, then begin with the lemongrass caramel ribs.

Morton's

050 **Steakhouse** XXX

551 Fifth Ave. (enter on 45th St. bet Fifth & Madison Aves.)

Subway: 5 Av
Phone: 212-972-3315
Web: www.mortons.com
Prices: $$$

Mon – Fri lunch & dinner
Sat – Sun dinner only

Part of a chain that started in Chicago and now extends across the globe, Morton's reigns as a well-respected chophouse. The Fifth Avenue location lies within easy walking distance of Grand Central Terminal and Times Square. In the crowded dining space, the soaring ceiling leaves room for a mezzanine overlooking the first floor. Clubby, masculine décor incorporates mahogany paneling, booths along the wall, and imposing chandeliers.

The menu, the same in all Morton's locations, centers on USDA prime aged beef, but also features crab cakes and lobster—all at rather beefy prices. California vintages are the focus of the extensive wine list. Morton's convenient Midtown location makes it popular with area business people and tourists alike.

Mr Chow

051 **Chinese** XX

324 E. 57th St. (bet. First & Second Aves.)

Subway: 59 St
Phone: 212-751-9030
Web: www.mrchow.com
Prices: $$$

Dinner daily

Actor, artist, interior designer and restaurateur, Michael Chow did the design for all four of his establishments (two of the others are in southern California; the fourth is in London). A striking mobile fashioned of red fabric hangs above the hip, black and white dining room, where even the waiters have trouble moving between the closely spaced tables.

Diners don't seem to mind the cramped quarters, as Mr. Chow lures a high-profile crowd night after night. It's not cool to ask for a menu; allow your waiter to order for you (though they will grudgingly bring a menu if you insist). Downtown residents need not venture north for Chow; a location at 121 Hudson Street in TriBeCa is open, and it's an equally trendy address.

Nicole's

American

052

10 E. 60th St. (bet. Fifth & Madison Aves.)

Subway: 5 Av - 59 St
Phone: 212-223-2288
Web: www.nicolefarhi.com
Prices: $$

Lunch daily

Food follows fashion at Nicole's, the restaurant located in the basement of Nicole Farhi's boutique. When you need a break from riffling through the racks of chic men's and women's clothing created by the Britain-based designer, follow the staircase down to the sleek restaurant. While you're deciding what to order, you can check out the action in the kitchen, housed in an ice-blue illuminated glass cube.

Here, a talented cooking team prepares seasonal dishes with a Cal-Med spirit. The menu, which changes daily, incorporates an array of premium ingredients ranging from local organic produce to fine imported food items. Just a stone's throw away from boutiques on Fifth and Madison avenues, Nicole's attracts a steady stream of ladies who lunch.

Osteria Laguna

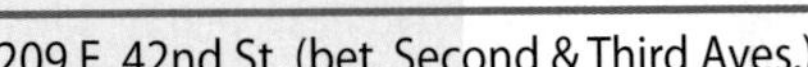

Italian

054

209 E. 42nd St. (bet. Second & Third Aves.)

Subway: Grand Central - 42 St
Phone: 212-557-0001
Web: www.osteria-laguna.com
Prices: $$

Mon – Fri lunch & dinner
Sat – Sun dinner only

Convenient to Grand Central Terminal and the United Nations, Osteria Laguna is tucked into the ground floor of a redbrick office building on a prime piece of Midtown real estate. Surprisingly charming for this stretch of 42nd Street, the dining space is separated into two rooms: a sunny, high-ceilinged front room with large windows and bare wood tables; and a back room where white-cloth-covered tables cluster.

A wide selection of homemade pasta and terrific, thin-crust, wood-oven-fired pizza star at lunch, when the room bustles with business diners. At dinner, additional entrées run from grilled branzino to veal saltimbocca, and a younger crowd composed of locals who work in the neighborhood holds sway, along with a cadre of tourists.

Oceana ✿

053 Seafood XXX

55 E. 54th St. (bet. Madison & Park Aves.)

Subway: 5 Av - 53 St
Phone: 212-759-5941
Web: www.oceanarestaurant.com
Prices: $$$$

Mon – Fri lunch & dinner
Sat dinner only

Oceana/Paul Johnson Photography

You'll think you're on the high seas when you step into Oceana. Both the name and the décor suggest a luxury ocean liner, complete with faux windows painted with murals of the glittering sea and passing ships.

At Oceana, simple seafood pairs with flavors that spark the natural taste of fresh fish and shellfish, as in a vibrant starter of bay scallop ceviche garnished with a composed salad, or an olive-oil-poached swordfish entrée served atop a scoop of black sticky rice. Desserts showcase sweets with modern flair and decadent combinations.

The wine list is extensive, with more than 1,000 labels, including one of the largest selections of white Burgundy in the city; the three-course tasting features exclusive pairings. At the bar, the short offering of oysters, cheeses and sashimi is perfect for an after-work snack.

Appetizers

- Cuttlefish Risotto, Fiddlehead Ferns, Cuttlefish Ink
- Nantucket Bay Scallop Ceviche, Fresh Hearts of Palm, Seaweed
- Florida Stone Crab Claws, Artichokes, Favas, Pancetta

Entrées

- Taro-wrapped Pompano, Baby Bok Choy, Coconut Cilantro Curry
- Nova Scotia Lobster, Wilted Baby Spinach, Malfatti Pasta
- Almond-crusted Snapper, Roasted Local Beets, Sunchokes

Desserts

- Roasted Caramel Pear Brioche, Vanilla Caramel Ice Cream
- Milk Chocolate Banana Sundae, Angel Food Cake, Maple Pecan Sauce
- Warm Vanilla-Grapefruit Cake, Earl Grey Ice Cream

P.J. Clarke's

Gastropub

055

915 Third Ave. (at 55th St.)

Subway: Lexington Av - 53 St — Lunch & dinner daily
Phone: 212-317-1616
Web: www.pjclarkes.com
Prices: ©©

Named for Patrick Joseph Clarke, who purchased the place in 1904, this saloon remains a slice of old New York, despite its change of ownership in 2002.

Pub fare still reigns at this former haunt of Frank Sinatra and Jackie O: big burgers, sandwiches, shepherd's pie and a long list of beers on tap. The bar scene, usually packed four deep with one of the city's best happy-hour crowds, overshadows the food, but this doesn't faze the good-looking young professionals who come to meet and greet. If you have to wait for a table, the bar is the place to be.

The latest additions to the family include P.J. Clarke's on the Hudson *(Four World Financial Center at Vesey St.)*, and P.J. Clarke's at Lincoln Center *(W. 63rd St. at Columbus Ave.)*.

Pampano

Mexican

056

209 E. 49th St. (bet. Second & Third Aves.)

Subway: 51 St — Mon – Fri lunch & dinner, Sat – Sun dinner only
Phone: 212-751-4545
Web: www.modernmexican.com/pampano
Prices: $$$

Chef Richard Sandoval has created a mini Mexican empire on this side of the border with a string of restaurants that spans the world serving his "modern Mexican" cuisine. Pampano is a duet between the chef and Placido Domingo and the team allows seafood to sing.

The white-walled upstairs dining room, with its sand-colored banquettes and light filtering in through the glass ceiling, evokes sun-bleached shores. Accordingly, fish takes top billing, and appears gracefully in almost every item on the menu. Top it off with a perfect margarita or a top-shelf tequila and it's almost like being by the beach in Acapulco.

During the week, get tasty lunch fare to go at nearby Pampano Taqueria, a welcome break from the sandwich and salad routine.

Pera

057 Turkish XX

303 Madison Ave. (bet. 41st & 42nd Sts.)

Subway: Grand Central - 42 St
Phone: 212-878-6301
Web: www.peranyc.com
Prices: $$

Mon – Fri lunch & dinner
Sat dinner only

At lunch and dinner, Midtown business types like to loosen their ties and shake things up a bit at Pera. This self-proclaimed "Mediterranean brasserie," named for an elegant neighborhood in Istanbul, brings a new dimension to eating in staid Midtown.

Like the owners, the cuisine here is primarily Turkish: meze of homemade grape leaves, beef and bulgur tartare, or smoked eggplant dip served with crispy lavash; mains like the signature spiced ground lamb Adana cooked on an open-flame grill.

Wood, marble and stone dominate the attractive interior, where an open kitchen and a hand-crafted communal table encourage a convivial spirit. Off the entrance, the zebrawood bar is a great place to grab a drink while you're waiting for friends to arrive.

Phoenix Garden

058 Chinese X

242 E. 40th St. (bet. Second & Third Aves.)

Subway: Grand Central - 42 St
Phone: 212-983-6666
Web: www.thephoenixgarden.com
Prices:

Mon – Fri lunch & dinner
Sat – Sun dinner only

You'll find this gem of a Chinese place tucked into the basement of a modest brick building in Murray Hill, where excellent Cantonese dishes keep locals coming back for more.

Since the menu cites some 200 different choices, it's worth requesting input from the friendly staff to assist in narrowing down your options. Whatever you decide on, don't miss the steamed shrimp and chive dumplings, pepper and salty shrimp, or any of the daily specials written on the board in the entryway (which may add the likes of Peking duck and steamed whole fish). The menu is meant for sharing, so bring as many friends as you can muster.

Prices can't be beat, especially considering that you can bring your own bottle (Phoenix Garden doesn't serve alcohol).

Picasso

Spanish XX

059

303 E. 56th St. (bet. First & Second Aves.)

Subway: 59 St — Lunch & dinner daily
Phone: 212-759-8767
Web: www.restaurantpicasso.com
Prices: $$

In a city where change is constant, it's comforting to find some things that remain exactly the same. Picasso hasn't changed a bit since it opened many years ago. There's no pretense here; this lively place with its warm and welcoming staff is straight out of Spain, from the olives marinating in giant jars atop the bar, to the aroma of garlic and the pitchers filled with sangria.

A dizzying array of tapas *(jamón Serrano,* beef *empanadillas, croquetas*) as well as traditional Spanish dishes (paella, veal *a la plancha*) fills the enormous menu; many entrées are served tableside from their cast-iron cooking pots. Quench your thirst with fruity red or white sangria, then choose from the list of full-bodied Riojas and other food-friendly Spanish wines.

Pietro's

Italian XX

060

232 E. 43rd St. (bet. Second & Third Aves.)

Subway: Grand Central - 42 St — Mon – Fri lunch & dinner, Sat dinner only
Phone: 212-682-9760
Web: www.pietros.com
Prices: $$$

Trendy it's not. Inexpensive? Not with a Midtown address in the shadow of the Chrysler Building. Founded in 1932 by Pietro Donini and his brother Natale, Pietro's is an old-fashioned Italian eatery. The plain dining room sports a patriotic (for Italy) red, green and white color scheme, and the food will be familiar: minestrone, chicken Parmigiana, spaghetti with meatballs, veal Marsala, shrimp scampi, along with steaks and chops. Your Italian grandmother probably didn't even cook food this good, but Pietro won't tell.

Pietro's may not have a chic décor or a fancy menu, but don't overlook this tried-and-true place. The service is good and preparations are rendered using excellent, fresh ingredients and homemade pasta—now that's Italian!

Riingo

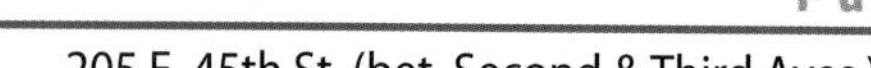

061 Fusion XX

205 E. 45th St. (bet. Second & Third Aves.)

Subway: Grand Central - 42 St — Lunch & dinner daily
Phone: 212-867-4200
Web: www.riingo.com
Prices: $$

Derived from the Japanese word for "apple" (as in the Big Apple), Riingo features celebrity chef Marcus Samuelsson's interpretation of Japanese and American cuisines. The stylish, contemporary restaurant, just off the lobby of the Alex Hotel, incorporates ebony wood, bamboo floor planks and thoughtful touches such as custom-made ceramic sake sets. At the front of the restaurant, a small bar, lounge and a few sidewalk tables offer a pleasant setting for a post-work cocktail or fast business lunch.

In addition to the creative kitchen menu and extensive raw-bar selection, Riingo offers a full range of sushi and maki of impressive quality. Open for all-day dining, Riingo and its original menu rise a cut above your typical hotel restaurant.

Rosa Mexicano

062 Mexican XX

1063 First Ave. (at 58th St.)

Subway: 59 St — Dinner daily
Phone: 212-753-7407
Web: www.rosamexicano.com
Prices: $$$

A sure crowd pleaser, Rosa Mexicano promises good food and a good time, and it always delivers. While outposts have popped up in New York and other cities, the East Side original still wins raves on a nightly basis. The place is always packed (reservations essential) with a mix of young and old, families and singles.

With its terrific margaritas and extensive tequila list, the bar is the place to wait for a table or unwind after work. Guacamole made to order tableside, along with authentic entrées like *budin Azteca* (multi-layer tortilla pie), and *crepas de camarón* (corn crêpes filled with shrimp and napped with chile pasilla sauce) keep 'em coming back for more. Appealing desserts are worth saving room for—at least order one to share.

Sakagura

Japanese

063

211 E. 43rd St. (bet. Second & Third Aves.)

Subway: Grand Central - 42 St
Phone: 212-953-7253
Web: www.sakagura.com
Prices: $$$

Mon – Fri lunch & dinner
Sat – Sun dinner only

It's all about sake at Sakagura. Although the restaurant is located in the basement of a Midtown office building (enter the lobby and walk down the back stairs), this is as authentic a sake den as you'll find in the city. Here, you'll be transported to Tokyo with traditional Japanese décor, secluded booths and tables filled with Japanese businessmen.

More than 200 kinds of sake are exquisitely presented in imported serving sets selected by the helpful staff. The menu plays a supporting role, designed to complement the sake list (no sushi is served, only sashimi, to best enjoy the sake). Other than that, the food doesn't skimp on variety, authenticity or quality. Share a few small plates as part of a lengthy ritual of nibbling and sake sipping.

San Pietro

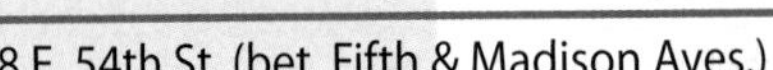

Italian

064

18 E. 54th St. (bet. Fifth & Madison Aves.)

Subway: 5 Av - 53 St
Phone: 212-753-9015
Web: www.sanpietro.net
Prices: $$$

Mon – Sat lunch & dinner

At San Pietro, the chef imports more than three-quarters of his ingredients, including cheeses and fish, from southern Italy. The three Bruno brothers run this traditional restaurant, where ancient recipes from Rome and Campania are revived and revitalized.

Vegetables figure prominently on the generous, seasonally changing menu: fresh fava beans are flavored with pecorino cheese and black truffles, broccoli rabe is sautéed in olive oil and garlic. Sure, there are pastas and risotto, but the signature dish is Pesce San Pietro, John Dory braised in garlic sauce scented with thyme and served with baked fennel and toasted hazelnuts.

Ceramic murals, decorative odes to the owners' native region of Campania, enhance the elegant dining area.

Sarge's

Deli

548 Third Ave. (bet. 36th & 37th Sts.)

Subway: 33 St — Lunch & dinner daily
Phone: 212-679-0442
Web: www.sargesdeli.com
Prices:

Opened many moons ago by former NYPD sergeant Abe Katz, Sarge's is a classic New York deli that pulls in a steady stream of locals. Pastrami is king here, but you can't go wrong with any of the choices, which range from blintzes to matzoh ball soup. If you can squeeze in dessert after a deli Wellington (a diet-busting combo of corned beef, pastrami and potatoes baked in a puff-pastry shell), Sarge's serves a mean cheesecake.
Abe is no longer on hand to chat up the customers, but the chipper waitstaff makes everyone feel like a regular, and children are welcome. Still run by the Katz family, Sarge's is a Murray Hill must for a real New York deli experience. For Long Island-bound commuters, Sarge's has a location in Syosset *(236 Jericho Tpk.)*.

Seo

Japanese 

249 E. 49th St. (bet. Second & Third Aves.)

Subway: 51 St — Mon – Fri lunch & dinner
Phone: 212-355-7722 — Sat – Sun dinner only
Web: N/A
Prices: $$

Seo is the lovely sort of neighborhood spot you'd like to be a regular at, so you could enjoy their authentic Japanese cuisine all the time. It's an understated place, located on a residential block near the United Nations, The Japan Society and the "Dag." In a neighborhood rich with Japanese eateries, Seo stands out for its excellent light dishes, such as miso-marinated cod, and sake-steamed clams and squid. They serve sushi and sashimi too, but don't let these dominate your meal or you'll miss out on the menu's variety.
Seo offers a good selection of sakes and beers to match the food. Sit at the sushi bar, or claim a table in the serene little dining room that overlooks a traditional Japanese garden behind the town house.

Shaburi

Japanese

067

125 E. 39th St. (bet. Lexington & Park Aves.)

Subway: Grand Central - 42 St
Phone: 212-867-6999
Web: www.shaburi.com
Prices: $$$

Mon – Fri lunch & dinner
Sat – Sun dinner only

In an age where everything is interactive, Shaburi fits right in with hands-on dining. Both the communal bar and individual tables are equipped with electric burners for making *shabu shabu*, the house specialty. Just order the ingredients that appeal (Matsuzaka beef, Kurobuta pork, seafood, veggies) and simmer them in hot broth at your table. While you're at it, you can use the tabletop burners to stir-fry bite-size pieces of meat or tofu, marinated in sugar or soy, for *sukiyaki* (served over rice or udon).
It's lots of fun for a group of friends—and a great ice-breaker for a first date. Wet your whistle with a sake, a house cocktail or Kirin on tap. The first American outpost of a Taiwanese chain, Shaburi opened in 2004.

Sip Sak

Turkish

068

928 Second Ave. (bet. 49th & 50th Sts.)

Subway: 51 St
Phone: 212-583-1900
Web: www.sip-sak.com
Prices: $$

Lunch & dinner daily

Turkish native and talented chef Orhan Yegen is notorious for loving and leaving the restaurants he opens. His current flame is Sip Sak, a homey place where a young Turkish waitstaff welcomes a crowd of international neighborhood residents.
Despite a recent remodeling, little has changed. The chef still seems to have a hand in every table, while overseeing the take-out orders and the kitchen. He may be peripatetic, but he produces some outstanding Turkish food—an excellent value, to boot. The best ingredients, handled with traditional Turkish techniques, yield well-balanced fare including meze, kebabs and a variety of lamb dishes. Will Yegen stay with Sip Sak? That remains to be seen, but with any luck, this romance will last a long time.

Smith & Wollensky

069 **Steakhouse** XX

797 Third Ave. (at 49th St.)

Subway: 51 St
Phone: 212-753-1530
Web: www.smithandwollensky.com
Prices: $$$$

Mon – Fri lunch & dinner
Sat – Sun dinner only

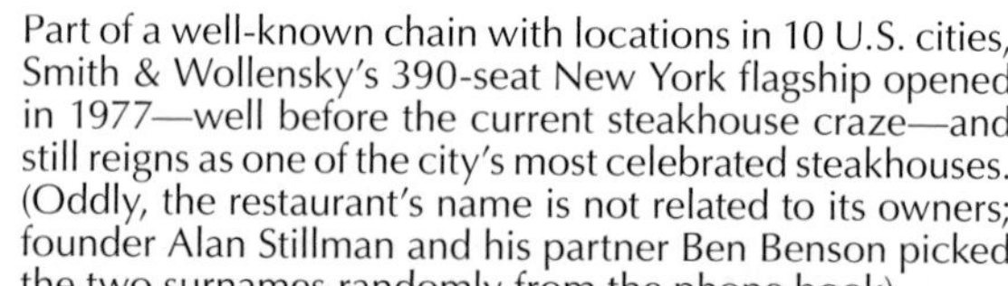

Part of a well-known chain with locations in 10 U.S. cities, Smith & Wollensky's 390-seat New York flagship opened in 1977—well before the current steakhouse craze—and still reigns as one of the city's most celebrated steakhouses. (Oddly, the restaurant's name is not related to its owners; founder Alan Stillman and his partner Ben Benson picked the two surnames randomly from the phone book).

USDA prime beef, which is dry-aged and hand-butchered on the premises, accounts for the constant crowds of agency types and other Midtowners who keep this place going strong. For night owls, adjoining Wollensky's Grill serves a less-expensive menu until 2am to nourish the raucus group of post-work partiers who hold sway at the wildly popular bar.

Sparks Steak House

070 **Steakhouse** XX

210 E. 46th St. (bet. Second & Third Aves.)

Subway: Grand Central - 42 St
Phone: 212-687-4855
Web: www.sparksnyc.com
Prices: $$$

Mon – Sat lunch & dinner

With seating for nearly 700 people, Sparks is well equipped to handle crowds. Indeed, it has drawn hordes of expense-account types for years. The bi-level dining space feels even more gigantic on an evening when the place is jamming—which is most of the time. There's a raucous, masculine vibe, enhanced by large tables and the 19th-century landscapes of the Hudson River Valley that line the wainscoted walls.

Unlike many steakhouses, Sparks doesn't offer a Porterhouse, but thick cuts of phenomenal prime sirloin and lamb or veal chops will satisfy your meat cravings (for seafood lovers, lobsters weigh in from 3 to nearly 6 pounds). Waiting for a table here is de rigueur, but speedy bartenders will shake a frosty martini for you in the meantime.

Sushi-Ann

Japanese XX

071

38 E. 51st St. (bet. Madison & Park Aves.)

Subway: 51 St — Mon – Fri lunch & dinner, Sat dinner only
Phone: 212-755-1780
Web: www.sushiann.com
Prices: $$

Located around the corner from Saks, Sushi-Ann is an unpretentious haven with its L-shaped sushi bar and blond varnished-wood tables, all set with fresh roses. This place next to the New York Palace Hotel is a good choice for a traditional sushi experience. Not to be overlooked, Sushi-Ann competes with the best sushi bars in the city.
Uniformed waiters cater to a casual clientele that includes business types as well as tourists, who all enjoy the excellent quality and variety of the sushi, sashimi and hand rolls served here. Those in the know take a seat at the sushi bar (where there's a $30 minimum) for individualized selections from the friendly and talented chefs.
Though pricey, the sake list highlights a number of good selections.

Sushiden

Japanese XX

072

19 E. 49th St. (bet. Fifth & Madison Aves.)

Subway: 5 Av - 53 St — Mon – Fri lunch & dinner, Sun dinner only
Phone: 212-758-2700
Web: www.sushiden.com
Prices: $$$

Inside Sushiden's windowed façade you'll find a long sushi bar, behind which the chefs work their magic, preparing raw fish with a legerdemain that proves the saying that the hand is quicker than the eye. Each piece of fish is sized perfectly over its tiny bed of rice, so the taste of one ingredient doesn't overwhelm the others (regulars recommend the *toro*, a fatty and flavorful cut of tuna taken from the fish's belly). A good selection of fixed-price meals are also offered, all at a good value. Young women in kimonos attend to customers in an efficient and pleasant manner.
The restaurant is closed on Saturdays, but is a good bet for weekday sushi. If you're on the West Side, there's a second Sushiden at 123 West 49th Street.

Sushi Ichimura

073 Japanese XX

1026 Second Ave. (bet. 54th & 55th Sts.)

Subway: Lexington Av - 53 St — Mon – Sat dinner only
Phone: 212-355-3557
Web: N/A
Prices: $$$$

Deep-pocketed Japanese diners and visiting dignitaries know to make a beeline for the sushi bar at this serene but often crowded restaurant. Here they throw frugality to the wind and abandon themselves to the *omakase*, a menu which features the chef's selection of the freshest sushi and sashimi (beakfish, needlefish, red clam, sweet shrimp, all depending on the market), prepared in perfect *Edo* style.
Guests can also order from the wider à la carte list of classic Japanese dishes (from fried burdock root to green-tea ice cream) or pick and choose from the sushi and sashimi menus.
The attentive staff sees to every last detail in an unobtrusive manner—just one of the reasons Ichimura makes regulars out of many a first-timer.

Sushi Yasuda

074 Japanese XX

204 E. 43rd St. (bet. Second & Third Aves.)

Subway: Grand Central - 42 St — Mon – Fri lunch & dinner, Sat dinner only
Phone: 212-972-1001
Web: www.sushiyasuda.com
Prices: $$$$

♿

Discreetly tucked away in the corridor between Grand Central Terminal and the United Nations, Sushi Yashuda appears almost Scandinavian with its blond woods and contemporary style. But look again: the walls, tables, ceiling and floor are all wrapped in solid bamboo planks. Even the sushi bar, the domain of Japanese chef Naomichi Yasuda, is made of unfinished bamboo.
Yasuda, whose years of experience include gigs in Tokyo and New York City, is a stickler for purity and simplicity. His raw fish offerings change daily, depending on the most pristine products available. Sushi and rolls are traditional *Edo* style, served in small pieces specifically seasoned to enhance the flavor of each. Friendly servers aim to please.

Taksim

Turkish

075

1030 Second Ave. (bet. 53rd & 54th Sts.)

Subway: Lexington Av - 53 St — Lunch & dinner daily
Phone: 212-421-3004
Web: www.taksim.us
Prices: ⊜

From the outside, Taksim looks more like a take-out joint than a sit-down restaurant. But come inside, take a seat at one of the colorful tables in the small room, and you'll discover a flavor-packed cuisine that more than compensates for the lack of atmosphere.

It's all about the food here. Specials augment a menu of Turkish fare that puts stock in such straightforward dishes as moussaka, shish kebabs, and a boneless lamb shank wrapped in eggplant and braised in tomato sauce. Although all the prices are reasonable, entrées from the grill are even less expensive when ordered as a sandwich. Taksim's flourishing take-out and delivery business often results in slow service, but the well-prepared, authentic food keeps locals coming back for more.

Tao

Asian

076

42 E. 58th St. (bet. Madison & Park Aves.)

Subway: 59 St — Mon – Fri lunch & dinner
Phone: 212-888-2288 — Sat – Sun dinner only
Web: www.taorestaurant.com
Prices: $$$

Asia's tastiest dishes star at this former movie theater. It's hard to imagine catching a flick in this dramatic dining playground today, outfitted as it is with a Chinese scroll draped across the ceiling and a 16-foot-high statue of Buddha towering over a reflecting pool in the main dining room. The theater's former balconies now accommodate diners too—some 300 of them on three levels.

The menu spotlights a combination of Hong Kong Chinese, Japanese and Thai dishes, including sushi and sashimi. Perfect for sharing, a host of small plates offers everything from dragon-tail spare ribs to lobster wontons. On weekend nights, Manhattan's young and restless turn out in droves to indulge in libations like the Zen-tini or Tao Love Potion #9.

Teodora

Italian XX

141 E. 57th St. (bet. Lexington & Third Aves.)

Subway: Lexington Av - 59 St — Lunch & dinner daily
Phone: 212-826-7101
Web: www.teodoranyc.com
Prices: $$

It's a pleasant surprise to discover this cozy restaurant on 57th Street, one of Midtown's busiest commercial thoroughfares. Equally conducive to a family dinner as a romantic date, the long, narrow dining room recalls a typical bistro with its wood bar, Belle Époque-style light fixtures and shelves lined with bottles of wine and carafes of vinegar.
Owners Giancarlo Quadalti (the chef) and his partner, Roberta Ruggini, both hail from the Emilia-Romagna area of Italy. The menu emphasizes an appealing array of Northern Italian dishes, including some rarely found treats such as *cotechino* (a rustic boiled pork sausage served atop a bed of perfectly puréed potatoes). Specials listed on the blackboards are particularly enjoyable.

Tsushima

Japanese X

141 E. 47th St. (bet. Lexington & Third Aves.)

Subway: Grand Central - 42 St — Mon – Fri lunch & dinner, Sat – Sun dinner only
Phone: 212-207-1938
Web: N/A
Prices: $$

There are few restaurant secrets left in New York, but Tsushima is one of them. Chances are, you haven't heard of it, but this place stands out among the competition in the thin slice of Midtown jammed with restaurants straight out of Tokyo. It's easy to walk right by Tsushima (it's located a few steps below street level), but once inside, you'll find a sultry décor that contrasts black wood with white leather seating.
Skilled chefs seamlessly juggle the standard table orders with the *omakase* offerings at the sushi bar, and the kitchen plays backup with an assortment of cooked courses. Though spicy tuna can be had, the chef's choice is the way to go, as Tsushima nets fantastic quality and interesting varieties of fish—all elegantly presented.

Vong ✿

Fusion XX

079

200 E. 54th St. (bet. Second & Third Aves.)

Subway: Lexington Av - 53 St
Phone: 212-486-9592
Web: www.jean-georges.com
Prices: $$$

Mon – Fri lunch & dinner
Sat – Sun dinner only

Jean-Georges Management

One of the nation's foremost chefs, Jean-Georges Vongerichten has made his mark on American cuisine with a galaxy of restaurants (just under 20 at last count) and several cookbooks to his credit.

You'll be introduced to the culinary concept at Vong as you enter the dining room, where bowls of aromatic spices decorate a long table. The Alsatian-born chef fuses Thai flavors—and 150 herbs and spices—with French technique here. It was a natural evolution for Vongerichten, who began cooking in France, then worked in Bangkok. An aromatic chicken and coconut soup appetizer epitomizes the chef's masterful technique, while main courses such as tamarind-glazed duck with pineapple fried rice consistently win fans.

From the Thai silks and louvered wooden panels in the dining room to the bamboo flatware and metal-accented serving pieces, Asian details permeate the design.

Appetizers

- Crab Spring Rolls with Tamarind Dipping Sauce
- Prawn Satay with Fresh Oyster Sauce
- Chicken and Coconut Milk Soup with Galangal and Shiitake Mushrooms

Entrées

- Spiced Cod Fish with Curried Artichokes and Tamarind Ketchup
- Lobster with Thai Herbs
- Chicken with Lemongrass, Asian Long Beans and Sweet Rice in Banana Leaf

Desserts

- Roasted Asian Pear, Licorice Ice Cream and Sableuse
- Coconut Sticky Rice, Mango and Coconut Reduction
- Passionfruit Soufflé and Passion Fruit Ice Cream

The Water Club

Seafood 

080

E. 30th St. (at the East River)

Subway: 33 St — Lunch & dinner daily
Phone: 212-683-3333
Web: www.thewaterclub.com
Prices: **$$$**

For years, birthdays, anniversaries and engagements have been celebrated at the Water Club, and, indeed, its setting is perfect for special occasions. Set on a barge in the East River, the dining room boasts floor-to-ceiling windows that overlook the river, and water views from every table. Marine signal flags hanging from the ceiling and a waitstaff dressed as a ship's crew complete the nautical theme.

The menu celebrates American dishes and spotlights seafood such as shrimp cocktail, grilled salmon and Maine lobster. Meat dishes like Colorado rack of lamb and Long Island duck please landlubbers. Live piano music entertains nightly, and in summer, the Crow's Nest on the restaurant's upper deck offers informal outdoor dining and river breezes.

Wolfgang's Steakhouse

Steakhouse XX

081

4 Park Ave. (at 33rd St.)

Subway: 33 St — Mon – Sat lunch & dinner; Sun dinner only
Phone: 212-889-3369
Web: www.wolfgangssteakhouse.com
Prices: **$$$$**

Wolfgang Zwiener worked for 41 years as a headwaiter at Brooklyn's Peter Luger steakhouse. Just as he was planning to retire, he got sidetracked into starting his own restaurant in Manhattan with his son and several other former waiters from Luger's. Opened in 2004, Wolfgang's occupies the main dining room of the 1912 Vanderbilt Hotel. What sets this space apart is its gorgeous vaulted and tiled ceiling, crafted by 19th-century artisan Rafael Guastavino.

It's all about meat here—strapping portions of Porterhouse served on the bone (or a three-pound lobster for fish fans). Wolfgang's hand-selects and dry-ages the meat in-house. Side dishes are à la carte, so you'll pay more to add the decadent creamed spinach or the signature German potatoes.

Yakitori Torys

Japanese

248 E. 52nd St. (bet. Second & Third Aves.)

Subway: 51 St
Phone: 212-813-1800
Web: www.torysnyc.com
Prices: $$

Mon – Fri lunch & dinner
Sat – Sun dinner only

Midtown has its fair share of Tokyo-quality restaurants and Torys is no exception. Positioned on the second floor of a busy block, this tranquil little yakitori place skewers up a remarkable variety of chicken parts and grills them expertly. The kitchen excels at yakitori, but is equally adept at other dishes so don't ignore the rest of the enormous menu. The chicken soup here easily competes with grandma's version and absolutely do not pass on *gyoza*, as they are a distant relative of the frozen versions found elsewhere. The attentive staff will present your parade of courses and quenching libations at a relaxed pace; everything is cooked to order and there's surely no rush.
Limited seating and fabulous food here make booking ahead a must.

Zarela

953 Second Ave. (bet. 50th & 51st Sts.)

Subway: 51 St
Phone: 212-644-6740
Web: www.zarela.com
Prices: $$

Mon – Fri lunch & dinner
Sat – Sun dinner only

Every day's a fiesta in this boisterous bistro, hung with bright paper garlands, ceremonial masks, puppets and other Mexican artifacts—Zarela Martinez sees to that. The chef opened her restaurant here in 1987, and it's still going strong. Her secret recipe for fantastic, powerful margaritas is just one of the reasons.
A native of Mexico, Zarela courts a carnival ambience with lively music and food that's served family-style, in case you wish to share. In the evenings, the place teems with regulars and post-work revelers who often spill out onto the sidewalk while they wait to dig into flavorful regional Mexican entrées like *Cochinita Pibil, camarones con coco* or a side of *arroz con crema,* whose enticing aromas fill the dining room.

Midtown West

When you think of Midtown West, Times Square probably comes to mind. True, brash **Times Square**, at Broadway and 42nd Street, demands your attention with its blazing marquees, but the neighborhood that runs from Fifth Avenue west to the Hudson River is so much more than that. Here you'll also find picturesque **Bryant Park**, the **Empire State Building**, and **Rockefeller Center**, home to NBC studios and the city's famous skating rink. For shoppers, **Macy's** anchors a frenetic shopping hub *(on Sixth Ave. at 34th St.)*, and **Diamond and Jewelry Way** *(W. 47th St., between Fifth & Sixth Aves.)* ranks as the world's largest district for diamonds and other precious stones.

If it's dining that interests you, look no farther. Midtown West holds a dense concentration of eateries, from Restaurant Row (as West 46th Street between Broadway and 9th Avenue is known) to the Time Warner Center (on Columbus Circle), home to some of New York's most celebrated restaurants.

A Bit of History

In the colonial era, this slice of Midtown belonged to the city but was actually the country, as New York's population was concentrated well below Canal Street. By the mid-19th century, the area was covered with brownstone town houses, home to upper-middle-class families who couldn't afford a mansion on Fifth Avenue. Upon the completion of the Sixth Avenue "El" (elevated railway) in 1878, a majority of these residents deemed the quarter too noisy and dirty, and, with their Fifth Avenue neighbors, began moving uptown.

The construction of **Rockefeller Center** between 1930 and 1940 permanently changed the character of the neighborhood. More than 225 buildings, mostly brownstones, were demolished to make room for the original 12 buildings of the complex, and the residential population

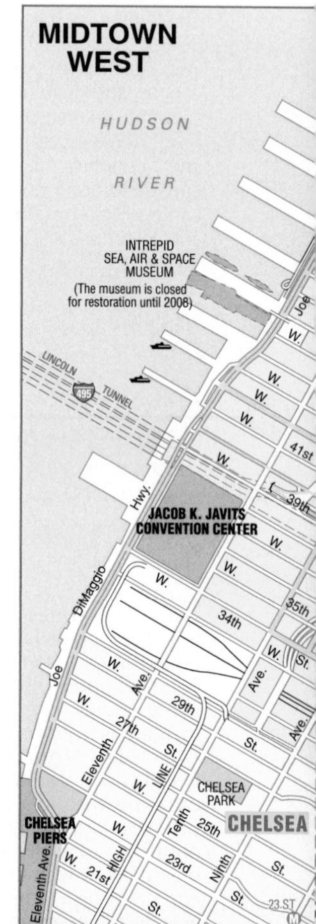

was dispersed to other parts of the city. But with that loss came significant gain. The center was hailed as an architectural triumph. Rockefeller's insistence that early tenants be affiliated with the television and radio industries soon attracted other media outlets to the district, boosting its worldwide visibility.

The Dividing Line

Although Fifth Avenue officially separates the east and west sides of Manhattan, it is the Avenue of the Americas (still known as Sixth Avenue to locals, though it was officially renamed in 1945) that actually feels like the dividing line. In part, that's because its neighbors are so distinct. One block east, the department stores of **Fifth Avenue** ooze gentility. One block west, the fabled **Theater District** (spreading north from Times Square along Broadway) teems with performance venues and restaurants, the latter touting pre- and post-theater menus.

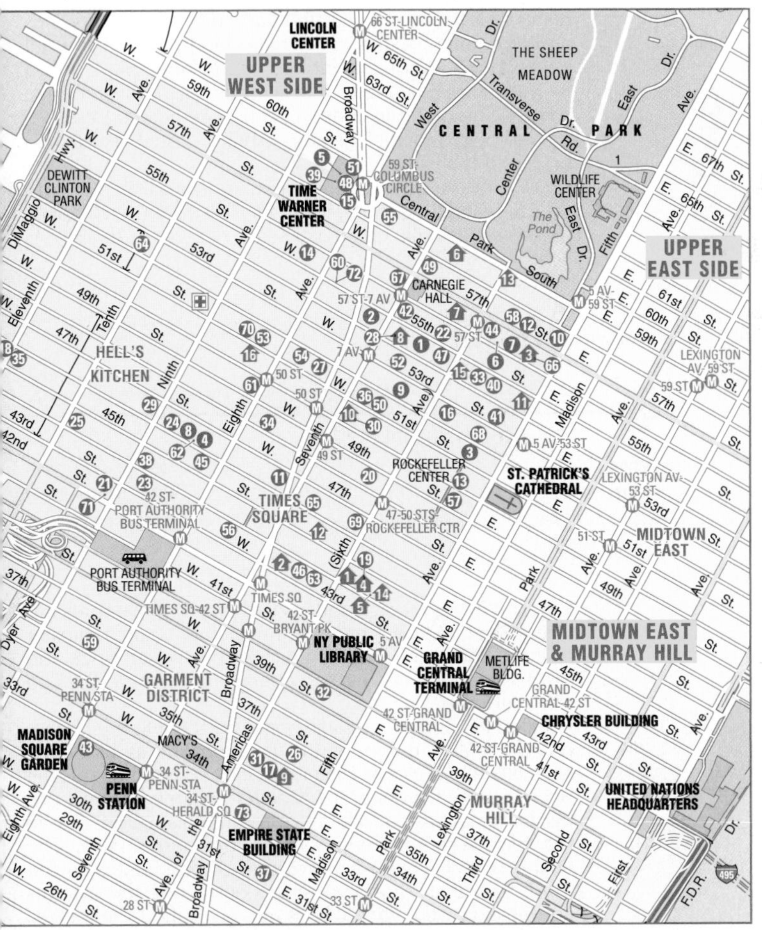

Abbocato

001 — **Italian** XX

136 W. 55th St. (bet. Sixth & Seventh Aves.)

Subway: 57 St — Mon – Sat lunch & dinner
Phone: 212-265-4000 — Sun dinner only
Web: www.abboccato.com
Prices: $$$

Brought to you by the Livanos family, whose stable includes Molyvos and Oceana, Abboccato bears the hallmarks of these experienced restaurateurs. Abboccato, located adjacent to the Blakely Hotel, combs the different regions of Italy for its cuisine and comes up with wines and tempting dishes such as half-moon pasta filled with beets and Gorgonzola dolce, or suckling pig cooked in milk and hazelnuts. If you're dining with someone special, the menu includes a section dedicated to dishes (grilled branzino, rack of lamb, whole-roasted veal shank) prepared tableside for two.
Chic, modern styling lends an understated elegance to the 75-seat dining room, while the 20-seat terrazza opens onto the sidewalk, creating a sense of alfresco dining.

Amalia

002 — **Mediterranean** XX

204 W. 55th St. (at Broadway)

Subway: 57 St - 7 Av — Mon – Fri lunch & dinner
Phone: 212-245-1234 — Sat – Sun dinner only
Web: www.amalia-nyc.com
Prices: $$$

Cloaked in high design and backed by nightlife impresario Greg Brier, Amalia has all the elements of a hipster lounge. The bi-level space dresses up exposed brick and distressed wood beams with ebony glass chandeliers and silk wallpaper.
Located in a former carriage house adjacent to the Dream hotel, Amalia's cuisine is just as appealing as its dining room's décor is glossy. Chef Ivy Stark's menu spotlights the warm, sunny flavors of the Mediterranean with creations like lamb osso buco with tangerine gremolata, and roasted sea bass with potatoes, rock shrimp and saffron. The well-selected wine list makes a fine complement to the food. And that's not surprising, considering the list was composed by the chef, who is also a certified sommelier.

Anthos ✿

Greek XXX

003

36 W. 52nd St. (bet. Fifth & Sixth Aves.)

Subway: 47-50 Sts - Rockefeller Ctr
Phone: 212-582-6900
Web: www.anthosnyc.com
Prices: $$$

Mon – Fri lunch & dinner
Sat dinner only

Anthos/Battman

Michael Psilakis presides over this Midtown temple of upscale Greek cuisine. It's not the first time we've seen the work of this Greek culinary god—he first made his mark in Manhattan with Onera and Dona, and his latest venture is also in partnership with Donatella Arpaia. Occupying the former Aqua Pazza space, Anthos (Greek for "to bloom") bursts with restrained elegance in its chocolate-brown chairs, and white- and pink-linen-topped tables.

Distinctive dishes depend on the market, and the menu reads like a tribute to Greek haute cuisine. Main courses are seafood-heavy (olive-oil-poached halibut over yogurt manti and caviar; crispy turbot with eggplant purée), while desserts, like a trio of baklava, are Olympic in stature.

Food this good is usually reserved for the expense-account crowd, but Anthos delights foodies on tighter budgets with its $28 prix-fixe lunch.

Appetizers

- Hilopita: Egg Noodles, Rabbit, Snails, Black Truffle, Manouri
- Five Raw Meze: Tuna, Yellowtail, Taylor Bay Scallop, Nairagi, Cobia
- Skordalia: Potato and Garlic Soup

Entrées

- Spicy Shellfish Yiouvetsi Stew, Orzo, Saffron
- Crispy Turbot, Iman Baldi, Cipollini, Pickled Fig Purée
- Baby Pork Chops, Belly, and Lahanodolma, Fennel, Avgolemono

Desserts

- Baklava Trio: Pistachio, Honey Custard, Walnut Cake
- Encased Sesame Ice Cream, Metaxa Caramel, Halva
- Chocolate And Coffee Torta, Milk Chocolate Mousse, Spiced Génoise

Barbetta

004 **Italian** XXX

321 W. 46th St. (bet. Eighth & Ninth Aves.)

Subway: 50 St (Eighth Ave.) — Lunch & dinner daily
Phone: 212-246-9171
Web: www.barbettarestaurant.com
Prices: **$$$**

In 2006 Barbetta celebrated its 100th birthday, still under the ownership of the Maioglio family who founded it. Inside the four 19th-century Maioglio-Astor town houses, you'll be transported to the heyday of 1950's continental dining in an ornate room decorated with 18th-century Piemontese furnishings and an antique crystal and gilded-wood chandelier.

The ample seasonal menu, featuring the specialties of Italy's Piemonte region—including some wonderful pastas—lists the date on which a particular dish first made its appearance. Pair your meal with one of the more than 1,700 different labels on the tremendous wine list.

Scented by gardenias, oleander and jasmine, the secluded garden is an oasis in the heart of the Theater District.

Bar Masa

005 **Japanese** X

10 Columbus Circle (in the Time Warner Center)

Subway: 59 St - Columbus Circle — Mon – Sat lunch & dinner
Phone: 212-823-9800
Web: www.masanyc.com
Prices: **$$$**

If you want upscale ingredients with elegant preparations served in a serene setting, head to Bar Masa. Adjacent to its pricey relative, Masa, Bar Masa features a long, thin dining room, with a bar on one side and a line of tables on the other. Japanese limestone tiles and dark woods lend an earthy element to the room, while a gauzy burgundy curtain separates the tables from the bar, (which accommodates diners and those just stopping by for a drink).

The structured seasonal menu provides a wide choice of appetizers, rolls, sushi, noodles and more. Dessert choices range from refreshing grapefruit granité to rich chocolate mousse. And while it's nowhere near the experience of Masa next door, prices here are certainly easier to swallow.

Bay Leaf

006 **Indian** XX

49 W. 56th St. (bet. Fifth & Sixth Aves.)

Subway: 57 St — Lunch & dinner daily
Phone: 212-957-1818
Web: N/A
Prices: $$

In a sea of ethnic restaurants on a busy Midtown street, Bay Leaf stands out for its classic Indian cooking and enjoyable setting. This Indian eatery, on the ground floor of an office tower, is popular at lunch with the business crowd who come here for the well-priced buffet. It's also a sure bet for dinner, with a diverse assortment of à la carte items, including traditional curries and tandoori dishes. Expertly managed, the service is smooth from start to finish, and the staff helps guests navigate the many choices.
Bay Leaf shies away from the predictable décor with an elegant display of rich paneled woods, framed black-and-white photography and discreet Indian music. Service is also available on the terrace during warmer months.

Beacon

007 **American**

25 W. 56th St. (bet. Fifth & Sixth Aves.)

Subway: 57 St — Mon – Fri & Sun lunch & dinner
Phone: 212-332-0500 — Sat dinner only
Web: www.beaconnyc.com
Prices: $$$

Open-fire cooking is the theme at Beacon, where big flavors result from food cooked in the wood-burning oven, rotisserie or grill. The reason it works so well is that chef and co-owner Waldy Malouf uses the best-quality raw ingredients he can find. Whether it's a simple Beacon burger, a sophisticated suckling pig or a homey Catskill trout, there's something to appeal to most every appetite—and bringing your appetite is de rigueur here, since portions are generous.
For those who want to enjoy the view of the bustling dining room, the mezzanine is the best place to sit; diners who consider cooking to be a spectator sport should grab one of the ringside seats by the open kitchen. The bar's sexy spirit and innovative cocktail menu always draws a crowd.

Becco

008 **Italian** XX

355 W. 46th St. (bet. Eighth & Ninth Aves.)

Subway: 42 St - Port Authority Bus Terminal — Lunch & dinner daily
Phone: 212-397-7597
Web: www.becconyc.com
Prices: $$

If you're seeking a quick bite before a show, this Restaurant Row town house in the Theater District can get you in and out with time to spare. If you have a free evening, come later to appreciate the hearty Italian cooking in less frenetic surroundings. Hanging copper pots, Italian landscapes and shelves full of country knickknacks dress the three separate dining spaces here, lending a homey air to this casual homestyle Italian restaurant.

Owned by Lidia Bastianich and her son, Joseph, Becco features a varied menu augmented by a list of specials. For those with big appetites, the *sinfonia di pasta* offers an abbondanza of unlimited portions of the chef's three daily pasta creations—just make sure your pants have an elastic waist.

Ben Benson's

009 **Steakhouse** XX

123 W. 52nd St. (bet. Sixth & Seventh Aves.)

Subway: 5 Av - 53 St — Lunch & dinner daily
Phone: 212-581-8888
Web: www.benbensons.com
Prices: $$$

If you grimace at the mere thought of fusion cooking, then this is the place for you. Since 1982, Ben Benson's has been serving prime cuts of USDA meats and other classic American fare to its contented macho clientele of power brokers and politicians (the names of the regulars are engraved on brass plaques set in the wainscoting). The huge menu includes the usual suspects (sirloin steaks, veal chops) but Southern fried chicken and crab cakes earn equal billing.

The high-ceilinged dining room is airier than many of the steakhouses in town, and this New York steakhouse remains stubbornly independent from chain ownership. For those who favor alfresco dining, the spacious sidewalk terrace provides a pleasant setting in nice weather.

BG

010 — American XX

754 Fifth Ave. (at 58th St.)

Subway: 5 Av - 59 St — Lunch & dinner daily
Phone: 212-872-8977
Web: www.bergdorfgoodman.com
Prices: $$$

Since Bergdorf Goodman is the center of the universe for the pampered and privileged, it goes without saying that BG, the store's seventh-floor dining room, serves as a cafeteria to New York's champagne-sipping set. In 2005, Bergdorf's closed their old restaurant in favor of this sleek salon, decorated in haute Parisian style with hand-painted wallpaper and 18th-century-style chairs. Soft shades of blue, green and yellow lend a feminine mystique to the light-filled room. The menu reads like an upscale country club—tomato and shrimp soup, chef's salad, soufflé—and afternoon tea is served daily.
For a less formal experience, try Bar III in the men's store across the street, where you can nosh on salads, sandwiches and soups while you sip a cocktail.

Blue Fin

011 — Seafood XX

1567 Broadway (at 47th St.)

Subway: 49 St — Lunch & dinner daily
Phone: 212-918-1400
Web: www.brguestrestaurants.com
Prices: $$$

You'd think it would be easy to spot this two-tier 400-seat restaurant on Times Square, but Blue Fin seductively conceals itself behind its glass-front bar. Connected to the W Hotel Times Square, the restaurant dazzles downstairs with its nightclub-like design incorporating ocean-blue walls, polished mirrors reflecting glittering light, and a fanciful mobile of fish that seem to swim above the diners. Follow the floating staircase upstairs, where the mood turns sultry in the lounge.
The extensive menu celebrates all creatures from the sea, from herb-crusted black bass to sesame-crusted bigeye tuna—including a selection of fresh oysters, clams, sushi, sashimi and seafood towers from the raw bar. New York labels are featured on the wine list.

Brasserie 8 1/2

012 **Contemporary** XXX

9 W. 57th St. (bet. Fifth & Sixth Aves.)

Subway: 57 St — Lunch & dinner daily
Phone: 212-829-0812
Web: www.brasserie8andahalf.com
Prices: $$$

Brasserie 8½'s individual style melds contemporary dash with a soupçon of decades past. You'll make a theatrical entrance down the brightly carpeted spiral staircase to reach the dining room. At the foot of the stairs, there's a circular lounge; a few more steps down, the brasserie is a big, bold, modern affair, with fabric-covered walls, leather booths, and a striking glass Léger mural walling off the kitchen.

Well-executed dishes are elegantly plated and take their inspiration from the Mediterranean (Riviera-style wild King salmon) to Asia (Japanese yellowtail tartare with passionfruit mayonnaise). Service is attentive but speedy, ideal for those who need to get back to the office, or to go home to practice their grand entrances.

Brasserie Ruhlmann

013 **French** XX

45 Rockefeller Plaza (bet. Sixth & Seventh Aves.)

Subway: 47-50 Sts - Rockefeller Ctr — Mon – Sat lunch & dinner
Phone: 212-974-2020 — Sun lunch only
Web: www.brasserieruhlmann.com
Prices: $$$

The right address is everything in Manhattan, and Brasserie Ruhlmann enjoys one of the city's most prestigious locations in the heart of Rockefeller Center. Owned by Jean Denoyer (of La Goulue fame), the restaurant pays tribute to French interior designer Émile-Jacques Ruhlmann. The Art Deco period shows through in the colorful mosaic tile floor, the elongated octagonal mirrors, and the alabaster lamps that cast a flattering glow.

Revamped by chef Laurent Tourondel (of the BLT empire) after the restaurant's rocky opening in early 2006, the bill of fare now focuses on appealing bistro dishes (a lobster club; a Kobe burger; poached skate wing) that are ideal for a power lunch. The wine list is mostly domestic, with plenty of by-the-glass pours.

Bricco

Italian XX

014

304 W. 56th St. (bet. Eighth & Ninth Aves.)

Subway: 57 St - 7 Av
Phone: 212-245-7160
Web: www.bricconyc.com
Prices: $$

Mon – Fri lunch & dinner
Sat – Sun dinner only

Amore comes to mind when you see the rose-red walls and autographed lipstick kisses that cover the ceiling in this romantic Italian place. The dining space spreads over two floors, with the upstairs room being the sunnier and more tranquil of the two. If it's action you want, stick to the first floor, where chefs fire pizzas in the wood-burning oven and waiters scurry around, skillfully managing to keep the dishes coming without rushing diners. The two Italian owners play host and professional flirt to a bevy of regulars, many of them women.
The strength of Bricco's straightforward menu lies in its selection of flavorful homemade pastas, augmented by daily specials. Leaning toward Italy, the wine list devotes an entire page to Gaja.

China Grill

Asian XX

016

60 W. 53rd St. (bet. Fifth & Sixth Aves.)

Subway: 5 Av - 53 St
Phone: 212-333-7788
Web: www.chinagrillmgt.com
Prices: $$$

Mon – Fri lunch & dinner
Sat – Sun dinner only

If ever a restaurant represented Midtown's corporate machismo, it's China Grill. Set within the CBS Building, the cavernous space, with its 30-foot ceilings, acres of black marble and an open kitchen can get awfully noisy, but that doesn't seem to dissuade the large numbers of business lunchers who pack the place every day.
The grill bills their food as "world cuisine," so appetizers and entrées take their influences from across Asia, and desserts bear assorted European accents. Enormous portions of dishes like barbecued salmon with Chinese mustard sauce or grilled Szechuan beef with sake and soy are perfect for sharing.
China Grill's recipe works, since the restaurant has gone global with locations in Miami, Las Vegas and Mexico City.

Café Gray ✿

Contemporary XXX

015

10 Columbus Circle (in the Time Warner Center)

Subway: 59 St - Columbus Circle — Dinner daily
Phone: 212-823-6338
Web: www.cafegray.com
Prices: $$$

Café Gray

The impersonal vibe of the Time Warner Center disappears as you walk through the book-lined, paneled hallway into the entrancing third-floor world of Café Gray. While the dining room sparkles with its mirrored columns and circular banquettes, its most eye-catching feature is the open stainless-steel kitchen, situated near the window wall that boasts spectacular Central Park panoramas.

Chef Gray Kunz's eclectic cuisine reflects his global background. He grew up in Singapore and worked in Europe and Asia before settling in New York, where he earned his reputation during his years at the legendary Lespinasse. Faced with the scrumptious offerings on the à la carte menu (available at dinner), you may have trouble deciding between the likes of lavender-skewered striped bass, and lamb roulade with coriander sauce. Just be sure to save room for the artful desserts.

Appetizers

- Truffled Mousseron and Porcini Ravioli with Madeira and Crème Fraîche
- Poached Lobster Salad with Artichokes, Harissa and Balsamic Pepper Oil
- Risotto with Mushroom Fricassée

Entrées

- Skate Schnitzel à la Grenobloise, Creamed Spinach
- Lavender Skewered Striped Bass, Fennel and Blood Orange
- Braised Short Rib of Beef, Soft Grits and Meaux Mustard

Desserts

- Chilled Rhubarb Soup, Floating Island, Elderflower Shaved Ice
- Caramelized Key Lime Pie, Candied Grapefruit Zest, Schlag
- Chocolate Rum Toast, Bananas, Rum Raisin Ice Cream

Cho Dang Gol

Korean

017

55 W. 35th St. (bet. Fifth & Sixth Aves.)

Subway: 34 St - Herald Sq — Lunch & dinner daily
Phone: 212-695-8222
Web: www.chodanggolny.com
Prices: $$

Named after a village in South Korea that's famed for its tofu, this unassuming eatery in Koreatown offers a break from the Korean barbecue served by the host of surrounding restaurants. Tofu, or soybean curd (*doo boo* in Korean) is the house specialty. Made fresh here each day, health-promoting tofu forms the basis of dishes from vegetable casseroles to pan-fried spicy octopus. Dishes are family-size and meant to be shared. An order of the *bulgogi* is easily big enough for several people, and appetizers can feed a hungry crowd. An abundance of plum wine, sake and *sochu* will liven up your meal in no time.

The friendly staff caters to a largely Korean clientele in a dining room decorated with wood beams and traditional Korean musical instruments.

Daisy May's BBQ

Barbecue

018

623 Eleventh Ave. (at 46th St.)

Subway: 50 St (Eighth Ave.) — Lunch & dinner daily
Phone: 212-977-1500
Web: www.daisymaysbbq.com
Prices: $$

Honey, grab your appetite and head straight for Daisy May's for some down-home finger-lickin'-good barbecue on Manhattan's wild West Side.

This sweet spot, complete with its barn-meets-school-cafeteria look, defies its location just northwest of the bright lights of Broadway. You'll find a motley bunch—everyone from bankers to bikers frequents this place for its fantastic food and friendly atmosphere.

Service-wise, you're on your own at Daisy's, where you place your order at the counter and are rewarded with a cardboard tray filled with chicken, ribs, pulled pork, or brisket with fixin's (Cajun dirty rice, baked beans, corn bread) alongside. They don't serve alcohol, but the minty iced tea served in mason jars will quench your thirst.

DB Bistro Moderne

019 **Contemporary**

55 W. 44th St. (bet. Fifth & Sixth Aves.)

Subway: 5 Av — Mon – Sat lunch & dinner
Phone: 212-391-2400 — Sun dinner only
Web: www.danielnyc.com
Prices: $$$

More *moderne* than bistro, Daniel Boulud's classy Midtown restaurant blends the freshest American ingredients with French recipes in a way that would make the U.N. proud. A glass bar divides the space into two dining rooms; the more informal front room boasts deep-red, rubbed-plaster walls hung with lustrous floral photographs that are reflected in the mirrors on the opposite wall.

Arranged by category (shellfish, asparagus, red meat, tuna), the menu singles out the house specialties—Boulud's smoked salmon, tomato tarte Tatin, *baeckeoffe* of escargots—as well as the dishes of the day. Boulud's irreverent takes on standards, like the hamburger stuffed with foie gras and black truffles, wins him rave reviews. Service is effortlessly efficient.

Del Frisco's

020 **Steakhouse**

1221 Sixth Ave. (at 49th St.)

Subway: 47-50 Sts - Rockefeller Ctr — Mon – Fri lunch & dinner
Phone: 212-575-5129 — Sat – Sun dinner only
Web: www.delfriscos.com
Prices: $$$

This sprawling bi-level steakhouse, with its wraparound floor-to-ceiling windows, exudes a strong aura of corporate muscle. Located on the ground level of the McGraw Hill Building (diagonally across from Radio City Music Hall), Del Frisco's attracts a suited clientele who look like they know their way around a balance sheet.

Start with a classic wedge of iceberg lettuce or a shrimp cocktail. Then it's straight to the prime aged, corn-fed steaks from the Midwest, in portions that would make a Texan proud. In fact, Del Frisco's has locations in the Lone Star state, as well as in Colorado, Florida and Las Vegas. After delivering your steak, the waiter will remain at your side until you have determined that it's cooked to your satisfaction.

Esca

Seafood XXX

021

402 W. 43rd St. (bet. Ninth & Tenth Aves.)

Subway: 42 St - Port Authority Bus Terminal — Mon – Sat lunch & dinner
Phone: 212-564-7272 — Sun dinner only
Web: www.esca-nyc.com
Prices: $$$

A bright spot in this traffic-clogged part of Midtown, Esca proves a sunny respite. The restaurant's name translates as "bait" in Italian, and the fish are indeed biting at this establishment founded by chef/partner David Pasternack, in league with Mario Batali and Joseph Bastianich.
On the changing menu, Italian-style seafood nets the starring role. In addition to the catches of the day, most of the inventive pasta dishes are tossed with various fruits of the sea, and the chef shows a deft hand in seasoning. Crudo tastings from the raw bar make great choices for a group. Wine bottles appear prominently displayed on shelves around the restaurant, and the day's antipasti tempts diners from a farm-style table in the front room.

Estiatorio Milos

Greek XXX

022

125 W. 55th St. (bet. Sixth & Seventh Aves.)

Subway: 57 St — Mon – Fri lunch & dinner
Phone: 212-245-7400 — Sat – Sun dinner only
Web: www.milos.ca
Prices: $$$

It's not nice to fool Mother Nature, and at Milos, they don't try—they carefully source organic ingredients, so there's no need to do much to improve on them. The concept here is simple: you choose your fish from the fresh-from-the-sea array displayed at the counter, decide how much you want (it's sold by weight), and specify whether you want it to be charcoal-grilled or baked in sea salt. Soon, it will appear at your table, adorned with olive oil and lemon sauce. The Milos Special is the best starter, and deliriously sweet baklava makes the perfect ending.
The cacophonous dining room melds touches of industrial modern with Greek taverna in a bright setting. Prices can be high, but it's still cheaper than a trip to the Greek Islands.

Etcetera Etcetera

Italian XX

352 W. 44th St. (bet. Eighth & Ninth Aves.)

Subway: 42 St - Port Authority Bus Terminal — Tue & Thu – Sat dinner only
Phone: 212-399-4141 — Wed & Sun lunch & dinner
Web: www.etcrestaurant.com
Prices: $$

ViceVersa's little sister opened in 2005, and shares the same combination of stylish surroundings and confident, affable service. Like its older sibling, Etcetera Etcetera's menu is Italian, but here they add Mediterranean accents. Ravioli filled with pumpkin, butter and sage, and homemade potato gnocchi are melt-in-your-mouth good. The Philippe Starck designed plastic chairs in pastel colors complement the ebony woodwork and the gray ceramic-tile wall in the dining room; modern artwork and sculptures complete the picture. Located just two blocks from The Great White Way, Etcetera Etcetera makes a convenient and pleasant place for a pre- or post-theater meal, and the nightly three-course prix-fixe menu will make your wallet happy.

Firebird

Russian XXX

024

365 W. 46th St. (bet. Eighth & Ninth Aves.)

Subway: 42 St - Port Authority Bus Terminal — Lunch & dinner daily
Phone: 212-586-0244
Web: www.firebirdrestaurant.com
Prices: $$$

Dramatic décor marks this "pre-Revolutionary" Russian establishment on Restaurant Row (as this block of West 46th Street is popularly known). Drama befits the place, though, standing as it does so near the theater district. The dining room is nearly as intricate as a Fabergé egg, every inch of it set about with Russian art, rare Russian books, plush fabrics and wall sconces dripping with crystals.
As you'd expect, the menu lists Russian specialties such as borscht, beef Stroganov, and an extensive selection of caviar. In addition to the à la carte selections, three- and seven-course tasting menus are available at lunch and dinner. The staff, costumed in Cossack garb, provides well-orchestrated formal service.

44 & X Hell's Kitchen

025 **Contemporary**

622 Tenth Ave. (at 44th St.)

Subway: 42 St - Port Authority Bus Terminal — Lunch & dinner daily
Phone: 212-977-1170
Web: www.44andx.com
Prices: $$

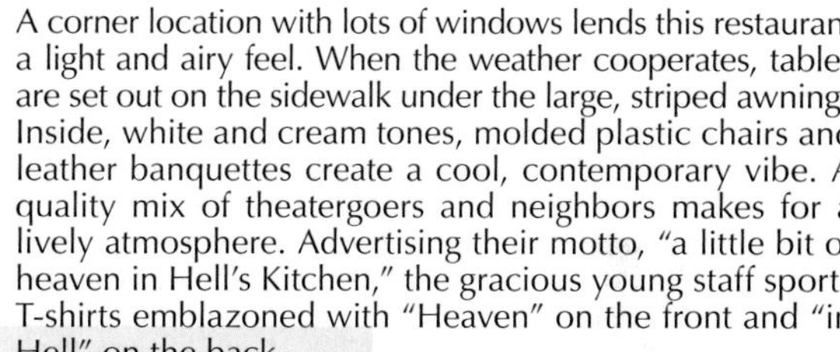

A corner location with lots of windows lends this restaurant a light and airy feel. When the weather cooperates, tables are set out on the sidewalk under the large, striped awning. Inside, white and cream tones, molded plastic chairs and leather banquettes create a cool, contemporary vibe. A quality mix of theatergoers and neighbors makes for a lively atmosphere. Advertising their motto, "a little bit of heaven in Hell's Kitchen," the gracious young staff sports T-shirts emblazoned with "Heaven" on the front and "in Hell" on the back.

American classics take on a 21st-century twist here; buttermilk fried chicken, for instance, comes with a chive waffle, and macaroni and cheese is given sophisticated oomph with Vermont cheddar.

Frankie & Johnnie's

026 **Steakhouse**

32 W. 37th St. (bet. Fifth & Sixth Aves.)

Subway: 34 St - Herald Sq — Mon – Fri lunch & dinner
Phone: 212-947-8940 — Sat dinner only
Web: www.frankieandjohnnies.com
Prices: $$$

The fourth location of Frankie & Johnnie's steakhouse empire (the first was established in 1926 on West 45th Street) offers diners a little bit of history in the heart of the Garment District. This renovated town house was once the home of John Drew Barrymore. In fact, Barrymore's library, with its coffered ceiling and original fireplace, forms part of the masculine, wood-paneled dining room on the second floor.

Diners with booming baritone voices feel no need to tone down their bonhomie while chowing down on some serious cuts of prime dry-aged beef, but no one seems to mind the din. The all-male brigade of waiters is especially accommodating, and the restaurant even has a limousine service to shuttle guests anywhere in Midtown.

Gallagher's

Steakhouse 

027

228 W. 52nd St. (bet. Broadway & Eighth Ave.)

Subway: 50 St (Broadway) — Lunch & dinner daily
Phone: 212-245-5336
Web: www.gallaghersnysteakhouse.com
Prices: $$$

Gallagher's, as they say, is truly "New York City to the bone." Established in 1927 next door to what is now the Neil Simon Theater, this culinary character satisfies carnivores with beef, beef and more beef. That focus becomes clear as you enter to see rows of assorted cuts of beef hanging in the glass-enclosed meat locker, patiently aging. Inside the wood-paneled dining room, waiters wear gold-trimmed blazers, tables wear red-checked cloths, and walls are lined with photographs of Broadway stars, politicians and athletes of both the human and equine varieties.

While it doesn't come cheap, the beef shows a quality that really stands out. Surf and Turf, with its 10-ounce filet mignon and 8-ounce lobster tail and claws, always wins raves.

Hell's Kitchen

Mexican

029

679 Ninth Ave. (bet. 46th & 47th Sts.)

Subway: 50 St (Eighth Ave.) — Tue – Fri lunch & dinner
Phone: 212-977-1588 — Mon & Sat – Sun dinner only
Web: www.hellskitchen-nyc.com
Prices: $$

As any New Yorker can tell you, this restaurant's name speaks to the 19th-century moniker for the surrounding neighborhood (between 34th and 59th streets, west of Eighth Avenue). At this hip Mexican eatery, the only thing devilish can be the wait you sometimes have to endure to get a table.

The "progressive Mexican" menu avoids the bland and predictable in favor of robust dishes executed with a true understanding of textures and flavors. Tamarind-marinated filet mignon chalupas and duck confit empanadas are light years away from the usual, while corn bread and black-bean purée provide a nice change from the ubiquitous chips and salsa.

A convivial atmosphere prevails in the narrow room, where tables line one side, and a bar lines the other.

Gordon Ramsay at The London ✿✿

Contemporary XXXX

028

151 W. 54th St. (bet. Sixth & Seventh Aves.)

Subway: 57 St
Phone: 212-468-8888
Web: www.gordonramsay.com
Prices: $$$$

Mon – Fri lunch & dinner
Sat – Sun dinner only

Gordon Ramsay/ Ben Anders

Gordon Ramsay, the hot-tempered, much-lauded Scottish chef, has finally brought his talents across the Pond with the New York debut of his restaurant at the recently renovated London hotel (see hotel listing).

Tucked off the less formal bar area, the intimate dining room, with seats for just 45 guests, is designed with the comfort of its privileged patrons in mind. Ramsay's obsession with detail extends beyond the kitchen to the perfectly orchestrated staff, who deliver gracious, polished service.

Gordon Ramsay attracts a posh crowd of A-listers who swoon while feasting on the chef's artful preparations, which memorably meld different textures and flavors. The pièce de résistance is the multicourse Prestige Menu. Ramsay's cooking mirrors its moneyed fans—you'll find yourself sampling everything from velvety foie gras and striped bass with caviar velouté to a fluffy apricot soufflé.

Appetizers

- Bluefin Tuna, Pickled White Radish, Peekytoe Crab, Herb Salad
- Foie Gras, Free Range Chicken, Truffled Quail's Egg
- Tiger Prawn Ravioli, Fennel Cream, Shellfish Vinaigrette

Entrées

- Black Bass, Chorizo Pays Basque, Artichokes Barigoule
- Cannon of Lamb, Confit Shoulder, Imam Bayildi
- Suckling Pig with Braised Belly, Confit Leg and Shoulder, Minted Peas

Desserts

- Slow Baked Quince with Crème Catalan and Pedro Ximénez Gelée
- Bitter Chocolate Mousse with Coffee Granité and Light Ginger Cream
- Apricot Soufflé with Amaretto Ice Cream

Insieme

Italian XX

030

777 Seventh Ave. (at 51st St.)

Subway: 50 St (Broadway)
Phone: 212-582-1310
Web: www.restaurantinsieme.com
Prices: $$$

Mon – Fri lunch & dinner
Sat dinner only

Lasagna verdi Bolognese and sea urchin risotto on the same menu? At Insieme, it makes perfect sense. The name translates as "together," echoing the dual personality of this Italian menu. Classic dishes like mamma used to make (linguini with clams, steak *Fiorentina*) are complemented by inspired contemporary fare. If it's too hard to choose between old and new, you can always opt for the tasting menu—it features a combination of both. The wine service is enthusiastic, so don't be shy about asking for assistance navigating through the extensive list.
Convenient to the Theater District, Insieme is located in The Michelangelo hotel *(see hotel listing)*, and is overseen by the same chef/sommelier partnership that runs Hearth in the East Village.

Keens Steakhouse

Steakhouse XX

031

72 W. 36th St. (bet. Fifth & Sixth Aves.)

Subway: 34 St - Herald Sq
Phone: 212-947-3636
Web: www.keens.com
Prices: $$$

Mon – Fri lunch & dinner
Sat – Sun dinner only

This macho palace of steaks and single-malt Scotch has been around since 1885, the lone survivor of the erstwhile Herald Square Theater District. A palpable sense of history (including the odor of pipe smoke) pervades the restaurant, which enforced a strict men-only rule until 1901. That's the year British actress Lillie Langtry challenged Keens' discriminatory policy in court, and won. Look up to see the restaurant's impressive collection of long-stemmed clay churchwarden pipes in racks lining the ceiling, another vestige of its men's-club days.
Hearty steaks and chops come in portions—and prices—hefty enough to satisfy the hungriest carnivores. A lighter pub menu of salads, burgers and sandwiches is also available at lunch and dinner.

Koi

Fusion

40 W. 40th St. (bet. Fifth & Sixth Aves.)

Subway: 42 St - Bryant Pk — Mon – Fri lunch & dinner
Phone: 212-921-3330 — Sat – Sun dinner only
Web: www.koirestaurant.com
Prices: $$$

This New York offshoot of the über-trendy flagship in West Hollywood opened in March 2005 in the Bryant Park Hotel, and it's always packed with the young, the restless and the affluent. The first thing you'll notice is the enormous white lattice canopy that dominates the dining room; underneath it, many of the elements of feng shui have been incorporated into the eye-popping design (with the exception of the pulsating music all day).

The menu is equally à la mode: an extensive choice of sushi, sashimi and rolls, as well as some original Pan-Asian fare. From the black-clad waitstaff and the chic plating to the A-list crowd, cool is the operative word at Koi. For a hipster's night out on the town, visit the equally trendy Cellar Bar.

La Bonne Soupe

033

French

48 W. 55th St. (bet. Fifth & Sixth Aves.)

Subway: 57 St — Lunch & dinner daily
Phone: 212-586-7650
Web: www.labonnesoupe.com
Prices: $$

A reference to a line in the eponymous 1950's French play by Félicien Marceau, the phrase *la bonne soupe* has come to mean the "good life," one abounding in health, happiness and wealth. That's the image that owners Jean-Paul and Monique Picot promote in their Midtown West bistro. Convenient to Fifth Avenue shopping and a brace of Midtown hotels, this spot provides out-of-towners—and residents—with a good meal at a reasonable price.

The long, narrow dining space ranges over two levels, both of which are often full at lunchtime. The kitchen does indeed whip up good soup, as well as a satisfying selection of savory crêpes, *croques monsieur,* salads, omelets, and such simple and tasty *plats du jour* as steak *frites* and *poulet au citron.*

La Masseria

034 Italian XX

235 W. 48th St. (bet. Broadway & Eighth Ave.)

Subway: 50 St (Eighth Ave.) Lunch & dinner daily
Phone: 212-582-2111
Web: www.lamasserianyc.com
Prices: $$

If you're looking for a relaxed meal, La Masseria operates at a less frenetic pace than many places in the neighborhood. With its wrought-iron chandeliers, beamed ceiling and walls plastered with an array of antique farming implements, La Masseria's décor takes its cue from the ancient farmhouses of Puglia. The overall effect creates a warm country feel in the dining room, which retains a hint of intimacy despite its large size.
The cooking adds another delightfully rustic note with dishes like sautéed calf's liver and onions given a pleasant tang from blueberry vinegar, and homemade stuffed fresh mozzarella—a house specialty. Italian comfort food, such as rigatoni with traditional "Sunday Grandmother's sauce," really hits the spot.

Landmark Tavern

035 Contemporary XX

626 Eleventh Ave. (at 46th St.)

Subway: 50 St (Eighth Ave.) Lunch & dinner daily
Phone: 212-247-2562
Web: www.thelandmarktavern.org
Prices: $$

Opened in 1868, the Landmark Tavern is one of the few original taverns remaining in New York. It's worth trekking to the far reaches of the West Side to experience this heritage restaurant, which still oozes with character. A recent renovation spiffed up the place, but its aged patina and historical charm rest intact, along with the original speakeasy door and the bar carved from a single piece of mahogany. What has changed is the menu. Forget about corned beef and cabbage or bangers and mash; sophisticated American cuisine tempts your taste buds with chargrilled baby octopus, and mahi mahi with raspberry vinaigrette and eggplant jam.

Le Bernardin ✿✿✿

Seafood

036

155 W. 51st St. (bet. Sixth & Seventh Aves.)

Subway: 47-50 Sts - Rockefeller Ctr

Phone: 212-554-1515

Web: www.le-bernardin.com

Prices: $$$$

Mon – Fri lunch & dinner
Sat dinner only

Le Bernardin/Shimon & Tammar Photography

In a city where chefs seem to change at the drop of a toque, it's remarkable that Le Bernardin has been under the same ownership since 1986, and that French-born chef Eric Ripert has been at the helm in the kitchen since 1994. Such stability shines through in the effortlessly efficient way that this acclaimed restaurant operates.

Ripert is a master in the treatment of fish. His exceptional and inventive cuisine incorporates the very freshest bounty of the sea as well as a depth of flavor netted from ingredients imported from around the globe. On the prix-fixe menu you can choose among categories of "almost raw" (carpaccio of tuna), "barely touched" (rustic, grilled salt cod salad) and "lightly cooked" (crispy black bass dusted with masala spices). If you're not up for decision-making, you may want to indulge in one of several tasting menus designed by the chef.

Appetizers

- Sliced Conch Marinated Peruvian Style
- Olive-Oil-Poached Hawaiian Escolar, Grapes, Sweet and Sour Saffron Shallot
- Sea Urchin Ravioli, Ostera Caviar, Sea Urchin Emulsion

Entrées

- Barely Cooked Alaskan Salmon; Black Trumpet and Porcini Pot-au-Feu
- Baked Lobster, Wilted Romaine, Squash, Candied Ginger
- Roasted Red Snapper, Ginger-Lemon-Scallion Broth

Desserts

- Dark Chocolate, Cashew and Caramel Tart
- Passionfruit Cream Enrobed in White Chocolate wisth Ginger Caramel
- Slow-baked Apple Confit, Almond Wafer, Crème Fraîche Sorbet

Mandoo Bar

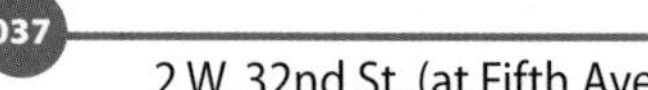

037 **Korean**

2 W. 32nd St. (at Fifth Ave.)

Subway: 34 St - Herald Sq — Lunch & dinner daily
Phone: 212-279-3075
Web: N/A
Prices:

The next time you've exhausted yourself looking through the racks at Macy's, head over to Koreatown's Mandoo Bar to rest and refuel. As soon as you spot this tidy restaurant, you'll know its specialty—*mandoo* is the Korean word for "dumpling"—since the large window grants a view of uniformed women busily rolling out and filling circles of dough.

Eight different kinds of silky dumplings (steamed or fried and filled with pork, vegetables, seafood, or tofu) are the real reason to visit this pleasant, if somewhat Spartan, restaurant, but noodle and rice dishes are available too. For a tasty snack, try the Pajeon pancake, pan-fried and filled with squid, mussels, shrimp and vegetables.

The best part? It doesn't cost a lot of dough to eat here.

Marseille

038 **French**

630 Ninth Ave. (at 44th St.)

Subway: 42 St - Port Authority Bus Terminal — Lunch & dinner daily
Phone: 212-333-2323
Web: www.marseillenyc.com
Prices: $$

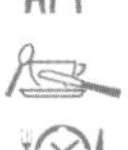

As vibrant and bustling as the southern French city for which it's named, Marseille boasts a brasserie feel with wicker chairs, handmade Art Deco floor tiles, stained glass, and a zinc bar. Dishes hail from the southern Mediterranean with Franco-Moroccan overtones. Appetizers include assorted meze, while lamb tagine and bouillabaisse number among the entrées.

Owing to Marseille's proximity to theaters (the restaurant is two blocks west of Times Square), it's busy almost constantly, often with out-of-towners. The waitstaff handles the crowds with visible ease, though.

Downstairs, the dimly lit lounge hints at something both secretive and alluring; while you're down there, check out the wine cellar—it's housed in a former bank vault.

Masa ✿✿

Japanese XX

039

10 Columbus Circle (in the Time Warner Center)

Subway: 59 St - Columbus Circle
Phone: 212-823-9800
Web: www.masanyc.com
Prices: **$$$$**

Tue – Fri lunch & dinner
Mon & Sat dinner only

Masa/Mikiko Kikuyama

Before you go to Masa, you should know that the price they charge for a meal here will strain any normal budget (the *omakase* will set you back more than $400).

What can you expect for your money here? Expect the most magnificent sushi you are ever likely to eat, each course a vivid study in texture, flavor and contrast. A memorable meal begins with several appetizers (perhaps toro tartare with black pearls of caviar, or spring clams with wild ramps). Then come course after course of exquisite sushi, all flown in fresh from Japanese waters. Pick one of the 10 seats at the sushi counter if you want to interact with master sushi chef Masa Takayama.

Tucked inside the Time Warner Center, 26-seat Masa is a temple of serenity. From the bamboo garden to the stunning Hinoki cypress imported from Japan, the restaurant's interior calls to mind the simple beauty of nature.

Appetizers

- Uni Risotto with Seasonal Truffles
- Toro Tartare with Caviar

Entrées

- From November through February Fugu Fish is on the menu prepared as a Sashimi Salad, as Fried Karaage, and as Sushi.
- From May through August, Hamo Fish is a seasonal item.

Michael's

040

Contemporary

24 W. 55th St. (bet. Fifth & Sixth Aves.)

Subway: 57 St
Phone: 212-767-0555
Web: www.michaelsnewyork.com
Prices: $$$

Mon – Fri lunch & dinner
Sat dinner only

East Coast expense accounts meet West Coast cooking at this busy Midtown institution. California style infuses the interesting array of American dishes. Chef/owner Michael McCarty, who founded the original Michael's near the beach in Santa Monica in 1979, developed his market-driven menu way before using fresh seasonal fare was fashionable. Enjoy dishes like pan-roasted salmon and dayboat monkfish tails at lunch or dinner.

In the airy dining room, light pours in from a wall of windows, illuminating the artwork on the peach-tone walls. Favored by media moguls, Michael's gets mobbed at lunchtime, and the waitstaff has to run at a big-city pace. The fact that everyone seems to be a regular here is proof enough that the brigade is up to the task.

Molyvos

042

Greek XX

871 Seventh Ave. (bet. 55th & 56th Sts.)

Subway: 57 St - 7 Av
Phone: 212-582-7500
Web: www.molyvos.com
Prices: $$

Lunch & dinner daily

An attractive Greek storefront façade beckons diners to Molyvos, named for the Greek village on the island of Lesvos, homeland of owner John Livanos. Inside, Greek artifacts, ceramics and family photographs dream up a homey ambience. Molyvos has been a Midtown staple for years, yet its quality and charm have never faltered. Close to Carnegie Hall, the restaurant makes a terrific pre- or post-performance gathering place.

Greek home-style dishes are the focus of the menu, which the kitchen reproduces with contemporary flair and delicious consistency. Many dishes are cooked in the wood-fired oven, and everything, including the phyllo dough, is made on the premises. Begin your meal with a round of shared meze, accompanied by a glass of ouzo.

The Modern ✿

Contemporary XXX

041

9 W. 53rd St. (bet. Fifth & Sixth Aves.)

Subway: 5 Av - 53 St
Phone: 212-333-1220
Web: www.themodernnyc.com
Prices: **$$$**

Mon – Fri lunch & dinner
Sat dinner only

The Modern/Louis Smeby

It's not easy to compete with works of art by Giacometti and Picasso, but that's the challenge that Alsatian-born chef Gabriel Kreuther faces at The Modern. Operated by Danny Meyer and housed in the boldly renovated Museum of Modern Art, the light-filled dining room with its huge window wall overlooks works displayed in the Abby Aldrich Rockefeller Sculpture Garden.

At lunch and dinner you have a choice between à la carte items or a prix-fixe menu, in addition to more elaborate chef's tastings. Either way, you'll relish intriguing ingredients and combinations like pork tenderloin marinated in wheat beer. The voluminous wine list cites some noteworthy Alsatian vintages.

If you enter through the street entrance, prepare to wade through the crowds in the informal bar, where you can order rustic small plates.

Appetizers

- Tuna and Diver Scallop Tartare, American Paddlefish Caviar
- Sweet Pea Soup, Morels, Foie Gras "Croquette"
- Escargot Ravioli, Slow-poached Farm Egg and Florida Frog Legs

Entrées

- Squab and Foie Gras "Croustillant", Caramelized Ginger Jus
- Chorizo-crusted Chatham Cod, Coco Bean Purée, Harissa Oil
- Curry Lamb Loin, Heirloom Shell Beans, Onion Rings

Desserts

- Lemon Napoleon, Exotique "Brunoise" and "Fromage Blanc" Sorbet
- Milk Chocolate Dacquoise and Raspberry Sorbet
- Citrus "Craquelin", Almond Mousseline and Mandarin Sorbet

Nick & Stef's

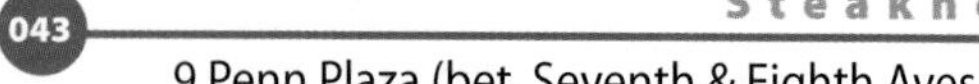

043 — **Steakhouse** XX

9 Penn Plaza (bet. Seventh & Eighth Aves.)

Subway: 34 St - Penn Station
Phone: 212-563-4444
Web: www.nickandstefs.com
Prices: $$$

Mon – Fri lunch & dinner
Sat – Sun dinner only

Sports fans going to Madison Square Garden to catch a Knicks or a Rangers game will no doubt appreciate the succulent cuts of prime beef served at Nick & Stef's, while evening revelers tend to celebrate with the unique bison-grass vodka cocktails. Although portions are hefty, you can still choose sides, from macaroni and cheddar to asparagus, to go with your steak. You'll find fresh seafood on the menu, too, in the form of Maine lobster, meaty crab cakes, shrimp scampi and more.

What sets this steakhouse apart is its contemporary feel. With its large windows, angled pine ceiling and warm tones, the Patina Group's version of a steakhouse—named for Joachim Splichal's twin sons—is less masculine than many others in the city.

Nobu Fifty Seven

044 — **Japanese** XXX

40 W. 57th St. (bet. Fifth & Sixth Aves.)

Subway: 57 St
Phone: 212-757-3000
Web: www.noburestaurants.com
Prices: $$$$

Mon – Fri lunch & dinner
Sat – Sun dinner only

Chef Nobu Matsuhisa has done it again, this time in Midtown. Nobu Fifty Seven's entrance may be sandwiched between two office buildings, but David Rockwell's sleek interior design incorporates sake jugs hanging above the bar, exotic woods and rattan wall coverings. Low lighting creates a sultry mood—not an easy feat in a place as large and busy as this one.

The restaurant pulls in a stylish business crowd whose expense accounts can handle the hefty prices. Specialties include rock shrimp tempura (plump, batter-fried shrimp in a creamy and piquant chile sauce), and black cod with miso, a dish that made Nobu famous.

Creative à la carte offerings feature great variety, but you can always opt for the chef's *omakase*.

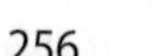

Orso

Italian

045

322 W. 46th St. (bet. Eighth & Ninth Aves.)

Subway: 42 St - Port Authority Bus Terminal — Lunch & dinner daily
Phone: 212-489-7212
Web: www.orsorestaurant.com
Prices: $$

A respected member of the Restaurant Row dining fraternity, Orso nestles on the ground floor of a charming brownstone just steps away from the Theater District. As at its two other branches, in Los Angeles and London, the restaurant offers diners a wide choice of Italian fare, running the gamut from pizza and penne to swordfish and sausages.

Dressed in warm pastel shades, tables are set with patterned earthenware. Gracious servers accommodate those who come in for a quick meal before the theater, as well as patrons who are devoting the evening to dining. Star gazers take note: the later you come here, the more likely you are to see an actor from one of the neighboring theaters catching a post-performance bite to eat.

Osteria Al Doge

Italian 

046

142 W. 44th St. (bet. Broadway & Sixth Ave.)

Subway: Times Sq - 42 St — Mon – Fri lunch & dinner
Phone: 212-944-3643 — Sat – Sun dinner only
Web: www.osteria-doge.com
Prices: $$

Set amid the hustle and bustle of Times Square, Osteria Al Doge presents an inviting, Mediterranean-style ambience enhanced by wrought-iron chandeliers, Italian ceramics and fresh flowers. This elegant Venetian-inspired restaurant is a terrific choice in an area filled with overpriced tourist traps. Homemade green pappardelle with lamb ragu, and tortellini filled with Atlantic salmon and goat cheese exemplify the authentic pasta dishes here. They are complemented by a good selection of fish and meat entrées—all served by a smiling and efficient staff of waiters. There's even a list of pizzas if you don't feel like bothering with multiple courses.

Staying in the Times Square area? Call in your order and the restaurant will deliver it.

Osteria Del Circo

047 — Italian XX

120 W. 55th St. (bet. Sixth & Seventh Aves.)

Subway: 57 St — Mon – Fri lunch & dinner
Phone: 212-265-3636 — Sat – Sun dinner only
Web: www.osteriadelcirco.com
Prices: $$$

From the Maccioni family, who brought you the famous Le Cirque (now in the Bloomberg Building), comes this less formal but exuberant Italian restaurant. A circus motif dominates the spirited décor, from the big-top tent billowing from the ceiling to the trapeze that swings down over the bar. Clown and monkey figurines abound, and a sculptural acrobat overlooks diners from his lofty platform.

Attractively displayed on ice in the dining room, the day's catch bolsters the regular menu, which spotlights Northern Italian fare. Specials change with the days of the week (come Monday for tripe, Thursday for osso buco), and pizzas make a great shared appetizer or a light entrée. As you leave, you can purchase a copy of the *Maccioni Family Cookbook*.

Petrossian

049 — French XXX

182 W. 58th St. (at Seventh Ave.)

Subway: 57 St - 7 Av — Lunch & dinner daily
Phone: 212-245-2214
Web: www.petrossian.com
Prices: $$$

Linger on the sidewalk to marvel at the ornate Renaissance-style 1907 Alwyn Court Building that frames the entrance to Petrossian. Opened in 1984, this is the New York sister to Petrossian Paris, which has been delighting French diners since the 1920s. It was then that the two Petrossian brothers from Armenia made caviar the toast of Paris, and founded the company that now ranks as the premier importer of Russian caviar—the restaurant's specialty.

Located a block from Carnegie Hall, Petrossian showcases ingredients that are as rich as its surroundings, which are adorned with Lalique crystal sconces, etched Erté mirrors and Limoges china. The contemporary French menu, peppered with caviar and foie gras, is perfect for lunch, brunch or dinner.

Per Se ✿✿✿

Contemporary

048

10 Columbus Circle (in the Time Warner Center)

Subway: 59 St - Columbus Circle
Phone: 212-823-9335
Web: www.perseny.com
Prices: $$$$

Mon – Thu dinner only
Fri – Sun lunch & dinner

Per Se

Having built his reputation at the storied French Laundry in Napa Valley, California, Thomas Keller took his talents to New York with Per Se. The restaurant's luxe Adam Tihany design is enhanced by the fabulous views of Central Park from its fourth-floor aerie in the Time Warner Center.

Precision reigns, from the choreographed service to the superlative cuisine. Diners are treated to a parade of sublime small courses (choose from a five- or a nine-course prix-fixe menu), and while the portions are diminutive, these tiny servings show astonishing attention to detail. Minimalist presentations amount to modern art on the plate, beautifully arranged with contrasting shapes, colors and textures. Exceptional wine pairings are worth the splurge.

With only 16 tables, Per Se plays hard-to-get with its reservations; they accept bookings two months in advance.

Appetizers

- Oysters and Pearls: Pearl Tapioca Sabayon, Island Creek Oysters, White Sturgeon Caviar
- Velouté de Cresson: "Ragoût" of New Crop Potatoes, "Pomme Maxim's", Black Truffle

Entrées

- Butter Poached Lobster, Caramelized Fennel Disc and Crystallized Chip, Noilly Prat Sauce
- Médaillon de Ris de Veau, Bacon Wrapped Mushroom, Caramelized Deer Tongue Lettuce

Desserts

- Sweet Grass Dairy's "Green Hill", Pickled "Fraises des Bois", Strawberry "Mignonnette"
- Passionfruit Sorbet, Coconut "Moelleux,", Hibiscus "Nuage", Coconut Custard

Piano Due

050 **Italian** XXX

151 W. 51st St. (bet. Sixth & Seventh Aves.)

Subway: 49 St
Phone: 212-399-9400
Web: N/A
Prices: $$$

Mon – Fri lunch & dinner
Sat dinner only

Piano Due and Palio Bar represent the perfect yin and yang, with dazzling bursts of color in one setting and soothing tones in another. The first floor Palio Bar (a survivor from the erstwhile Palio restaurant) dazzles with riotous reds and oranges, while Sandro Chia's powerful frescoes dominate the design. Whereas Palio Bar sets the scene with its energetic spirit, Piano Due sports a luscious design upstairs with off-white hues punctuated by red jewel tones.
Tasting menus offer an excellent way to sample several dishes of Piano Due's contemporary Italian cuisine, though an à la carte menu is also available. The signature dish is soft egg-yolk ravioli filled with fluffy ricotta cheese and spinach, topped with a decadent shaving of black truffles.

Porter House

051 **Steakhouse** XXX

10 Columbus Circle (in the Time Warner Center)

Subway: 59 St - Columbus Circle
Phone: 212-823-9500
Web: www.porterhousenewyork.com
Prices: $$$

Lunch & dinner daily

Filling the void left by V Steakhouse, Porter House New York is one of the newest members of the Time Warner Center's restaurant collection. Run by chef Michael Lomonaco of Windows on the World fame, Porter House takes the concept of a classic steakhouse and hones it with a modern edge.
Rich chocolate-brown leather, gleaming cherrywood, and cool stainless-steel accents give the dining room a clean, sophisticated look, but it is the panoramic views of Central Park that command your attention.
Porter House's menu raises the stakes for meat lovers, but Lomonaco makes concessions for non-carnivores with a generous selection of fish entrées. Save room for the rich and retro-chic desserts.

Remi

Italian 

145 W. 53rd St. (bet. Sixth & Seventh Aves.)

Subway: 7 Av — Lunch & dinner daily
Phone: 212-581-4242
Web: N/A
Prices: **$$**

Dreams of Venice come to mind when you enter this perennially busy Italian restaurant. Between the Venetian-glass chandelier, the mural of Venice that covers one wall, and the bright sunlight streaming in through the large front windows, there's much to suggest that lovely city. Indeed, *remi* means "oars" in Italian, a reference to the famous canals of Venice.

In keeping with this theme, the food derives much of its influence from the Veneto region. Dishes such as sautéed calf's liver, and ravioli stuffed with tuna are just two of Remi's signature dishes. Homemade pastas are particularly good, but be sure to leave room for *dolci* such as tiramisu and white-chocolate hazelnut semifreddo. Managers run the dining room with a watchful eye.

René Pujol

French

321 W. 51st St. (bet. Eighth & Ninth Aves.)

Subway: 50 St (Eighth Ave.) — Tue – Sun lunch & dinner
Phone: 212-246-3023
Web: www.renepujol.com
Prices: **$$**

In a city where trendy establishments of the moment seem to eclipse tried-and-true eateries, René Pujol stands out as a 30-year Theater District veteran. Classic French fare (sole meunière; cassoulet; snails in garlic, parsley and tomato butter), remains true to its roots by respecting Gallic culinary tradition. Dinner is based on a three-course prix-fixe menu (at lunch you have a choice of a fixed or à la carte menu), but within that structure you can choose among the list of appetizers, entrées and desserts.

Normally, there's a calm atmosphere in the carpeted dining room, with its lace curtains and working fireplace. The pre-theater rush can be a little overwhelming for newcomers, but the proficient waitstaff handles it all without a fuss.

Russian Samovar

054 — Russian

256 W. 52nd St. (bet. Broadway & Eighth Ave.)

Subway: 50 St (Broadway) — Lunch & dinner daily
Phone: 212-757-0168
Web: www.russiansamovar.com
Prices: $$

It's no surprise that Russian Samovar borders the Theater District; this restaurant, with its flashy mix of Russian celebrities, bigwigs and hockey players, provides enough entertainment to rival Broadway. The crowd is raucous and the vodka is strong; guests can sample many varieties of the house-infused spirit available by the shot, the carafe or the bottle. Though the décor is one part Old World and one part Russian grandmother, this place shows diners a good time.

The staff can seem standoffish but are helpful even so. Authentic favorites, like crisp chicken Kiev, beef Stroganoff, hearty *pelmeni* (ground veal and beef dumplings in a light chicken broth), and the perfectly prepared blini, provide a taste of Moscow in the middle of Manhattan.

San Domenico NY

055 — Italian

240 Central Park South (bet. Broadway & Seventh Ave.)

Subway: 59 St - Columbus Circle — Mon – Fri lunch & dinner, Sat – Sun dinner only
Phone: 212-265-5959
Web: www.sandomeniconewyork.com
Prices: $$$

There's no denying that San Domenico has a lot going for it: its enviable location across from Central Park; its sumptuous ambience; and its memorable Italian cuisine. Opened by restaurateur Tony May (formerly of the Rainbow Room) in 1988, San Domenico shows off a style that is matched by its well-heeled patrons and its team of waiters in ties and waistcoats. Tihany's redesign displays leather-wrapped columns, fabric-covered light "boxes" and furnishings imported from Italy.

Elegant Italian food is spotlighted here, and house-made pastas shine with a delicacy and lightness all their own. In season, you can even partake in dishes luxuriously made with white truffles. If you're watching your wallet, go for the set-price lunch.

Sardi's

American XX

056

234 W. 44th St. (bet. Broadway & Eighth Ave.)

Subway: Times Sq - 42 St — Tue – Sun lunch & dinner
Phone: 212-221-8440
Web: www.sardis.com
Prices: $$$

Grand dame of New York's theater-district restaurants, Sardi's has been serving patrons of the Great White Way since the 1920s. Stage-curtain red is the color scheme in the dining room, from the walls to the leather banquettes to the jackets worn by the mature brigade of waiters. And, of course, no self-respecting show-biz star can claim to have made it on Broadway until they see their caricature hanging among the framed portraits that paper Sardi's walls.

Exemplified by "Sardi's Traditions" like cannelloni au gratin, shrimp Sardi (sautéed in garlic sauce), and steak tartare, the American fare here provides ample sustenance to get you through a show. If you prefer to dine after the theater, Sardi's even offers a late supper seating.

The Sea Grill

Seafood XX

057

19 W. 49 St. (bet. Fifth & Sixth Aves.)

Subway: 47-50 Sts - Rockefeller Ctr — Mon – Fri lunch & dinner, Sat dinner only
Phone: 212-332-7610
Web: www.rapatina.com/seaGrill
Prices: $$$

You'll descend in an elevator like a deep-sea diver down to this Rockefeller Center seafood emporium, where the blues and beiges of the stylish décor capture the colors of the sand and sea. You can enjoy the Sea Grill's magical setting overlooking Rock Center's skating rink (open October to April). Large windows peer out over the ice, where golden lights sparkle at night. In summer, the rink's space is filled with umbrella-shaded tables.

Offerings include everything from oysters and clams from the seafood bar to roasted whole fish and seafood prepared *a la plancha* (on a traditional cast-iron griddle). Whatever you choose, you'll savor a daily changing selection of fish and shellfish, fresh off the boat. Sides are sized for sharing.

Shelly's

058 — Italian XX

41 W. 57th St. (bet. Fifth & Sixth Aves.)

Subway: 57 St — Lunch & dinner daily
Phone: 212-245-2422
Web: www.shellysnewyork.com
Prices: $$

Yes, Virginia, there really is a Shelly in the kitchen here, and she sure knows how to cook. Visible from the street through large windows, fresh oysters, clams, shrimp and fish cool their heels on a bed of ice—a good advertisement for the raw bar and the Italian-style oven-roasted seafood that share menu space with traditional pastas and hearty steaks. Do as the Tuscans do and dig into a *bistecca Fiorentina* (a 28-day dry-aged ribeye for two). If you're feeling patriotic, you can order the Cobb salad or a cheeseburger *à la Americana*—proof that this place has something for everyone.

Although brunch and lunch are popular, Shelly's stays packed in the evening, when Midtown office workers stop by for cocktails and dinner.

Staghorn Steakhouse

059 — Steakhouse XX

315 W. 36th St. (bet. Eighth & Ninth Aves.)

Subway: 34 St - Penn Station — Mon – Fri lunch & dinner, Sat dinner only
Phone: 212-239-4390
Web: www.staghornsteakhouse.com
Prices: $$$

Shrimp cocktail, Caesar salad, baked clams, creamed spinach, onion rings and aged prime steak: there's a reason the oldies-but-goodies never go out of style. Staghorn Steakhouse is the place to go when visions of filet mignon and veal chops dance in your head.

Pay no attention to the Garment District location close to Penn Station and the Javits Center—although it's great for hungry conventioneers. Inside, the dining room eschews dark and clubby for a black and tan color scheme warmed by light wood floors and a handsome bar.

The staff is well dressed, professional and friendly. Be sure to ask your server about the daily specials, as well as wines available by the glass, since the menu only lists bottles and half-bottles.

Sugiyama

Japanese

251 W. 55th St. (bet. Broadway & Eighth Ave.)

Subway: 57 St - 7 Av — Tue – Sat dinner only
Phone: 212-956-0670
Web: www.sugiyama-nyc.com
Prices: $$$

When you walk into Sugiyama, the first thing you'll notice is the cloud of smoke rising from the red-hot stones on the tabletops, where beef or seafood are cooking. Welcome to the world of *kaiseki*, a traditional Japanese dining experience that ignites your taste buds with a parade of small dishes having an amazing richness and depth of flavor. If there's a time to splurge, this is it. Put yourself in chef Nao Sugiyama's hands and allow his talent to wow you.

Waiters explain the dishes and the concept; all you have to do is decide how many courses your appetite or wallet can accommodate. Reserve a space at the counter, where you can interact with the personable chefs and take in all the action. This is unquestionably the best seat in the house.

Sushi Jun

Japanese

302 W. 50th St. (at Eighth Ave.)

Subway: 50 St (Eighth Ave.) — Mon – Fri lunch & dinner
Phone: 212-315-4800 — Sat – Sun dinner only
Web: N/A
Prices: $$

Sushi Jun proves the adage that good things come in small packages. This sliver of a restaurant, located on the ground floor of a Midtown tower, has just four tables and a small bar with seating for up to eight customers. What this place lacks in size it more than makes up for in substance, delivering some of the freshest and tastiest sushi around.

Chef Jun mans the sushi bar alongside two other sushi chefs who plate the rolls and sashimi on attractive pottery and sleek porcelain dishes. Fish is the focus, but sparkling clear clam soup, and vegetarian *namasu* illustrate the diversity of the dishes. You can order à la carte, or tuck into the sushi deluxe, which offers a market-based sampling that might include tuna, salmon, eel and fluke.

Sushi of Gari 46

062 — Japanese XX

347 W. 46th St. (bet. Eighth & Ninth Aves.)

Subway: Times Sq - 42 St
Phone: 212-957-0046
Web: N/A
Prices: $$$

Tue – Fri lunch & dinner
Sat – Sun dinner only

Chef Masatoshi "Gari" Sugio struts his stuff at the third in his mini-empire of sushi restaurants, this one on Restaurant Row in the Theater District. Here, he reels in fans of fantastically fresh and diverse sushi (think salmon with tomato; bluefin toro with tofu). The best seats in the house are at the sushi bar, where you can watch the chef perform his magic while you indulge in the day's *omakase*.
Count on consistency in piece after piece of splendid sushi, which hit their highest notes in the chef's 130 signature creations (there is no printed list; ask the chefs, if you're not familiar with Gari's cuisine).
A note for sake fans: the blended sakes available at Gari's other two restaurants are also available here.

Sushi Zen

063 — Japanese XX

108 W. 44th St. (bet. Broadway & Sixth Ave.)

Subway: 42 St - Bryant Pk
Phone: 212-302-0707
Web: www.sushizen-ny.com
Prices: $$$

Mon – Fri lunch & dinner
Sat dinner only

Chef/owner Toshio Suzuki creates delicately textured sushi and sashimi, which, while it certainly tastes good, is also good for you (that's the Zen part). There's a wealth of different menus here. If you're new to raw fish, try the Introduction to Sushi from the sushi bar. Teriyaki, hand rolls, sashimi and more are all available à la carte, but you can also choose among three fixed-price tasting menus. The latter provide a good way to experience the kitchen's expertise, and you can sample the impressive sake selection to accompany your meal.
As the restaurant's name implies, decoration is minimal, albeit bright and comfortable. Grab a seat at one of the outdoor tables on a nice day and watch the hustle and bustle of Midtown.

Taboon

Middle Eastern

064

773 Tenth Ave. (at 52nd St.)

Subway: 50 St (Eighth Ave.) Dinner daily
Phone: 212-713-0271
Web: N/A
Prices: **$$**

With its car dealerships and industrial spaces, Tenth Avenue in Midtown may lack the personality of many other New York neighborhoods, but it's worth visiting just for a meal at Taboon. This inviting Middle Eastern restaurant, named for its crackling wood-burning brick oven (*taboon* in Arabic), adds character to an otherwise barren street in Hell's Kitchen.
Taboon is that rare restaurant ideal for those dining alone or in groups. Meals begin with heavenly flatbreads, slathered with olive oil, sprinkled with rosemary and sea salt, and brought to the table still warm from the oven; fresh tzatziki serves as a sparkling accompaniment. Middle Eastern accents enliven delicious dishes, from a salad of red-wine-braised octopus to lamb osso buco.

Tintol

Portuguese

065

155 W. 46th St. (bet. Sixth & Seventh Aves.)

Subway: Times Sq - 42 St Lunch & dinner daily
Phone: 212-354-3838
Web: www.tintol.com
Prices: **$$**

The area surrounding Times Square is a difficult place for a serious restaurant to survive. Challenges are many, including astronomical rents, an abundance of kitschy themed restaurants, and a customer base of budget-minded tourists. Yet this new tapas bar's location makes Tintol a good bet for a pre- or post-theater nosh. Plates are small, ingredients are tasty, service is good, and the setting says urban-chic with its inviting bar, exposed brick, and black wood tables.
At Tintol, tapas come in several forms: cold, as in the *escabeche* of plump Portuguese sardines; hot, like the fried *bolos de bacalhua* (cod fritters); and in casserole-style dishes such as braised goat in red wine, served in traditional clay *casuellas*.

Town

066 **Contemporary**

15 W. 56th St. (bet. Fifth & Sixth Aves.)

Subway: 57 St — Mon – Fri & Sun lunch & dinner
Phone: 212-582-4445 — Sat dinner only
Web: www.townnyc.com
Prices: **$$$**

At the Chambers Hotel *(see hotel listing)*, "a night on the town" translates as a meal at the property's stylish restaurant, located downstairs from the lobby bar. The understated yet hip décor, designed by David Rockwell in blond woods and cascades of beads, appeals to Gotham fashionistas and well-heeled tourists. Town opened in 2001 as the first independent venture of chef Geoffrey Zakarian, who also runs Country in Gramercy.
Modern and healthy cuisine depends on market availability, influencing menu selections that could include grilled sea bass served over artichoke leaves, or fresh asparagus salad. Many of the dishes are presented in a colorful neo-Californian style. Service is well-timed and courteous at this serious restaurant.

Trattoria Dell'Arte

067 **Italian**

900 Seventh Ave. (bet. 56th & 57th Sts.)

Subway: 57 St - 7 Av — Lunch & dinner daily
Phone: 212-245-9800
Web: www.trattoriadellarte.com
Prices: **$$**

The nose knows. Take your cue from the much-larger-than-life nose sculpture that tops the entrance to Trattoria Dell'Arte. Designed as an idiosyncratic artist's studio, the interior exhibits unfinished paintings, sculptural body parts and a gallery of works depicting Italian noses. The trattoria, bigger than it first appears, sits opposite Carnegie Hall, a location that assures the restaurant's constant buzz.
A long antipasto bar teems with assorted seafood, cured meats, and cheeses, while the menu offers a substantial selection of Italian favorites from pappardelle to *pesce*. Tasty pizza choices include *d'aragosta,* topped with a one-pound lobster, tomatoes and mozzarella. Confident service adds to the contagiously exuberant air of the place.

21 Club

American XX

068

21 W. 52nd St. (bet. Fifth & Sixth Aves.)

Subway: 5 Av - 53 St — Mon – Sat lunch & dinner
Phone: 212-582-7200
Web: www.21club.com
Prices: $$$

A dowager among New York City restaurants, the 21 Club started as a speakeasy during Prohibition. In the 1950s, the club debuted in its first film, *All About Eve*. Since then, the restaurant has starred in a multitude of movies, as well as playing host to a galaxy of stars, including Humphrey Bogart, Frank Sinatra and Helen Hayes.

With its dim lighting and once-secret wine cellar (in a basement vault in the building next door), 21 Club still exudes a clandestine air. It's a place for power brokers, and the presence of a Bloomberg terminal in the lounge reminds guests that, in New York, money is big business. Cuisine sticks to the tried and true; 21 Classics, including the burger favored by Ari Onassis, provide the best traditional experience.

Utsav

Indian 

069

1185 Sixth Ave. (entrance on 46th St.)

Subway: 47-50 Sts - Rockefeller Ctr — Lunch & dinner daily
Phone: 212-575-2525
Web: www.utsavny.com
Prices: ⊜

Don't let the plain bar area mislead you; climb the carpeted stairs to the upstairs dining room and you'll discover a posh formal setting, hovering above the 46th Street fray in an elevated bridge between two Manhattan office buildings. In this airy room, billowing fabric covers the ceiling, and leafy green plants soak up natural light from floor-to-ceiling windows.

Those in the know come for the bounteous lunch buffet (noon to 3pm daily), laden with a variety of meat (fish curry, tandoori chicken) and vegetable dishes *(daal bukhari)*, plus salads, condiments, naan and dessert. Theatergoers can take advantage of the Broadway Special, a three-course pre-theater dinner (with a choice of appetizer, entrée and dessert) for less than $30.

ViceVersa

070 **Italian**

325 W. 51st St. (bet. Eighth & Ninth Aves.)

Subway: 50 St (Eighth Ave.) — Mon – Fri lunch & dinner
Phone: 212-399-9291 — Sat dinner only
Web: www.viceversarestaurant.com
Prices: $$

Run by the experienced team of three Italian gents who cut their teeth at San Domenico on Central Park South, ViceVersa (pronounded VEE-chay versa) celebrates *la dolce vita*. The restaurant fashions an urbane ambience in its earth-tone dining space, highlighted by a zinc bar and softly lit wall alcoves displaying terra-cotta urns. Locals love the enclosed back terrace for summer dining.

Approachable fixed-price menus complement extensive à la carte offerings, all of which come to the table in artful array. Pastas are consistently good, and entrées (breadcrumb-and-caper-crusted veal tenderloin; sesame-coated salmon) show a deft hand. Desserts, perhaps a dark-chocolate cake with vanilla gelato or panna cotta with sour cherries, prove irresistable.

West Bank Café

071 **American**

407 W. 42nd St. (bet. Ninth & Tenth Aves.)

Subway: 42 St - Port Authority Bus Terminal — Lunch & dinner daily
Phone: 212-695-6909
Web: www.westbankcafe.com
Prices: $$

Open for some 30 years, the West Bank Café is clearly doing something right. Located on the edge of the Theater District, this standby blends Italian influences with American know-how. Tasty selections might include refreshing tuna tartare, and homemade pappardelle topped with spicy sausage, tomato sauce and Greek yogurt.

From the framed windows and the pleasant jazz tunes piped in the background to the leather banquettes and soft lighting, the look is classic bistro. Though it attracts a larger and livelier crowd in the evenings, the West Bank Café makes an ideal choice for lunch as well. There's even a brunch menu featuring breakfast favorites ranging from eggs Benedict to brioche French toast, in addition to sandwiches and salads.

Yakitori Totto

Japanese

251 W. 55th St. (bet. Seventh & Eighth Aves.)

Subway: 59 St - Columbus Circle — Dinner daily
Phone: 212-245-4555
Web: N/A
Prices: $$$

Far from the offerings of New York City's ubiquitous hot-dog carts, yakitori is one of the most popular street foods of Japan. The term refers to a style of grilled meat, mainly chicken, that is marinated in a soy-based sauce and then cooked on a smoky charcoal grill. The result is tender, juicy and tasty morsels, many presented on skewers. Not for the faint of stomach, unconventional selections—chicken knees, bleeding chicken hearts on a stick, and chicken sashimi—are all specialties of the house.
Enjoy the sounds of Japanese pop and sultry jazz while you discover delectable treasures. Although the restaurant is well staffed, don't expect hovering service. Japanese culture dictates that servers stand back and wait to be summoned by patrons.

Yang Pyung Seoul 

Korean

43 W. 33rd St. (bet. Broadway & Fifth Ave.)

Subway: 34 St - Herald Sq — Lunch & dinner daily
Phone: 212-629-5599
Web: N/A
Prices: 

Near the Empire State Building in the area known as Little Korea, Yang Pyung Seoul brings an authentic slice of Korea to this section of Midtown. What draws many people from New York's Korean community to this nondescript little place, which is open 24 hours a day, is the quality and authenticity of its cuisine.
Don't worry if your Korean is a little rusty; the menu includes helpful photographs of the various dishes. *Banchan,* complimentary offerings that are served before your meal, are tasty as well as generous in size. Specialties of the house here include the rich and robust broths, particularly the *hae jang gook,* which is reputed to stave off winter colds and even cure hangovers. Finish it all off with a "shot" of sweet liquid yogurt.

SoHo & Nolita

The heart of Manhattan's downtown fashion scene, SoHo—short for South of Houston—is New York at its trendiest and most colorful. Visitors throng the district *(bounded by West, Houston, Lafayette and Canal streets)* on weekends, making even walking down the sidewalk difficult—especially given the proliferation of sidewalk tables full of purses and jewelry, sunglasses and scarves, and "outsider" art. The restaurant scene is a lively one here, as eclectic as SoHo itself. You'll find everything from designer-decorated, high-end restaurants to tiny, decidedly untrendy eateries.

Nolita (for North of Little Italy), Little Italy's über-fashionable sister, actually sits within that district's former boundaries; four blocks long and three blocks wide, it stretches from Kenmare to Houston streets on Mulberry, Mott and Elizabeth streets. The moniker Nolita came courtesy of real-estate developers, who in the 1990s wanted to distinguish it from the red-sauce joints of the old neighborhood. Today Nolita is chock-a-block with chic cafes that are ideal for people-watching.

A Bit of History

Site of the first free black community in Manhattan, SoHo was settled in 1644 by former slaves of the Dutch West India Company, who were granted land for farms. In the early 19th century, Broadway was paved and a number of prominent citizens, including *Last of the Mohicans* author James Fenimore Cooper, moved in, bringing cachet to the district. In the late 1850s, stores such as Tiffany & Co. and Lord & Taylor were joined on Broadway by grand hotels. Theaters, casinos and brothels entertained visitors—and drove respectable middle-class families uptown. The exodus made room in the late 1800s for a slew of new warehouses and factories, many built with ornamented cast-iron façades, which looked like carved stone. The area thrived as a commercial center until the 1890s, when fashionable businesses began relocating to Fifth Avenue.

Art Brings a New Start

By the late 1950s the neighborhood was a slum known as "Hell's Hundred Acres," and city planners slated it for demolition to make room for an expressway until residents objected. Often in violation of building codes, painters and sculptors converted vacant warehouses into studios, galleries and living quarters. An underground art scene took root and thrived until the early 1980s, when uptown galleries, boutiques and affluent professionals began to push out the very artists who made the neighborhood so desirable in the first place.

Today few artists can afford to live or work in SoHo, and the migration of galleries northward to Chelsea continues. Locally owned boutiques have been largely supplanted by international couturiers, making SoHo a Mecca for moneyed fashionistas. Overflowing with traffic, pedestrians and sidewalk vendors, **Broadway** is SoHo at its most commercial. The west end of Broadway ranks as the neighborhood's premier corridor for fashion and art as well as dining.

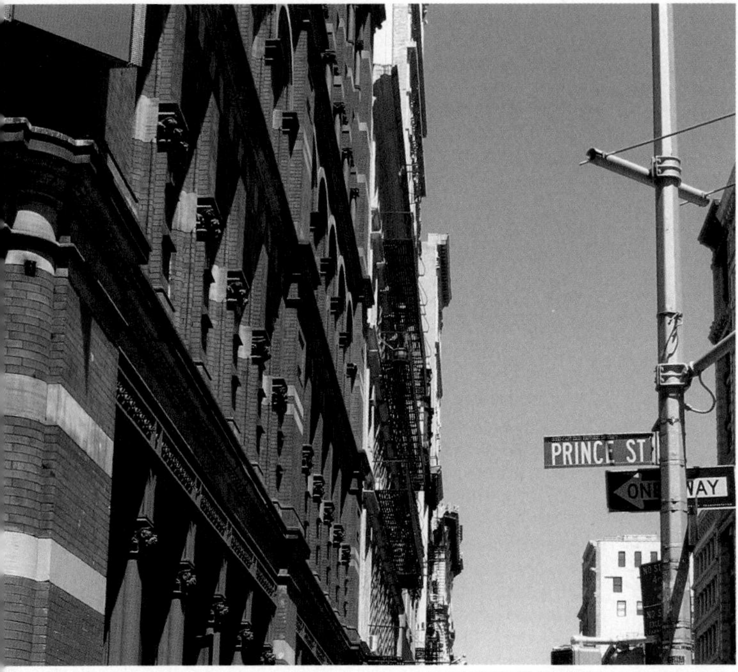

Brigitta L. House/MICHELIN

SOHO & NOLITA

Ama

Italian 

001

48 MacDougal St. (bet. Houston & Prince Sts.)

Subway: Spring St (Sixth Ave.) — Lunch & dinner daily
Phone: 212-358-1707
Web: www.amanyc.com
Prices: $$

How appropriate that a restaurant whose name derives from the Italian word for love should open on Valentine's Day (2005). Passers-by are drawn here by the warm glow coming from within. Once inside, you'll find a narrow room balanced by mirrors and an impressionistic painting of pink blossoms on the ceiling; tables cluster close together, adding to the intimate feel.

The menu avoids run-of-the-mill Italian fare in favor of cooking that takes its influences from Puglia. Unusual creations, such as the mushroom-and-blueberry-filled *mezzelune*, or the signature dessert made with Amaretto-soaked sponge cake and cherry crème brulée, are standard at Ama. Drop by for happy hour Italian-style, complete with complimentary olives, crostini and cheese.

Antique Garage

Turkish

002

41 Mercer St. (bet. Broome & Grand Sts.)

Subway: Canal St (Broadway) — Lunch & dinner daily
Phone: 212-219-1019
Web: www.antiquegaragesoho.com
Prices: ⚭

The name of this place tells you just what to expect: it's set in a former auto-repair garage converted to an antique store/restaurant. Filled with antique furniture, china and light fixtures—many of which are for sale—the cozy dining room feels more like a little country restaurant than a chic SoHo eatery. Seating is at tiny tables, or on low sofas, with coffee tables in between.

The food is the only thing notably Turkish here, and it's quite authentic and packed with flavor. Eggplant salad, grilled Turkish meatballs made with ground lamb and beef, and Mediterranean shrimp could be ordered as a meze selection to share or as progressive courses. Mint lemonade is freshly squeezed, and they brew an excellent cup of heady Turkish coffee.

Aquagrill

Seafood XX

003

210 Spring St. (at Sixth Ave.)

Subway: Spring St (Sixth Ave.) — Lunch & dinner daily
Phone: 212-274-0505
Web: www.aquagrill.com
Prices: $$

From the staggering selection of oysters at the raw bar to simple grilled fish, Jeremy and Jennifer Marshall's establishment aims to please all seafood lovers. The husband-and-wife team divides up the work here: chef Jeremy watches over the kitchen while Jennifer oversees the dining room, decorated with lamps made with seashells.
The chef treats his fresh supplies with due deference, adding subtle Asian accents to enhance the preparations. Clever combinations, like falafel-crusted salmon, are a hallmark of Aquagrill. Brunch is a real treat on weekends and lunch is always busy, but it's at dinner that the kitchen staff really struts their stuff. Service is smoothly choreographed, and an air of professionalism pervades the whole operation.

Balthazar

French 

80 Spring St. (bet. Broadway & Crosby St.)

Subway: Spring St (Lafayette St.) — Lunch & dinner daily
Phone: 212-965-1414
Web: www.balthazarny.com
Prices: $$$

As one of the city's first French bistros, Balthazar reigns unrivaled for its authentic ambience, constantly animated by lively conversation. All the requisite late-19th-century Paris décor elements are here (red leatherette banquettes, mosaic tile floors), along with an eclectic crowd that runs from trendsetters to tourists. Part of Keith McNally's restaurant empire, Balthazar is still where the cool crowd hangs.
As for the menu, it's classic bistro; products are fresh, dishes are well prepared, and specials correspond to the day of the week. Baskets piled with fresh breads (baked at the restaurant's own bakery) and the shellfish towers are both as impressive to look at as they are to eat. Served in a paper cone, the crispy *frites* are a must.

Blue Ribbon

005 **Contemporary**

97 Sullivan St. (bet. Prince & Spring Sts.)

Subway: Spring St (Sixth Ave.) Dinner daily

Phone: 212-274-0404
Web: www.blueribbonrestaurants.com
Prices: $$$

Simple comforts here create a convivial atmosphere that makes you feel like a SoHo insider, although the closeness of the tables means that conversation is rarely private. Denizens of late-night New York will appreciate the fact that the restaurant serves until 4am.

The kitchen turns out an eclectic but winning array of dishes that range from all-American (fried chicken, hamburgers) to Mediterranean (paella, sautéed skate). Blue Ribbon's success has spawned several offspring over the years, with a Blue Ribbon Sushi just a few doors down, Blue Ribbon Bakery a few blocks west, and a sister to Blue Ribbon and Blue Ribbon Sushi, both in Park Slope. Then there's the newest member of the family, Downing Street Bar, in the West Village.

Blue Ribbon Sushi

006 **Japanese**

119 Sullivan St. (bet. Prince & Spring Sts.)

Subway: Spring St (Sixth Ave.) Lunch & dinner daily
Phone: 212-343-0404
Web: www.blueribbonrestaurants.com
Prices: $$

A few doors down from its sister, Blue Ribbon, the equally popular Blue Ribbon Sushi bears a sign so discreet you'd think they were trying to keep the place a secret. Inside the cozy, compact room, the chefs jostle for space to prepare their specialties behind the sushi counter.

Divided into sections by ocean (Atlantic and Pacific), the extensive menu of sushi can appear bewildering at first glance, but what sets it apart are unusual offerings such as jellyfish and spicy lobster with egg wrapper. The requisite cooked dishes are also available, as is a tempting array of seasonal specials. If you're going for dinner, be sure to get there early; the no-reservations policy means the restaurant fills up quickly in the evening.

Café El Portal

Mexican

007

174 Elizabeth St. (bet. Kenmare & Spring Sts.)

Subway: Spring St. (Lafayette St.) — Mon – Sat lunch & dinner
Phone: 212-226-4642
Web: N/A
Prices: ֍

There is something comforting about a place that doesn't try to compete with its fancy neighbors. In an area known for being a fashionista's Mecca, Cafe El Portal defies Nolita's hipper-than-thou vibe with its low-key design and casual ambience. Despite its less than impressive digs, this restaurant serves up some of the most authentic Mexican dishes in the city. Everything is made in-house at the tiny family-run place, from the fantastic tortillas to the piquant salsas.
The tiny bar boasts a tequila collection with more bottles than the restaurant has seats, and the cocktail menu goes well beyond your run-of-the-mill margarita. Reasonable prices and hearty portions are just a couple more reasons why locals love El Portal.

Cendrillon

Asian

008

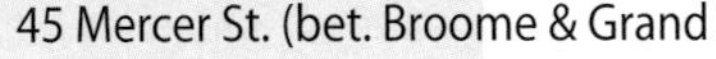

45 Mercer St. (bet. Broome & Grand Sts.)

Subway: Canal St (Broadway) — Tue – Sun lunch & dinner
Phone: 212-343-9012
Web: www.cendrillon.com
Prices: $$

All too often, fusion cuisine merely reflects where the chef took his last vacation, but at this roomy SoHo restaurant, a real understanding of Asian culinary culture underscores the cooking. With Filipino cooking at its core, Cendrillon surprises with zesty and vivacious flavors, guaranteed to cheer the most sullen taste buds. Noodle dishes and Asian barbecue compete with tantalizing entrées, like grilled oxtail and salt-roasted duck. Although portion size is on the generous side, you'll definitely want to leave room for dessert. Check out the impressive selection of exotic Asian teas to round out your meal.
Like the fairy tale from which its name derives (*Cendrillon* is French for "Cinderella"), Cendrillon assures diners of a happy ending.

Downtown Cipriani

009 Italian XX

376 West Broadway (bet. Broome & Spring Sts.)

Subway: Spring St (Sixth Ave.) Lunch & dinner daily
Phone: 212-343-0999
Web: www.cipriani.com
Prices: $$$

Part of the Cipriani group, the Downtown satellite seems right at home in its oh-so-SoHo surroundings. On sunny days, the Euro crowd is in top form outside, where tables perch on the sidewalk to afford great people-watching. Don't be surprised if you recognize some faces among the well-heeled regulars; this place attracts a high-profile set. Inside, despite the luxurious atmosphere, seating is unnecessarily cramped.

Downtown Cipriani features a casual menu of hearty Italian fare. Be sure to try a Bellini (Prosecco with peach purée), the cocktail created by Giuseppe Cipriani at the famed Harry's Bar in Venice. Siblings include Cipriani Dolci *(Grand Central Terminal)*, and Harry Cipriani, in the Sherry Netherland hotel *(781 Fifth Ave.)*.

Ed's Lobster Bar

010 Seafood X

222 Lafayette St. (bet. Kenmare & Spring Sts.)

Subway: Spring St. (Lafayette St.) Tue – Sun lunch & dinner
Phone: 212-343-3236
Web: www.lobsterbarnyc.com
Prices: $$

Finally East Siders have a simple seafood spot to call their own without having to trek to Mary's Fish Camp or Pearl Oyster Bar. It's not quite a shack, though it's certainly casual with its New England-style décor and inviting marble bar.

Ed McFarland (an alumnus of Pearl) is throwing his hat in the "best lobster roll" ring, where his version deftly competes. Lobster meat piled on a bun slathered with butter, accompanied by perfect fries and Ed's pickles, brightens any stormy day. The kitchen is equally skilled with other sea creatures, and daily specials feature the freshest catch. Wines and beers harmonize with the saltwater menu. Though Ed's doesn't accept reservations, with a little more lobster to go around, the wait won't hurt so much.

Giorgione

Italian

307 Spring St. (bet. Greenwich & Hudson Sts.)

Subway: Spring St (Sixth Ave.)
Phone: 212-352-2269
Web: N/A
Prices: $$

Mon – Fri & Sun lunch & dinner
Sat dinner only

All the buzz occurs inside rather than outside Giorgione, given its location on a quiet block in SoHo. Giorgio DeLuca (of Dean & DeLuca) owns this lively place, which you enter via the sleek bar. The narrow space continues, lined with chrome tables, white-leather seats and ice-blue walls that contribute to the cool vibe. Staff may be young and hip but don't give a whiff of attitude.

A cool, downtown crowd drops in for a select menu of terrific oven-fired pizzas, pastas, and fresh catch from the oyster bar. After dinner, you'll find it difficult to resist the sweet temptations of simple *dolci* with a perfectly brewed espresso.

Just around the corner, Giorgione 508 *(508 Greenwich St.)* serves simple yet delicious fare in a relaxed cafe setting.

Jean Claude

French 

137 Sullivan St. (bet. Houston & Prince Sts.)

Subway: Spring St (Sixth Ave.)
Phone: 212-475-9232
Web: N/A
Prices: $$

Dinner daily

Just add a plume of Gauloise smoke, and this little bistro could be on the Left Bank in Paris instead of planted in the heart of SoHo. Simply decorated with wine bottles and Gallic-themed posters, the dining room sports a lively, yet romantic, atmosphere—complete with French music playing in the background. Brown paper covers white linens on tables that snuggle so close together that if you like the looks of your neighbor, it wouldn't be difficult to start up a conversation about the tasty, classic French fare.

Don't be deterred by the fact that Jean Claude only accepts cash. If you don't mind eating early, you won't need oodles of the green stuff to afford the inexpensive, three-course, fixed-price dinner menu (offered from 6pm to 7:30pm).

Kittichai

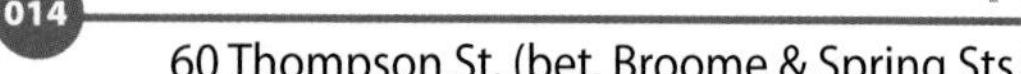

014 Thai

60 Thompson St. (bet. Broome & Spring Sts.)

Subway: Spring St (Sixth Ave.) — Lunch & dinner daily
Phone: 212-219-2000
Web: www.kittichairestaurant.com
Prices: $$$

Located in the fashionable Sixty Thompson Hotel *(see hotel listing)*, this sensual SoHo newcomer offers subtly spiced Thai cooking, thanks to chef Ian Chalermkittichai, who came to New York from the Four Seasons Hotel in Bangkok.
The food is as appealing as this exotic setting, where orchids float in bottles on lighted shelves, lush silk fabrics and Thai artifacts adorn the walls, and a reflecting pool forms the centerpiece of the dining room. Appetizers and entrées are modern and approachable, balancing European technique with New York accents and Thai inflections. Black-clad waiters can help you sort out which is which.
At times, the food seems more fusion than Thai, as the chopsticks on the table and the sashimi-style appetizers suggest.

L'Ecole

015 French

462 Broadway (at Grand St.)

Subway: Canal St (Broadway) — Mon – Fri lunch & dinner
Phone: 212-219-3300 — Sat dinner only
Web: www.frenchculinary.com
Prices: $$

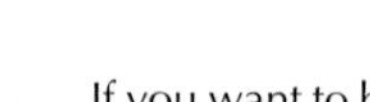

If you want to be a guinea pig, this is the place to do it. The restaurant associated with The French Culinary Institute provides the opportunity for its students to show off what they've learned. They've certainly mastered the first rule of good cooking: use the best ingredients you can find and don't mess around too much with a good thing.
The kitchen earns top marks for its four- or five-course dinner menus, and the prix-fixe lunch menu is a great—and inexpensive—way to sample the flavorful regional French fare, which changes every six weeks (be sure to make reservations). A conscientious student waitstaff caters to customers in a soothing yellow room decorated with photographs depicting the bustling world of a restaurant kitchen.

Lure Fishbar

Seafood XX

016

142 Mercer St. (at Prince St.)

Subway: Prince St — Lunch & dinner daily
Phone: 212-431-7676
Web: www.lurefishbar.com
Prices: $$$

If your credit card's not maxed out from visiting the Prada shop above this restaurant, Lure Fishbar makes a great place to drop anchor. It's decked out in a fantastic tiki-trendy style with angular porthole windows, semi-circular booths, teak paneling and tropical-print fabrics, reminiscent of a luxury ocean liner. The only thing missing from the maritime motif is the sound of waves crashing and the feel of sand between your toes.

Have a seat at the sushi bar and order a sushi-sashimi combo, or sit at the raw bar to share a shellfish plateau (in sizes small, medium and large). In the main dining room, you can net one of the fresh catches, which are as pleasing to the eye as they are to the palate. Just one visit and you'll be hooked.

Mercer Kitchen

Contemporary X

017

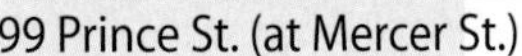

99 Prince St. (at Mercer St.)

Subway: Prince St — Lunch & dinner daily
Phone: 212-966-5454
Web: www.jean-georges.com
Prices: $$

When it opened in the basement of SoHo's Mercer Hotel *(see hotel listing)* in 1998, Mercer Kitchen took a position at the head of the culinary new wave. Today the restaurant, which owes its existence to wunderkind Jean-Georges Vongerichten, remains fiercely fashionable. This is the quintessential SoHo experience: a Prada-clad crowd, chic décor and a staff all dressed in black.

The menu appeals day and night with raw-bar selections, salads, sandwiches, and entrées that have roots in France but travel to faraway locales for inspiration. Raw tuna and wasabi dress up pizza; thinly shaved fennel forms a perfect salad; salmon swims with miso and bok choy. Take a seat at the bar for a glass of rose or a cool draft and you may even make a new friend.

Mezzogiorno

018 — Italian

195 Spring St. (at Sullivan St.)

Subway: Spring St (Sixth Ave.) — Lunch & dinner daily
Phone: 212-334-2112
Web: www.mezzogiorno.com
Prices: $$

A SoHo veteran established more than 12 years ago by Vittorio and Nicola Ansuini, Mezzogiorno (the name means "midday") re-creates the warm, vibrant atmosphere of the owners' native Florence. More than 100 Italian artists were asked to interpret the restaurant's logo, a smiling sun; their collection of collages, paintings and small objets d'art are displayed at one end of the room.
The Florentine theme continues in the menu that follows the seasons and reads straight from Italy. An extensive collection of pastas proves enticing, while meats are classically prepared. Pizzas are perfectly cooked in the woodburning oven and topped simply. Outside, the raised terrace provides a great vantage point for people-watching when the weather cooperates.

Peasant

019 — Italian

194 Elizabeth St. (bet. Prince & Spring Sts.)

Subway: Spring St (Lafayette St.) — Tue – Sun dinner only
Phone: 212-965-9511
Web: www.peasantnyc.com
Prices: $$

Chef Frank DeCarlo named his restaurant for his cooking style. Peasant emphasizes honest, Italian country fare, much of which is cooked in the wood-burning brick oven and served in terra-cotta pots.
Comforts are simple here, too, with church-pew seating, exposed brick walls and tabletop candles providing the main source of light. (Okay, the restaurant is dark, but who doesn't look good in dim, romantic candlelight? Besides, the menu is entirely in Italian, so you can always use the lack of light as an excuse to ask for a translation.) Rustic entrées include lamb with polenta, gnocchi with meaty wild mushrooms and steak Florentine. Pizza, with pepperoncini and soppressata or mortadella, among other toppings, is a sure-fire hit.

Public

Fusion

020

210 Elizabeth St. (bet. Prince & Spring Sts.)

Subway: Spring St (Lafayette St.)
Phone: 212-343-7011
Web: www.public-nyc.com
Prices: **$$$**

Mon – Fri dinner only
Sat – Sun lunch & dinner

Here's your chance to sample Tasmanian sea trout, grilled kangaroo or New Zealand venison, complemented by a good selection of boutique wines from Down Under. Public's kitchen takes its cue from London restaurant The Providores (owned by the same pair of chefs who founded Public) in creating a unique style of cooking that fuses Australian and New Zealand ingredients with influences that span the globe. Brunch is eye-opening, with selections ranging from toasted oat pancakes to grilled chorizo and salad.

Designed by AvroKO, this bright, airy Nolita spot incorporates salvaged pieces of public buildings into the former muffin factory it occupies, adding whimsical touches like shelves of library books and vintage card catalogs.

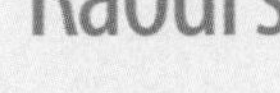

Raoul's

French

021

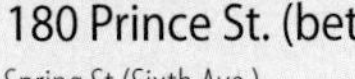

180 Prince St. (bet. Sullivan & Thompson Sts.)

Subway: Spring St (Sixth Ave.)
Phone: 212-966-3518
Web: www.raouls.com
Prices: **$$$**

Dinner daily

For any restaurant to survive for 30 years in this fickle business, they must be doing something right—and Raoul's does many things right. For starters, the kitchen turns out good classic French food, from skate with Manila clams to Colorado lamb with sweetbreads; the day's selection is presented on individual blackboards. You can't help but get caught up in the energetic atmosphere in the dimly lit main room, but if you're seeking a calmer spot for a quiet conversation, try the bright upstairs space or the tiny covered garden room.

This authentic bistro, its walls covered with arresting artwork, had its 15 minutes of fame in 2006 when it stood in for an upscale Beacon Hill eatery in Martin Scorcese's film, *The Departed*.

Salt

022 **Contemporary**

58 MacDougal St. (bet. Houston & Prince Sts.)

Subway: Spring St (Sixth Ave.) Mon – Fri lunch & dinner
Phone: 212-674-4968 Sat dinner only
Web: www.saltnyc.com
Prices: $$

The term "neighborhood restaurant" is bandied about on a pretty casual basis these days, but Salt genuinely deserves the moniker. Here diners are encouraged to sit at one of three communal tables in the middle of the room, where they can rub elbows with the locals—and maybe even eavesdrop on some juicy SoHo gossip.

From salt-crusted venison loin and Alaskan King salmon to grilled Newport steak, this short menu is a showpiece of contemporary American cooking. It contains a section called "Protein + 2," which is perfect for South Beach dieters, since it allows you to choose your entrée and pair it with any two side items. You'd do equally well to trust the kitchen, though; the chef's selections are always fresh and seasonal.

Savoy

023 **Contemporary**

70 Prince St. (at Crosby St.)

Subway: Prince St Mon – Sat lunch & dinner
Phone: 212-219-8570 Sun dinner only
Web: www.savoynyc.com
Prices: $$

Like a fine wine, Savoy has only improved with age. Peter Hoffman and his wife, Susan Rosenfeld, opened in 1990 with the intention of creating memorable meals from the best local ingredients. They still make good on their concept, which relies on their relationships with local growers. Elegant country cooking is expertly crafted from top-quality products here, taking care that the flavors of the main ingredients stand out. The same care applies to the wine list, which offers an intriguing selection by both the bottle and the glass.

The place occupies two floors of an 1830s town house, with a boisterous bar downstairs and a more peaceful dining area upstairs. If Savoy wasn't so successful, locals would gladly keep it as their own little secret.

Snack

Greek

024

105 Thompson St. (bet. Prince & Spring Sts.)

Subway: Spring St (Sixth Ave.)
Lunch & dinner daily
Phone: 212-925-1040
Web: N/A
Prices: $$

Don't blink, or you might walk right past Snack. Seating just ten people at five lime-green tables, this sweet little Greek place offers a refreshing antidote to SoHo's über-trendy temples of gastronomy. Enveloped by photographs of Hellenic landmarks and shelves of Mediterranean grocery items, you'll feel transported to sunnier climes.
When you taste the fresh, authentic Greek cuisine, you'll half expect to feel sand between your toes. The friendly staff is more than willing to advise diners trying to choose from the delectable array of meze, sandwiches and savory pies (offerings are scrawled on a blackboard).
If you're craving souvlaki or stuffed grape leaves while in the West Village, visit the bigger Snack at 63 Bedford Street.

Tasting Room

Contemporary

025

264 Elizabeth St. (bet. Houston & Prince St.)

Subway: Broadway - Lafayette St
Tue – Thu dinner only
Phone: 212-358-7831
Fri – Sun lunch & dinner
Web: www.thetastingroomnyc.com
Prices: $$

Opened in 1999, Colin and Renee Alevras' East Village eatery developed a devoted following through the years. Now fans of the Tasting Room will have to go to Nolita to find their favorite haunt. In summer 2006, the restaurant relocated to a bigger space on Elizabeth Street. The new, 80-seat Tasting Room features a full bar pouring classic cocktails made with boutique spirits and house-made mixers. (The original East Village space is now a wine bar/cafe.)
Chef Colin takes inspiration from farm-fresh products (Max Creek Hatchery trout, Stone Church Farm duck, Eckerton Hill Farm lettuces), and the varied menu changes daily. Items are sized to "taste" (appetizers) or "share" (main courses) so bring some friends and sample away.

Woo Lae Oak

Korean

148 Mercer St. (bet. Houston & Prince Sts.)

Subway: Prince St — Lunch & dinner daily
Phone: 212-925-8200
Web: www.woolaeoaksoho.com
Prices: $$

Want to go out to cook tonight? Each of the marble-topped tables in stylish Woo Lae Oak contains a built-in griddle for customers to barbecue anything from tuna loin and tiger prawns to shiitake mushrooms and free-range chicken breast. For those whose idea of cooking is making reservations, the restaurant offers Korean specialties (beef short ribs; stuffed, braised chicken breast) prepared with a flair for depth of flavor.
It's not just the cooking that sets this place apart from more traditional eateries in Koreatown; it's the attractive dining space, too, with its roomy, open floor plan—the décor still sparkles—and glam downtown crowd. A great value, the fixed-price lunch special features some of the restaurant's most popular dishes.

Zoë

Contemporary

90 Prince St. (bet. Broadway & Mercer St.)

Subway: Prince St — Tue – Sun lunch & dinner, Mon lunch only
Phone: 212-966-6722
Web: www.zoerestaurant.com
Prices: $$

With its terra-cotta columns, rich colors and mosaic tile, Zoë's bold surroundings have been packing 'em into this 19th-century landmark since 1992. The prime location on SoHo's Prince Street, with its high-end stores and galleries, can't be beat. The cuisine is American at heart, but it roams from the Far East to the Mediterranean for inspiration. Fish is a popular menu staple, and Zoë offers more than 35 wines by the glass as accompaniment. Just be sure to leave room for such goodies as caramelized banana tart and cappuccino cheesecake.
Clad in blue suits, the waitstaff boasts the courteous and unflustered manner that comes from proficiency at working a busy room. As a whole, the operation possesses the confidence of a well-oiled machine.

Peter L. Wrenn / MICHELIN

TriBeCa

An intriguing wedge of warehouses, loft residences, art galleries and oh-so-chic restaurants, TriBeCa was named in the 1970s by a real-estate agent hoping to create a hip identity for the area. The acronym—which stands for Triangle Below Canal—stuck, and true to expectations, TriBeCa has become a trendy place. So far, it has not been commercialized nearly to the extent that SoHo has, despite being home to dozens of celebrities, most notably actor Robert DeNiro. For paparazzi-dodging starlets, that is precisely its appeal.

Technically, TriBeCa is not a triangle but a trapezoid. Its boundaries are *(clockwise from north)* Canal Street, Broadway, Murray Street, and the Hudson River. Greenwich and Hudson streets are the main thoroughfares for dining and nightlife; art and interior-design stores are scattered throughout the district.

A Bit of History

Once used as farmland by Dutch settlers, the area now known as TriBeCa was included in a large tract granted to Trinity Church in 1705. In the ensuing century, wealthy families built elegant residences around Hudson Square (now the Hudson River Tunnel traffic rotary). A fruit and produce market opened in 1813 at the western edge of the neighborhood, but the quarter remained primarily residential until the mid-19th century, when the shipping and warehousing industries formerly located at the South Street Seaport moved to deepwater piers on the Hudson River. Five- and six-story "store and loft" buildings were built around the district to accommodate the new trade. By 1939, Washington Market, as the area along Greenwich Street came to be known, boasted a greater volume of business than all the other markets in the city combined.

In the 1960s, city planners approved urban-renewal projects that called for the demolition of many buildings along the waterfront. Luckily, enough of the old commercial warehouses remained to attract artists pushed out of SoHo and others seeking cavernous industrial living space. Today, those same artists would be hard-pressed to afford such a space in TriBeCa; loft-apartment prices now start at around $1 million.

Trendy TriBeCa

Catering as they do to a local clientele of creative types, TriBeCa is a cool place to eat. You can splurge on a meal here in expensive restaurants whose reputations precede them, or go for more modest fare. If it's a sunny day, snag an umbrella-shaded table outside—TriBeCa's wide sidewalks accommodate lots of them.

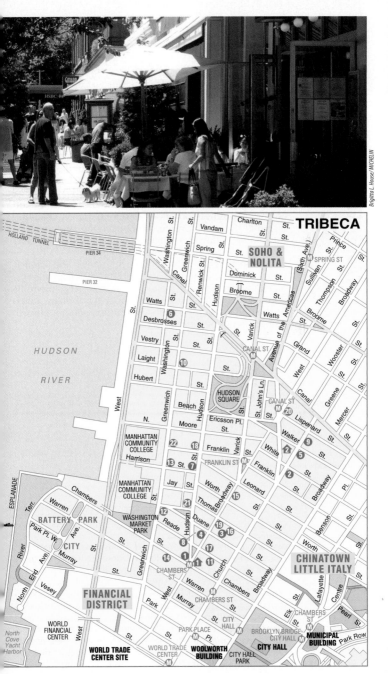

Brigitta L. House/MICHELIN

TRIBECA

SOHO & NOLITA

HUDSON RIVER

HOLLAND TUNNEL

PIER 34

PIER 32

HUDSON SQUARE

MANHATTAN COMMUNITY COLLEGE

WASHINGTON MARKET PARK

BATTERY PARK CITY

ESPLANADE

CHINATOWN LITTLE ITALY

FINANCIAL DISTRICT

WORLD FINANCIAL CENTER

North Cove Yacht Harbor

WORLD TRADE CENTER SITE

WOOLWORTH BUILDING

CITY HALL

CITY HALL PARK

MUNICIPAL BUILDING

Acappella

Italian 

001

1 Hudson St. (at Chambers St.)

Subway: Chambers St (West Broadway)
Phone: 212-240-0163
Web: www.acappella-restaurant.com
Prices: $$$

Mon – Fri lunch & dinner
Sat dinner only

If this restaurant, with its stately columns, antique tapestries and large windows in front, looks familiar, you may have seen it in the first episode of the HBO series *The Sopranos*, part of which was filmed here. A reproduction of the imposing portrait of Federico da Montefebre, erstwhile Duke of Urbino, dominates the brick wall of the dining room (the original, painted by Piero della Francesca in 1645, is on display in Florence).
Overseen by chef/owner Sergio Acappella, the kitchen turns out carefully prepared northern Italian dishes, including homemade pastas. In winter, the menu is peppered with the likes of wild boar and buffalo meat. At the end of your meal, enjoy a complimentary glass of grappa alongside your dessert.

Arqua

Italian XX

002

281 Church St. (at White St.)

Subway: Franklin St
Phone: 212-334-1888
Web: www.arquaristorante.com
Prices: $$

Mon – Fri lunch & dinner
Sat – Sun dinner only

Recalling small hill villages in Italy's Veneto region, this corner trattoria celebrates northern Italy in its sunny-colored, light-filled space.
Thanks to chef/owner Leonard Pulito, who named his restaurant after the Italian town where he and his family raised their own livestock and grew their own produce, the food at Arqua is executed with an eye for excellence. House-made pappardelle may be married to an earthy sauce made with duck and mushrooms, and sprinkled with parmesan to finish the dish; branzino is brushed with lemon and olive oil and grilled whole; thin scallops of veal have a natural affinity for wild mushrooms and Marsala. Desserts from ricotta cheesecake to semifreddo do Italy proud, and gelati and sorbetti are made on-site.

Blaue Gans

Austrian

139 Duane St. (bet. Church St. & West Broadway)

Subway: Chambers St (West Broadway) — Lunch & dinner daily
Phone: 212-571-8880
Web: www.wallse.com
Prices: $$

Taking over the space formerly occupied by Le Zinc, chef Kurt Gutenbrunner (also of Wallsé) may have saved the zinc bar and the vintage art posters of the former tenant, but he has turned the menu upside-down with his Austro-German cooking.
Open for three meals as well as late-night noshing, the restaurant focuses on Austrian specialties, including an entire section devoted to sausages. The kitchen eschews the heavy hand often used in this style of cooking and instead offers light preparations of Austrian classics like Wiener Schnitzel, with each ingredient perfectly represented—down to the fresh-grated horseradish.
For dessert, the likes of cherry strudel, homemade ice-cream coupes, and Salzburger Nockerl will leave you smacking your lips.

Bread Tribeca

Italian 

301 Church St. (at Walker St.)

Subway: Canal St (Sixth Ave.) — Lunch & dinner daily
Phone: 212-334-8282
Web: www.breadtribeca.com
Prices: $$

Inside this windowed façade on the corner of Church and Walker streets, you'll find a simple, contemporary décor trumped by good Italian cuisine that's a pleasure to eat any time of the day. As you'd guess from the name, Bread Tribeca specializes in a variety of tasty sandwiches, with fillings such as Sicilian sardines, homemade mozzarella and prosciutto di Parma stuffed between crusty ciabatta bread or baguettes.
But wait, there's more. The menu also cites an impressive collection of non-sandwich items at lunch, brunch and dinner. Don't overlook the fresh salads, pastas, seafood entrées and thin-crust pizzas cooked in the wood-burning oven. And be sure to leave room for the delicious caramelized banana tart, served with vanilla ice cream.

Bouley ✿✿

Manhattan ▶ TriBeCa

004 — **French** ✕✕✕✕

120 West Broadway (at Duane St.)

Subway: Chambers St (West Broadway) — Lunch & dinner daily
Phone: 212-964-2525
Web: www.davidbouley.com
Prices: $$$$

Bouley

David Bouley's culinary skill reflects two different cultures. Born and raised in Connecticut, Bouley nourished his love of cooking at the stove of his French grandmother. After stints in a number of U.S. establishments, he went to France, where he trained with some of Europe's finest chefs.

At Bouley, two vaulted rooms cosset diners: the intimate red room, with its claret-colored Venetian-plaster walls; and the airy white room, accented by an antique French fireplace. The innovative menu reflects the chef's travels to Japan, along with his strong grounding in French technique. Tasting menus allow diners to sample a treasure trove of culinary delights, and the flurry of little extras from the kitchen rounds out the progression of courses.

Across the street, Bouley's three-level food emporium houses the Upstairs dining room, Bouley Bakery/Café, and Bouley Market.

Appetizers

- Florida Shrimp, Fava Beans, Turkish Morels, White Asparagus, Spring Sweet Pea Sauce
- Seared New York Foie Gras, Pruneaux d'Agen, Rosemary Apple Purée, Quince Purée

Entrées

- Chatham Cod, Black Truffle Dashi, Hon Shimeji, Porcini, and Shiitake, Scallion Sauce
- Roast Lamb, Ramps, Sheep's Milk Ricotta Gnocchi, Zucchini Mint Purée, Rosemary Sauce

Desserts

- Vanilla Crème Brûlée Strudel, Strawberries, Poached Rhubarb, Sour Cream-Meyer Lemon Sorbet
- Raspberry Meringue, Lime and Goat Yogurt, Vanilla and Rose Petal Ice Creams

Capsouto Frères

French XX

451 Washington St. (at Watts St.)

Subway: Canal St (Sixth Ave.)
Phone: 212-966-4900
Web: www.capsoutofreres.com
Prices: $$

Tue – Sun lunch & dinner
Mon dinner only

Before you enter Capsouto Frères, stop and take a gander at the striking 1891 landmark structure in which the restaurant is housed. A handsome mix of Romanesque and Flemish Revival styles, this brick and stone building on the corner of Watts Street once held a shoe factory. Inside the ground-floor restaurant, the owners have preserved the building's old-fashioned charm.

Since 1980, Capsouto Frères has been pleasing diners at lunch, brunch and dinner with the likes of sole meunière, duck confit and cassoulet. Light-as-air soufflés—a house specialty—are the best choice if your sweet tooth is crying for dessert, while savory soufflés, like wild mushroom and spinach and cheese varieties, make a satisfying snack or a light meal.

Chanterelle

French XXX

2 Harrison St. (at Hudson St.)

Subway: Franklin St
Phone: 212-966-6960
Web: www.chanterellenyc.com
Prices: $$$$

Mon – Wed & Sun dinner only
Thu – Sat lunch & dinner

It's not easy to keep a restaurant going for more than 20 years, but owners Karen and David Waltuck have managed to do it, and do it well. Set within the 19th-century New York Mercantile Exchange, the Art Nouveau-style dining room reflects Karen's feminine touch in its peach tones, sheer balloon shades, fresh flowers and the menu's handwritten script.

David's take on French cuisine adds light contemporary accents. Seasonal selections change monthly, but the signature grilled seafood sausage is available all the time. Check out Chanterelle's collection of menu covers near the reception desk; Keith Haring, Roy Lichtenstein and Louise Nevelson number among the famous artists who have designed covers for the restaurant.

Danube ✿

008 **Austrian** XXX

30 Hudson St. (bet. Duane & Reade Sts.)

Subway: Chambers St (West Broadway) Mon – Sat dinner only
Phone: 212-791-3771
Web: www.thedanube.net
Prices: **$$$**

Danube/Tobias Everke

Named for the river that flows through Vienna, Danube represents David Bouley's Austrian fantasy, realized by designer Jacques Garcia and architect Kevin White. In the stately dining room, you'll be immersed in the luxury of late-19th-century Vienna. Here, plush sofas stand in for banquettes, ceilings are covered in Venetian plaster, and dark drapes dress tall, arched windows.

À la carte menus include weekly market choices, an Austrian menu, and a "modern eclectic" menu. All blend Austrian ingredients or preparations with contemporary and even Asian elements. Japanese yellowtail makes frequent appearances, as do Wiener Schnitzel, Spätzle and Kavalierspitz. A sampling of the chef's favorites, the tasting menu weaves together a delicious symphony of flavors and styles. Of course, dessert is de rigueur here, with deliciously updated versions of Austrian pastry.

Appetizers

- Scallop, Crabmeat, Paradeiser Coriander, Lemon-Thyme Sauce
- Bluefin, Hamachi, Key Lime Pickled Onion, Pumpkin Seed Oil
- Smoked Salmon, Potato Salad, Watercress Dressing

Entrées

- Yellowtail, Austrian Crescent Potato, Vodka, Caviar
- King Salmon, Styrian Wurzelgemüse, Apple Rosemary Purée
- Wiener Schnitzel, Crescent Potato, Lingonberries

Desserts

- Caramel Strudel, Bartlett Pears, Moscato d'Asti Ice Cream
- Huckleberry Crêpes, Huckleberry Sour Cream Sorbet
- Chocolate Hazelnut Soufflé, Chocolate Chip Ice Cream

Dennis Foy

Contemporary XXX

009

313 Church St. (bet. Lispenard & Walker Sts.)

Subway: Canal St (Sixth Ave.) — Mon – Sat dinner only
Phone: 212-625-1007
Web: www.dennisfoynyc.com
Prices: $$$

Chefs are often compared to artists, but in the case of Dennis Foy, the analogy is unquestionable. Foy, both chef and owner, shows off his talents in the kitchen, where his cutting-edge cooking wins rave reviews, as well as in the dining room, where his paintings proudly hang.

The chef's adventurous spirit shines in his signature warm crab tian, a riff on crab cakes. Occasionally, he makes forays into molecular gastronomy, as in a "salt-cured terrine of foie gras, prunes, Eis and Snow."

Foy opened his eponymous TriBeCa restaurant in December 2006 in the space formerly occupied by Lo Scalco. The cathedral-like space, with its colorful arches, church-pew-like banquettes, and gold-leaf wallpaper, echoes the owner's creative soul.

Dylan Prime

Contemporary XX

010

62 Laight St. (at Greenwich St.)

Subway: Canal St (Varick St.) — Mon – Fri lunch & dinner
Phone: 212-334-4783 — Sat & Sun dinner only
Web: www.dylanprime.com
Prices: $$$

Dylan Prime is a bit off the beaten track from the hub of TriBeCa's action, but you won't regret the detour. The menu is contemporary American with an emphasis on meat: prime cuts of filet mignon, aged prime rib and a huge 32-ounce Porterhouse are all served with your choice of sauces. Then there's the Carpetbagger steak, the chef's creation of an 11-ounce filet mignon stuffed with Blue Point oysters. You'll also find a few seafood entrées, but meat is the main reason to come here.

Low, moody lighting provides an intimate vibe, and a window wall affords diners a look at the impressive wine selection, which consists mainly of California vintages. The new "Pie-tini" list entices with apple pie, lemon-meringue and mud-pie cocktails.

Fresh

Seafood XX

011

105 Reade St. (bet. Church St. & West Broadway)

Subway: Chambers St (West Broadway) — Mon – Fri lunch & dinner

Phone: 212-406-1900 — Sat – Sun dinner only

Web: www.freshrestaurantnyc.com

Prices: $$

It's easy to ensure that your restaurant serves the freshest seafood possible when you own your own seafood company. That's the case with Eric Tevrow, the proprietor of Fresh. His company is the sole provider of fish to Fresh, so it's no wonder that this sea-themed dining room nets a steady stream of loyal fish lovers.

The menu changes each day to feature the daily catch, which might include the likes of Maine peekytoe crab, Nantucket striped bass and Florida Keys grouper. Simply grilled entrées are delicious, while everything from soy-ginger dressing to orange-ponzu sauce tops the daily specials. The lobster roll and the New England clam chowder embody American simplicity at its best; they're both prepared authentically with an elegant hand.

Gigino Trattoria

Italian XX

012

323 Greenwich St. (bet. Duane & Reade Sts.)

Subway: Chambers St (West Broadway) — Lunch & dinner daily

Phone: 212-431-1112

Web: www.gigino-trattoria.com

Prices: $$

Picture a little trattoria in Italy. When you walk in, you receive a warm greeting from the staff; the décor is unpretentious, but cheery, with a wood-beamed ceiling, yellow walls and a wood-burning oven. This is the ambience you'll find at Gigino, hidden away in lower TriBeCa.

With an extensive list of reasonably priced dishes ranging from oven-fired pizzas to the signature pasta—*spaghetti del Padrino*, made with beets, escarole, garlic and anchovy-flavored olive oil—Gigino tries to satisfy the appetites of its wide audience. The menu reads like a collection of favorite family recipes, yet the artful plating is far from ordinary.

The restaurant is featured in the movie *Dinner Rush* with Danny Aiello.

The Harrison

Contemporary

013

355 Greenwich St. (at Harrison St.)

Subway: Franklin St — Dinner daily
Phone: 212-274-9310
Web: www.theharrison.com
Prices: $$

Chef/owner Jimmy Bradley has a magic touch creating warm, welcoming restaurants—like The Red Cat in Chelsea—with widely appealing food. He's done it again at The Harrison, which opened on this corner in 2001.

At The Harrison the professional team is always ready to help; the staff keeps a constant lookout around the rustic-chic dining room to make sure their customers have everything they want. From the kitchen here comes contemporary American cuisine that doesn't take itself too seriously; the menu always looks to the seasons with a wink of fun.

Desserts, like chocolate-filled beignets or strawberry-rhubarb crisp, are worth the wait. To top off your meal, choose a wine by the glass or a selection from the 300-bottle wine list.

Kitchenette

American 

014

156 Chambers St. (bet. Greenwich St. & West Broadway)

Subway: Chambers St (West Broadway) — Lunch & dinner daily
Phone: 212-267-6740
Web: N/A
Prices:

For a taste of home, visit Kitchenette. This casual cafe, now in a larger space, brings the taste of mom's kitchen to trendy TriBeCa. Affordable and attractive, the luncheonette-style restaurant with its kitschy-cool country appeal has attracted a loyal following for more than 10 years. Guests are met by the aroma of fresh baked goods upon entering, and those in the know save room for a slice of one of the scrumptious pies or cakes.

The soul of American cooking is alive and well here, where meatloaf, chili and blue-plate specials number among the most-requested dishes. Far from fancy, Kitchenette's meals are stick-to-your-ribs good and perfect for lunch, weekend brunch or weeknight dinner. And kids are welcome, an asset in Manhattan.

Landmarc

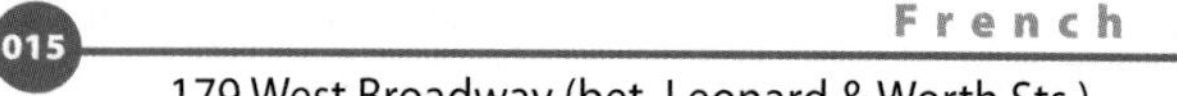

015 French XX

179 West Broadway (bet. Leonard & Worth Sts.)

Subway: Franklin St — Lunch & dinner daily
Phone: 212-343-3883
Web: www.landmarc-restaurant.com
Prices: $$

Established by chef Marc Murphy and his wife, Pamela, in 2004, Landmarc stars innovative bistro-style fare. As the son of a diplomat, Murphy grew up traveling in France and Italy, a heritage that is reflected in the restaurant's menu and well-priced wine list.

Landmarc is a rare treat, offering adults upscale cuisine like grilled quail or rock-shrimp risotto while their little ones munch on kid-friendly food. Be sure to try dessert here; kids can have an ice-cream cone while, for one low set price, you can sample every sweet on the menu.

With its exposed brick walls, sleek booths and contemporary artwork, the two-story dining room blends well with the neighborhood's trendy ambience. A second location in the Time Warner Center *(10 Columbus Circle, 3rd floor)* is now open.

Megu

016 Japanese XXX

62 Thomas St. (bet. Church St. & West Broadway)

Subway: Chambers St (West Broadway) — Mon – Fri lunch & dinner
Phone: 212-964-7777 — Sat & Sun dinner only
Web: www.megunyc.com
Prices: $$$

For an awe-inspiring experience, follow the kimono-clad hostess downstairs to the two-story space Megu reserves for diners. Ultra-sleek design meets traditional Japanese elements in this capacious room, which centers on an ice carving of Buddha floating over a rose-petal-strewn pool. Above the Buddha hangs a huge *bonsho*, an exact replica of Japan's largest temple bell. White porcelain columns, made from rice bowls and sake vases, line the room's upper tier.

The progression of courses in Megu's different tasting menus may include skewered meat or fish grilled over *bincho-tan* charcoal, as well as meat seared on hot Japanese river stones. Megu's other location in the posh Trump World Tower is equally impressive, and caters to an expense-account crowd.

Nam

Vietnamese

017

110 Reade St. (bet. Church St. & West Broadway)

Subway: Chambers St (West Broadway)
Phone: 212-267-1777
Web: www.namnyc.com
Prices: $$

Mon – Fri lunch & dinner
Sat & Sun dinner only

Nam attracts hosts of diners who come for generous, tasty and inexpensive Vietnamese cooking that balances yin and yang in its serene dining space. The likes of chile-lime sauce, coconut, curry powder, and fresh herbs flavor the delicate dishes. Classic starters are light and flavorful, but don't pass up the *Bun* dishes (various ingredients served over rice vermicelli) as an entrée. To end your meal, toasted coconut and banana bread is a warm, satisfying treat.
Efficient service by a young staff, and a simple but pleasant atmosphere, filled with bamboo trees and black-and-white photographs of Vietnam, are a few more reasons to like this place. If Chelsea is more convenient for you, visit Nam's sister, Omai *(158 Ninth Ave.)*.

Nobu

Japanese

018

105 Hudson St. (at Franklin St.)

Subway: Franklin St
Phone: 212-219-0500
Web: www.myriadrestaurantgroup.com
Prices: $$$$

Mon – Fri lunch & dinner
Sat – Sun dinner only

In partnership with Drew Nieporent and actor Robert DeNiro, celebrity chef Nobu Matsuhisa opened Nobu in 1994 to a large fanfare, and the restaurant continues to enjoy success today. Architect David Rockwell imagined the Japanese countryside in Nobu's dining room, replete with stylized birch trees and a wall of black river stones (although the décor looks a bit tired these days).
Nobu is best known for its seductive sushi and sashimi, but don't pass up Matsuhisa's appealing specialties like the miso-glazed black cod or monkfish pâté with caviar. Sharing dishes is the best way to "do" Nobu. The chef's expanding empire now includes Nobu Next Door, offering similar food in a simpler setting, and Nobu Fifty Seven in Midtown *(40 W. 57th St.)*.

The Odeon

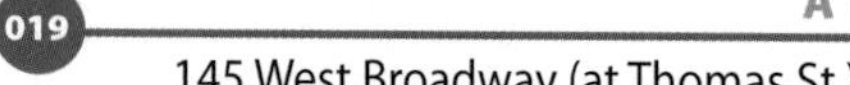

019 — American

145 West Broadway (at Thomas St.)

Subway: Chambers St (West Broadway) — Lunch & dinner daily
Phone: 212-233-0507
Web: www.theodeonrestaurant.com
Prices: $$

A red neon marquee above the door marks The Odeon, a TriBeCa hotspot since the 1980s. Now as then, you can still catch a glimpse of big-name entertainers and artists here, but regular folks are welcome, too.

The Art Deco-style space uses Formica-topped tables, wood paneling and 1930s light fixtures to suggest a Parisian bistro, and the kitchen interprets American dishes with a discreet French flair (*moules frites*, lamb chops, roast chicken). Check out the weekday fixed-price lunch menu; it's the perfect way to snag refined cuisine at reasonable prices.

If you're out late, drop by for croque monsieur sandwiches, French onion soup or crispy calamari available on the brasserie menu of light fare, served every night beginning at midnight.

Pepolino

020 — Italian

281 West Broadway (bet. Canal & Lispenard Sts.)

Subway: Canal St (Sixth Ave.) — Lunch & dinner daily
Phone: 212-966-9983
Web: www.pepolino.com
Prices: $$

A variety of thyme that grows wild in the hills of Tuscany, pepolino makes a fitting namesake for this rustic Italian eatery on TriBeCa's northern edge.

Indeed, herbs play a big part in the cooking here, and *pepolino* is the favorite of owner Patrizio Siddu, who shares the kitchen with partner Enzo Pezone. Both chefs grew up in Italy, where they mastered the nuances of regional Italian cooking before opening Pepolino in 1999. Their homemade spinach and ricotta gnocchi tossed with butter and sage melts in your mouth.

Charming country décor complements reasonably priced Tuscan recipes enhanced by extra-virgin olive oil, aged balsamic vinegar and fresh ricotta and mozzarella. Weekend brunch brings favorites from frittatas to panini.

Scalini Fedeli

Italian ✗✗

165 Duane St. (bet. Greenwich & Hudson Sts.)

Subway: Chambers St (West Broadway)
Phone: 212-528-0400
Web: www.scalinifedeli.com
Prices: $$$

Tue – Fri lunch & dinner
Mon & Sat dinner only

In the space formerly occupied by Bouley, Scalini Fedeli has an old-fashioned Tuscan ambience embellished with graceful vaulted ceilings and light yellow hues. Flickering candles and roses on each white-linen-draped table spell a European sophistication that seems a bit dated in today's TriBeCa.
Chef/owner Michael Cetrulo offers diners a choice of fixed-price menus, including a "regional (as in Italy) tasting." If the sound of wild striped bass in a Sicilian olive tomato jus, or pappardelle with a game sauce made with venison and hare, finished with Barolo wine and bitter chocolate makes your mouth water, make tracks for Scalini Fedeli.
For chocoholics, a separate section of the dessert menu is solely devoted to chocolate sweets.

Tribeca Grill

Contemporary ✗✗

375 Greenwich St. (at Franklin St.)

Subway: Franklin St
Phone: 212-941-3900
Web: www.myriadrestaurantgroup.com
Prices: $$$

Mon – Fri & Sun lunch & dinner
Sat dinner only

Another venture by Drew Nieporent and Robert DeNiro, Tribeca Grill burst on the scene in 1990. One of the first restaurants to cement TriBeCa's reputation as a gourmet-dining destination, it still draws crowds. The building that now houses the grill as well as DeNiro's TriBeCa film company was home to the Martinson Coffee factory in the early 1900s. Recalling its industrial origins, pipes and brickwork are left exposed inside.
Today the first two floors pay homage to wine. The voluminous wine list cites 1,700 labels at prices starting as low as $30; selections include more than 250 vintages of Châteauneuf-du-Pape. The kitchen showcases the bright, natural flavors of regional ingredients (peekytoe crab, Hudson Valley foie gras).

Upper East Side

An enclave for the wealthy and fashionable, the Upper East Side represents a broad cross section of New York neighborhoods and contains an impressive concentration of restaurants. In the area that stretches from Fifth Avenue to the East River, and from 60th Street to 96th Street, you'll find food to please every palate, from Austrian cuisine to vegetarian fare.

Rimming the east edge of Central Park, the Metropolitan Museum of Art, the Guggenheim Museum, the Jewish Museum, the Whitney Museum of American Art, the Frick Collection, the Neue Galerie, and the Cooper-Hewitt National Design Museum are collectively known as **Museum Mile**. An impressive concentration of galleries, along with elegant shops, upscale restaurants, clubs, exclusive private schools and fabulous residences grace this area as well.

East of Lexington Avenue, where there's a significant population of single people, the atmosphere becomes more casual. Here, modern high-rise apartment buildings dominate, sharing space with a variety of pubs, sports bars and pizza joints.

A Bit of History

In the late 19th century, rich industrialists including Andrew Carnegie and Henry Clay Frick began building mansions on the large lots along Fifth Avenue, abutting Central Park. One of the first sections to be developed was around East 86th Street, where several prominent families of German descent, including the Schermerhorns, the Astors and the Rhinelanders, built country estates. Yorkville, as it was known, soon moved east past Lexington Avenue and became a suburb of middle-class Germans, many of whom worked in nearby piano factories and breweries—although hardly a rathskeller survives today. In the 1950s, waves of immigrants from Hungary and Eastern Europe established their own communities, only to disappear as gentrification set in a couple of decades ago.

Over the years, the posh East Side has been a magnet for celebrities—Greta Garbo, Andy Warhol, Richard Nixon and Woody Allen among them. Today, **Fifth Avenue** remains the neighborhood's most impressive thoroughfare, **Madison Avenue** is chock-a-block with chi-chi shops and art galleries; and **Park Avenue** is an elegant residential boulevard.

Brigitta L. House/ MICHELIN

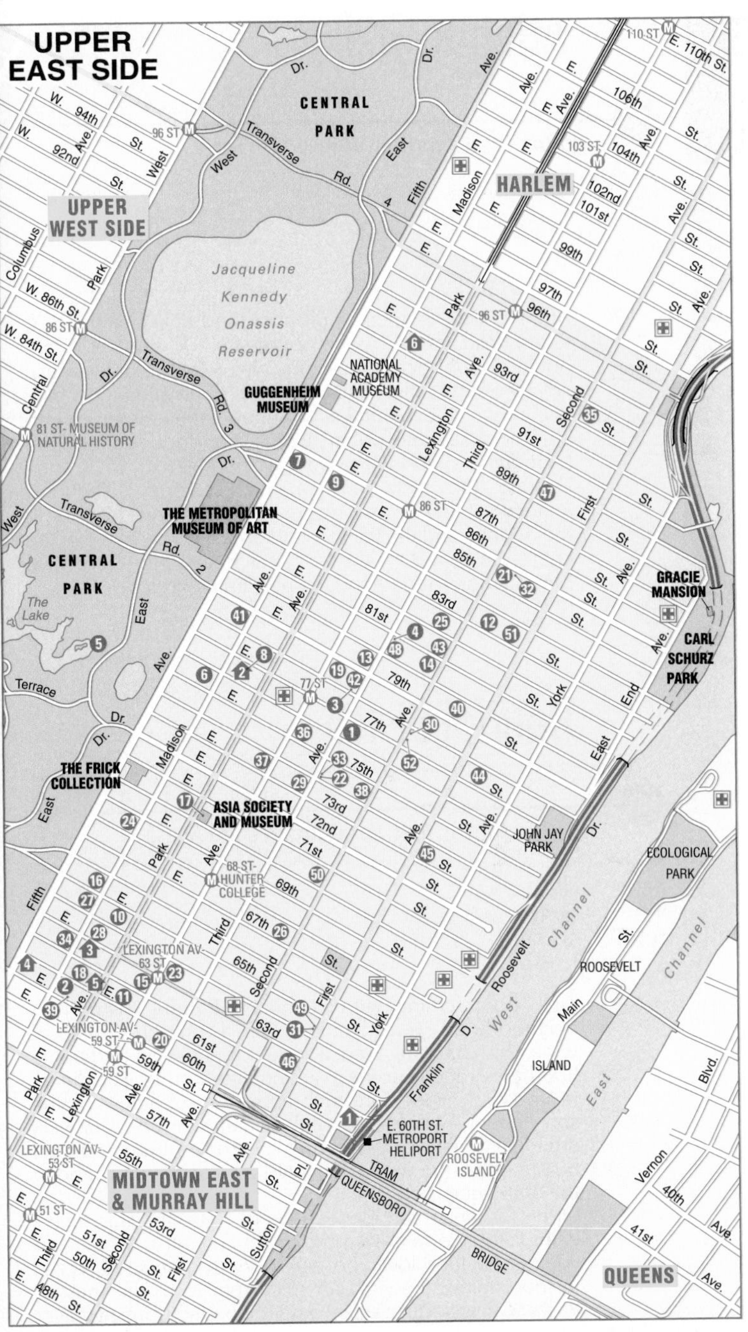
UPPER EAST SIDE
CENTRAL PARK
HARLEM
UPPER WEST SIDE
Jacqueline Kennedy Onassis Reservoir
NATIONAL ACADEMY MUSEUM
GUGGENHEIM MUSEUM
81 ST-MUSEUM OF NATURAL HISTORY
THE METROPOLITAN MUSEUM OF ART
GRACIE MANSION
CARL SCHURZ PARK
The Lake
THE FRICK COLLECTION
ASIA SOCIETY AND MUSEUM
JOHN JAY PARK
ECOLOGICAL PARK
68 ST-HUNTER COLLEGE
LEXINGTON AV-63 ST
LEXINGTON AV-59 ST
59 ST
LEXINGTON AV-53 ST
51 ST
ROOSEVELT ISLAND
E. 60TH ST. METROPORT HELIPORT
TRAM
QUEENSBORO BRIDGE
MIDTOWN EAST & MURRAY HILL
QUEENS
West Channel
East Channel

Atlantic Grill

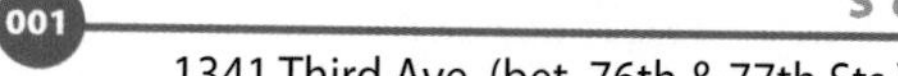

001 **Seafood** XX

1341 Third Ave. (bet. 76th & 77th Sts.)

Subway: 77 St
Phone: 212-988-9200
Web: www.brguestrestaurants.com
Prices: $$

Lunch & dinner daily

Atlantic Grill is another drop in the bucket of the B.R. Guest Restaurant Group. The popular 200-seat restaurant hooks a sophisticated East Side clientele (be sure to make advance reservations). One room is done in nautical blue and white; the other has a sunny aspect with cream-colored walls and potted palms. Outdoor seating is in high demand during the warmer months.

Despite the restaurant's name, seafood selections, including raw-bar and sushi offerings, come from both the Atlantic and the Pacific. For dinner, go with one of the chef's entrées or try the fresh catch (anything from wild King salmon to Alaskan halibut), simply grilled.

Bandol Bistro

003 **French** X

181 E. 78th St. (bet. Lexington & Third Aves.)

Subway: 77 St
Phone: 212-744-1800
Web: www.bandolbistro.com
Prices: $$

Wed – Sun lunch & dinner
Mon – Tue dinner only

Tiny, but teeming with character, Bandol Bistro is a neighborhood gem. Named for a prized Provençal wine, this charming French restaurant delivers traditional Southern French cuisine in an intimate setting. The dining room's dark woods and rich tones are set aglow by the soft lighting, while a handful of tables on the sidewalk are ideal for enjoying a warm New York afternoon. Don't be put off by the well-worn interiors—they simply add to the ambience.

Open for lunch and dinner, Bandol Bistro delights diners with its made-from-scratch French country cooking. If you're a seafood lover, be sure to try the fish soup served in the traditional style with spicy rouille, or the mussels Provençal accompanied by a side of perfectly crispy *frites*.

Aureole ✿

Contemporary XXX

002

34 E. 61st St. (bet. Madison & Park Aves.)

Subway: 5 Av - 59 St
Phone: 212-319-1660
Web: www.aureolerestaurant.com
Prices: $$$$

Mon – Fri lunch & dinner
Sat dinner only

Aureole/Vitaly Agibalov

Housed in a 1920s brownstone, this Upper East Side beauty belongs to Charlie Palmer's restaurant kingdom (there's a second Aureole in the Mandalay Bay Resort and Casino in Las Vegas). The romantic atmosphere of the bi-level dining room, with its hanging ferns, honey-colored woods and contemporary artwork, goes hand in hand with the prestigious neighborhood.

Artisan food items and products from small local farms form the foundation of what is billed as "progressive American cuisine." This might translate into cornmeal-crusted softshell crab with Romesco sauce or a velvety spiced duck breast with elegant Moroccan flavors. In addition to the three-course prix-fixe menu, the chef also whips up wonderful creations for his multicourse tastings. More than 700 selections from around the globe fill the well-selected wine list.

Appetizers

- Lobster Tortellini in Fragrant Broth with Thyme and Lemongrass
- Oakwood-smoked Salmon with Chickpea Blini and Roe
- American Caviar and Smoked Trout with Poached Quail Egg

Entrées

- Lobster Cannelloni, Tomato Confit and Clamshell Mushrooms
- Moulard Duck Breast, Confit and Date "B'steeya"
- Grilled Loin and Slow Braised Shoulder of Lamb, Asparagus Tart

Desserts

- Milk Chocolate Mousse, Peanut Butter Crunch, Caramel Peanuts, Brittle Ice Cream
- Passionfruit Cream, Rice Milk Parfait, Coconut Sorbet, Kaffir Lime Gelée, Kiwifruit

Beyoglu

004 — Turkish

1431 Third Ave. (at 81st St.)

Subway: 77 St — Lunch & dinner daily
Phone: 212-650-0850
Web: N/A
Prices: $$

Small plates star at this meze house, where low prices and a casual, convivial atmosphere add to the appeal. The simple dining room with its bright walls and inlaid-tile tables sets the scene for sharing meze (the focus of the menu) from tangy homemade yogurt with cucumber and garlic to smooth stuffed grape leaves to a crunchy shepherd's salad. Most of the recipes—and some wine and beer offerings—come from Turkey, though Greek and Lebanese accents are found in many of the items.

If the idea of small plates doesn't float your boat, there's also a short list of daily specials, including meat kebabs and grilled fish. Your waiter will fill you in on the delightful desserts, such as baklava, and *kadayif* filled with almonds, pistachios and honey.

Boathouse Central Park

005 — American

The Lake at Central Park (E. 72nd St. & Park Dr. North)

Subway: 68 St - Hunter College — Lunch & dinner daily
Phone: 212-517-2233
Web: www.thecentralparkboathouse.com
Prices: $$

You couldn't dream up a more romantic setting for a first date or a special occasion. Nestled on the shore of the lake in the middle of Central Park, the Boathouse features peaceful water views through its floor-to-ceiling windows. Built in the 1950s, Loeb Boathouse replaced the original two-story Victorian structure designed by architect Calvert Vaux in the 1870s.

Today the Boathouse is the only place in Manhattan for a lakeside meal. And the American fare (jumbo lump crab cakes, house-made pasta) makes it all the more worthwhile.

On a sunny day, sit out on the deck (be sure to make reservations) and watch the boats float by. After lunch, why not hit the water with a gondola ride (advance notice required) or a rowboat rental?

Café Boulud ✿

French

006

20 E. 76th St. (bet. Fifth & Madison Aves.)

Subway: 77 St
Phone: 212-772-2600
Web: www.danielnyc.com
Prices: $$$$

Tues – Sun lunch & dinner
Mon dinner only

Café Boulud/B. Hirsch

Set in the Surrey Hotel, Café Boulud brings a taste of the Old Country to the heart of the Upper East Side. Operated by Daniel Boulud, this restaurant pays homage to the cafe that the chef's family owned just outside Lyon in France.

Boulud's cooking exhibits a controlled creativity and an intelligent marriage of ingredients. Two- and three-course prix-fixe lunch options offer good selection and quality, while four menu categories appeal to different moods. Feeling old-fashioned? Choose *La Tradition*, made up of French country classics. If you want to dine according to the season, try *La Saison*. For vegetarians, there's *Le Potager*. Armchair travelers will favor *Le Voyage*, culled from around the world.

Recalling 1930s Paris, Café Boulud caters to a sophisticated Upper East Side crowd of ladies who lunch and soigné Europeans. Service is always polished and professional.

Appetizers

- Portuguese Octopus Salad, Orange, Caper Vinaigrette
- Veal Agnolotti, Braised Endive, Leeks, Pecorino
- Seared and Poached Hudson Valley Foie Gras, Savoy Cabbage

Entrées

- Moroccan Lamb Trio, Almond-stuffed Prune, Red Lentils
- Ricotta Ravioli, Tomato Compote, Fava Leaves, Aged Pecorino
- Snapper, Soba Noodles, Seaweed, Daikon, Shiitake Broth

Desserts

- Pear Pistachio Tart, Spiced Pear, Sangria Sorbet
- Devils Food Cupcake, Caramel Gratin, Salted Caramel Ice Cream
- Sticky Toffee Pudding, Pineapple, Cilantro, Vanilla Ice Cream

Café Sabarsky

Austrian

1048 Fifth Ave. (at 86th St.)

Subway: 86 St (Lexington Ave.)
Phone: 212-288-0665
Web: www.wallse.com
Prices: $$

Thu – Sun lunch & dinner
Mon, Wed lunch only

Art alone is reason enough to visit the Neue Galerie, founded in 2001 by cosmetics mogul Ronald Lauder to display his collection of early 20th-century Austrian and German art, as well as the collection of his friend, art dealer Serge Sabarsky. Besides fine art, you'll find a real gem in this 1914 Beaux Arts mansion, in the form of Café Sabarsky.

Old World charm oozes from the cafe, modeled on a late-19th-century Viennese *Kaffeehaus*. In the dining room, adorned with reproductions of Josef Hoffmann sconces, Otto Wagner fabrics and a Bösendorfer piano, chef Kurt Guntenbrunner (of Wallsé and Blaue Gans) offers fine Austrian cuisine. You'll find the likes of bratwurst and beef goulash here, but whatever you do, don't pass up the pastries!

The Carlyle

Contemporary

35 E. 76th St. (at Madison Ave.)

Subway: 77 St
Phone: 212-570-7193
Web: www.thecarlyle.com
Prices: $$$$

Lunch & dinner daily

Few places say old New York like The Carlyle *(see hotel listing)*. Opulent and well-mannered, The Carlyle exudes refinement, and its dining room proves a perfect complement to the hotel's sophistication. As far as luxury goes, this handsome space pulls out all the stops, from the tuxedo-clad waitstaff to the Cartier dessert cart. Tones of mushroom and chocolate-brown, lush fabrics, fresh flowers and soft lighting make the restaurant an equally ideal spot for staging a romantic tête-à-tête, a ladies' lunch, or a business deal.

The traditional menu is almost as classy as the crowd. French-influenced favorites such as seared Hudson Valley foie gras with roasted Mission figs, prime aged ribeye and simple fish dishes number among the choices.

Centolire

Italian XX

1167 Madison Ave. (bet. 85th & 86th Sts.)

Subway: 86 St (Lexington Ave.) — Lunch & dinner daily
Phone: 212-734-7711
Web: www.pinoluongo.wordpress.com
Prices: $$$

With 100 (*cento* in Italian) lire, you can go to America, or so an old Italian song goes. Accordingly, Tuscan-born restaurateur Pino Luongo (of Tuscan Square) opened Centolire in 2001 to honor those Italians who, like himself, came to America to start a new life. Two dining spaces present different options: the more cozy and quiet downstairs room or the larger, more colorful upstairs area, accessed via a glass elevator.

At lunch, Centolire proposes a three-course menu of appealing Italian fare at a price you can't refuse. Dinner brings a range of well-prepared entrées from osso buco to *Cacciucco alla Toscana* brimming with fresh fish and shellfish. Before you leave, check out the cookbooks written by Pino, which are displayed near the entrance.

Davidburke & Donatella

Contemporary XXX

133 E. 61st St. (bet. Lexington & Park Aves.)

Subway: Lexington Av - 59 St — Lunch & dinner daily
Phone: 212-813-2121
Web: www.dbdrestaurant.com
Prices: $$$

Opened by David Burke and Donatella Arpaia, this restaurant reconfigures a traditional town house with geometric patterns, ebony parquet floors and a palette that runs from chocolate brown to lipstick red. The place is constantly mobbed with a chi-chi cadre of diners.

Burke, who oversees the kitchen, describes his cooking style as "David Burke unplugged." You'll know what this means when you taste dishes such as day-boat scallops "Benedict," a take on the popular egg dish (in Burke's version, scallops replace the eggs, chorizo stands in for the ham, and a potato pancake masquerades as an English muffin). At lunch, the set menu is the best value.

The entire staff operates with noteworthy efficiency and grace.

Daniel ✿✿

010 French XXXXX

60 E. 65th St. (bet. Madison & Park Aves.)

Subway: 68 St - Hunter College
Phone: 212-288-0033
Web: www.danielnyc.com
Prices: $$$$

Mon – Sat dinner only

Daniel/Peter Medilek

Raised on a farm outside Lyon, Daniel Boulud worked with some of the best chefs in France before landing in the States as executive chef of Le Cirque. It was fitting that he opened Daniel in 1993 in the former Mayfair Hotel—the space once filled by Le Cirque. An arched colonnade defines the Italian Renaissance-style dining room, designed with an 18-foot-high coffered ceiling and a bronze chandelier with alabaster globes that seem to float above the room.

It is in this palatial setting that Boulud turns the best domestic and imported seasonal products into artful dishes prepared in the French tradition. The talented kitchen team adds a soupçon of American flair to the seasonal menus. The offerings are mouthwatering with even a separate menu dedicated to vegetables. And given the lush setting, foie gras and caviar are always appropriate.

Appetizers

- Peekytoe Crab Salad, Avocado, "Carotte Fondante"
- Guinea Hen and Foie Gras Terrine, Port Gelée, Poached Quince
- Tai Snapper Ceviche, Wasabi Cream, Radishes

Entrées

- Paupiette of Black Sea Bass in a Crisp Potato Shell
- Duo of Dry Aged Beef: Braised Short Ribs and Seared Ribeye
- Honey-glazed Liberty Farms Duck Breast with Leg "Craquelins"

Desserts

- Tahitian Vanilla Bavaroise, Passion Fruit Banana Sorbet
- Warm Chocolate Financier, Lady Gray Ice Cream
- Caramelized Banana, Chantilly, Caramel Sauce, Candied Hazelnuts

Donguri

Japanese

012

309 E. 83rd St. (bet. First & Second Aves.)

Subway: 86 St (Lexington Ave.) — Tue – Sun dinner only
Phone: 212-737-5656
Web: www.donguri nyc.com
Prices: $$$

Owned by Ito En, a Japanese tea company (which also owns Kai), Donguri offers an extensive menu of authentic Japanese cuisine. With only 24 seats, this nondescript little place fills up quickly with a grown-up crowd who can afford the prices and appreciate the light, flavorful food.

Try one of the fixed menus, which might start with miso soup and a delightful plate of assorted appetizers, then progress through several more courses. Dinner may also be ordered à la carte—with a huge assortment of dishes to share—or go all out and order the chef's *omakase* (tasting menu). All products are ultra-fresh and specials change daily.

Due

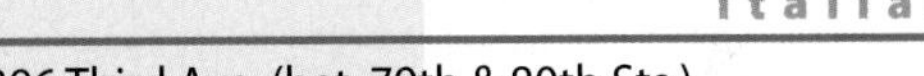

Italian

013

1396 Third Ave. (bet. 79th & 80th Sts.)

Subway: N/A — Lunch & dinner daily
Phone: 212-772-3331
Web: N/A
Prices: $$

While it may seem that the Upper East Side drowns in a sea of spaghetti sauce with its many Italian restaurants, one spot worth its salt is Due. This light-filled place dishes out classic, well-prepared Northern Italian cuisine. Decorated in traditional bistro style with colorful ceramics, photographs, and Italian tourism posters, Due sports a relaxed elegance. Large French windows open out to the hustle and bustle of Third Avenue.

Waiters are professional and deliver rapid and efficient service to eager customers who feast on everything from veal piccata to seafood-topped squid-ink linguine scented with roasted garlic. Don't commit to anything before you consider the plentiful daily specials—especially the enticing risotto of the day.

Etats-Unis ✿

014 **Contemporary**

242 E. 81st St. (bet. Second & Third Aves.)

Subway: 77 St — Dinner daily
Phone: 212-517-8826
Web: www.etatsunisrestaurant.com
Prices: $$$

Etats-Unis

Delightful food here comes without pretentious surroundings. The little shoebox of a dining room is done in rustic-chic style with bare light bulbs hanging from the ceiling, molded plastic chairs and uncovered varnished-wood tables. The open kitchen and the warm, family-run atmosphere combine to make dining here feel a bit like an intimate dinner party in your own home, minus all of the work.

Conceived by owners Tom and Jonathan Rapp, the limited menu changes daily to reflect the market. Simply prepared, without the fussy style often found in this neighborhood, the food at Etats-Unis defines approachable gourmet cuisine. Flavors stand out in the balanced dishes, and the homey yet sophisticated desserts constitute a worthy excuse for going off that diet.

If you can't get a table, the charming Bar at Etats-Unis across the street offers the same menu.

Appetizers

- Twice-risen Shropshire Blue Cheese Soufflé Pudding with Chives
- Scalloped Blue Point Oysters with Freshly Grated Horseradish, Sautéed Onions, Crumbled Saltines and Cream

Entrées

- Grilled Atlantic Halibut, Celery Root and Parsnip Purée, Roasted Granny Smith Apples, Haricots Verts
- Grilled Rack of Lamb, Mint Pesto, Roasted Potatoes, Baby Artichokes

Desserts

- Date Pudding, Caramelized Rum Sauce, Freshly Whipped Cream
- Chocolate Soufflé with Warm Molten Center
- Light and Fluffy Lemon Pudding Cake, Freshly Whipped Cream

Fig & Olive

Mediterranean

015

808 Lexington Ave. (bet. 62nd & 63rd Sts.)

Subway: Lexington Av - 63 St — Lunch & dinner daily
Phone: 212-207-4555
Web: www.figandolive.com
Prices: $$$

At this Mediterranean restaurant and olive oil shop (now with a second location in the Meatpacking District at 420 W. 13th St.), olive oil is treated with the same attention afforded fine wine. Each dish—from grilled lamb to mushroom carpaccio—is accented with a specific extra virgin oil. You'll find fragrant oils from France, Italy and Spain here, and the wine list echoes the same regions (with many selections by the glass).

Settle into the pleasant dining room on a time-out from strenuous shopping at nearby Bloomingdale's, and dig into tartines, carpaccio, crostini, or a charcuterie platter brimming with prosciutto, *jamón Iberico* and *saucisson sec*. The bright food will revive you for further shopping adventures without an expanded waistline.

Frederick's Madison

Contemporary

016

768 Madison Ave. (bet. 65th & 66th Sts.)

Subway: 68 St - Hunter College — Lunch & dinner daily
Phone: 212-737-7300
Web: www.fredericksnyc.com
Prices: $$$

Brothers Frederick and Laurent Lesort, known for Frederick's Bar & Lounge *(8 W. 58th St.)*, also preside over Frederick's Madison. The menu focuses on Mediterranean fare in the form of small plates, tartares, charcuterie and cheeses. Signature dishes include foie gras chaud-froid, which comes seared, and in a cold terrine served with kumquat jam; open ravioli of braised rabbit; and slow-baked cod with clam nage. In the dining room, blond woods, red velvet chairs, and Lalique light fixtures bespeak an elegance befitting the Upper East Side.

Spin-off Frederick's Downtown *(637 Hudson St.)* sits on a quiet Greenwich Village corner and offers a French bistro feel with plenty of outdoor seating.

Garden Court Café

017 **Asian**

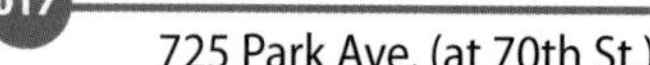

725 Park Ave. (at 70th St.)

Subway: 68 St - Hunter College — Tue – Sun lunch only
Phone: 212-570-5202
Web: www.asiasociety.org
Prices: $$

Flooded by natural light in the glass-enclosed, plant-filled lobby of the Asia Society, this cafe is a far cry from your garden-variety museum restaurant. You may not hear much about it, but the Garden Court is worth seeking out, not only for its airy ambience but for the Asian dishes that expertly fuse elements of east and west.

Serving lunch Tuesday through Sunday, the Garden Court balances salads and sandwiches with seasonal entrées (Korean BBQ duck; steamed mahi mahi in a banana leaf). It's a quality show, right down to the careful presentation and good service – and the museum's entry fee is not required to access the cafe.

Don't miss the museum gift shop for cookbooks, teas and wonderful gifts.

Geisha

018 **Japanese**

33 E. 61st St. (bet. Madison & Park Aves.)

Subway: Lexington Av - 59 St — Mon – Fri lunch & dinner, Sat dinner only
Phone: 212-813-1112
Web: www.geisharestaurant.com
Prices: $$$

Named for the sensuous world of the geisha, this restaurant is owned by the same team—Vittorio Assaf and Fabio Granato—who introduced Serafina to the New York dining scene. Four individually decorated dining spaces on two floors incorporate elements of Japanese costumes, Oriental flowers (cherry blossom light fixtures), and origami (a "3-D" wall of stacked, fabric-covered cubes).

The result is a cool, seductive space in which to savor the menu of French-accented Asian fare originally conceived by Eric Ripert of Le Bernardin. Coconut-marinated fluke, and hamachi and bluefin patchwork are two of the enticing selections. Sure, there's also sushi galore, but why not try something different, like grilled shrimp lollipops on sugarcane skewers?

Il Riccio

Italian

019

152 E. 79th St. (bet. Lexington & Third Aves.)

Subway: 77 St — Lunch & dinner daily
Phone: 212-639-9111
Web: N/A
Prices: $$

Located four blocks from the Metropolitan Museum of Art, Il Riccio makes a great lunch spot when you've had your fill of fine art. A shiny brass door beckons you into the restaurant, which sits on a busy street, surrounded by boutiques and eateries. Two different dining rooms here offer a comfortable respite from trekking through museum galleries.

Diners are cosseted at Il Riccio, where the chef takes great care in preparing Italian classics. Although the menu is not extensive, it does offer a nice range of dishes—the emphasis here is on pasta, from spaghetti with crab meat and tomato to gnocchi tossed in a bright pesto—along with a roster of daily specials. The short wine list celebrates Italian *vino,* including a page of pricey reserves.

Isle of Capri

Italian

020

1028 Third Ave. (at 61st St.)

Subway: Lexington Av - 59 St — Mon – Sat lunch & dinner
Phone: 212-223-9430
Web: www.isleofcapriny.com
Prices: $$

Tradition reigns in this stylish Upper East Side establishment, started in 1955 by Vincenzo and Maria Lammana, and still going strong. When the original owners died in the 1990s, Isle of Capri passed to their two daughters, who run the restaurant today. There's a joyful air in the pleasant dining room, set about by Greco-Roman-style statues recalling the island where Roman emperors Octavian Augustus and Tiberius both had residences.

A table in the center of the dining room displays baskets full of seasonal and imported Italian products, hinting at the ingredients used in the dishes here. Excellent house-made pastas, broiled veal chops, shrimp scampi and *trippa alla calabrese* (tripe braised in tomato sauce) are all authentic and satisfying.

Ithaka

021 Greek

308 E. 86th St. (bet. First & Second Aves.)

Subway: 86 St (Lexington Ave.)
Phone: 212-628-9100
Web: www.ithakarestaurant.com
Prices: $$

Mon – Fri dinner only
Sat – Sun lunch & dinner

A Mediterranean-blue awning welcomes visitors to Ithaka, the way the sea would greet them in Greece. Inside, live music and an amiable staff makes Ithaka an endearing spot.

This cozy place, with beamed ceiling, brick walls and stone floors, presents an authentic Old World cuisine. Greek favorites like moussaka and pasticcio share with *kalamari scharas* (grilled calamari) and *arni youvetsi* (baby lamb baked in a clay pot with orzo, tomato sauce and feta). Perhaps best of all, the prices will leave some change in your pocket.

If you still have room for dessert, the creamy house-made yogurt *(yiaourti sakoulas)* is as good as any you'll get in Greece; here, it's drizzled with perfumed honey and topped with crunchy hazelnuts.

J.G. Melon

022 American

1291 Third Ave. (at 74th St.)

Subway: 77 St
Phone: 212-744-0585
Web: N/A
Prices:

Lunch & dinner daily

Preppies still wanting a taste of the college life haunt J.G. Melon, where burgers and beers are the staples. The cheeseburger, cooked to order and served on a toasted English muffin, is arguably one of the best in the city, and the crispy, golden, cottage fries that accompany it perfectly round out the meal (literally, since the fries are round!). Cold nights bring customers begging for Melon's chili.

This place has been a New York institution for generations, and is always packed with neighborhood residents, including recent college graduates and young families with kids. Checkered tablecloths, wood floors and a long wooden bar give Melon's an amiable local pub feel, while the old-school staff makes everyone feel like a regular.

JoJo ✿

Contemporary XX

023

160 E. 64th St. (bet. Lexington & Third Aves.)

Subway: Lexington Av - 63 St
Lunch & dinner daily
Phone: 212-223-5656
Web: www.jean-georges.com
Prices: $$$

Jean-Georges Management

JoJo will always be special to its "father," superstar chef Jean-Georges Vongerichten. After all, this bistro was his first restaurant in New York, launched in 1991. Given the nickname that Vongerichten knew as a boy, JoJo got a major overhaul for its tenth birthday. Now the two-story town house drips with plush velvets, rich tapestries and fine silks. Low lighting from crystal chandeliers casts a sultry glow on the room's deep hues, and the closely spaced tables amplify the feeling of intimacy

In this romantic lair, the chef presents a confident and skilled version of modern French cuisine, in dishes like a savory and flaky porcini mushroom tart, or a slow-baked salmon served on a pillow of chive mashed potatoes with pickled wild ramps and earthy morels.

JoJo's daytime small-plate menu is popular with the ladies who lunch.

Appetizers

- Tuna Roll with Soy Bean Emulsion
- Goat Cheese and Potato Terrine, Mesclun and Arugula Juice
- Shrimp Dusted in Orange Power, Artichokes and Arugula

Entrées

- Codfish, Marinated Vegetables, Aromatic Sauce
- Sirloin Steak, Gingered Mushrooms, White Asparagus, Soy Caramel Sauce
- Ginger Chicken, Green Olives

Desserts

- Green Apple Pavlova, Thai Basil Seeds
- Warm Chocolate Cake with Vanilla Ice Cream
- Banana Brioche Pudding, Candied Pecans, Nutmeg Ice Cream

Kai

024 Japanese XXX

822 Madison Ave. (bet. 68th & 69th Sts.)

Subway: 68 St - Hunter College — Tue – Sat lunch & dinner
Phone: 212-988-7277
Web: www.itoen.com
Prices: $$$

You'll find Kai hidden away on the second floor of the Upper East Side tea shop owned by Ito En, one of the best-known tea companies in Japan. A serene setting marked by clean lines and soothing tones creates just the right vibe in which to experience kaiseki cuisine.

Centuries ago, *kaiseki* originated in the temples of Kyoto as small dishes served during a traditional Japanese tea ceremony. Kai modernizes this tradition with a *kaiseki* that balances offerings between land and sea with secondary ingredients vital to the dish. Order the *kaiseki* in advance if this is your preference; or go with the seasonal prix-fixe menu offered nightly. Additionally, the à la carte is perfect for those who prefer to create their own menu.

Kings' Carriage House

025 Contemporary XX

251 E. 82nd St. (bet. Second & Third Aves.)

Subway: 86 St (Lexington Ave.) — Lunch & dinner daily
Phone: 212-734-5490
Web: N/A
Prices: $$

This restored carriage house is about as far from New York as you can get in New York. Run by Elizabeth King and her husband Paul Farell (who hails from Dublin), Kings' Carriage House resembles an Irish country manor, set about with Chinese porcelains, antique furnishings and hunting trophies on the walls. Its lovely ambience and personal service is perfect for charming a loved one or friend, or impressing out-of-town guests.

Simple and old-fashioned American dishes (as in a salad of grilled chicken breast and asparagus spears fanned over frisée; a dessert of ripe seasonal fruit) dominate the daily changing fixed-price menu. The lunch menu is especially inexpensive, but if you can't make it for a meal, do drop 'round for afternoon tea.

L'Absinthe

French XX

026

227 E. 67th St. (bet. Second & Third Aves.)

Subway: 68 St - Hunter College — Lunch & dinner daily
Phone: 212-794-4950
Web: www.labsinthe.com
Prices: $$$

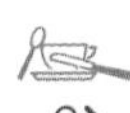

Remember the good old days, when you sat around cafes all day, railing on the political system and sipping the mind-blowing liquor, absinthe, until you could no longer see? Of course you don't—unless you happened to grow up in late-19th-century Paris. Though absinthe has long since been replaced by the gentler aperitif Pernod, the Art Nouveau age lives on at Jean-Michel Bergougnoux's brasserie. Chandeliers with tulip-shaped light fixtures, large framed mirrors and sprays of bright flowers bring to mind Belle Époque Paris.

Meanwhile, the kitchen interprets timeless French dishes from cold pâté of quail to *choucroute Alsacienne*, for 21st-century patrons. Beef tartare and steamed mussels are featured at brunch, which also has a children's menu.

La Goulue

French XX

027

746 Madison Ave. (bet. 64th & 65th Sts.)

Subway: Lexington Av - 63 St — Lunch & dinner daily
Phone: 212-988-8169
Web: www.lagouluerestaurant.com
Prices: $$$

Few places in New York say "Paris" more than this venerable bistro, opened in 1972. Named for the 19th-century Moulin Rouge dancer immortalized in paintings by Henri de Toulouse-Lautrec, La Goulue re-creates La Belle Époque with framed vintage posters, lace cafe curtains, and Art Nouveau light fixtures.

Well-rendered classics fill the menu with the likes of a rich foie gras terrine or steaming onion soup to start, followed by a hearty coq au vin or steak *frites*. Desserts are not to be missed, from the tarte Tatin to the floating island. A steady supply of celebrities and well-heeled New Yorkers frequent this place, and the closely spaced bistro tables make eavesdropping de rigueur. From spring to fall, the sidewalk tables are highly coveted.

Le Bilboquet

French 

25 E. 63rd St. (bet. Madison & Park Aves.)

Subway: Lexington Av - 63 St — Lunch & dinner daily
Phone: 212-751-3036
Web: N/A
Prices: $$

There's no sign indicating Le Bilboquet's presence, but this swanky French restaurant is perpetually populated nightly with a sexy international crowd. Once inside, you'll observe that most of the patrons (many of them are French) seem to know each other, adding to the private-club ambience. This hotspot, with its tight quarters and loud music, is not the place for a quiet conversation, but if you're looking for a party, it's an ideal place to be.

The kitchen turns out French bistro cuisine and leaves the modern interpretations and fussy presentations to the competition. Steak tartare, roast chicken, *moules frites* and *salade Niçoise* are among the most-requested dishes. An insouciant attitude pervades the service, but the crowd never seems to care.

Lenox Room

029

Contemporary XX

1278 Third Ave. (bet. 73rd & 74th Sts.)

Subway: 77 St — Mon – Fri & Sun lunch & dinner, Sat dinner only
Phone: 212-772-0404
Web: www.lenoxroom.com
Prices: $$

Looking for good food in a cocoon-like ambience? You've come to the right place. Opened in 1995 by maitre d' Tony Fortuna and hotelier Edward Bianchini, the Lenox Room wraps diners in cozy comfort with its claret-red walls, cushy banquettes and wood-paneling.

The updated American cuisine fits right in with this sophisticated environment, and the service is pleasant and professional. Lunch brings salads, sandwiches and a short list of entrées; the three-course "I Love New York" menu is such a deal. At dinner, there's a nice balance of choices, including "Tiers of Taste," a combination of three small plates for one set price. Dinner entrées travel the globe for inspiration, from Wiener Schnitzel to rigatoni with duck sausage ragoût.

Lusardi's

030 **Italian** XX

1494 Second Ave. (bet. 77th & 78th Sts.)

Subway: 77 St
Phone: 212-249-2020
Web: www.lusardis.com
Prices: $$

Mon – Fri lunch & dinner
Sat – Sun dinner only

Both the décor and the service are warm at Lusardi's, an Upper East Side staple since Luigi and Mauro Lusardi founded the restaurant in 1982. Decorated with vintage Italian posters, the well-kept yellow dining room is quiet at lunch; it comes alive in the evening, though, with a loyal following of diners who pack the place.

An ample choice of classic northern Italian fare attracts customers year-round, while special menus designed around white truffles or wild game are tuned to the season. Pasta lovers will find a wide range of alternatives, and fish and meat dishes are given equal face time. Lusardi's fans will be glad to know that they can purchase bottles of the family's own marinara sauce and extra virgin olive oil at the restaurant.

Maya

031 **Mexican** XX

1191 First Ave. (bet. 64th & 65th Sts.)

Subway: 68 St - Hunter College
Phone: 212-585-1818
Web: www.modernmexican.com
Prices: $$

Dinner daily

Maya practically defines casual elegance. Few restaurants are able to carry off being informal enough for a weeknight while being upscale enough for a weekend, but Maya expertly straddles that line. This spirited Mexican restaurant's pastel walls and vibrant artwork make it feel like an elegant private home, and its lively scene lures the right mix of a crowd.

Far from the burrito-laden menus of the competition, Richard Sandoval's menu reads like a love letter to Mexico. Time-honored culinary traditions are updated with a contemporary twist in many of the dishes, and a seemingly limitless margarita menu complements the elegant yet zesty creations from the devoted chef. Bursting with powerful flavors, meals here go well beyond fajita fare.

Maz Mezcal

Mexican

032

316 E. 86th St. (bet. First & Second Aves.)

Subway: 86 St (Lexington Ave.)
Phone: 212-472-1599
Web: www.mazmezcal.com
Prices: $$

Mon – Fri dinner only
Sat – Sun lunch & dinner

Simple Mexican food—and lots of it—leaves locals eager to return to Maz Mezcal, located on a busy restaurant block. Eduardo Silva now runs his family's East Side stalwart; after he took the reins, he renamed the place Maz Mezcal, then expanded it several years ago.

Flavorful Tex-Mex fare includes combination plates, as well as favorites such as enchiladas and fajitas. Dishes are tailored to mild palates in this family-friendly place, but if you prefer your food *picante*, the kitchen will be happy to spice things up. With more than 50 types of tequila, and its cousin, mezcal, available from the bar, you can count on a lively atmosphere almost every night. In warm weather, the party spills out to the backyard garden and the sidewalk seats.

Mezzaluna

Italian

033

1295 Third Ave. (bet. 74th & 75th Sts.)

Subway: 77 St
Phone: 212-535-9600
Web: www.mezzalunany.com
Prices: $$

Lunch & dinner daily

Mezzaluna is a restaurant that takes it name seriously. So much so, that they offered 20 meals to any artist (many of them Italian) who would agree to render his or her version of the restaurant's namesake crescent-shaped chopping knife. As you'll see, the 77 different versions that paper the walls each depict a unique take on this design and provide an eye-catching backdrop for well-prepared seasonal Italian dishes.

Founded by Aldo Bozzi, the restaurant has been around since 1984. Antiques imported from Italy and tables nesting close together add to the simple comfort and convivial atmosphere. From black linguine topped with fiery tomato sauce to brick-oven pizza, it's easy to see why the crowds line up here.

Nello

Italian XX

034

696 Madison Ave. (bet. 62nd & 63rd Sts.)

Subway: 5 Av - 59 St — Lunch & dinner daily
Phone: 212-980-9099
Web: N/A
Prices: $$$$

It's all about the Beautiful People at Nello. This place appeals to a moneyed, dress-to-impress clientele, who don't flinch at the restaurant's uptown prices. (Nello seems to keep pace with neighbors Givenchy, Christofle, Hermès and Lalique.) Inside, black-and-white photographs of an African safari adorn the walls, and little crystal vases of fresh flowers brighten the tabletops. Tables are tight, but with this chic crowd, it's all the more pleasing.

Nello is worth the splurge, not only for the delectable Italian cuisine and the charming waitstaff, but for the opportunity to see how the "other half" lives. Before you leave, pause inside the entrance to check out photographs of the rich and famous patrons who have dined here before you.

Nick's

Pizza 

035

1814 Second Ave. (at 94th St.)

Subway: 96 St (Lexington Ave.) — Lunch & dinner daily
Phone: 212-987-5700
Web: N/A
Prices:

New York has long been known for its pizzerias, and this one takes the cake—or, rather, the pie. The Manhattan satellite of the Forest Hills (Queens) original, Nick's is everything you want a pizza place to be. The dining room is pleasant and cozy, the service is jovial and efficient, and you can watch the cooks hand-tossing the dough and firing your pizza in the wood-burning oven.

Pies turn out thin and crispy, spread with a good balance of tomato sauce, herbs and your choice of toppings. On the list of pasta (properly called "macaroni" in the traditional Italian-American lexicon) and meat entrées, half portions accommodate those with less hearty appetites—but with food this good at such reasonable prices, you'll want to rethink your diet.

Orsay

036 **French**

1057 Lexington Ave. (at 75th St.)

Subway: 77 St — Lunch & dinner daily
Phone: 212-517-6400
Web: www.orsayrestaurant.com
Prices: $$

In true Parisian fashion, this smart brasserie at the corner of 75th Street overflows onto the sidewalk terrace through its large French doors. Inside, the Paris of the 1950s comes alive through the zinc bar, fan-patterned mosaic tile floor, mahogany paneling and frosted-glass partitions.

The chef takes a few liberties with modern preparations, but the origins are French to the core. Lamb navarin, escargots, and steak tartare speak to the classic technique, while the likes of citrus-cured hamachi, or wild Duclair duckling with blood-orange glaze show contemporary flair.

Ideal for business or pleasure, Orsay's attractive bar provides a comfortable spot for guests dining alone to enjoy a glass of wine and a bountiful shellfish platter.

Payard

037 **French**

1032 Lexington Ave. (bet. 73rd & 74th Sts.)

Subway: 77 St — Mon – Sat lunch & dinner
Phone: 212-717-5252
Web: www.payard.com
Prices: $$$

Famous for its handmade chocolates and mouth-watering French pastries, Payard is also a notable restaurant. Since you have to walk past the cases of tempting sweets to reach the dining room, there's always a danger that you'll decide to forget the main course altogether. If you do resist (until the end of the meal, that is), you'll be treated to modernized French dishes such as sautéed East Coast halibut with classic ratatouille, roasted rack of lamb with Provençal vegetable bayaldi, and a tasty tart topped with rich duck confit, sweet parsnip purée and meaty lardons.

And don't even think of leaving without a sweet souvenir—perhaps a box of French *macarons*, some champagne truffles or a selection of *pâtes de fruits*—to tide you over until breakfast.

Persepolis

038

Persian

1407 Second Ave. (bet. 73rd & 74th Sts.)

Subway: 77 St

Phone: 212-535-1100

Web: www.persepolisnyc.com

Prices: $$

Mon – Sat lunch & dinner
Sun dinner only

In summer 2006, Persepolis (which bears the name of one of the ancient capitals of Persia, established in the late 6th century BC) moved to new digs a few doors down. This larger space sports a bistro feel with its tinned ceiling, white linens and wood accents. Even the presentation has been updated with sparkling white china.

What hasn't changed is the menu. Olive oil, lemon, garlic, saffron, cinnamon—and even a few secret ingredients—flavor a tasty assortment of traditional dishes. Begin your meal with *khumus* or fresh feta cheese and market vegetables before tucking into saffron chicken or baby lamb barg—and be sure to order the sour cherry rice with any entrée.

Takeout and delivery are a popular option for Upper East Side residents.

Philippe

039

Chinese

33 E. 60th St. (bet. Madison & Park Aves.)

Subway: 5 Av - 59 St

Phone: 212-644-8885

Web: www.philippechow.com

Prices: $$$

Mon – Sat lunch & dinner
Sun dinner only

After more than 25 years at Mr. Chow in Midtown, Philippe Chow opened his eponymous restaurant in RM's appealing space. The main room now has a clean, contemporary look, with leather banquettes lining the walls and vases of artfully arranged branches decorating the niches between the dining room and the bar.

Upscale Chinese cuisine ranges from striped bass Bejing to crispy duck. Entrées are sized—and priced—for two to three people (half-orders are available on some items). Noodles and dumplings merit a separate section on the menu; most every evening at 8pm, you can watch the chef craft traditional noodle dishes at a station in the middle of the dining room.

Quatorze Bis

French XX

040

323 E. 79th St. (bet. First & Second Aves.)

Subway: 77 St — Tue – Sun lunch & dinner
Phone: 212-535-1414 — Mon dinner only
Web: N/A
Prices: $$

This French bistro has changed its location, but not its name—which refers to its former address on 14th Street (*quatorze* in French). The word "bis" was added to the title when the restaurant moved in 1989 (*bis* is French for "once again").

Regulars hope Quatorze Bis is on the Upper East Side to stay, so they can keep enjoying the likes of homemade pork terrine, beef Bourguignon, cassoulet, and cream-filled profiteroles in their own backyard. Open for dinner nightly and lunch every day except Monday, Quatorze Bis is a gracious neighborhood restaurant.

The marble-topped bar, French posters and cozy banquettes make for an oh-so-Parisian atmosphere. Be sure to check out the two caricatures of King Louis XIV of France that hang on the wall.

Serafina Fabulous Pizza

Italian X

041

1022 Madison Ave. (bet. 78th & 79th Sts.)

Subway: 77 St — Lunch & dinner daily
Phone: 212-734-1425
Web: www.serafinarestaurant.com
Prices: $$

After browsing the tony boutiques of Madison Avenue, the Beautiful People head for Serafina Fabulous Pizza. People-watching is fantastic at this trendy Italian spot, best known for specialties cooked in its wood-burning oven. The second-floor dining room has a lively and energetic feel, while the third level boasts a retractable roof for alfresco dining in warmer months.

Snagging a seat at this popular spot may prove difficult in the evening, but great pizzas, fresh pastas, and grilled meats and fish make it well worth the wait. The gracious staff encourages those who wish to linger to sit back and enjoy a glass of the house sangria.

Four other Serafinas (all with the same menu) in Manhattan ensure that the party never ends.

Shanghai Pavilion

042 **Chinese** XX

1378 Third Ave. (bet. 78th & 79th Sts.)

Subway: 77 St

Lunch & dinner daily

Phone: 212-585-3388

Web: N/A

Prices: $$

While so many of the Upper East Side's restaurants seem to tailor their prices to an upscale clientele, Shanghai Pavilion is a real gem if you're looking for reasonably priced and sophisticated Chinese cuisine served in a pleasing, contemporary setting. Shanghai and Cantonese specialties cover all the bases, from pan-fried bean curd to steamed juicy buns filled with the likes of pork, with or without crabmeat. There's something for everyone on the generous menu, which also accommodates more westernized tastes.

If it's a traditional banquet you crave, call ahead to arrange it with the restaurant, then round up a group of friends for a multicourse feast. This isn't your average take-out joint—its food and décor rise well above the standard.

Spigolo

043 **Italian** XX

1561 Second Ave. (at 81st St.)

Subway: 86 St (Lexington Ave.)

Sun - Mon & Thurs - Sat dinner only

Phone: 212-744-1100

Web: www.spigolo.net

Prices: $$

Even at the beginning of the week, this sliver of a dining room is packed. The draw? Upper East Siders want to be among the lucky few (there are less than 20 tables) to relish the inspired Italian cooking at Spigolo.

Husband-and-wife team Scott and Heather Fratangelo met at the Union Square Café before opening this place. Food and wine are like religion here, and Scott pays serious attention to quality. Unusual yet rustic presentations, such as hake *acqua pazza* (served in a tomato-and-fish-based broth made with garlic and hot chile) are a sure bet, while more familiar dishes like light sheep's-milk-ricotta gnocchi with cream and pancetta are crowd pleasers. Heather plays the charming hostess when she's not whipping up delectable pastries.

Sushi of Gari ✿

044 — Japanese

402 E. 78th St. (bet. First & York Aves.)

Subway: 77 St — Tue – Sun dinner only
Phone: 212-517-5340
Web: www.sushiofgari.com
Prices: $$$

Sushi of Gari

Nestled on a quiet street, Sushi of Gari is named for its genius chef, Masatoshi "Gari" Sugio. Sushi connoisseurs, including devoted regulars, know that the innovative sushi and sashimi here—rich with ingredients flown in from Japan—is well worth a detour.

For a piece of the action, belly up to the sushi bar, where the expert chefs will explain each ingredient and tailor your *omakase* (tasting menu) to your liking. If you prefer table seating, head for the two small, sparsely furnished dining rooms.

If you choose the omakase, be prepared to spend a bundle. Rest assured though, from red snapper with fried lotus root to toothsome squid with sea urchin sauce, a succession of fantastic and distinctive signature dishes will enchant your senses. The food here remains consistent and creative, and the chefs will feed you, piece by piece, until you say "uncle."

Appetizers

- Bluefin Tuna with Creamy Tofu Sauce
- Salmon with Sautéed Tomato and Onion Sauce
- Miso-marinated Kanpachi with Daikon, Mint Paste and Garlic

Entrées

- Torched Yari-Squid with Creamy Sea Urchin Sauce
- "Shabu Shabu" Snow Crab with Yuzu Sauce
- Herb-marinated Lobster with Mo-Jio

Desserts

- Tempura Ice Cream with Strawberry Sauce
- Yuzu Panna Cotta

Sushi Sasabune

Japanese ✕

401 E. 73rd St. (at First Ave.)

Subway: 77 St
Phone: 212-249-8583
Web: N/A
Prices: $$$

Mon – Fri lunch & dinner
Sat dinner only

This third outpost of the Sasabune family is paradise for sushi devotees who appreciate top quality with a palatable price tag.
Since Sasabune only offers sushi *omakase*, or chef's tasting, it's not the place for newcomers or picky eaters. In fact, the restaurant posts a sign stating "No Spicy Tuna. No California Roll. TRUST ME," so those hankering for tempura should steer clear. However, true sushi lovers will delight in a parade of sparkling flavors and textures, from the albacore sashimi and briny oysters with citrus soy sauce to the blue-crab hand roll with toasted nori and creamy filling.
At times, there may be a wait for a seat in the small dining room, but the chefs will make up for it with gracious service and wonderful sushi.

Sushi Seki

Japanese ✕✕

1143 First Ave. (bet. 62nd & 63rd Sts.)

Subway: Lexington Av - 59 St
Phone: 212-371-0238
Web: N/A
Prices: $$$

Mon – Sat dinner only

A longtime neighborhood favorite, Seki is all about sushi, and the quality is just terrific. It can be a tough reservation to get, as the restaurant is both popular and small, but it's worth the advance booking to sample creations of the namesake chef, who once worked in the kitchen at Sushi of Gari.
In the modest dining rooms, the waitstaff keeps up a steady tempo, while at the sushi bar, chefs craft fresh-from-the-boat products into tasty morsels. Regulars know to ask about the unique chef's sushi and daily specials that aren't on the menu, but even the spicy-tuna set is well-fed here.
Late hours accommodate revelers who hanker for sushi after most places have closed. If you want first-rate sushi to go, Seki offers takeout.

Taco Taco

Mexican

1726 Second Ave. (bet. 89th & 90th Sts.)

Subway: 86 St (Lexington Ave.)
Phone: 212-289-8226
Web: N/A
Prices:

Lunch & dinner daily

If you're lucky enough to live within its delivery zone, chances are you've enjoyed a meal from Taco Taco, but this colorful Mexican restaurant isn't just for take-out.

Authentic Mexican and Tex-Mex dishes are some of the best in the city, and the prices here are as palatable as the food. Come hungry and tuck into everything from quesadillas served up Mexico City-style to huevos rancheros. Tacos are the house specialty; either the fried-fish taco or the "taco taco" (shredded pork cooked in a chipotle sauce) is sure to please.

You'll find many of the elements—tableside guacamole, a full bar offering tasty margaritas and many varieties of tequila—popular at pricier Mexican restaurants, but this neighborhood spot keeps it real.

Taste

American

1411 Third Ave. (at 80th St.)

Subway: 77 St
Phone: 212-717-9798
Web: www.elizabar.com
Prices: $$

Lunch & dinner daily

Youngest son of the founders of Zabar's (New York's landmark West Side deli), Eli Zabar launched his second fresh-food market, Eli's, in 1998. Taste is adjacent to the market, a restaurant devised to pair small plates and changing entrées with Eli's favorite regional wines.

Drop in after work to sample affordable wines by the glass, and be sure to order something (like roasted eggplant and tomato tart or baby burgers on brioche) to nosh on. Dinner and brunch are full-service with appealing American cooking that's always full of flavor. At breakfast and lunch the setting is more relaxed and food is presented cafeteria-style. The menu always represents the tasty, home-style fare Eli's is known for—cooked better at his place than yours.

Tori Shin

Japanese XX

1193 First Ave. (bet. 64th & 65th Sts.)

Subway: 68 St — Dinner daily
Phone: 212-988-8408
Web: N/A
Prices: $$$

From the outside this place doesn't look like much, but the sign reading "Authentic Japanese Food Culture" is your first indication that this team isn't fooling around. The sophisticated crowd of aficionados here reserves a seat at the counter, in order to catch the chefs in action.
You'll quickly find that this isn't your average yakitori and beer joint. The kitchen uses top-quality chicken and expertly seasons and grills every part of the bird from heart to skin. The chefs will adjust your menu upon request, but be open to necks or livers as they might turn out to be your favorites.
Note that before 10pm only fixed menus are offered. These include a dinner set and an *omakase,* and are truly the best way to sample the fare here.

Trata Estiatorio

Greek XX

1331 Second Ave. (bet. 70th & 71st Sts.)

Subway: 68 St - Hunter College — Lunch & dinner daily
Phone: 212-535-3800
Web: www.trata.com
Prices: $$$

Everything about this bright trattoria will remind you of the sea, from the crisp blue-and-white façade to the stone-washed white walls and the colorful mosaics of sea life above the bar. The design lures a fashionable clientele who also frequent its sister in the Hamptons.
With the Greek Islands as a theme and fresh seafood displayed on ice by the open kitchen, what else would you expect but a daily changing list of fruits of the sea? Whole fish from around the globe are the house specialty; fresh catches like Alaskan Arctic char and African tiger shrimp are charcoal-grilled and priced per pound. Go for lunch if you want a bargain.
Don't overlook the wine list here; many Greek varietals are cited with descriptions of their characteristics.

Triangolo

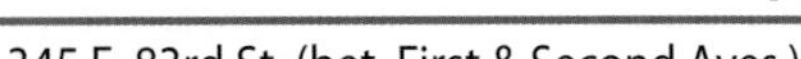

Italian

051

345 E. 83rd St. (bet. First & Second Aves.)

Subway: 86 St (Lexington Ave.) — Dinner daily
Phone: 212-472-4488
Web: www.triangolorestaurant.com
Prices: $$

Although it's tucked away off the beaten track of upscale shops and world-class museums, Triangolo nonetheless keeps customers lining up outside. Why? Attentive service might be one reason. The warm décor in the simple dining room is another.

The greatest draw, though, is the generous menu of pastas, topped with hearty homemade sauces; *rotolo di pasta montanara* (rolled pasta filled with spinach, porcini and parmesan) is one of the signature dishes. Of course, you won't want to dive into the pastas without first sampling something from the long list of antipasti. And, by all means, save room for the tasty tiramisu.

Reasonable prices make one more reason why Triangolo might just be better than dining at your Italian grandmother's house.

Uva

Italian

052

1486 Second Ave. (bet. 77th & 78th Sts.)

Subway: 77 St — Mon – Fri dinner only
Phone: 212-472-4552 — Sat – Sun lunch & dinner
Web: www.uvawinebarnewyork.com
Prices: $$

You'd never guess that this intimate little wine bar, with its mixed crowd, lively ambience, and impressive wine list (*uva* is Italian for "grape") was related to Lusardi's, an Italian stalwart in the Upper East. In Uva's rustic, dimly lit dining room, the friendly Italian staff wends their way around the tightly spaced tables, delivering plates and offering advice about the wine and food.

Surprisingly good cuisine, served in generous portions at reasonable prices, is a far cry from the generic Italian-American standards. Instead, Uva's menu encompasses a creative selection of house-made pastas, entrées, cheeses and cured meats. There always seems to be a crush at the bar, where patrons can taste more than 30 wines by the glass.

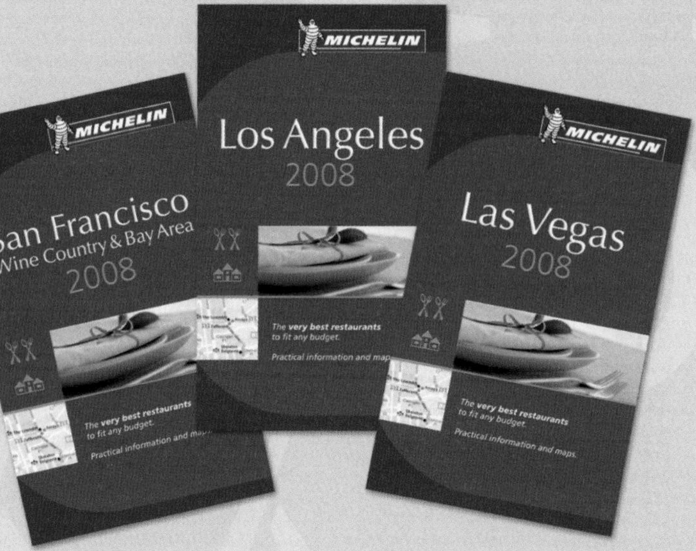
MICHELIN
San Francisco
Wine Country & Bay Area
2008
The very best restaurants
to fit any budget.
MICHELIN
Los Angeles
2008
The very best restaurants
to fit any budget.
Practical information and maps
MICHELIN
Las Vegas
2008
The very best restaurants
to fit any budget.
Practical information and maps.

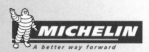

Upper West Side

Great cultural institutions and good food are what you can expect from the Upper West Side, along with tidy rows of restored brownstones and stunning apartment buildings bordering Central Park. Reaching from Central Park West to the Hudson River between 59th Street and 110th Street, the Upper West Side is home to the **Lincoln Center for the Performing Arts** and the **American Museum of Natural History**. This neighborhood is also where you'll run into some of the city's favorite food markets, such as Zabar's *(80th St. & Broadway)*, a family-run New York institution for more than 75 years.

A Bit of History

Development has been relatively recent in this neighborhood. In the late 19th century, shantytowns, saloons and stray goats populated the area. This all changed in 1884 when Henry Hardenbergh built New York's first luxury apartment house—the celebrated **Dakota**—at 1 West 72nd Street. With its eclectic turrets, Gothic gables and ornate finials, the Dakota made a fitting setting for the 1968 film *Rosemary's Baby*. Over the years, the Dakota housed many celebrities, including Leonard Bernstein, Lauren Bacall and John Lennon, who was shot outside the 72nd Street entrance by a crazed fan in 1980.

After the Dakota came the ornate **Ansonia Hotel** *(2101-2119 Broadway)* and the elegant **San Remo** *(145 Central Park West)*, with its stunning Central Park views. These sumptuous digs appealed to bankers, lawyers and other well-to-do professionals, who were followed in the 1930s by prosperous Jewish families relocating from the Lower East Side.

Gentrification of the older row houses has made the cross streets desirable, particularly among young professionals and college students. Today the Upper West Side's tree-lined residential blocks provide a quiet contrast to the bustle of Broadway, the area's commercial spine.

Brigitta L. House/ MICHELIN

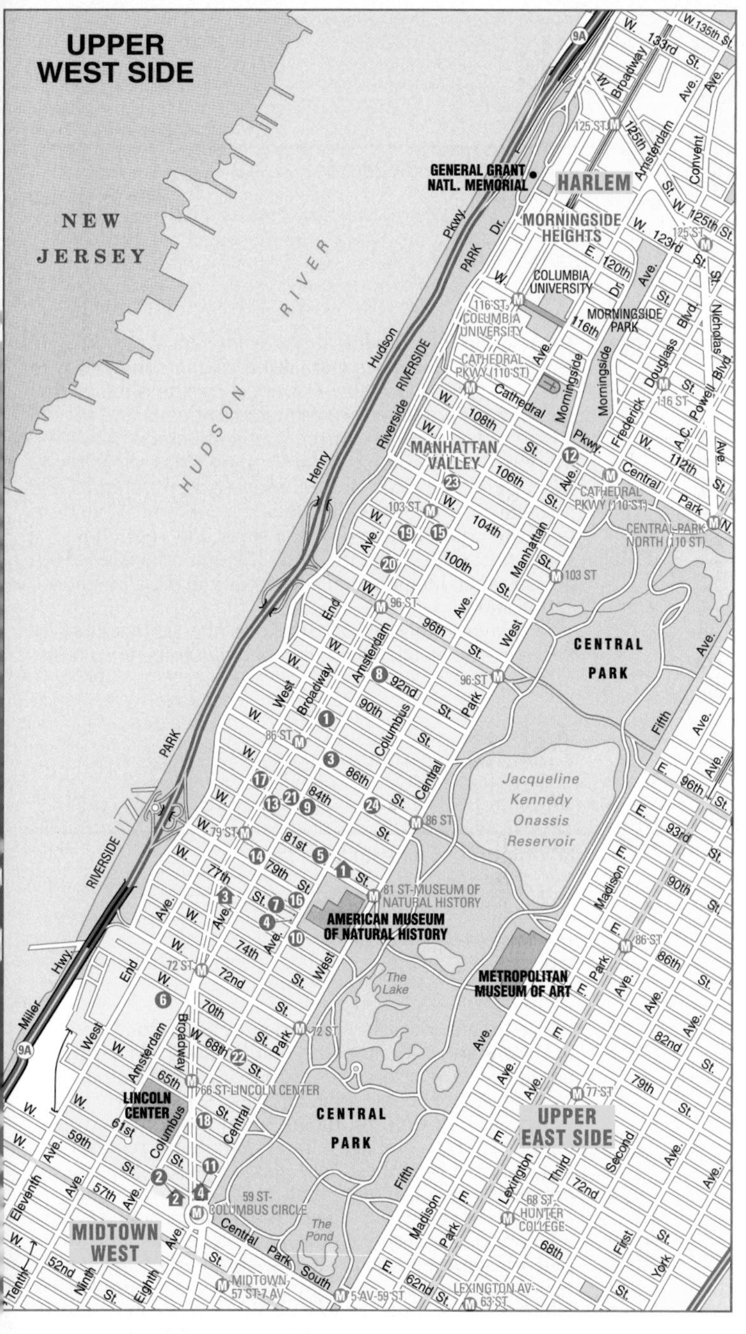
UPPER WEST SIDE
NEW JERSEY
HUDSON RIVER
GENERAL GRANT NATL. MEMORIAL
HARLEM
MORNINGSIDE HEIGHTS
COLUMBIA UNIVERSITY
MORNINGSIDE PARK
MANHATTAN VALLEY
CENTRAL PARK
Jacqueline Kennedy Onassis Reservoir
AMERICAN MUSEUM OF NATURAL HISTORY
METROPOLITAN MUSEUM OF ART
The Lake
LINCOLN CENTER
The Pond
UPPER EAST SIDE
MIDTOWN WEST
125 ST
116 ST-COLUMBIA UNIVERSITY
CATHEDRAL PKWY (110 ST)
116 ST
CENTRAL PARK NORTH (110 ST)
103 ST
96 ST
86 ST
79 ST
81 ST-MUSEUM OF NATURAL HISTORY
72 ST
66 ST-LINCOLN CENTER
59 ST-COLUMBUS CIRCLE
MIDTOWN 57 ST-7 AV
5 AV-59 ST
LEXINGTON AV-63 ST
68 ST-HUNTER COLLEGE
77 ST
Henry Hudson Pkwy.
RIVERSIDE PARK
Riverside Dr.
Miller Hwy.
Broadway
Amsterdam Ave.
Columbus Ave.
West End Ave.
Central Park West
Manhattan Ave.
Morningside Ave.
Cathedral Pkwy.
Central Park South
Central Park North
Fifth Ave.
Madison Ave.
Park Ave.
Lexington Ave.
Third Ave.
Second Ave.
First Ave.
York Ave.
Eleventh Ave.
Tenth
Ninth
Eighth Ave.
Frederick Douglass Blvd.
A.C. Powell Blvd.
St. Nicholas Ave.
Convent Ave.
W. 135th St.
W. 133rd St.
W. 125th St.
W. 123rd St.
W. 120th St.
W. 116th St.
W. 112th St.
W. 108th St.
W. 106th St.
W. 104th St.
W. 100th St.
W. 96th St.
W. 92nd St.
W. 90th St.
W. 86th St.
W. 84th St.
W. 81st St.
W. 79th St.
W. 77th St.
W. 74th St.
W. 72nd St.
W. 70th St.
W. 68th St.
W. 65th St.
W. 61st St.
W. 59th St.
W. 57th St.
W. 52nd St.
E. 96th St.
E. 93rd St.
E. 90th St.
E. 86th St.
E. 82nd St.
E. 79th St.
E. 72nd St.
E. 68th St.
E. 62nd St.
9A

Aix

001 **French** XX

2398 Broadway (at 88th St.)

Subway: 86 St (Broadway) — Mon – Sat dinner only
Phone: 212-874-7400 — Sun lunch & dinner
Web: www.aixnyc.com
Prices: $$$

To describe the cooking at Aix as Provençal would send any French culinary traditionalist crying into their copy of *Larousse Gastronomique*. Provençal cuisine is merely the jumping-off point for this restaurant's original and playful takes on the best dishes from southern France.

Modern yet classic pastas and sandwiches share menu space with the likes of parmesan-crusted daurade and roasted duck breast with Alsatian sauerkraut. Selections from the grill are served with a smile and your choice of sauce and sides. Even the brunch menu retains a French accent, often including quiche, crêpes, and Gallic-infused egg dishes.

The split-level dining space reflects the vibrant hues of Provence. Sidewalk tables are much requested in summer.

Asiate

002 **Fusion** XXX

80 Columbus Circle (at 60th St.)

Subway: 59 St - Columbus Circle — Lunch & dinner daily
Phone: 212-805-8881
Web: www.mandarinoriental.com
Prices: $$$$

Asiate reigns over the city from its 35th-floor aerie in the Mandarin Oriental *(see hotel listing)*. Wrap-around windows showcase breathtaking views of Central Park, making Asiate a top spot for view seekers. Thanks to designer Tony Chi, the dining room has a modern feel, capped off by a ceiling of transparent tubes representing stylized tree branches. Two glass-enclosed walls by the entrance showcase more than 1,300 bottles of wine.

Headed by Noriyuki Sugie, the kitchen staff fashions adventurous cuisine (tuna and fluke sashimi on a bed of seaweed salad; curry-crusted Ahi tuna with a risotto croquette) with an exotic, yet approachable allure. Discreet and professional servers cater equally well to business people, hotel guests and tourists.

Barney Greengrass

Deli

541 Amsterdam Ave. (at 86th St.)

Subway: 86 St (Lexington Ave.) — Tue – Sun lunch only
Phone: 212-724-4707
Web: www.barneygreengrass.com
Prices:

Open since 1908, Barney Greengrass is a New York institution. This Upper West Side eatery offers a slice of history with its Jewish comfort food. Old-fashioned décor, which wears the patina of time, includes Formica-topped tables. While this might put off style seekers, those who appreciate real deli food keep coming back for more.

Matzoh ball soup and hearty chopped liver are just like your Bubbie used to make, and deli sandwiches, piled high with thinly sliced meats and cheeses, are among the best in the city. Ignore the servers' attitude and don't forget to save room for a big, crunchy pickle.

The restaurant is open until 4pm weekdays and 5pm on weekends, but the store remains open until 6pm if you're taking your comfort food to go.

Café Frida

Mexican

368 Columbus Ave. (bet. 77th & 78th Sts.)

Subway: 81 St - Museum of Natural History — Lunch & dinner daily
Phone: 212-712-2929
Web: www.cafefrida.com
Prices: $$

From its bright walls to its inspired and authentic cuisine, Café Frida turns your perception of the average Mexican restaurant on its head. Classic regional dishes, including seasonal specialties, are a far cry from the fried chimichangas and sizzling fajitas often associated with standard Mexican establishments. The kitchen isn't afraid to turn up the heat in many of the dishes, including the *papatdzules*, chicken-filled tortillas topped with a flavorful green pumpkin-seed sauce. From pan-seared duck breast to marinated lamb shanks, the menu manages to stay upscale without being fussy.

Colorful walls and traditional furnishings transport visitors to sunny Mexico, and while the approach to service is casual, the staff is friendly and helpful.

Calle Ocho

446 Columbus Ave. (bet. 81st & 82nd Sts.)

Subway: 81 St - Museum of Natural History
Phone: 212-873-5025
Web: www.calleochonyc.com
Prices: $$

Mon – Sat dinner only
Sun lunch & dinner

Looking for good food and good fun? You've come to the right place. Calle Ocho pulls in the partyers with its winning mix of salsa music, potent caipirinhas and mojitos, and zesty food—borrowing influences from Argentina to Puerto Rico and from Cuba to Peru. Named for the bustling main drag in Miami's Little Havana neighborhood, Calle Ocho (Spanish for "Eighth Street") is always jumping.

The 200-seat dining room sets the tone for a good tim with the vivid Cuban-themed mural that lines one wall, and the bold cuisine follows suit by balancing such ingredients as chipotles, calabaza squash, yuccas and plantains. Your taste buds will salsa after enjoying dishes like jerk pork chop, banana-leaf-wrapped snapper and panela-glazed salmon.

Compass

Contemporary XX

006

208 W. 70th St. (bet. Amsterdam & West End Aves.)

Subway: 72 St (Broadway)
Phone: 212-875-8600
Web: www.compassrestaurant.com
Prices: $$

Mon – Sat dinner only
Sun lunch & dinner

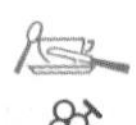

Head North-Northwest from Midtown and point yourself in the direction of Compass. Slate-covered square pillars, marble floors, bright-red high-backed banquettes, and modern artwork combine with subtle, recessed lighting to create a décor that oozes urban sophistication.

Not far from Lincoln Center, Compass makes a great spot for a pre- or post-theater nosh, or a cocktail at the popular bar. You can order from the à la carte menu (think Maine lobster bolognese; terrine of foie gras with candied cocoa nibs) or choose from two appetizers, two entrées and two desserts on the reasonably priced prix-fixe menu. There's also a seasonal chef's tasting.

Stored behind frosted glass, the impressive wine collection is well worth investigating.

Gari

007 Japanese

370 Columbus Ave. (bet. 77th & 78th Sts.)

Subway: 81 St - Museum of Natural History — Dinner daily
Phone: 212-362-4816
Web: N/A
Prices: $$$

At Gari, the Upper West Side chi-chi sister of Sushi of Gari *(402 E. 78th St.)*, it's not just about the sushi. It's about the combination of the Zen-like ambience and upscale crowd, the preparation and presentation of the fish, and the ritual of eating it. This location of Gari is also known for it's elegant cooked items such as seared foie gras and beef short ribs, but to miss out on Gari's impeccably fresh sushi—especially the *omakase* showcasing the chef's creations—is, after all, to miss the point. Either way, the wide menu is a sure crowd pleaser and the dining room perpetually busy as a result.

The communal setting alongside, rather than facing, the sushi bar provides the best seats in the house for watching the masters at work.

Gennaro 

008 Italian

665 Amsterdam Ave. (bet. 92nd & 93rd Sts.)

Subway: 96 St (Broadway) — Dinner daily
Phone: 212-665-5348
Web: www.gennarorestaurant.com
Prices: $$

New York may be known for its high-priced cuisine, but you don't always need a thick wallet to afford a rewarding meal. Gennaro is proof of that. Set on an unassuming stretch of Amsterdam Ave., this place delivers fantastic food at a palatable price.

Diners pack the tiny restaurant, but everyone is in such a good mood that the close quarters never seem to matter. The cavalcade of Italian classics is surely the reason for their smiles—everything from the grilled octopus appetizer and fresh mussel-topped bucatini to the warm pear tart is sensational. Many of the dishes, including the wonderful pasta specials, reflect a Sicilian heritage.

The wine list offers an exceptional selection of bottles, with half of the list priced under $30.

Good Enough to Eat

American

483 Amsterdam Ave. (bet. 83rd & 84th Sts.)

Subway: 79 St — Lunch & dinner daily
Phone: 212-496-0163
Web: www.goodenoughtoeat.com
Prices: $$

Comfort food, home cooking: call it what you want, it still means food like mom used to make. During the day, this cute little place is known for its bountiful breakfasts (they serve light lunches, too). At night it morphs into a cozy, full-service restaurant serving up ample portions of perennial favorites—meatloaf, pumpkin pie and turkey dinner with all the trimmings—that really hit the spot when you're tired of trendy.

Sweet-natured servers deliver your order in a scene out of a Norman Rockwell painting, complete with folk art, quilts and antiques; there's even a white picket fence outside. The case of homemade cakes may remind you so much of home that, after a meal here, you'll be tempted to ask chef/owner Carrie Levin to adopt you.

Isabella's

Mediterranean

359 Columbus Ave. (at 77th St.)

Subway: 79 St — Lunch & dinner daily
Phone: 212-724-2100
Web: www.brguestrestaurants.com
Prices: $$

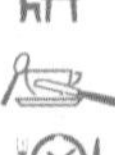

With its appealing location, friendly staff and broad menu, Isabella's maintains a genuine neighborhood feel. It should—the restaurant has been attracting a loyal following for more than fifteen years. One of the few places that's open for lunch in this part of town, Isabella's makes a great spot to take a break if you're touring the nearby Museum of Natural History. In summer, the airy bi-level dining space with its wicker chairs and French doors adds a pleasant outdoor terrace.

The menu leans to the Mediterranean, offering the likes of chicken, pasta and fish but also includes the usual crowd pleaser salads and sandwiches. Drop by Sunday for the popular brunch, or have a late lunch or early dinner from the sunset menu (from 4pm to 5:30pm).

Jean Georges ✿✿✿

011 **Contemporary** XXXX

1 Central Park West (bet. 60th & 61st Sts.)

Subway: 59 St - Columbus Circle Lunch & dinner daily
Phone: 212-299-3900
Web: www.jean-georges.com
Prices: $$$$

Jean-Georges Management

Jean-Georges Vongerichten owns a galaxy of restaurants in New York City, but this one shines above the rest. On the ground floor of the Trump International Hotel, Jean-Georges wraps its space with huge window walls looking out on Columbus Circle. Adam Tihany sculpted the minimalist geometric motif, orchestrating the interior lighting to mimic natural light at different times of the day. Extraordinary marriages of flavors and textures surprise in each course, and sublime ingredients are transformed by the hand of a master. Tender morsels of squab might be accompanied by Asian pear, candied tamarind, microgreens and orange jus, or red snapper crusted with crushed nuts, seeds and coriander. For quality and value, go for the prix-fixe lunch menu.
Adjacent to the dining room, casual Nougatine cafe serves breakfast, lunch and dinner sans the formality or the hefty price tag.

Appetizers

- Bluefin Ribbons, Avocado, Spicy Radish, Ginger Marinade
- Goat Cheese Royale, Beet Marmalade, Crushed Pistachios
- Sea Scallops, Caramelized Cauliflower, Caper-Raisin Emulsion

Entrées

- Black Bass Crusted with Nuts and Seeds, Sweet and Sour Jus
- Red Snapper, Lily Bulb-Radish Salad, White Sesame, Lavender
- Smoked Squab à l'Orange, Asian Pear, Candied Tamarind

Desserts

- A Composition of Four Different Seasonal Desserts
- A Composition of Four Different Chocolate Desserts
- A Composition of Four Different Exotic Fruit Desserts

Miss Mamie's Spoonbread Too

Southern

012

366 W. 110th St./Cathedral Pkwy.
(bet. Columbus & Manhattan Aves.)

Subway: Cathedral Pkwy (110 St) — Lunch & dinner daily
Phone: 212-865-6744
Web: www.spoonbreadinc.com
Prices: ⚭

Columbia students in search of Southern-style cooking count on Miss Mamie's for finger-licking-good vittles. A country-diner décor highlighted by yellow Formica tables, yellow and red checkered floors, and vintage kitchen utensils takes guests back to the 1950s.
Southern fried chicken is a stand-out, its juicy meat covered in a crispy deep-fried coating, but don't overlook the daily specials on the blackboard. Side dishes include Dixie favorites like black-eyed peas and collard greens. Of course, you can't leave Miss Mamie's without a taste of the red velvet cake slathered in white cream frosting—or a cup of dark, cinnamon-scented coffee, one of the best deals in town at only $1.
Check out Harlem sister, Miss Maude's, at 547 Lenox Avenue.

Nëo Sushi

Japanese

013

2298 Broadway (at 83rd St.)

Subway: 86 St (Broadway) — Dinner daily
Phone: 212-769-1003
Web: www.neosushi.com
Prices: $$$

You'll recognize Nëo Sushi by all the framed accolades that hang in the restaurant's window at the corner of Broadway and 83rd Street. But don't take someone else's word for it; step inside the minimalistic space and see for yourself.
Organized according to "Special Cold Dishes," hot items "From the Kitchen," and "Nëo Fusion" (à la carte sushi, rolls and tempura), New Age takes on Japanese cuisine are highlighted by unique sauces (chipotle sauce for an oyster roll; blueberry vinaigrette for sea bass) that set this place apart. Count on signature dishes, including lobster mango salad, baby shrimp tempura bites, and fluke with ponzu sauce, for a sure bet.
Note to the budget-minded: dinner here can add up to the triple digits before you know it.

Nice Matin

Mediterranean

201 W. 79th St. (at Amsterdam Ave.)

Subway: 79 St — Lunch & dinner daily
Phone: 212-873-6423
Web: www.nicematinnyc.com
Prices: $$

Named after the daily newspaper published in the major city on France's Côte d'Azur, Nice Matin transports diners to the sun-drenched Mediterranean coast.

Niçoise dishes here exhibit as many vibrant colors as appear in the room's luminous décor. Done up as a French cafe, the place asserts its unique personality by avoiding all the decorative clichés you find in many Gallic-style restaurants; lights dangle from the tops of high pillars that spread umbrella-like against the ceiling, and tables sport Formica tops.

The menu, like a tanned French lothario, wanders the wider Mediterranean region for its inspiration. *Plats du jour (moules Provençal* on Monday, old-fashioned roast duck on Saturday) bring fans in on specific days of the week.

Noche Mexicana

Mexican

852 Amsterdam Ave. (bet. 101st & 102nd Sts.)

Subway: 103 St (Broadway) — Lunch & dinner daily
Phone: 212-662-6900
Web: www.noche-mexicana.com
Prices:

Tucked in between small restaurants and bodegas, Noche Mexicana is a great find. Bright and cheery, the restaurant's walls are papered with posters of artwork by Diego Rivera.

The dining room is small, but authentic Mexican food is the real focus here, where an engaging staff with a warm spirit attends to guests. The *taco de lengua* may be messy, but the tender, tasty beef tongue dressed with cilantro, onions and tomatoes, and wrapped in corn tortillas, is worth the laundry bill. You won't go wrong with the great tamales, tingas or the *taco cesina* (filled with preserved beef). If you like your food *caliente*, make sure to request it spicy.

Grab a seat in the back of the restaurant, where you can watch those delicious tamales being made.

Ocean Grill

Seafood XXX

016

384 Columbus Ave. (bet. 78th & 79th Sts.)

Subway: 79 St — Lunch & dinner daily
Phone: 212-579-2300
Web: www.brguestrestaurants.com
Prices: $$

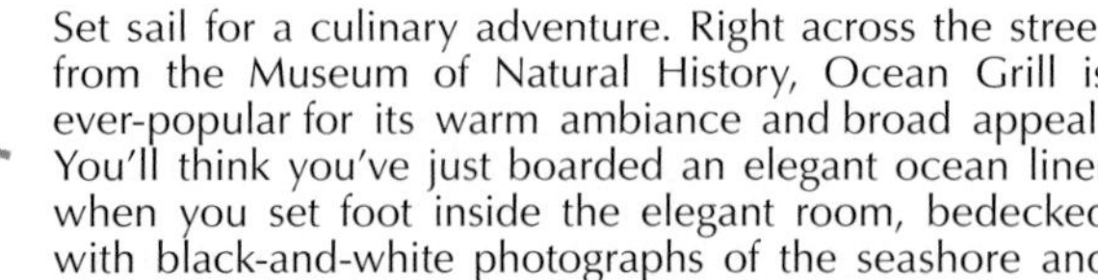

Set sail for a culinary adventure. Right across the street from the Museum of Natural History, Ocean Grill is ever-popular for its warm ambiance and broad appeal. You'll think you've just boarded an elegant ocean liner when you set foot inside the elegant room, bedecked with black-and-white photographs of the seashore and porthole windows peeking in on the kitchen.

You'll find something for every fish lover here, whether it's a plate of oysters from the raw bar, simply grilled fish, Maine lobster or maki rolls. And be sure to sample one of the scrumptious desserts (perhaps a lemon meringue tart, or the house chocolate fondue). Egg dishes, pancakes and French toast compete with crab cakes and caviar at the popular weekend brunch.

Ouest

Contemporary XXX

017

2315 Broadway (bet. 83rd & 84th Sts.)

Subway: 86 St (Broadway) — Mon – Sat dinner only; Sun lunch & dinner
Phone: 212-580-8700
Web: www.ouestny.com
Prices: $$$

This polished restaurant from chef Tom Valenti draws celebrities, media moguls and neighborhood denizens alike. Past the perennially busy bar, you'll reach the large room at the back, which peers into the open kitchen. Bring some friends so you'll be more likely to snag one of the terrific circular booths covered in deep-red tufted leather. Low lighting turns Ouest into a romantic spot for dinner, while green-apple martinis and poached eggs with house-smoked duck star at the lively weekend brunch.

Behind the stoves, a veritable army of chefs riffs on American comfort food, resulting in dishes (such as prosciutto-wrapped halibut with mashed Yukon potatoes and pickled asparagus) that are high on originality and strong on presentation.

Picholine ✿✿

018 Mediterranean XXXX

35 W. 64th St. (bet. Broadway & Central Park West)

Subway: 66 St-Lincoln Center — Dinner daily
Phone: 212-724-8585
Web: www.picholinenyc.com
Prices: $$$

Picholine

Elegant older sister to Artisanal—chef/proprietor Terrance Brennan's Murray Hill brasserie—Picholine pulls in a cadre of smartly dressed regulars who come for Brennan's sophisticated Mediterranean cuisine. A major facelift in fall 2006 has re-made this staid beauty in sleek tones of lilac, cream and gray.

The menu, too, has been updated, but it still features the best products (squab, pea shoots, blood oranges, Maine lobster) that each season brings to bear. Picholine strikes gold with signatures such as sea urchin panna cotta or wild mushroom risotto, which stand out as much for their elegance as for their surprising counterpoints in texture and flavor. Don't pass up the cheese course—it's one of the best in the city thanks to Brennan's custom-designed Artisanal Cheese Center.

Early evenings here can be frantic; if you can't get a table, go for a seat at the new wine bar.

Appetizers

- Sea Urchin Panna Cotta, Ocean Consommé, Caviar
- "Bacon and Eggs", Polenta, Tuna Bacon, Truffle Toasts
- Maine Lobster, Caramelized Endive, Kumquat, Vanilla Brown Butter

Entrées

- Heirloom Chicken "Kiev", Braised Mushrooms, Liquid Foie Gras
- Hand-harvested Sea Scallops, Blood Orange Grenobloise
- Red-legged Partridge, Tokyo Turnips, Foie Gras Sabayon

Desserts

- Caramel Apple Brioche, Apple Salad, Salted Caramel Ice Cream
- Chocolate Soufflé, Peanut Butter Sorbet, Malt Foam
- Pear "Torchon", Chocolate Soup, Confiture de Lait Sorbet

PicNic Market & Café

American

2665 Broadway (bet. 101st & 102nd Sts.)

Subway: 103 St (Broadway) — Lunch & dinner daily
Phone: 212-222-8222
Web: www.picnicmarket.com
Prices: $$

Close to Columbia University, this cafe grew out of a picnic-basket business that catered to Central Park concertgoers. Fans can now enjoy heartier meals in the pleasant room, decorated with a colorful mural by Peter Marks. Daily specials add to the short menu of main courses such as coq au vin, steak au poivre, and pan-fried trout. Salmon tartare with ginger vinaigrette, and crostini topped with plump calamari make good places to start.
Everyone from Columbia professors to Upper West Side families gathers here, and the neighborhood regulars are chummy with the chef and the waitstaff. Charcuterie, cheese, and salad plates are still available to go, as are the oils, vinegars, coffees and teas displayed on shelves alongside the bar area.

Regional

020

Italian

2607 Broadway (bet. 98th & 99th Sts.)

Subway: 96 St (Broadway) — Mon – Fri dinner only
Phone: 212-666-1915 — Sat – Sun lunch & dinner
Web: N/A
Prices: $$

The area above 96th Street is seeing more and more independent restaurants opening these days, and Regional makes a noteworthy addition to this artsy, academia-oriented neighborhood.
In keeping with its name, the restaurant spotlights specialties from all 20 regions of Italy. Recipes stay true to their geographical origins, with honest fare like *involtini di vitello* (scaloppini of veal stuffed with parmesan and Italian pork sausage) and *pasta al pesto di Trapani* (tossed with fresh tomatoes and a pesto made from almonds and basil) representing the best of each area.
Made in-house, desserts like the wonderful *torta di Capri* (a rich, moist flourless chocolate cake covered with molten chocolate sauce), are worth abandoning your diet for.

Spiga

021 **Italian** XX

200 W. 84th St. (bet. Amsterdam Ave. & Broadway)

Subway: 86 St (Broadway) — Dinner daily
Phone: 212-362-5506
Web: www.spiganyc.com
Prices: $$$

Multiple rich dimensions emerge from unlikely pairings at Spiga. Chef Salvatore Corea suprises diners with his original takes on Italian favorites, as in a pan-roasted breast of duck served over turnip purée with apples, dried fruit and chocolate sauce. Canneloni may be reinvented as sheets of fresh pasta wrapped around baccala purée, while tender, stewed baby squid lie on a bed of soft, white polenta. The short, Italian-focused wine list cites excellent offerings by the glass.

Tucked away on a quiet Upper West Side block, this delightful restaurant nestles tables in every available nook, and its gracious owner gives guests a warm welcome. The peaceful little dining room lies in stark contrast to the bustling vibe created in the kitchen.

Telepan

022 **American** XX

72 W. 69th St. (bet. Central Park West & Columbus Ave.)

Subway: 66 St - Lincoln Center — Wed – Sun lunch & dinner
Phone: 212-580-4300 — Mon – Tue dinner only
Web: www.telepan-ny.com
Prices: $$$

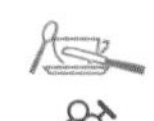

From décor to dishes, Telepan shows off all that is modern American. Located on a quiet Upper West Side block, this restaurant is the culinary child of chef Bill Telepan. Grass-green walls hung with small paintings and large-format photography set a simple tone for the dining room, where closely spaced tables leave little room for privacy. Contemporary American cooking here has generated well-deserved interest, and Telepan has garnered a loyal following for its farm-fresh ingredients. Little fuss and lots of flavor characterize selections like house-smoked brook trout served atop a buckwheat and potato blini accented by tangy sour cream and crunchy black radish.

American, European and New World labels are well represented on the wine list.

Tokyo Pop

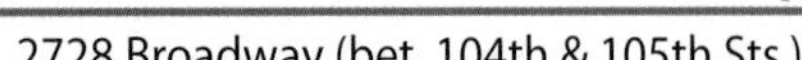

023 **Japanese**

2728 Broadway (bet. 104th & 105th Sts.)

Subway: 103 St (Broadway) Lunch & dinner daily
Phone: 212-932-1000
Web: N/A
Prices: $$

The name says it all at Tokyo Pop, where a burst of bright colors creates a mood-lifting atmosphere. Diners who prefer to have a front-row seat to the action should head straight for the sushi bar, where the chef dazzles with his sharp skills. Sushi figures largely on the menu here, but the entrées are what really show off the chef's talent for combining textures and tastes. Unexpected items, such as the chile lobster roll (lobster tempura and chile peppers wrapped in an edamame "net") and the glazed eggplant dessert, are standouts.

Although Columbia University reigns over the neighborhood, Tokyo Pop is far from a commissary for undergrads. This hip Japanese place can be a bit pricey, but its sushi and Asian-fusion fare is worth the price.

Zeytin

024 **Turkish**

519 Columbus Ave. (at 85th St.)

Subway: 86 St (Central Park West) Lunch & dinner daily
Phone: 212-579-1145
Web: www.zeytinny.com
Prices: $$

Step off the hubbub of Columbus Avenue into Zeytin and step into a sultry world of romantic, purple-hued walls and low lighting. This seductive space is welcoming and intimate—perfect for a date.

Zeytin's traditional Turkish cuisine (the restaurant's name is Turkish for "olive") breathes new life into an area of the Upper West Side formerly dominated by run-of-the-mill restaurants. Ethnic-food lovers should head straight for this place, where intoxicating flavors and textures seduce diners. Eggplant-wrapped veal shank is unbelievably tender, while veal-, mushroom-, and cheese-stuffed pastries *(pachanga borek)* are delicate, yet receive high marks for flavor.

The best part? No passport is required for this culinary journey.

John Peden/ The New York Botanical Garden

The Bronx

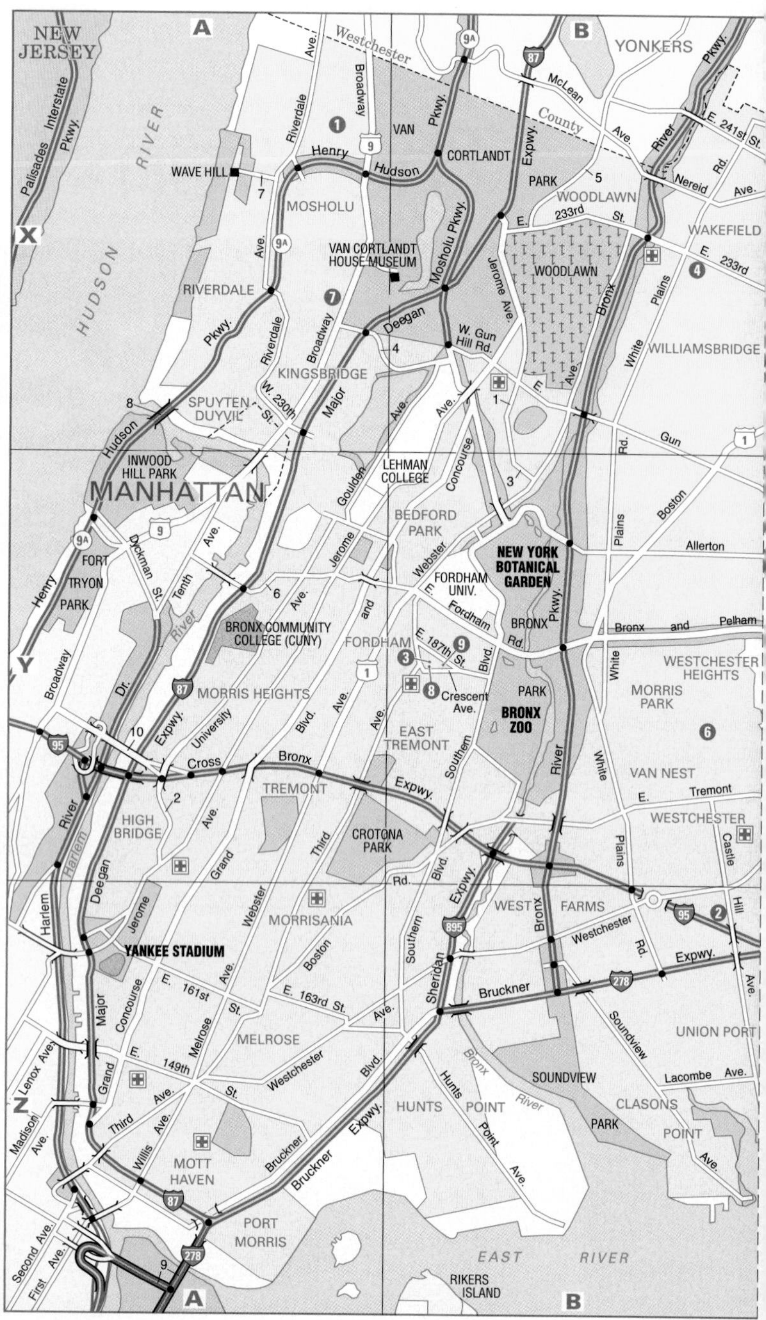
NEW JERSEY
YONKERS
HUDSON RIVER
WAVE HILL
MOSHOLU
VAN CORTLANDT PARK
VAN CORTLANDT HOUSE MUSEUM
RIVERDALE
KINGSBRIDGE
SPUYTEN DUYVIL
WOODLAWN
WAKEFIELD
WILLIAMSBRIDGE
INWOOD HILL PARK
MANHATTAN
LEHMAN COLLEGE
BEDFORD PARK
NEW YORK BOTANICAL GARDEN
FORDHAM UNIV.
FORT TRYON PARK
BRONX COMMUNITY COLLEGE (CUNY)
FORDHAM
BRONX PARK
BRONX ZOO
WESTCHESTER HEIGHTS
MORRIS PARK
MORRIS HEIGHTS
EAST TREMONT
TREMONT
VAN NEST
WESTCHESTER
HIGH BRIDGE
CROTONA PARK
WEST FARMS
MORRISANIA
YANKEE STADIUM
UNION PORT
MELROSE
SOUNDVIEW PARK
CLASONS POINT
HUNTS POINT
MOTT HAVEN
PORT MORRIS
EAST RIVER
RIKERS ISLAND
Cross Bronx Expwy.
Bruckner Expwy.
Major Deegan Expwy.
Bronx River Pkwy.
Henry Hudson Pkwy.
Mosholu Pkwy.
Grand Concourse
Crescent Ave.
E. 187th St.
E. 161st St.
E. 163rd St.
E. 149th St.
E. 233rd St.
E. 241st St.
W. 230th St.
W. Gun Hill Rd.
Westchester County
A
B
X
Y
Z

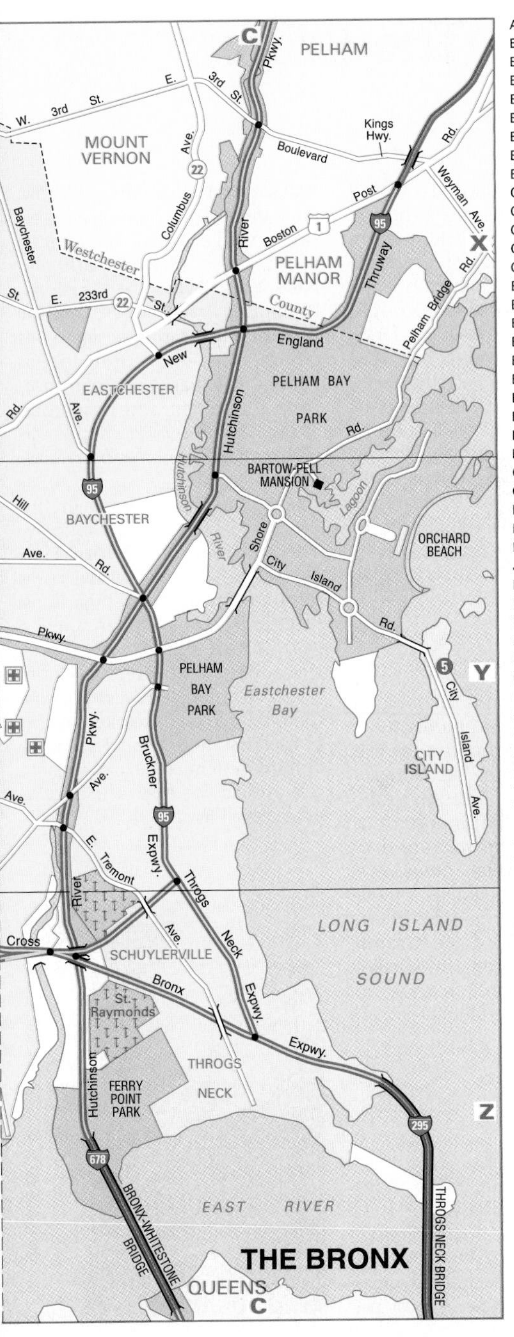

Allerton Ave.	BCY
Bainbridge Ave.	1 BX
Baychester Ave.	CX
Boston Rd.	AZCX
Broadway	AX
Bronx and Pelham Pkwy.	BCY
Bronx River Pkwy.	BXZ
Bruckner Blvd.	AZ
Bruckner Expwy.	AZCY
Castle Hill Ave.	BYZ
City Island Ave.	CY
City Island Rd.	CY
Crescent Ave.	BY
Cross Bronx Expwy.	AYCZ
Edw. L. Grant Hwy.	2 AY
E. Gun Hill Rd.	BXCY
E. Fordham Rd.	ABY
E. Tremont Ave.	BYCZ
E. 149th St.	AZ
E. 161st St.	AZ
E. 163rd St.	AZ
E. 204th St.	3 BY
E. 233rd St.	BCX
E. 241st St.	BX
Goulden Ave.	ABXY
Grand Blvd. and Concourse	ABXZ
Henry Hudson Pkwy.	ABXY
Hunts Point Ave.	BZ
Hutchinson River Pkwy.	CXZ
Jerome Ave.	AZBX
Major Deegan Expwy.	AZBX
Melrose Ave.	AZ
Mosholu Pkwy.	BX
Nereid Ave.	BX
New England Thruway	CX
Pelham Bridge Rd.	CX
Riverdale Ave.	AX
Sheridan Expwy.	BZY
Shore Rd.	CXY
Soundview Ave.	BZ
Southern Blvd.	BYZ
Third Ave.	ABYZ
Throgs Neck Expwy.	CYZ
University Ave.	AY
Van Cortlandt Park South	4 ABX
Van Cortlandt Park East	5 BX
Webster Ave.	ABXZ
Westchester Ave.	AZCY
W. Fordham Rd.	6 AY
W. 230th St.	AX
W. 252nd St.	7 AX
W. Gun Hill Rd.	BX
White Plains Rd.	BXZ
Willis Ave.	AZ

BRIDGES

Bronx-Whitestone Bridge	CZ
Henry Hudson Bridge	8 AX
Throgs Neck Bridge	CZ
Triborough Bridge	9 AZ
Washington Bridge	10 AY

The Bronx

The only borough attached to the mainland, the Bronx is marked by contrasts. Run-down apartment buildings and massive housing projects characterize the southern part of the borough, although, in recent years, funds have been allocated to make the area more livable. To the north, grand mansions and lush gardens fill prosperous sections such as Riverdale and Fieldston. Thanks to journalist John Mullaly, who led a movement in the late 1800s to buy inexpensive parcels of land and preserve them as parks, 25 percent of the Bronx today consists of parkland.

A Bit of History

Named after Jonas Bronck, a Swede who settled here in 1639, the borough developed in the late 1800s. In 1904, the first subway line connecting the Bronx to the island of Manhattan opened, causing significant migration to this outlying borough. Grand Art Deco apartment buildings sprang up along the wide tree-lined thoroughfare called the **Grand Concourse**, attracting Jews from Eastern and Central Europe; a few of their descendents remain here to this day.

A Modern Melting Pot

Hispanics make up more than half of the population of the Bronx today. African-Americans, Irish-Americans, West Indies immigrants and others round out the cultural stew. A host of Italians settled in the Belmont area, though now they share their streets with Albanian immigrants. Located near the **Bronx Zoo** and **New York Botanical Gardens**, Belmont's main street, **Arthur Avenue**, lures diners from all over town, who come to eat authentic Italian-American fare, shop for salami and provolone at their favorite food shops, and pick up fresh produce in the mid-avenue arcade.

The biggest food news in the Bronx today is the fact that New York's venerable **Fulton Fish Market**, where most of the city's restaurateurs purchase their finny fare, has moved from Lower Manhattan (where it's been since 1869) to new digs in Hunts Point. Spanning the length of four football fields, the market facility boasts a state-of-the-art climate-control system, which maintains the indoor temperature at a constant 41°F.

© Martha Cooper

Beccofino

001 Italian

5704 Mosholu Ave. (at Fieldston Rd.)

Dinner daily

Subway: 231 St (& bus BX9)
Phone: 718-432-2604
Web: N/A
Prices: $$

Beccofino is a charmer in Riverdale. Located on a quiet tree-lined street, Beccofino, with its quality Italian food and warm service, fits perfectly in the residential neighborhood.

There are less than 20 tables in this intimate restaurant, where exposed brick walls, terra-cotta floors and soft lighting add to the appealing rustic ambience. Locals and regulars cram this place for generous portions of tasty Italian creations like fettuccine topped with fresh peas, prosciutto and tomato in a cream sauce, and tender veal Forestier. Lemony ricotta cheesecake makes a perfect end to any meal here.

Beccofino doesn't accept reservations, but it charms customers with its friendly service, which makes even first-time visitors feel like regulars.

Brisas Del Caribe

002 Puerto Rican

1207 Castle Hill Ave. (bet. Ellis & Gleason Aves.)

Lunch & dinner daily

Subway: Castle Hill Av
Phone: 718-794-9710
Web: N/A
Prices:

Brisas Del Caribe delivers a good bang for the buck. This large, lively restaurant in a vibrant Latin neighborhood is always full with people waiting for tables (the restaurant doesn't take reservations) or grabbing take-out orders. While you're waiting, review the menu, posted on a large board above the counter.

Come armed with a big appetite to tackle huge portions of delicious Latin- and Caribbean-influenced food like *mofongo de cerdo*, a mashed plantain and pork dish accompanied by *pastel* (a smooth masa of cassava steamed in banana leaves). Most of the staff speak Spanish, and their generous spirit will make anyone feel welcome. Brisas Del Caribe draws from all walks of life—you'll find everyone from bikers to babies here.

Enzo's Café

Italian

2339 Arthur Ave. (bet. Crescent Ave. & 187th St.)

Subway: Fordham Rd (Grand Concourse) — Lunch & dinner daily
Phone: 718-733-4455
Web: N/A
Prices: $$

It's all in the family at Enzo's. This restaurant is run by Enzo DiRende, son of one of the founders of Dominick's, a veritable institution on storied Arthur Avenue—the Little Italy of the Bronx.

New kid on the block, Enzo's is tucked between eateries that have been serving here for decades, but in this case, youth has the advantage. A stickler for hospitality, the manager fusses over the guests, and every staff member has a smile. Expect the familiar—linguine with red sauce and clams, whole fish Livornese, tiramisù—but the food is just like your *nonna* whipped up. The delicious, crusty bread and desserts come fresh from bakeries in the neighborhood. Enzo's has two locations in the Bronx; the original one is at 1998 Williamsbridge Road.

Gabrielle's Dining

004

Jamaican

748 E. 233rd St. (bet. Byron Ave. & White Plains Rd.)

Subway: 233 St — Lunch & dinner daily
Phone: 718-395-3045
Web: www.gabriellesdining.com
Prices: ☺☺

One bite of curried goat chased with ginger-pineapple punch at Gabrielle's, and you'll think you've died and gone to Jamaica. Slightly under the radar in an area populated by Caribbean take-out joints and jerk spots, Gabrielle's is a true find.

Just inside the entrance, there's a take-out section where prices are a bit lower, but it's worth dining in for service that is as warm as the Jamaican sun. Friendly faces and special touches, like the complimentary appetizer that accompanies each meal, soften even the hardest New Yorkers.

Well-grounded in its knowledge of Jamaican cooking, the kitchen turns out hearty fare (crispy coconut shrimp; curried conch; "Rasta pasta"). The bill even leaves you with some change for your next island vacation.

Le Refuge Inn

French

586 City Island Ave. (bet. Bridge & Cross Sts.)

Subway: Pelham Bay Park (& bus BX29) — Tue – Sun lunch & dinner
Phone: 718-885-2478
Web: www.lerefugeinn.com
Prices: $$

City Island, an oasis of marinas, yacht clubs, fried-seafood eateries and Victorian homes, forms the setting for Le Refuge. The inn, which overlooks the harbor, occupies a lovely white French Empire-style house, built c.1876.

While Le Refuge operates as a bed-and-breakfast, its charming restaurant is open to the public (lunch and brunch by reservation only). Several different rooms downstairs accommodate diners in Victorian style with antiques, crystal chandeliers, and classic window treatments. On the plate, chef/owner Pierre Saint-Denis proffers a taste of France, from *mousse de foie gras* to *canard à l'orange*. All menus are prix-fixe, but modestly priced.

Upstairs, seven guestrooms are individually designed with comfort in mind.

Patricia's Pizza & Pasta

006

1080 Morris Park Ave. (bet. Haight & Lurting Aves.)

Subway: Pelham Pkwy (& bus BX8) — Lunch & dinner daily
Phone: 718-409-9069
Web: N/A
Prices: $$

For a small-town feel in the heart of the Bronx, check out Patricia's Pizza and Pasta. This trattoria is tucked away in an Italian-American section of the Bronx, where neighbors congregate outdoors to catch up on local gossip while kids play baseball in the small playground down the street. Patricia's, with its laid-back style and good home cooking (and no-reservations policy), is a natural addition to this endearing area.

Seating is limited here, where, as the name suggests, pizza and pasta form the focus of the menu. You can expect old-fashioned Italian-American comfort food—in enormous quantities with hearty flavors—served by an efficient, no-nonsense waitstaff.

Patricia's has a sibling, Nonno Tony's, in the Bronx.

Riverdale Garden

007

4576 Manhattan College Pkwy.
(bet. Broadway & Waldo Ave.)

Subway: Van Cortlandt Park - 242 St — Mon – Sat dinner only
Phone: 718-884-5232 — Sun lunch & dinner
Web: www.theriverdalegarden.com
Prices: $$

Close to Van Cortlandt Park at the edge of Riverdale, this restaurant sits on a quiet street adjacent to the train depot. Go on a warm, sunny day, when you can enjoy the outdoor garden, filled with greenery, flowers and tile-inlaid tables.
Chef/owner Michael Sherman updates his menu daily, but favors game dishes in season (venison, quail, wild boar); his wife, Lisa, creates the luscious desserts. It's worth leaving Manhattan for the likes of Long Island duck breast with red lentils, local zucchini and rhubarb compote, or lime-poached striped bass with grilled plums. On weekends, "Blunch" features the best of breakfast along with typical lunch entrées.
Can't do without your laptop? The Riverdale Garden offers wireless internet access.

Roberto's

Italian

008

603 Crescent Ave. (at Hughes Ave.)

Subway: Fordham Rd (Grand Concourse) — Mon – Thu lunch & dinner
Phone: 718-733-9503 — Fri lunch only
Web: www.robertobronx.com
Prices: $$

With the Italian food shops of Arthur Avenue nearby, it's no wonder that Roberto Paciullo's restaurant is the epicenter for Italian food in the Bronx. This is traditional Italian fare, simply the best you can find in this borough. House-made pastas share the menu with some familiar entrées and an extensive list of wines—the majority of them Italian. Check out the daily specials, but note that they're not advertised with prices (be sure to ask if you don't want to be surprised).
Amid the nondescript commercial buildings in this Bronx neighborhood, Roberto's stands out with its coral-colored façade and wrought-iron balcony. Inside, the rustic dining room mixes farmhouse tables with marvelous ceramic urns, some of them used as planters.

Tra Di Noi

Italian

622 E. 187th St. (bet. Belmont & Hughes Aves.)

Subway: Fordham (Grand Concourse)
Phone: 718-295-1784
Web: N/A
Prices: $$

Tue – Fri lunch & dinner
Sat – Sun dinner only

Just between us, there's no haute cuisine here, no contemporary twists or bursts of innovation. There is good, classic Italian-American fare, served in a neighborhood surrounded by Italian markets where vendors sell *salumi*, baked goods and artisan cheeses as their families have for generations.

This type of Italian food never goes out of style. People come from miles around, with kids in tow, to sample chef/owner Marco Coletta's marvelous lasagna, linguini carbonara, or veal chop on the bone, served with a side of artichokes and sweet-and-sour *caponatina*. And don't forget the homemade ricotta cheesecake.

The waitstaff speaks Italian, and the owner's wife will shower you with attention—just like the old days in this Little Italy of the Bronx.

©Martha Cooper

Brooklyn

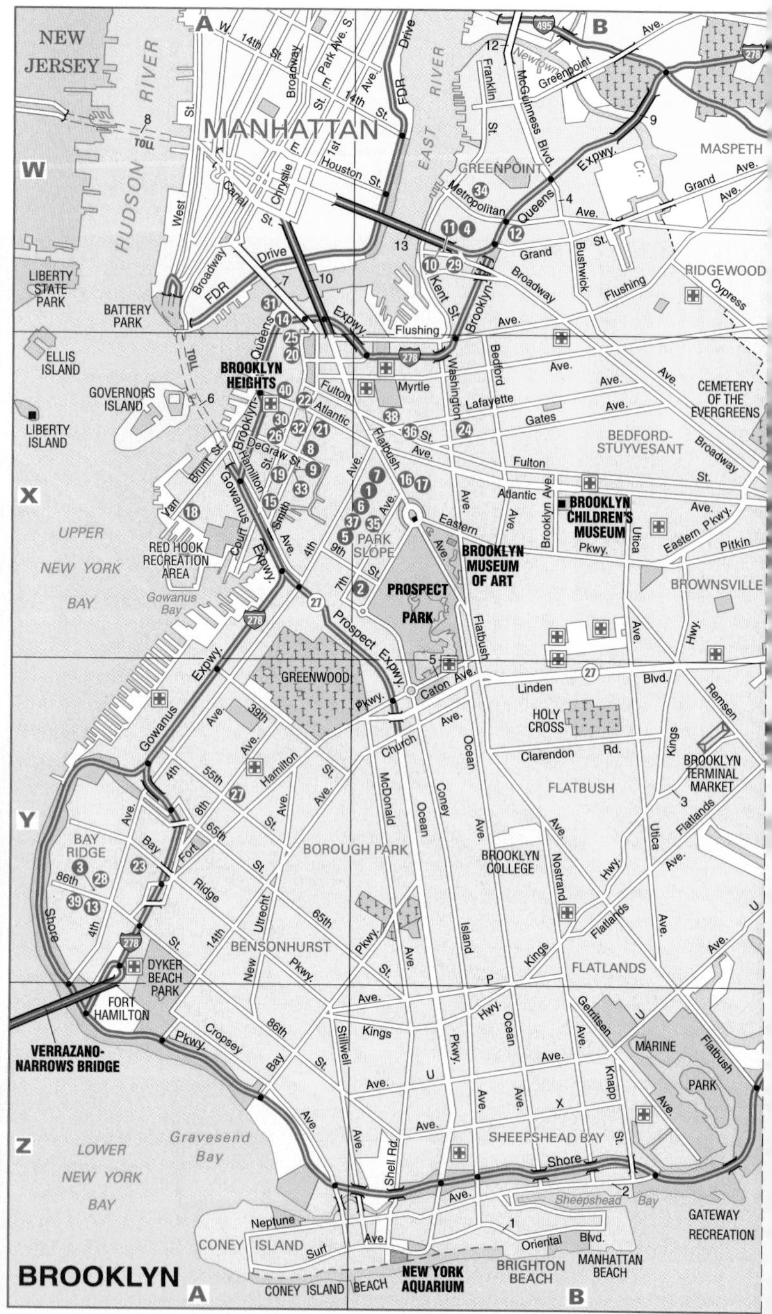
BROOKLYN
NEW JERSEY
MANHATTAN
HUDSON RIVER
EAST RIVER
LIBERTY STATE PARK
BATTERY PARK
ELLIS ISLAND
GOVERNORS ISLAND
LIBERTY ISLAND
BROOKLYN HEIGHTS
GREENPOINT
MASPETH
RIDGEWOOD
CEMETERY OF THE EVERGREENS
BEDFORD-STUYVESANT
BROOKLYN CHILDREN'S MUSEUM
BROOKLYN MUSEUM OF ART
PROSPECT PARK
PARK SLOPE
BROWNSVILLE
UPPER NEW YORK BAY
Gowanus Bay
RED HOOK RECREATION AREA
GREENWOOD
HOLY CROSS
BROOKLYN TERMINAL MARKET
FLATBUSH
BAY RIDGE
BOROUGH PARK
BROOKLYN COLLEGE
BENSONHURST
FLATLANDS
DYKER BEACH PARK
FORT HAMILTON
VERRAZANO-NARROWS BRIDGE
MARINE PARK
Gravesend Bay
LOWER NEW YORK BAY
SHEEPSHEAD BAY
Sheepshead Bay
GATEWAY RECREATION
CONEY ISLAND
CONEY ISLAND BEACH
NEW YORK AQUARIUM
BRIGHTON BEACH
MANHATTAN BEACH
TOLL

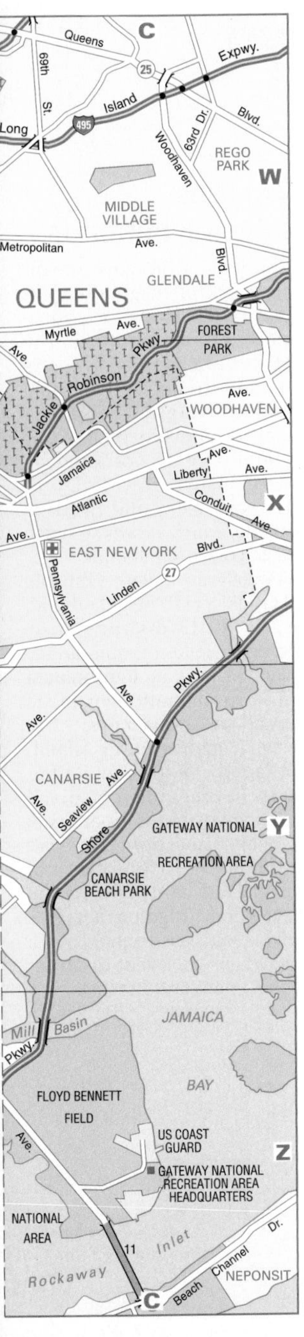

Atlantic Ave.	ACX
Avenue P	BYZ
Avenue U	BZCY
Avenue X	BZ
Bay Pkwy.	AZBY
Bay Ridge Pkwy.	AYZ
Beach Channel Dr.	CZ
Bedford Ave.	BX
Brighton Beach Ave.	**1** BZ
Broadway	BWCX
Brooklyn Ave.	BX
Brooklyn-Queens Expwy.	AXCW
Bushwick Ave.	BWX
Caton Ave.	BY
Church Ave.	BY
Clarendon Rd.	BY
Coney Island Ave.	BYZ
Court St.	AX
Cropsey Ave.	AZ
Eastern Pkwy.	BX
Emmons Ave.	**2** BZ
Flatbush Ave.	BXCZ
Flatlands Ave.	BCY
Flushing Ave.	BXCW
Foster Ave.	**3** BY
Franklin St.	BW
Fort Hamilton Pkwy.	ABY
Fulton St.	ACX
Gates Ave.	BX
Gerritsen Ave.	BZ
Gowanus Expwy.	AXY
Grand Ave.	BW
Grand St.	BW
Greenpoint Ave.	BW
Humboldt St.	**4** BW
Jamaica Ave.	CX
Kent Ave.	BW
Kings Highway	AZBX
Knapp St.	BZ
Linden Blvd.	BYCX
McDonald Ave.	BYZ
McGuinness Blvd.	BW
Metropolitan Ave.	BCW
Myrtle Ave.	AXCW
Neptune Ave.	ABZ
New Utrecht Ave.	AYZ
Nostrand Ave.	BYZ
Ocean Ave.	BYZ
Ocean Pkwy.	BYZ
Oriental Blvd.	BZ
Parkside Ave.	**5** BY
Pennsylvania Ave.	CXY
Pitkin Ave.	BCX
Prospect Expwy.	AXBY
Remsen Ave.	BXCY
Seaview Ave.	CY
Shell Rd.	BZ
Shore Pkwy.	ACYZ
Smith St.	AX
Stillwell Ave.	ABZ
Surf Ave.	ABZ
Utica Ave.	BXY
Washington Ave.	BX
4th Ave.	AYBX
9th St.	ABX
14th Ave.	AYZ
39th St.	AY
65th St.	AYBZ
86th St.	ABZ

BRIDGES AND TUNNELS

Brooklyn-Battery Tunnel	**6** AX
Brooklyn Bridge	**7** AW
Holland Tunnel	**8** AW
Kosciuszko Bridge	**9** BW
Manhattan Bridge	**10** AW
Marine Parkway Bridge	**11** CZ
Pulaski Bridge	**12** BW
Verrazano-Narrows Bridge	AZ
Williamsburg Bridge	**13** BW

Brooklyn

New York's most populous borough, with 2.5 million residents, Brooklyn sits on the western tip of Long Island. Its landmass extends from the East River to Coney Island and from the Narrows to Jamaica Bay. Although almost half a million Brooklynites commute to Manhattan, the borough retains a distinctive, country-village atmosphere in its eclectic mix of neighborhoods.

A Bit of History

Founded by the Dutch in 1636, the area now called Brooklyn was first christened Breuckelen ("broken land" in Dutch) after a small town near Utrecht. By the time it became part of New York City in 1898, Brooklyn was flourishing as a center of industry and commerce. Its first direct link to Manhattan came in 1883 in the form of the **Brooklyn Bridge**. Then came the Williamsburg Bridge (1903), the Manhattan Bridge (1909), and the first subway, in 1905. The 13,700-foot-long **Verrazano-Narrows Bridge**, completed in 1964, further facilitated travel between Brooklyn and the other boroughs.

A Taste of the Neighborhoods

A close look at Brooklyn reveals a patchwork of neighborhoods. Verdant **Park Slope**, a choice residential community, is the most recent haven for the diaper-and-stroller crowd. Staid **Brooklyn Heights** reigns as a wealthy enclave of narrow, tree-lined streets bordered by historic brownstones. Don't miss a walk along the riverside **Esplanade**, which affords stunning views of Lower Manhattan.

Traditionally an Italian, Hispanic and Hasidic Jewish neighborhood, hipster **Williamsburg** now welcomes an influx of young artists. Brooklyn's Little Italy, **Bensonhurst** boasts a proliferation of pizza joints and pasta restaurants.

You can't ignore **Coney Island**. A bit faded since its mid-20th-century heyday, this place still brings crowds to its boardwalk for Coney Island hot dogs—not to mention the wide expanse of beach. Less than a mile east of Coney Island, **Brighton Beach** is a thriving Russian neighborhood; this is where you want to go for authentic blinis and borscht.

Brooklyn

Brigitta L. House/MICHELIN

Al Di Lá

Italian

248 Fifth Ave. (at Carroll St.)

Subway: Union St
Phone: 718-783-4565
Web: www.aldilatrattoria.com
Prices: $$

Wed – Sun & Mon dinner only

In a world of laminated menus, it's always a joy to find a daily changing bill of fare that actually bears the day's date. At this perennially busy Park Slope trattoria, husband-and-wife team Emiliano Coppa and Anna Klinger offer a balanced selection of seasonal Italian dishes that are both robust in flavor and generous in size. New Yorkers, not often known for their patience, wait quietly just to taste Klinger's risotto.

The high-ceilinged room boasts a faded chic, with its church-pew seats and eccentric touches, such as the coffee pots hanging from the walls. If you have questions about the menu, the knowledgeable staff can offer sound advice. Plan to get here early, though, since Al Di Lá's no-reservations policy means it fills up quickly.

Applewood

002

Contemporary

501 11th St. (bet. Seventh & Eighth Aves.)

Subway: 7 Av
Phone: 718-768-2044
Web: www.applewoodny.com
Prices: $$

Tue – Sat dinner only
Sun lunch only

Park Slope real-estate agents hoping to convince Manhattanites to make the big move across the river should bring them to Applewood. Set within a turn-of-the-century house, this place is a real neighborhood jewel, where everyone seems to know each other. David and Laura Shea run the restaurant with a passion that shines through in everything they do.

The pretty dining room boasts a fireplace to warm diners in winter, and a changing exhibit of works by local artists gives the place a homespun feel. In the kitchen, the best local organic produce, hormone-free meats and wild fish are transformed into excellent seasonal dishes, like vibrant pan-seared skate, and grilled Vermont pork loin, that are well balanced and full of flavor.

Areo

Italian

8424 Third Ave. (bet. 84th & 85th Sts.)

Subway: 86 St — Tue – Sun lunch & dinner
Phone: 718-238-0079
Web: N/A
Prices: $$

With its large windows and attractive façade, this Bay Ridge Italian eatery packs in diners in the evening (lunch is more subdued). The bar divides the two dining rooms, which are decorated with dried flowers and Roman-themed wall stencils. Although the tables are well separated, the din at dinnertime rules out any hope of whispered conversation.

Prices seem more Manhattan than Brooklyn, but that doesn't deter the crowds that flock here for their favorite Italian dishes. Settle back and enjoy the complimentary plate of bruschetta, olives and salami while you consider the list of daily specials, which best shows off the kitchen staff's abilities.

Baci & Abbracci 

Italian

204 Grand St. (bet. Bedford & Driggs Sts.)

Subway: Bedford Av — Mon – Fri dinner only
Phone: 718-599-6599 — Sat – Sun lunch & dinner
Web: www.baciny.com
Prices: $$

Dinner at this intimate, contemporary spot in the heart of the Williamsburg buzz will leave you giving kisses and hugs all around. The loveable menu welcomes with wide-open arms, offering enticing choices at each course. Final decisions are only further complicated by the daily specials created in the rustic, Italian style at which the kitchen excels.

Pizzas are the standout, with perfectly cooked thin crusts and an enticing assortment of toppings. The restaurant also serves a lovely brunch best enjoyed in the garden behind the restaurant, a supreme warm-weather setting. Inside, the lighting is low and the ambience inviting, but if you live nearby and prefer to eat in, Baci & Abbracci will deliver its affectionate flavors right to your door.

Belleville

French

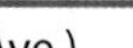

330 5th St. (at Fifth Ave.)

Subway: 4 Av - 9 St — Lunch & dinner daily
Phone: 718-832-9777
Web: www.bellevillebistro.com
Prices:

Belleville executes the informal French bistro concept perfectly in Park Slope, from décor to ambience to food. Decorated to appear old, Belleville looks comfortably worn, with mosaic floors, mirrored walls displaying the wine list, rows of wood-paneled banquettes, and tables nuzzled close together. In nice weather, windows open out on Brooklyn's busy Fifth Avenue and sidewalk seating.

The reasonably priced menu features well-prepared bistro fare from bourride to steak tartare to lusciously tender duck confit served beside a bundle of frisée and roasted baby potatoes. This is a welcoming neighborhood place for a lingering lunch, a romantic dinner or a weekend brunch. There's even a kids menu for little gourmands-in-training.

Blue Ribbon Sushi

Japanese

278 Fifth Ave. (bet. 1st St. & Garfield Pl.)

Subway: Union St — Dinner daily
Phone: 718-840-0408
Web: www.blueribbonrestaurants.com
Prices: $$

Brooklyn sushi lovers need not venture to Manhattan anymore with a Blue Ribbon Sushi located in Park Slope. This neighborhood favorite is the sister of the SoHo original *(119 Sullivan St.)* and is right next door to the casually elegant Blue Ribbon Brooklyn, just as the two are neighbors in SoHo.

This location provides equally delicate fare with original touches—but in larger surroundings and at a less frenetic pace (and with a no-reservations policy). Delight in the freshest sushi (which changes daily), or go beyond the status quo with the Blue Ribbon roll (half of a lobster topped with caviar). To help you narrow down your choices, sushi and sashimi are classified according to which ocean—the Atlantic or the Pacific—the fish comes from.

Brooklyn Fish Camp

Seafood

162 Fifth Ave. (bet. De Graw & Douglass Sts.)

Subway: Union St — Lunch & dinner daily
Phone: 718-783-3264
Web: www.brooklynfishcamp.com
Prices: $$

Since many Brooklynites work in Manhattan, the borough tends to be pretty sleepy during the day, and it can be hard to find a good place for lunch. Brooklyn Fish Camp has solved that problem for fish lovers in Park Slope.

Although the décor is inspired by the simple fish shacks of the rural South, the menu is a seriously focused celebration of the sea. An offshoot of the original Mary's Fish Camp in the West Village, this casual eatery sails away with top-notch seafood and enthusiastic service. The menu changes daily, based on the market, but owner Mary Redding's famous lobster rolls, fried-fish sandwiches, fresh grilled fish and selection of steamed or fried shellfish are always available. Order a side of spicy Old Bay fries to share.

Chance

Asian

223 Smith St. (bet. Baltic & Butler Sts.)

Subway: Bergen St — Lunch & dinner daily
Phone: 718-242-1515
Web: www.chancecuisine.com
Prices:

If you visit this Boerum Hill eatery, chances are you'll be enchanted. Brooklyn chef and restaurateur Ken Li runs the show at this modern Asian restaurant, which marries China and France for both its name and its inspiration.

Inside, the dining room says sleek with dark wood floors and walls, red chairs, and tables set with chopsticks on woven placemats. Large windows up front take in the street scene, while out back there is a small outdoor dining area.

The menu finds its heart in China, in a long list of dishes such as steamed pork dumplings, hot and sour soup, and Peking duck, but it ends up in France with foie gras and chocolate soufflé. Offering some 20 different choices, the Lunch Box special leaves nothing to chance.

Chestnut

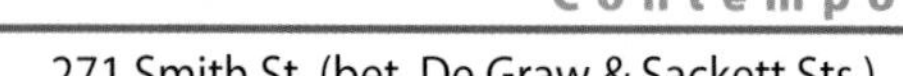

009 **Contemporary**

271 Smith St. (bet. De Graw & Sackett Sts.)

Subway: Carroll St — Tue – Sat dinner only
Phone: 718-243-0049 — Sun lunch & dinner
Web: www.chestnutonsmith.com
Prices: $$

Some proprietors name their restaurants with bad puns and some use their street address, but the owners of Chestnut christened their Carroll Gardens eatery with a moniker that perfectly sums up their philosophy. The name, like the place, is comforting, seasonal and reminds diners that the best supermarket is nature itself. Time has been well spent here sourcing the best ingredients, whose natural flavors are allowed to shine.

Come on Tuesday or Wednesday night to take advantage of Chestnut's prix-fixe value menus, or order à la carte and feast on halibut with guanciale and wild mushrooms or stuffed pork chop with agrodolce figs.

Down-home style characterizes the dining room, and the young team provides personable and chatty service.

Diner

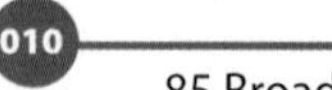

010 **American**

85 Broadway (at Berry St.)

Subway: Marcy Av — Lunch & dinner daily
Phone: 718-486-3077
Web: www.dinernyc.com
Prices: $$

Williamsburg may be the current epicenter of hip and trendy, but this simple little corner spot is none of those things. Mark Firth and Andrew Tarlow painstakingly renovated the 1920s Kullman Diner, and though the result may be a little rough around the edges, its casual warmth brings regulars back time and time again.

Chef Caroline Fidanza provides them a skeleton menu of favorites including the excellent burger and the refreshing goat-cheese salad, both seen on more tables than not. Abundant daily specials are also offered, including both market-driven dishes and whimsical, fusion comfort food. Sure, the prices are reasonable and the service informal but this is no ordinary diner; they even publish a quarterly, aptly named, *Diner Journal*.

Dressler ✿

American

149 Broadway (bet. Bedford & Driggs Aves.)

Subway: Marcy Av
Phone: 718-384-6343
Web: www.dresslernyc.com
Prices: $$

Mon – Sat dinner only
Sun lunch & dinner

Brooklyn

Dressler/Jason Joseph

There's more to Williamsburg's dining scene than just a great steak. With the addition of Dressler, the neighborhood's culinary landscape forges ahead. Housed in a former printer's shop, this inviting space features dark wood furnishings, mosaic tile floors and a wall covered in mirrors. The warmly lit room is detailed throughout with swirls of intricate metalwork crafted by local artisans.

Overseen by the team behind DuMont, the deftly prepared cuisine and thoughtful service keeps the energetic ambience in check, making a trip over the Williamsburg Bridge a rewarding one. The zinc-topped bar lined with high cushioned chairs is a comfortable perch to sip one of the creative cocktails, like the "Brooklyn," made with rye, maraschino and a twist of orange.

A fabulous Sunday brunch packs in the locals for everything from steak and eggs to goat-cheese and leek quiche.

Appetizers

- Beet Salad, Tomato Tart, Chevrot, Micro Greens
- Artichoke Heart Salad, Cranberry Beans, Arugula, Parmesan
- Quail, Stoneground Grits, Crisp Country Ham, Wild Mushrooms

Entrées

- Halibut, Asparagus, Favas, Sugar Snaps, Country Ham
- Short Rib and Ribeye, Horseradish Whipped Potato, Onion Jam
- Rack of Lamb, Roasted Garlic Flan, Spinach, Ratatouille

Desserts

- Chocolate Tart, Marshmallows, Chocolate Mint Ice Cream
- Banana Soufflé, Passion Fruit Caramel
- Cheesecake Ice Cream Sandwich, Rhubarb Rose Soup, Strawberry Granita

DuMont

012 — American

432 Union Ave. (bet. Devoe St. & Metropolitan Ave.)

Subway: Lorimer St — Lunch & dinner daily
Phone: 718-486-7717
Web: www.dumontrestaurant.com
Prices: $$

DuMont may look like just one more Williamsburg restaurant, but don't pass this one by. Inside, an antique sheen is reflected in the tile floor, and the weathered tin walls and ceiling. Rock music brings the atmosphere up to the present.

Chefs Cal Elliott and Polo Dobkin are DuMont's two hidden secrets. Formerly of Gramercy Tavern, they propose a list of seasonal specials along with a short menu of all-American fare such as barbecue ribs, and DuMac and cheese (made with radiatore pasta and cheddar, parmesan and gruyère cheeses, studded with bits of bacon). Even the specialty cocktail list is unique, with espresso martinis, Moscow mules and Grand Dad's lemonade.

For a weeknight burger and a beer, try DuMont Burger at 314 Bedford Avenue.

Eliá

013 — Greek

8611 Third Ave. (bet. 86th & 87th Sts.)

Subway: 86 St — Tue – Sun dinner only
Phone: 718-748-9891
Web: www.eliarestaurant.org
Prices: $$

You've spent the day on your scooter tooling around Santorini; the sun is starting to set, and now it's time for dinner... Okay, so you're in Brooklyn, and it's a cold Tuesday in February, but the sunny feel of this Bay Ridge taverna will nonetheless transport you to warmer climes. Whitewashed brick walls and marine blues in the modest dining room evoke sun-washed stucco buildings and the color of the Aegean Sea.

Along with the usual Greek favorites, the menu lists items (like the fish of the day) that come simply prepared and well flavored—as they do in the Greek islands—with bounteous amounts of fragrant olive oil and lemon. The best part? The upscale cuisine served here also comes with a palatable price tag.

Five Front

Contemporary

5 Front St. (bet. Dock & Old Fulton Sts.)

Subway: High St — Mon – Fri dinner only
Phone: 718-625-5559 — Sat – Sun lunch & dinner
Web: www.fivefrontrestaurant.com
Prices: $$

Tucked into the up-and-coming neighborhood dubbed DUMBO (for Down Under the Manhattan Bridge Overpass), Five Front takes its name from its address on busy Front Street. The restaurant is located just a block or so from the esplanade, with its fantastic views of Lower Manhattan. Weather permitting, the best seats at Five Front are in its spacious bamboo-filled garden, which nestles under the span of the Brooklyn Bridge.

Locals favor this pleasant space to savor sophisticated American fare, much of it interpreted with Italian accents. Inspired choices include Moroccan braised lamb, and monkfish with manila clams and chorizo. At dinner, the three-course, fixed-price meal adds another option to the already reasonably priced menu.

Frankies 457 Spuntino 

Italian

457 Court St. (bet. 4th Pl. & Luquer St.)

Subway: Carroll St — Lunch & dinner daily
Phone: 718-403-0033
Web: www.frankiesspuntino.com
Prices: 

Although *spuntino* loosely translates as "snack," Frankie's offers serious dining in a cozy setting. The initial food preparation takes place in the basement kitchen, while the rustic meals are assembled in the casual dining room, behind a counter stacked with charcuterie and crusty breads. This practice fills the room with mouth-watering aromas, as meatball parmigiana sandwiches and warm bowls of house-made pastas are plated and brought to the table.

Frankies attracts diners from young area newcomers to old-school Brooklynites, who know red sauce as "gravy." Weather permitting, the best spot to dine is the inviting back garden, illuminated by strings of tiny lights. Visit the Manhattan location at 17 Clinton Street on the Lower East Side.

Brooklyn

Franny's

016 **Italian**

295 Flatbush Ave. (bet. Prospect Pl. & St. Marks Ave.)

Subway: Bergen St — Tue – Fri dinner only
Phone: 7118-230-0221 — Sat – Sun lunch & dinner
Web: www.frannysbrooklyn.com
Prices: $$

Run by husband-and-wife team Franny Stephens and Andrew Feinberg, who share a passion for sustainable agriculture, Franny's is an inviting spot. A comfortable bar up front and a stack of highchairs for seating little ones imply all ages are welcome here.

The centerpiece of the open kitchen is the wood-burning brick oven from whose confines the individual-size pizzas emerge puffed and crispy. Affable servers will likely tempt you with at least one of the daily specials, but remember that the chef's selection of house-cured meats and small plates is also worth considering.

Decorated with greenery, strings of white lights, and a neatly arranged pile of wood to feed the pizza oven, the patio out back is the place to be on a warm evening.

Garden Café

017 **Contemporary**

620 Vanderbilt Ave. (at Prospect Pl.)

Subway: 7 Av — Tue – Sat dinner only
Phone: 718-857-8863
Web: N/A
Prices: $$

This unassuming gem of a restaurant has operated for some 20 years in Prospect Heights, a neighborhood which is now mostly gentrified. Owner John Policastro does the cooking, using premium ingredients; his charming wife, Camille, runs the front of the house.

It may not be trendy, but this family-run cafe draws an epicurean crowd with its excellent cuisine. At night there's but one set menu, and it's a bargain considering the high quality of the food. Don't expect fancy presentations or fussy ingredients, but do expect to be dazzled by simplicity.

Oddly, there's no garden here; the name comes from the ambience inside the restaurant, which is set about with lots of green plants, cane chairs, candlelight and soft music playing in the background.

The Good Fork

Contemporary

391 Van Brunt St. (bet. Coffey & Van Dyke Sts.)

Subway: Smith – 9 Sts (& bus B77) Tue – Sun dinner only
Phone: 718-643-6636
Web: www.goodfork.com
Prices: $$

Red Hook, with its yet-to-be-gentrified warehouses and pot-holed streets, is not always easy to access (it's best to come by bus or car), but those who come to enjoy a cozy dinner at The Good Fork in this up-and-coming neighborhood will be deliciously rewarded.

Run by Ben Schneider (he built the restaurant) and his wife, Sohui Kim, this is the kind of adorable place where everything is as good as it looks. The eclectic menu zigzags from onion rings to pappardelle with wild boar, and if it seems scattered, that's the point. Showing the split personality between chef Kim's classic training (braised rabbit, ravioli with butternut squash) and her proud Korean heritage (Korean-style steak and eggs over kimchee rice), the menu here truly has something for everyone.

The Grocery

Contemporary

019

288 Smith St. (bet. Sackett & Union Sts.)

Subway: Carroll St Mon – Sat dinner only
Phone: 718-596-3335
Web: N/A
Prices: $$

Can you tell a restaurant by its façade? In this case, you can. The inviting Grocery, its name etched on the glass window in front, beckons diners to experience the warm hospitality and charming ambience inside.

Co-owners and chefs Sharon Pachter and Charles Kiely run this Carroll Gardens establishment with watchful eyes. This pair lends flair to flavorful American dishes, and their concise, contemporary menu changes frequently to showcase the best of local farmers' markets (think semolina-crusted fluke or slow-rendered duck breast). The well-chosen international wine list thoughtfully includes a few half-bottles.

Reservations are a must in this tiny place. In summer, though, the pleasant garden out back increases the seating capacity.

Henry's End

020 **American**

44 Henry St. (bet. Cranberry & Middagh Sts.)

Subway: High St — Dinner daily
Phone: 718-834-1776
Web: www.henrysend.com
Prices: $$

Nearly under the bridge in Brooklyn Heights, two blocks from the esplanade with its views of Lower Manhattan, Henry's End serves up American dishes in a casual atmosphere. Bistro tables are tightly packed in the small room, where the décor is fading and the walls are lined with black-and-white photographs of Brooklyn through the years.

Whether your tastes run to simple American classics (Southern fried chicken) or to more sophisticated preparations (wild Alaskan salmon), Henry's has something for you—and lots of it. Sample barbecued rattlesnake or antelope *au poivre* during the annual wild game festival (October through February). The ever-changing list of American wines by the glass is sure to provide a fitting accompaniment.

Jolie

021 **French**

320 Atlantic Ave. (bet. Smith & Hoyt Sts.)

Subway: Bergen St — Lunch & dinner daily
Phone: 718-488-0777
Web: www.jolierestaurant.com
Prices: $$

Set on a rather nondescript stretch of Atlantic Avenue, Jolie beckons diners in Boerum Hill with its planters of greenery that decorate the sidewalk out front. Inside, a semi-circular marble-topped bar dominates the front of the restaurant, while the large dining room is in back. Walls do double duty as an art gallery; changing exhibits fill the space, lending an élan and sophistication to this *petit* bistro. As pleasant as the place is, the pièce de résistance is the walled garden area, *très jolie* indeed with its shade trees, flowering vines and market umbrellas.

Classic bistro fare fills the menu with such French favorites as roasted chicken breast stuffed with ricotta and fresh herbs, *escargots de Bourgogne*, and steak tartare *au Cognac*.

Ki Sushi

022 **Japanese**

122 Smith St. (bet. Dean & Pacific Sts.)

Subway: Bergen St — Mon – Sat lunch & dinner
Phone: 718-935-0575 — Sun dinner only
Web:
Prices: $$

Ki Sushi proves that you don't need to go across the river to Manhattan to get great Japanese food. The highlight of this solid Japanese cuisine is its fantastic sushi—the *omakase* features seafood flown in from Tokyo's famous Tsukiji Market—but with items such as Chilean sea bass and grilled ribeye steak with truffle mashed potatoes, there's plenty to satisfy those who prefer their food cooked. House specialty sushi rolls include some eye-catching selections—Spicy Girl or Foxy Lady Roll, anyone?
The interior's Zen-chic design, complete with a water wall and potted orchids, may look the part of a hip hotspot, but the excellent service from welcoming servers shows that style doesn't trump substance.

La Maison du Couscous

023 **Moroccan**

484 77th St. (bet. Fourth & Fifth Aves.)

Subway: 77 St — Lunch & dinner daily
Phone: 718-921-2400
Web: www.lamaisonducouscous.com
Prices: $$

The spirit of the Casbah infuses this Bay Ridge find, where Moroccan lanterns, bright pillows and a mosaic tile fountain festoon the tiny room. Music keeps the mood lively, despite the fact that the restaurant doesn't serve alcohol (guests are welcome to bring their own).
Start with little gems like the cumin- and paprika-spiced hummus, or deep-fried morsels of phyllo stuffed with tasty goat cheese and black-olive tapenade. Entrées focus on couscous and tagines, as well as kebabs from the grill and sandwiches like the *kefta*, made with chopped lamb mixed with parsley, onion and spices.
Run by a dedicated team, La Maison du Couscous adds an exotic note to the plethora of contemporary American restaurants found in other parts of this borough.

Locanda Vini & Olii

024 Italian X

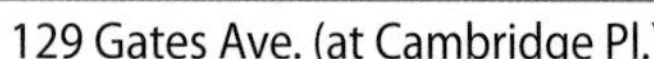

129 Gates Ave. (at Cambridge Pl.)

Subway: Clinton - Washington Avs — Tue – Sun dinner only
Phone: 718-622-9202
Web: www.locandany.com
Prices: $$

Gracious host François Louy and his wife, Catherine, are not strangers to the restaurant business. Both from northern Italy, the couple comes with good credentials. François worked for the Cipriani restaurant group, and Catherine was a manager for Balthazar before the pair opened their own place in Clinton Hill. Located in a restored 100-year-old pharmacy, Locanda uses the old apothecary shelves and drawers to hold wine bottles, antique crockery and other supplies.

The menu changes daily, but the likes of house-made gnocchi in fresh tomato sauce, and branzino steamed *en papillote* in white wine and perfumed with fennel make a healthy prescription for a good meal. If you're dining with four or more, you can call ahead and request a tasting menu.

Noodle Pudding

025 Italian XX

38 Henry St. (bet. Cranberry & Middagh Sts.)

Subway: High St — Tue – Sun dinner only
Phone: 718-625-3737
Web: N/A
Prices: $$

Look for a warm greeting and friendly service once you find this restaurant, but don't look for a sign on the door—there isn't one. Brooklyn Heights cognoscenti know where to come for good conversation and generous portions of rustic Italian fare, including hearty pastas and grilled meats.

Diners at well-spaced bistro tables have a view of the Henry Street scene through the restaurant's picture window. From risotto to osso buco, all the Italian favorites are on the menu. You can drink in the scene while you sip a cup of strong espresso after your meal.

The restaurant (which doesn't accept reservations) takes its name from a baked dish that resembles kugel, a savory pudding baked with noodles and traditionally served on the Sabbath.

Osaka

Japanese

026

272 Court St. (bet. De Graw & Kane Sts.)

Subway: Bergen St — Lunch & dinner daily
Phone: 718-643-0044
Web: www.osakany.com
Prices: $$

Osaka's plain brick façade blends in well with the village atmosphere of Cobble Hill. Inside the intimate, always-crowded dining room, black linens and bamboo accents play against pistachio-colored walls.

Named for Osaka-style sushi, featuring larger pieces of fish over smaller beds of rice, the restaurant offers an extensive selection of maki and chef's special rolls (there's even a "Viagra roll," with eel, avocado and sea urchin—the latter prized as an aphrodisiac) as well as raw seafood (sushi and sashimi are available as entrées or à la carte). Cooked courses include tempura, teriyaki, broiled black cod and grilled duck breast. If you're looking for a deal, try the combination boxes available for lunch and dinner.

Pacificana

Chinese

027

813 55th St. (at Eighth Ave.)

Subway: 8 Av — Lunch & dinner daily
Phone: 718-871-2880
Web: N/A
Prices: $$

The next time you're thinking dim sum, visit Sunset Park. This Brooklyn neighborhood, home to a fast-growing Asian population, is quickly becoming New York City's newest spot for Chinese food. Pacificana, with its crimson walls, vaulted ceilings, and semi-open kitchen framed by floor-to-ceiling fish tanks, is an elegant alternative to the bustle of Chinatown's Canal Street.

Sit back and relax while the smiling staff brings the parade of food to you. Carts overflow with a tempting array of typical dim sum fare—steamed dumplings, braised crab- and pork-filled tofu skin, crispy pork. There's also a full regular menu with house specialties like scallops with apples and macadamia nuts in a noodle nest, or lamb chops with black-peppercorn sauce.

The Pearl Room

Seafood XX

028

8201 Third Ave. (at 82nd St.)

Subway: 86 St — Lunch & dinner daily
Phone: 718-833-6666
Web: www.thepearlroom.com
Prices: $$

The wave-shaped awning is your first clue to the type of cuisine you'll enjoy at this Bayside fish emporium. Fresh from seas around the globe comes a large array of well-prepared dishes, from seafood paella to jumbo Panama shrimp. And speaking of jumbo, the portions here are nothing to sneeze at. On weekends, the family-style brunch includes everything from homemade pastries and pancakes to steak and eggs.

Large windows add to the luminous feel of the room, with its shell-pink luster and aquatic-themed ceiling mural. This is a place that is as inviting in winter, with its open fireplace, as it is in the summer, when diners appreciate the spacious, covered terrace out back. Expect the service to be gracious and attentive any time of year.

Quercy

French X

030

242 Court St. (bet. Baltic & Kane Sts.)

Subway: Bergen St — Tue – Sun lunch & dinner, Mon dinner only
Phone: 718-243-2151
Web: N/A
Prices: $$

Bistro décor in this attractive Cobble Hill eatery hearkens back to the 1950s with its blue and white linoleum floor, Formica bar, and red vinyl-covered banquettes. The food is classic bistro, too—think sautéed skate, steak au poivre, and for dessert, warm tarte Tatin topped with caramelized apples. Chef/owner Jean-François Fraysse named his establishment after his hometown in southwest France; in true French fashion, the day's specials are written on a blackboard and presented to you along with a basket of country bread accompanied by butter and homemade strawberry jam.

Hip Brooklyn residents frequent Quercy for that intangible *je ne sais quoi*, or perhaps it's just for the good French comfort food served in an inviting atmosphere.

Peter Luger 

Steakhouse

029

178 Broadway (at Driggs Ave.)

Subway: Marcy Av
Lunch & dinner daily
Phone: 718-387-7400
Web: www.peterluger.com
Prices: $$$

$

Peter Luger

Don't be fooled by the beer-hall ambience: Peter Luger serves some of the best steaks in the country. Famed for its velvety USDA prime beef, dry-aged on the premises, this Williamsburg institution has been catering to carnivores since 1887. Brooklyn factory-owner Sol Forman purchased the restaurant in the 1940s, after namesake Peter Luger passed away. Today the Forman family hand-selects every cut of meat.

You'll have to trek to Brooklyn to experience this place, but who cares, when you can have steak this good? Sharing is de rigueur, and the menu offers Porterhouse steak for 2, 3 or 4 people (there's a steak for one if you're dining alone). Creamed spinach, served in a crock big enough to feed two people, is a Luger tradition, along with the French fries. Wonderful cheesecake, the gold standard for this New York-style dessert, comes with a generous dollop of Schlag.

Appetizers

- Jumbo Shrimp Cocktail
- Sizzling Canadian Bacon
- Sliced Salad of Tomatoes and Onions with Peter Luger Sauce

Entrées

- Dry Aged, Family Selected, USDA Prime Porterhouse Steak for Two, Three or Four
- Double Thick Loin Lamb Chops
- Creamed Spinach for Two

Desserts

- Cheese Cake, Served with Homemade Schlag
- Pecan Pie, Served with Homemade Schlag
- Holy Cow Sundae, Served with Homemade Schlag

Brooklyn

River Café

031 **Contemporary** XXX

1 Water St. (bet. Furman & Old Fulton Sts.)

Subway: High St — Lunch & dinner daily
Phone: 718-522-5200
Web: www.rivercafe.com
Prices: $$$$

Location, location, location: these are the three best reasons to eat at the River Café. Housed in a barge on the East River with the Statue of Liberty and Brooklyn Bridge in its sights, this landmark has been around since 1977. Spectacular views stretching across the river to Manhattan's Financial District make this a favorite spot of romantics who book tables by the window for special dates or marriage proposals.

At lunch you can order à la carte, while at dinner you must choose between three- or six-course tasting menus that spotlight products like wild King salmon, Maine lobster and Hudson Valley foie gras. For dessert, the chocolate marquise Brooklyn Bridge is topped with a chocolate model of the span that looms nearby.

Savoia

033 **Italian** X

277 Smith St. (bet. De Graw & Sackett Sts.)

Subway: Carroll St — Lunch & dinner daily
Phone: 718-797-2727
Web: N/A
Prices: $$

Colorful earthenware plates, bare wooden tables and exposed brick enhance the rustic atmosphere of this Carroll Gardens charmer. At the pizza counter, a cook tearing leaves of fresh basil fills the room with a wonderful aroma, while the wood-burning pizza oven glows in the background.

No wonder that pizza is a hot item here. Toppings stray from the standard, with hot sopressata, fried eggplant and boiled egg among the many choices. There are plenty of other entrées, too—most of them focusing on Southern Italian traditions—from hearty fettucine *boscialo* (with a flavorful meat sauce kicked up with slivers of fried eggplant and nuggets of mozzarella) to a Sicilian-style beef cutlet. Personable and relaxed service adds to Savoia's casual vibe.

Saul ✿

Contemporary XX

032

140 Smith St. (bet. Bergen & Dean Sts.)

Subway: Bergen St — Dinner daily
Phone: 718-935-9844
Web: www.saulrestaurant.com
Prices: $$$

Saul/Ellen Wallop

Saul Bolton named his restaurant after himself, and in this case, the vanity is well deserved. The chef honed his skills in the kitchens of no less than Eric Ripert and David Bouley before setting out on his own in Brooklyn's Boerum Hill. Today his 35-seat dining room is a magnet for the area's cosmopolitan mix of intellectuals, professionals and young families.

Bolton offers top-quality seasonal ingredients sourced from local markets and New England farms. Dishes such as seared day-boat scallops with organic polenta, pan-roasted Vermont-raised veal with spring garlic and fava beans, and the signature baked Alaska—served over a dark-chocolate cookie drizzled with caramel sauce—illustrate the chef's considerable prowess in the kitchen. À la carte selections are always a sure bet, but there's also a prix-fixe menu—a good value—and a chef's tasting.

Appetizers

- Prosciutto-wrapped Foie Gras Terrine with Green Raisins, Artichokes, Meyer Lemon Marmalade
- Salad of Bluefin, Avocado, Pickled Red Onions, Apples and Smoky Tomato Jelly

Entrées

- Broken Arrow Ranch Axis Venison with Porcinis and Gingered Pear Chutney
- Three Corner Field Farms Lamb Tasting: Braised Shoulder Wrapped in Socca, Merquez, Chop and Liver

Desserts

- Gratin of Valrhona Araguani Chocolate, Anise Scented Caramel Ice Cream, Autumn Fruit Compote
- Three Corner Fields Farm Sheep's Milk Panna Cotta, Sauterne Soaked Apricots

Sea

Thai

114 N. 6th St. (bet. Berry & Wythe Sts.)

Subway: Bedford Av — Mon – Fri lunch & dinner
Phone: 718-384-8850 — Sat – Sun dinner only
Web: www.searestaurant.com
Prices: $$

You could call this cool Williamsburg Thai restaurant bubbly, since the bubble is Sea's logo. This shape appears on the menu and on the cutouts of the wooden partitions dividing the dining spaces, and it reflects from the disco ball that hangs from the ceiling. Admire the life-size Buddha that overlooks a pool in the middle of the dining room, but be forewarned that all this Zen-like ambience dissolves at night into pulsing DJ music.

Whatever time you go to this restaurant-cum-nightclub, the menu cites a wide selection of spicy Thai fare, from crispy basil spring rolls to an array of curries and stir-frys. The volcanic chicken topped with spicy "lava sauce" is a surefire hit.

There's another Sea in the East Village *(75 Second Ave.)*.

Sette Enoteca & Cucina

035

Italian

207 Seventh Ave. (at 3rd St.)

Subway: 7 Av — Lunch & dinner daily
Phone: 718-499-7767
Web: www.setteparkslope.com
Prices: $$

Craving some Chianti and capellini? Then head straight for Sette Enoteca & Cucina, where the talented kitchen crew turns out consistently tasty Italian fare.

This Park Slope restaurant is popular with the neighbors—you'll find everyone from hip moms and their offspring to cool couples dining on pizza, pasta, and a host of entrées that includes crisp duck breast, wood-oven-roasted fish, and grilled hanger steak. The all-Italian wine list touts its *venti per venti,* 20 bottles for $20 each, and wines are also available by the quartino.

Don't expect exposed brick and candle-wax-covered Chianti bottles, though. Sette Enoteca & Cucina bucks the trend with its contemporary design (think blond wood tables and metallic-fabric-covered banquettes).

The Smoke Joint

Barbecue

87 S. Elliot Pl. (bet. Fulton St & Lafayette Ave.)

Subway: Lafayette Av — Lunch & dinner daily
Phone: 718-797-1011
Web: www.thesmokejoint.com
Prices:

You may leave smelling of hickory smoke, but the taste left in your mouth from this fantastic barbecue joint is worth the hungry stares you'll get from fellow subway riders. Settle down, grab a beer and dig into seriously smoky ribs coated with "jointrub"—a secret house recipe—and sandwiches, all served with a variety of sauces, including the lip-smacking-good "jointsmoke" and the spicy "hollapeno" varieties. Sides include the usual suspects, but the cayenne-spiked mac and cheese and the smoky, molasses-flavored barbecued beans are fantastic.

Despite its location near the esteemed Brooklyn Academy of Music, the setting is laid-back, and the staff is energetic, smiling, and just plain fun. Great prices leave an even better taste in your mouth.

Stone Park Cafe

Contemporary

324 Fifth Ave. (at 3rd St.)

Subway: Union St — Mon – Fri dinner only
Phone: 718-369-0082 — Sat – Sun lunch & dinner
Web: www.stoneparkcafe.com
Prices: $$

A run-down Park Slope bodega was given a facelift in fall 2004 and opened as this delightful place that marks another example of Fifth Avenue's culinary coming of age. Named for the Old Stone House historical museum set in the park across the street, Stone Park Cafe emits a casual vibe, with brown paper covering the tablecloths.

Service reflects the pride that the waitstaff clearly feels about the place, while the menu offers a selection of dishes well balanced between simple fare and more ambitious preparations. Best of all, the kitchen uses market-fresh ingredients, and knows when to leave well enough alone. Go for weekend brunch and start your day off with a Bellini, followed by the likes of house-smoked salmon or short-rib hash and eggs.

Thomas Beisl

Austrian

038

25 Lafayette Ave. (bet. Ashland Pl. & St. Felix St.)

Subway: Atlantic Ave – Pacific St
Phone: 718-222-5800
Web: N/A
Prices: $$

Tue – Sun lunch & dinner
Mon dinner only

Fort Greene is alive with the smell of strudel at Thomas Beisl. This Austrian *beisl*, or bistro, is run by chef/owner Thomas Ferlesch, who manned the stove for 11 years as executive chef of the Upper West Side institution, Café des Artistes.

Located across from the Brooklyn Academy of Music, Thomas Beisl has the bistro look down with its white-paper-topped tables, terrazzo floor, and blackboard scrawled with the daily specials. Not to mention the engaging and attentive staff.

The menu reads like a love letter to Vienna with traditional Wiener Schnitzel, beef goulash, and homemade bratwurst rounding out the selections. Concertgoers drop in after the performance for Linzer torte, strudel, and *kaiserschmarren*, a souffléd pancake.

Tuscany Grill

Italian

039

8620 Third Ave. (bet. 86th & 87th Sts.)

Subway: 86 St
Phone: 718-921-5633
Web: N/A
Prices: $$

Dinner daily

Many restaurants lay claim to being romantic, but there's something about the combination of candlelight and a plate of pasta (remember that scene in Disney's *Lady and The Tramp?)* that just seems to naturally foster *amore*. For more than a decade, Tuscany Grill has been providing such an ambience for its customers, who come to this Brooklyn Little Italy not only from the surrounding Bay Ridge area but from Manhattan as well.

The room has a rustic appeal with its dried flowers, pine sideboards and yellow-hued walls, while the menu, as the restaurant's name suggests, celebrates the robust fare of Tuscany (grilled pizza, roasted fish). Expect a wait at this cozy spot—especially on weekends—if you don't have a reservation.

Water Falls Café

Middle Eastern

040

144 Atlantic Ave. (bet. Clinton & Henry Sts.)

Subway: Atlantic Av — Lunch & dinner daily
Phone: 718-488-8886
Web: www.waterfallscafe.com
Prices: ⊖⊖

Brooklyn

Of the smattering of Middle Eastern restaurants on Brooklyn's Atlantic Avenue, Water Falls Cafe is the best of the bunch. It's not much on décor—simple white walls, basic black chairs, minimal artwork—but this family-run place dishes up terrific food at a great value.

Feisty and good-humored, the owner makes sure you are well taken care of, even if her mothering encourages you to eat every last bite—or at least take any leftovers home. The menu features typical Middle Eastern fare—hummus, shish kabob, kibbeh, and some of the best fattoush this side of the Arabian Sea.

There's an extensive list of freshly squeezed juices along with strong Arabic coffee and sweet mint tea. Alcohol is not served here, though you are welcome to bring your own.

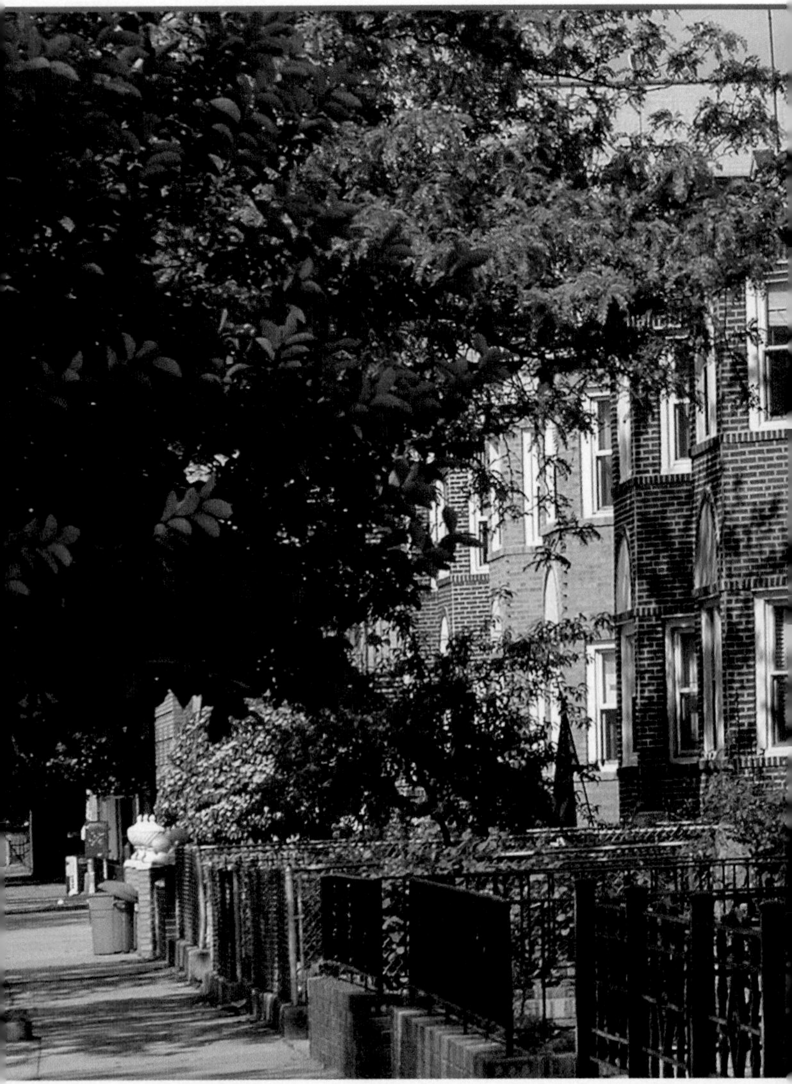

©Martha Cooper

Queens

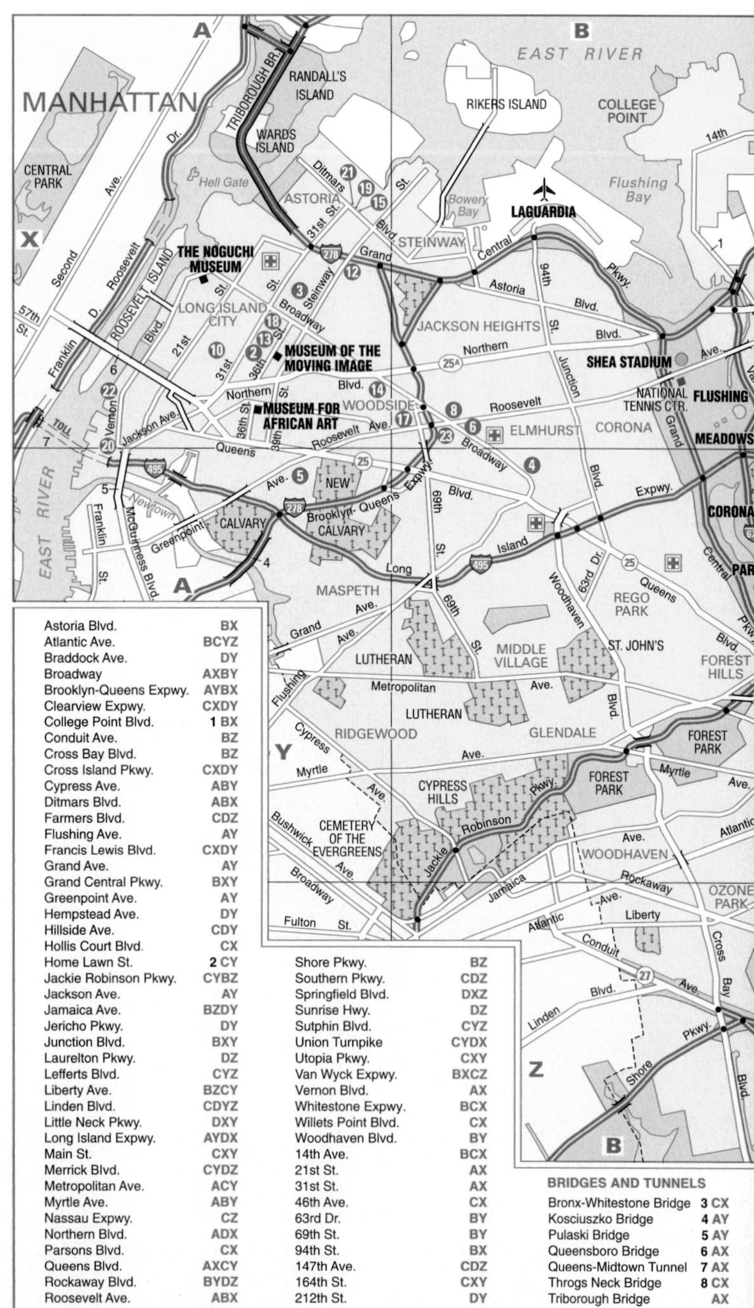

Astoria Blvd.	BX
Atlantic Ave.	BCYZ
Braddock Ave.	DY
Broadway	AXBY
Brooklyn-Queens Expwy.	AYBX
Clearview Expwy.	CXDY
College Point Blvd.	1 BX
Conduit Ave.	BZ
Cross Bay Blvd.	BZ
Cross Island Pkwy.	CXDY
Cypress Ave.	ABY
Ditmars Blvd.	ABX
Farmers Blvd.	CDZ
Flushing Ave.	AY
Francis Lewis Blvd.	CXDY
Grand Ave.	AY
Grand Central Pkwy.	BXY
Greenpoint Ave.	AY
Hempstead Ave.	DY
Hillside Ave.	CDY
Hollis Court Blvd.	CX
Home Lawn St.	2 CY
Jackie Robinson Pkwy.	CYBZ
Jackson Ave.	AY
Jamaica Ave.	BZDY
Jericho Pkwy.	DY
Junction Blvd.	BXY
Laurelton Pkwy.	DZ
Lefferts Blvd.	CYZ
Liberty Ave.	BZCY
Linden Blvd.	CDYZ
Little Neck Pkwy.	DXY
Long Island Expwy.	AYDX
Main St.	CXY
Merrick Blvd.	CYDZ
Metropolitan Ave.	ACY
Myrtle Ave.	ABY
Nassau Expwy.	CZ
Northern Blvd.	ADX
Parsons Blvd.	CX
Queens Blvd.	AXCY
Rockaway Blvd.	BYDZ
Roosevelt Ave.	ABX
Shore Pkwy.	BZ
Southern Pkwy.	CDZ
Springfield Blvd.	DXZ
Sunrise Hwy.	DZ
Sutphin Blvd.	CYZ
Union Turnpike	CYDX
Utopia Pkwy.	CXY
Van Wyck Expwy.	BXCZ
Vernon Blvd.	AX
Whitestone Expwy.	BCX
Willets Point Blvd.	CX
Woodhaven Blvd.	BY
14th Ave.	BCX
21st St.	AX
31st St.	AX
46th Ave.	CX
63rd Dr.	BY
69th St.	BY
94th St.	BX
147th Ave.	CDZ
164th St.	CXY
212th St.	DY

BRIDGES AND TUNNELS

Bronx-Whitestone Bridge	3 CX
Kosciuszko Bridge	4 AY
Pulaski Bridge	5 AY
Queensboro Bridge	6 AX
Queens-Midtown Tunnel	7 AX
Throgs Neck Bridge	8 CX
Triborough Bridge	AX

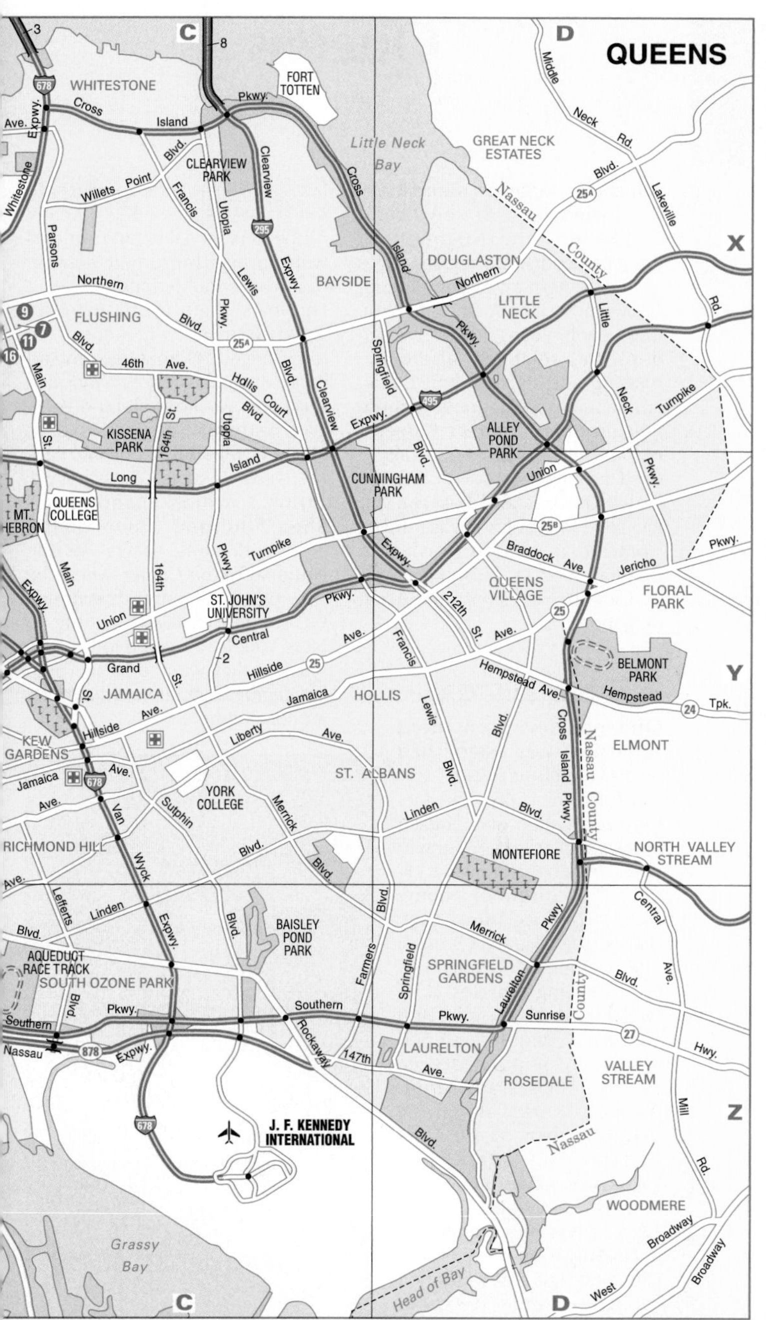
QUEENS
C
D
X
Y
Z
WHITESTONE
FORT TOTTEN
Little Neck Bay
GREAT NECK ESTATES
CLEARVIEW PARK
DOUGLASTON
BAYSIDE
LITTLE NECK
FLUSHING
ALLEY POND PARK
KISSENA PARK
CUNNINGHAM PARK
QUEENS COLLEGE
MT. HEBRON
QUEENS VILLAGE
FLORAL PARK
ST. JOHN'S UNIVERSITY
BELMONT PARK
JAMAICA
HOLLIS
ELMONT
KEW GARDENS
ST. ALBANS
YORK COLLEGE
RICHMOND HILL
MONTEFIORE
NORTH VALLEY STREAM
BAISLEY POND PARK
AQUEDUCT RACE TRACK
SOUTH OZONE PARK
SPRINGFIELD GARDENS
LAURELTON
ROSEDALE
VALLEY STREAM
J. F. KENNEDY INTERNATIONAL
WOODMERE
Grassy Bay
Head of Bay
Nassau County
Whitestone Expwy.
Cross Island Pkwy.
Clearview Expwy.
Willets Point Blvd.
Francis Lewis Blvd.
Utopia Pkwy.
Parsons Blvd.
Northern Blvd.
Main St.
46th Ave.
Hollis Court Blvd.
Springfield Blvd.
Long Island Expwy.
164th St.
Union Turnpike
Grand Central Pkwy.
Hillside Ave.
Jamaica Ave.
Liberty Ave.
Hempstead Ave.
Hempstead Tpk.
Braddock Ave.
Jericho Tpk.
212th St.
Van Wyck Expwy.
Sutphin Blvd.
Merrick Blvd.
Linden Blvd.
Lefferts Blvd.
Farmers Blvd.
Laurelton Pkwy.
Southern Pkwy.
Sunrise Hwy.
Rockaway Blvd.
147th Ave.
Nassau Expwy.
Middle Neck Rd.
Lakeville Rd.
Little Neck Pkwy.
Central Ave.
Mill Rd.
Broadway
West Broadway
678
295
495
878
25A
25B
25
24
27
3
8
2
9
7
11
16

Queens

Almost as large as Manhattan, the Bronx, and Staten Island combined, the borough of Queens covers 120 square miles on the western tip of Long Island. Thousands of immigrants come here each year, drawn by the borough's relatively affordable housing and its tight-knit ethnic communities. Restaurants in these neighborhoods reflect Queens' ethnic diversity as well. Take a stroll through Astoria to find Greek grilled octopus and baklava. Try Jackson Heights for foods ranging from Indian tandoori dishes to Bolivian *arepas*. Flushing reigns as Queens' most vibrant Asian neighborhood.

A Bit of History

Queens' first permanent settlement was established by the Dutch at present-day Flushing in 1645. Clashes between Dutch and English settlers marked its early years. When the English took over the colony of Nieuw Amsterdam in 1664, they named this county Queens, after Catherine of Braganza, wife of King Charles II of England. Until the mid-19th century, Queens remained a sparsely populated area of small villages and farms. As New York City grew, urbanization of Queens accelerated, attracting successive waves of German and Irish immigrants. In 1898, Queens was incorporated as a borough of New York City, and new transportation facilities made it easier for residents to commute to Manhattan. By the 1970's, nearly 30 percent of Queens' residents were foreign born; that number has nearly doubled today.

For years, there wasn't much to attract tourists to Queens. That has changed as film studios and art museums make use of abandoned factories in Long Island City and Astoria. Sports thrive in **Flushing Meadows Corona Park** *(between 111th St. & Van Wyck Expwy.)*, which encompasses **Shea Stadium**, home of the New York Mets, as well as the **National Tennis Center**, where the U.S. Open is held each summer. Of course, visitors traveling to New York by air come to Queens whether they want to or not: both LaGuardia and Kennedy airports are located here.

©Martha Cooper

Arharn Thai

Thai

32-05 36th Ave. (bet. 32nd & 33rd Sts.)

Subway: 36 Av — Mon – Fri lunch & dinner
Phone: 718-728-5563 — Sat – Sun dinner only
Web: N/A
Prices:

An easy train ride leaves you a block from this sleepy Thai place, surrounded by a lineup of restaurants that would suit the United Nations. Expect a room simply decorated with Thai handicrafts—many for sale—and service that is warm and eager to please.

The extensive menu offers a variety of chef's specialties and classics. *Mee Grob,* a contradictory composition of fried rice noodles, shrimp and tofu in a sticky tamarind sauce makes a bright starter, as does *Yum Koon Chieng,* a salad of Chinese sausage, cucumber, tomato and scallion tossed with lime juice and chile. Authentic spice levels may be toned down for Western palates, but large portions leave tasty leftovers to bring home. Traditional family-style dining is the best way to go here.

Brick Cafe

Mediterranean

30-95 33rd St. (at 31st Ave.)

Subway: Broadway — Mon – Fri dinner only
Phone: 718-267-2735 — Sat – Sun lunch & dinner
Web: www.brickcafe.com
Prices: $$

Resembling a European country inn, with its lace curtains, chunky wood tables, tin ceiling and knick-knacks set around the room, the Brick Cafe wraps diners in a rustic, romantic atmosphere. This storefront eatery, set on a residential street in Astoria, is a good place to take a date.

In the candlelit room, you can share plates that take their cues from the southern regions of France and Italy. Salads range from Caprese to Niçoise, while entrées include everything from penne alla vodka to striped bass oreganata. For dessert, tiramisu and crêpes Suzette represent the cafe's Franco-Italian tendencies.

Locals favor the weekend brunch, which includes everything from omelets and French toast to octopus carpaccio and tuna tartare.

Chao Thai

Thai

85-03 Whitney Ave. (at Broadway)

Subway: Elmhurst Av — Wed – Mon lunch & dinner
Phone: 718-424-4999
Web: N/A
Prices:

One of the best Thai restaurants in the five boroughs, Chao Thai makes up in taste what its décor lacks in style. It's a tiny spot of real estate in the heart of Elmhurst, sandwiched between Asian markets and restaurants of all types. Don't get distracted by piles of durian and jackfruit beckoning your wallet; save your *baht* for a coconut ice cream.

Skip the printed menu and ask staff to translate the long list of daily specials; this is where the kitchen's talent lies. These dishes are closer to Bangkok than New York and reflect the restaurant's commitment to feed a typically Thai clientele properly. Prices are low enough to order an extra dish or two.

This popular place has limited seating, takes cash only, and is BYOB, so plan ahead.

De Mole

Mexican 

45-02 48th Ave. (at 45th St.)

Subway: 46 St — Lunch & dinner daily
Phone: 718-392-2161
Web: N/A
Prices:

If you lived in Sunnyside, you'd likely be a regular at this charming Mexican bistro. Even if you don't, you might want to stop by the cozy brick-walled spot for its flavorful food and its surprising, European-influenced setting.

De Mole perfectly fuses real Mexican cuisine with a Balthazar-like touch on the details. The reasonably priced menu—supplemented by inviting daily specials—brings forth the best of Mexico, while fajitas, nachos and such are a nod to Mexican-American tastes. Even chips and salsa get bistro treatment as freshly fried tortillas are presented SoHo-style in a paper bag and served with an addictive smoky salsa.

If you need a kick to quench your thirst, you'll have to stop by the nearest bodega to pick up some *cervesas*; De Mole is BYOB.

Fiesta Mexicana

006 Mexican

75-02 Roosevelt Ave. (at 75th St.)

Subway: 74 St - Broadway — Lunch & dinner daily
Phone: 718-505-9090
Web: N/A
Prices: $$

Just a few blocks from the Jackson Heights station, Fiesta Mexicana indulges sit-down diners as well as those on the run—the latter with its booming take-out business. A loyal clientele haunts this place for the delicious authentic Mexican food here. Although it's tempting, don't fill up on the chips and fantastic smoky salsa, so you'll have room for tasty *tacos de tinga* (soft corn tortillas stuffed with shredded roast pork and cooked in a chipotle tomato sauce). For dessert, the chocolate *tres leches* cake is a signature.

The restaurant has no liquor license, but the seasonal *agua frescas*, blends of fresh fruit juices and water served over ice, are great thirst-quenchers. Be sure to bring cash; Fiesta Mexicana doesn't accept credit cards.

Gum Fung

007 Chinese

136-28 39th Ave. (bet. Main & 138th Sts.)

Subway: Flushing - Main St — Lunch & dinner daily
Phone: 718-762-8821
Web: N/A
Prices: $$

For any dim sum die-hard in the New York area, Gum Fung is Mecca. The huge, bright dining room sits in the heart of Flushing's Chinatown, easily accessible by either train or car. Diners here are greeted with open arms, and groups and families pack this place for the bite-size offerings served from carts that are maneuvered around the room by members of the waitstaff. Once you're seated, settle in and pay careful attention to the procession of steamed and fried concoctions passing by your table. Spring rolls, sticky-rice packets, and steamed buns number among the multitude of delectable dim sum selections.

Corral some friends and sample a little bit of everything. Just remember, for the best quality and variety, you have to get here early.

Jackson Diner 

Indian

37-47 74th St. (bet. Roosevelt & 37th Aves.)

Subway: Jackson Hts - Roosevelt Av — Lunch & dinner daily
Phone: 718-672-1232
Web: www.jacksondiner.com
Prices: ⊜

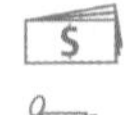

You could call the décor in this Jackson Heights diner whimsical, or you could say it was gaudy, depending on your point of view. Either way, it's colorful and modern, from the 3-D leaves on the ceiling to the multi-hued chairs that are more functional than comfortable.

Don't come expecting burgers and milkshakes, though, since this diner is all about Indian cooking. If you like curries, masala dosa and tandoori dishes, Jackson Diner won't disappoint. The inexpensive lunch buffet offers a wide variety of Southern Indian dishes, including dessert, for one low price.

After lunch, spend some time exploring the immediate neighborhood, which teems with jewelry stores, sari shops and groceries, all peddling Indian wares.

KumGangSan

138-28 Northern Blvd. (bet. Bowne & Union Sts.)

Subway: Flushing - Main St — Lunch & dinner daily
Phone: 718-461-0909
Web: www.kumgangsan.net
Prices: $$

Having hunger pangs in the middle of the night? If you happen to be near Flushing, make a beeline for KumGangSan; it's open 24/7. Named for a range of mountains (translated as "Diamond Mountains" in English) in North Korea, the restaurant offers simple comforts, but that's of little matter to the lines of faithful customers who come here to dine on the large selection of noodles, bowls of steaming broth, barbecued meats and casseroles, all made with seasonings imported from Korea. Meals begin here with a series of *panchan* (small dishes) before moving on to appetizers and main courses. In summer, snag a table on the terrace, with its burbling fountain.

There's another location in Midtown West, which is open all night, too.

Malagueta

Brazilian

010

25-35 36th Ave. (at 28th St.)

Subway: 36 Av
Phone: 718-937-4821
Web: N/A
Prices: ⊜

Tue – Fri dinner only
Sat – Sun lunch & dinner

The neighborhood may be nondescript and the comfort may be basic here, but those aren't the reasons for coming to this tiny South American eatery. Good Brazilian food and reasonable prices are the reasons, and it would be a shame to visit Queens and miss this place. While most people associate Astoria with Greek food, you'll be rewarded for trying something different here.

At Malagueta, chef/owner Herbet Gomes, who grew up in northern Brazil, dishes up the likes of *acaraje* (black-pea fritters), *salpicao* (traditional Brazilian salad) and *moqueca de camarão* (shrimp stew with palm oil, onions, peppers and coconut milk); *feijoada*, the national dish of Brazil, is offered only on Saturday. Whenever you go, save room for the passion fruit mousse.

Pho'Hoang

Vietnamese

011

41-01 Kissena Blvd. (at Main St.)

Subway: Flushing - Main St
Phone: 718-762-6151
Web: N/A
Prices: ⊜

Lunch & dinner daily

$

Just blocks from the 7 train in the heart of Flushing, Pho'Hoang brings a taste of Saigon to a section of Queens where an Asian-American population and good Asian restaurants predominate.

The dining room may be basic, but prices are very reasonable, and this place is usually packed with people slurping bowls of *pho* or digging into succulent barbecued meats and poultry. Food here is authentically prepared, and a brisk take-out trade keeps the cooks at the steam counter on their toes. The enormous menu covers everything from excellent Vietnamese spring rolls to hearty rice and noodle dishes. Pho, the seemingly bottomless bowls of rice-noodle soup, come in two sizes—but with prices this good, why get the small?

Sabry's

Seafood

24-25 Steinway St. (bet. Astoria Blvd. & 25th Ave.)

Subway: Astoria Blvd — Lunch & dinner daily
Phone: 718-721-9010
Web: N/A
Prices: $$

Located in an area of Astoria that's fast becoming known as Little Egypt, Sabry's serves seafood with Egyptian accents—starting with the large ice-filled case where the day's fresh catch is displayed. Prepared in the style of many Greek eateries, fish from this case are grilled or baked whole, here with Middle Eastern flavorings like garlic, cumin, cardamom and red pepper. Aromatic tagines, such as the shellfish version cooked in a heady tomato sauce, are another good option. Baba ganoush is packed with flavor, and the freshly made pita bread makes a fantastic accompaniment.

If you must have a glass of wine, be aware that the restaurant doesn't serve alcohol and you cannot BYOB. There are plenty of other options, though, like tasty mint tea.

S'Agapo

Greek

013

34-21 34th Ave. (at 35th St.)

Subway: Steinway St — Lunch & dinner daily
Phone: 718-626-0303
Web: N/A
Prices: $$

When in Astoria, go where the Greeks go, and in the case of S'Agapo ("I love you" in Greek), you'll quickly discover why this place is always crammed with Greeks, locals and Manhattanites sipping ouzo or a great bottle of wine.

Located on a quiet residential block bordering Astoria and Long Island City, S'Agapo is owned and managed by a charming couple from Crete. The taverna focuses on providing authentic food at palatable prices, with personal service.

Rustic preparations of perfectly grilled fish, lamb, and an extensive assortment of cold and hot appetizers mean that no diner goes away hungry. A number of Cretan specialties (house-made lamb sausage, Cretan cheese dumplings), as well as the quiet outdoor terrace, set S'Agapo apart.

Sapori d'Ischia

Italian

55-15 37th Ave. (at 56th St.)

Subway: Northern Blvd — Tue – Sun lunch & dinner
Phone: 718-446-1500
Web: N/A
Prices: $$

Remember the movie *Big Night*? Like the Baltimore Italian restaurant that starred in that film, Sapori d'Ischia doesn't serve sides of spaghetti. In fact, their "house rules," posted at the bar, spell out a number of other things the restaurant doesn't do (for instance, they don't serve butter, grate cheese atop seafood or put lemon peel in espresso).

Set on an industrial-looking block in Woodside, Sapori d'Ischia started out as a wholesale Italian foods business. Over the years, owner Frank Galano (who runs the place with his son Antonio), added a market and then a small trattoria to the premises. Today, delectable pastas, low prices and a convivial atmosphere complete with live piano entertainment keep customers coming back for more.

718 - Seven One Eight

015

French

35-01 Ditmars Blvd. (at 35th St.)

Subway: Astoria - Ditmars Blvd — Lunch & dinner daily
Phone: 718-204-5553
Web: www.718restaurant.com
Prices: $$

What's in a name? In this case, 718 refers to the Queens' area code. No matter. This cozy French bistro provides a welcome addition to the Greek and Italian places that pervade the Astoria dining scene.

With its solid French base, the cuisine displays Spanish and American influences, all realized with fresh, seasonal products: shrimp meets mango in a salad, rack of lamb pairs with piquillo peppers, and thin-crust *tarte flambée* pay homage to that traditional Alsatian dish. Banana and chocolate bread pudding, and warm apple tart round out the scrumptious dessert menu.

Come Friday night to watch the belly dancer and listen to music from the Casbah. If you're out partying late, 718 offers a tapas menu every day until 2am.

Spicy & Tasty

Chinese

39-07 Prince St. (at 39th Ave.)

Subway: Flushing - Main St — Lunch & dinner daily
Phone: 718-359-1601
Web: N/A
Prices: ⓢⓢ

Teeming with a dizzying array of restaurants, bakeries and shops all catering to Flushing's booming Asian population, this Chinatown block draws a mix of New Yorkers in search of real Chinese food.

Spicy & Tasty fills that bill with fiery Szechuan cuisine that is remarkably consistent. Delicious dishes blend different degrees of heat, ranging from the mouth-numbing effect of Szechuan peppercorns to whole chilies marinated in sour vinegar that are merely warm by comparison. A few mild selections, which are no less tasty, will appeal to more prudent palates. Count on the kind staff for sound guidance regarding what to order.

The spacious dining room eschews Chinese lanterns and red walls in favor of light colors and wood sculptures.

Sripraphai 

Thai

64-13 39th Ave. (bet. 64th & 65th Sts.)

Subway: Woodside - 61 St — Mon – Tue & Thu – Sun lunch & dinner
Phone: 718-899-9599
Web: N/A
Prices: ⓢⓢ

The Thai crowd is your first hint that owner Sripraphai Tipmanee serves the real thing at her eponymous restaurant. Her food is spicy, and she doesn't cop out by catering to American tastes. Probably the most authentic Thai restaurant in New York City, Sripraphai is well worth the ride out to Woodside (street parking is available nearby, and the restaurant is a short walk from the train).

All the accolades here go to the premium ingredients. Succulent pork and sweet shrimp fill the bean thread casserole; a julienne of fresh green papaya pairs perfectly in a salad with crispy catfish; and green-and-white-speckled Thai eggplant makes the green curry a delight.

On a warm, sunny day, the garden out back makes an appealing place to dine.

Stamatis

018 — Greek

3114 Broadway (bet. 31st & 32nd Sts.)

Subway: Broadway — Lunch & dinner daily
Phone: 718-204-8964
Web: N/A
Prices: $$

Who says there's no longer any good Greek food to be found in Astoria? *Au contraire*, the neighborhood's Mediterranean heritage is alive and well at Stamatis. A block away from the subway, Stamatis delivers all the standards to an eager crowd, many of whom are Greek.

If you're hankering for spanikopita, hop on the train and head straight here. The restaurant's enormous menu runs all the bases, from meze to grilled whole fish, and each entrée comes with your choice of a classically Greek side item. Presentations are simple, but dishes are large on portion, flavor and quality.

After your meal, a complimentary dessert based on the daily selection of sweets (perhaps a cinnamon honey cake or a custard-filled pastry), will arrive at your table.

Taverna Kyclades

019 — Greek

33-07 Ditmars Blvd. (bet. 33rd & 35th Sts.)

Subway: Astoria - Ditmars Blvd — Lunch & dinner daily
Phone: 718-545-8666
Web: www.tavernakyclades.com
Prices: ⊜

Known for its large Greek population, Astoria doesn't lack for tavernas. This one, located on one of the commercial hubs of Greek Astoria, stands out for its seafood. A trophy swordfish decorates the exposed brick wall of the tiny dining room, where the waitstaff is clad appropriately in blue and white (the colors of the Greek flag).

Lunch is simple here, with a short menu of fish entrées supplemented by a few Greek grills and, of course, *spanikopita* (spinach pie layered with feta cheese and phyllo). Dinner presents a wider choice of main courses emphasizing the fruits of the sea, though concessions are made to landlubbers with lamb chops, chicken kebabs, and steaks. Desserts are only offered in the evening, and reservations are not accepted.

Tournesol

French

020

50-12 Vernon Blvd. (bet. 50th & 51st Aves.)

Subway: Vernon Blvd - Jackson Av

Phone: 718-472-4355

Web: N/A

Prices: $$

Tue – Sun lunch & dinner
Mon dinner only

A sunflower grows in Long Island City, in the form of this art-filled bistro, whose name means "sunflower" in French. Not far outside the Queens-Midtown Tunnel, Tournesol defies its unappealing concrete-jungle location. With only 40 seats, the family-run restaurant was a pioneer in this section of Queens and paved the way for other neighborhood eateries here.

In the simple, cheery dining room, you can feast on dishes from the South of France (the changing menu may offer sautéed snails, terrine of duck liver, braised beef cheeks, and warm bread pudding). The good news is that you only have to travel a single stop on the 7 train from Grand Central Station to get here. If you're around on the weekend, try Tournesol's French-style brunch.

Trattoria l'Incontro

Italian

021

21-76 31st St. (at Ditmars Blvd.)

Subway: Astoria - Ditmars Blvd

Phone: 718-721-3532

Web: www.trattorialincontro.com

Prices: $$

Tue – Sun lunch & dinner

From the warm welcome you receive at Trattoria l'Incontro, you'll know immediately how important the customers are to Abruzzi native Tina Sacramone and her son, Rocco. Indeed, at this Astoria restaurant, the hospitality is as important as the food. The chef is frequently spotted in the dining area, greeting regulars and making sure everyone is happy with dishes such as Tina's homemade pastas. Risotto here is served in a crisp parmesan "bowl," a good example of how the chef improves on classic Italian fare.

In the dining room, beams punctuate the ceiling, and paintings of the Italian countryside fill the walls. The brick pizza oven, which is visible to diners, turns out a host of savory pies—and even a sweet one stuffed with chocolate.

Water's Edge

022 — American

4-01 44th Dr. (at the East River)

Subway: 23 St - Ely Av — Mon – Fri lunch & dinner
Phone: 718-482-0033 — Sat dinner only
Web: www.watersedgenyc.com
Prices: $$$

Waterside dining with magnificent Manhattan views draws patrons to the Water's Edge. The entire back wall of the restaurant is made of windows, affording superb views of the East River and the skyscrapers of Midtown. Elegant table settings, Louis XV-style chairs, and live piano music fill the dining room, decked out with original artwork and Oriental rugs.

Menus change seasonally; expect skillfully prepared contemporary dishes like grilled sturgeon with sorrel whipped potatoes, and duck with caramelized peaches and braised endive.

If you're coming from Manhattan, make dinner reservations at Water's Edge, and take the complimentary boat shuttle to the restaurant from the 34th Street pier.

Zabb Queens

023 — Thai

71-28 Roosevelt Ave. (bet. 70th & 72nd Sts.)

Subway: 74 St - Broadway — Dinner daily
Phone: 718-426-7992
Web: www.zabbqueens.com
Prices: $$

Expect the unexpected at Zabb. The place may not be much to look at, but if you want to taste some fantastic Thai food, take a trip to Jackson Heights.

Showcasing the cuisine of the Issan region of northeastern Thailand, this family-run restaurant aims to please. Abandon yourself to adventure, and try specialties such as catfish *larb* (crispy ground catfish mixed with mango, cashews, chile and lime juice) or *Esan Thai* sausage, garnished with ginger, peanuts and slivers of red onion. Fantastic homemade coconut ice cream is rich with coconut milk and chunks of coconut meat; it's served with battered and fried bananas drizzled with honey and sprinkled with sesame seeds.

The staff is sweet as pie, eager to assist whenever they can.

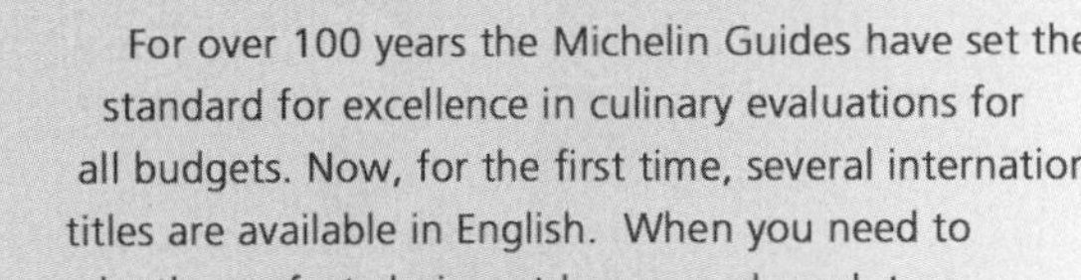

For over 100 years the Michelin Guides have set the standard for excellence in culinary evaluations for all budgets. Now, for the first time, several international titles are available in English. When you need to make the perfect choice, at home or abroad, turn to the world's most obsessively researched guide series. The Michelin Guide. How to find perfect.

www.michelinguide.com

Staten Island

Staten Island

New York City's "forgotten borough," Staten Island is primarily a bedroom community, culturally and economically related more to New Jersey than New York. The island, 14 miles long and 8 miles wide, boasts more wide-open green space than anywhere else is in the city.

To reach any of the restaurants here, you'll have to drive over the Verrazano-Narrows Bridge, or take the ferry. The borough's biggest attraction, the celebrated Staten Island Ferry carries over three-and-a-half-million tourists and commuters a year between Manhattan's South Ferry and St. George terminals, passing the Statue of Liberty each way. Stunning views of the Manhattan skyline and New York Harbor, especially at night, are priceless. So is the fare—the ride is free!

A Bit of History

Staten Island got its name in the early 1600s from Dutch merchants, who dubbed it Staaten Eyelandt (Dutch for "State's Island"). The first permanent settlement was established at Oude Dorp by Dutch and French Huguenot families in 1661. Over the next two centuries, the island thrived on farming and agriculture, ferrying goods to nearby Manhattan and New Jersey.

Staten Island's economy grew considerably in 1898, after its citizens voted to incorporate as one of the five boroughs of Greater New York City. This move attracted hardworking immigrants—many of Italian and Irish descent—to its farms and factories, and hard-playing society folks to its resort hotels. The boom went bust after World War I, when many residents left to make their fortunes on the mainland. The borough blossomed once again when the Verrazano-Narrows Bridge opened in 1964, linking the island with Brooklyn and bringing an influx of Manhattanites seeking refuge from the buzzing energy of the city.

Today's Staten Island

Though isolated, Staten Island is not without its attractions. Its sandy, relatively uncrowded beaches, especially South Beach, make for a lovely outing. **Historic Richmond Town**, a 25-acre village *(441 Clarke Ave.)*, marks the site of one of the earliest settlements on the island. History comes alive here, thanks to costumed guides who demonstrate crafts (printmaking, tinsmithing, weaving) and regale visitors with tales about 19th-century life in the former county seat. An unexpected treasure, the **Jacques Marchais Museum of Tibetan Art** houses rare objects from Tibet, Nepal, China, Mongolia and India in an enchanted setting atop Lighthouse Hill.

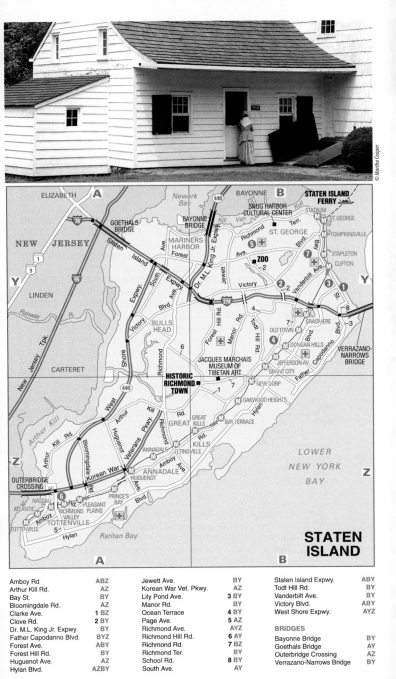

© Martha Cooper

STATEN ISLAND

Street		Grid
Amboy Rd		ABZ
Arthur Kill Rd.		AZ
Bay St.		BY
Bloomingdale Rd.		AZ
Clarke Ave.	1	BZ
Clove Rd.	2	BY
Dr. M.L. King Jr. Expwy.		BY
Father Capodanno Blvd.		BYZ
Forest Ave.		ABY
Forest Hill Rd.		BY
Huguenot Ave.		AZ
Hylan Blvd.		AZBY
Jewett Ave.		BY
Korean War Vet. Pkwy.		AZ
Lily Pond Ave.	3	BY
Manor Rd.		BY
Ocean Terrace	4	BY
Page Ave.	5	AZ
Richmond Ave.		AYZ
Richmond Hill Rd.	6	AY
Richmond Rd.	7	BZ
Richmond Ter.		BY
School Rd.	8	BY
South Ave.		AY
Staten Island Expwy.		ABY
Todt Hill Rd.		BY
Vanderbilt Ave.		BY
Victory Blvd.		ABY
West Shore Expwy.		AYZ

BRIDGES

Bridge	Grid
Bayonne Bridge	BY
Goethals Bridge	AY
Outerbridge Crossing	AZ
Verrazano-Narrows Bridge	BY

Aesop's Tables

Staten Island

001 — **Contemporary**

1233 Bay St. (bet. Maryland & Scarboro Aves.)

Bus: 51 & 81
Phone: 718-720-2005
Web: N/A
Prices: $$

Tue – Sat dinner only
Sun lunch & dinner

Aesop's Tables occupies a renovated storefront on the island's east shore. Since it opened in 1991, this place has attracted a mixed crowd who have become fans of this charming restaurant.
The menu changes regularly, following seasonal ingredients from Long Island and New Jersey farms, but American fare here can include anything from meatloaf to salmon roasted on a cedar plank. The simple, garlicky baked clams perfectly define this restaurant's appealing country cooking.
In the cozy dining room, where blue-and-white bistro chairs nuzzle up to little square tables, the specials are posted on a blackboard framed by silk flowers. Out back, the leafy garden, lit by candles at night, makes a great setting in which to eat on a balmy summer evening.

American Grill

002 — **American**

1180 Victory Blvd. (at Clove Rd.)

Bus: 53, 61, 62
Phone: 718-442-4742
Web: N/A
Prices: $$

Lunch & dinner daily

Red neon letters announce this neighborhood restaurant run by husband-and-wife team Charles and Melissa Santangelo, graduates of the Culinary Institute of America. Charles mans the stoves, while Melissa manages the front of the house with an expert eye.
Inside, the dining room sports a simple décor, pleasantly embellished with dark woods, deep red tones, and color caricatures of its famous local patrons. The food is all-American, prepared with good products; the service is warm and doting without being pushy. Herb- and mustard-crusted salmon, crab cakes, and New York strip steak with beer-battered onion rings represent the menu's variety. American Grill's loyal followers also turn out for the restaurant's reasonably priced lunch and brunch.

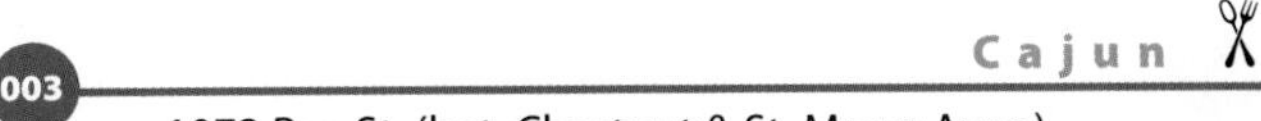

Bayou Restaurant

Cajun

003

1072 Bay St. (bet. Chestnut & St. Marys Aves.)

Bus: 51 & 81
Phone: 718-273-4383
Web: www.bayoustatenisland.com
Prices: $$

Mon – Sat lunch & dinner
Sun dinner only

Hop the ferry from Manhattan to Bayou, where the good times roll and the down-home Creole cooking will make you yearn for The Big Easy. Despite its location in a nondescript neighborhood, if you close your eyes and step inside this faithfully recreated New Orleans bistro, you might think you're in the French Quarter. Exposed brick walls make a gallery for trumpets, banjos, Mardi Gras beads, and portraits of favorite son, Louie Armstrong.

Here, the party never ends, and the mood is infectious. The menu showcases what N'awlins does best, offering chicken and andouille gumbo, catfish po' boys with roasted-pecan gravy, seafood jambalaya, and crawfish étouffée. There's even grilled alligator, and for dessert, don't forget the fried cheesecake.

Carol's Cafe

American

004

1571 Richmond Rd. (at Four Corners Rd. & Seaview Ave.)

Bus: X15, 74, 76, 84, 86
Phone: 718-979-5600
Web: www.carolscafe.com
Prices: $$$

Wed – Sat dinner only

Well-known on Staten Island for the cooking school she operates above her restaurant, owner Carol Frazzetta presides over the kitchen here. Frazzetta graduated from Le Cordon Bleu and studied at the Culinary Institute of America before opening Carol's Cuisine (the cooking school) in 1972. It was only natural that she would follow suit with her own cafe.

Decorated with a feminine touch, evident in the pink-linen napkins, fresh flowers and hanging plants that decorate the interior, Carol's only serves dinner. The seasonal menu travels through the U.S. and Europe for inspiration, fixing on the chef's favorite dishes. With entrées like oven-roasted beef brisket and pancetta- and mushroom-stuffed veal chop, homework never tasted quite so good.

Nurnberger Bierhaus

005 German

817 Castleton Ave. (at Davis Ave.)

Bus: 46, 96 — Lunch & dinner daily
Phone: 718-816-7461
Web: www.nurnbergerbierhaus.com
Prices: $$

Tradition reigns at this friendly Staten Island restaurant, complete with an Oktoberfest spirit and a waitstaff clad in German garb. Rustic German food is what the restaurant does best, and the meat-heavy menu focuses on generous portions of stick-to-your-ribs dishes like *Jägerschnitzel* and *Wurststellar mit allem drum & dran,* four types of sausage accompanied by sauerkraut and red cabbage. Desserts pile on more calories, in the form of German chocolate cake and *Apfelstrudel.*

Groups and families (a children's menu is available) are particularly drawn to the bierhaus, where they are welcomed with open arms and a full stein. The beer is reason alone to visit this place; several imported brews are available on draft, and even more by the bottle.

Panarea Ristorante

006 Italian

35 Page Ave. (bet. Boscombe Ave. & Richmond Valley Rd.)

Bus: 74 — Lunch & dinner daily
Phone: 718-227-8582
Web: www.panarearistorante.com
Prices: $$

Don't be fooled by this restaurant's location in a strip mall; one step inside the etched-glass door, and you'll be won over by its casual elegance. Named for one of the more beautiful islands off the coast of Sicily, Panarea is owned by two Italian couples. From the wood-paneled bar topped with flower-filled Italian ceramic vases to the elegant dining room with its cozy fireplace to the lovely covered veranda, Panarea makes any occasion special.

The kitchen turns out well-prepared Italian classics, like tender grilled baby octopus and spaghetti *chitarra* with lobster sauce. All of the pastas are made from scratch, and the delectable desserts are homemade. Be sure to save room for one of the latter, washed down with a cup of the heady espresso.

Vida

Contemporary

007

381 Van Duzer St. (bet. Beach & Wright Sts.)

Bus: 78 — Tue – Sun lunch & dinner
Phone: 718-720-1501
Web: N/A
Prices: $$

Vida ("life" in Spanish) is an appropriate name for a restaurant at the center of a neighborhood's revitalization. Just five minutes from the waterfront in an area filled with faded, but soon-to-be-revamped Victorian homes, endearing Vida breathes new life into this promising locale.

Terrific food at honest prices is the mantra here, and succulent, spicy-sweet pulled pork on crostini shares the menu with delicious salmon croquettes napped with saffron aïoli. Desserts, like the creamy pumpkin cheesecake, are baked in-house, and while the printed menu is full of delights, the best way to experience Vida is by ordering one of the daily specials.

Friendly service at this casual place cements its reputation as a true neighborhood restaurant.

Where to **stay**

Alphabetical list of Hotels

The Maritime

001

363 W. 16th St. (at Ninth Ave.)

Subway: 14 St - 8 Av
Phone: 212-242-4300 or 800-466-9092
Fax: 212-242-1188
Web: www.themaritimehotel.com
Prices: $$$

121 Rooms

4 Suites

The Maritime Hotel

Ocean liner or hotel? The Maritime, designed for the National Maritime Union in 1966, was meticulously renovated in 2003 to blend the atmospheres of both. Striking five-foot porthole windows, warm teak walls and built-ins, and details in deep blues and greens enhance the air of nautical nostalgia. The lobby, in elegant yet simple retro style, exudes a relaxed and cool ambience.

Most of the cabinlike rooms, each with a marble bath, face the Hudson River and all offer CD/DVD players, flat-screen LCD TVs and wireless Internet access. Sybarites will love the feel of the custom-made cotton sheets, while business travelers will appreciate the spacious work desk and the hotel's on-site business center.

The hotel houses La Bottega, an Italian trattoria (where you can have breakfast), and chic Matsuri *(see restaurant listing)* for Japanese food. And to work off all that food, there's a 24-hour fitness room on-site, or you can borrow a bicycle from the hotel.

Relax with a drink at Cabanas rooftop bar or visit trendy Hiro to experience the hip Chelsea scene. The Maritime is well situated for gallery hopping, as well as sampling Chelsea nightlife and upscale shopping.

The Bowery Hotel

335 Bowery (at 3rd St.)

Subway: Astor Pl
Phone: 212-505-9100 or 866-726-9379
Fax: 212-505-9700
Web: www.theboweryhotel.com
Prices: **$$$$**

The Bowery Hotel/Gregory Goode

This nondescript block of what was once known as Skid Row might seem an unlikely location for a trendy boutique hotel, but Eric Goode and Sean MacPherson (who brought you the Maritime in Chelsea) are betting that their new East Village property will draw hordes of hipsters and Europeans. Though the block can be dodgy late at night, it's within easy walking distance of New York's coolest 'hoods (East Village, SoHo, Nolita, Greenwich Village, Lower East Side).

From the outside, the hotel's new redbrick façade towers castle-like above neighboring structures. Giant black-paned windows give the building a pre-war charm. Step inside and you'll be engulfed in the dim, sultry lobby, where dark woods, fireplaces, velvet couches and mosaic mirrors create a distinctly Old World air.

Those huge, sound-proofed windows afford great city views, and paired with whitewashed brick walls, make the rooms seem larger. A mix of period and contemporary pieces add to the Art Deco-meets-21st-century design, while 500-thread-count bed linens, hi-def TV, and rainfall showerheads add luxury.

Look for the outdoor courtyard bar and restaurant Gemma to be popular with the in-crowd.

Best Western Seaport Inn

001

33 Peck Slip (at Front St.)

Subway: Fulton St
Phone: 212-766-6600 or 800-937-8376
Fax: 212-766-6615
Web: www.seaportinn.com
Prices: $$

72 Rooms

Best Western Seaport Inn

Hard by the Brooklyn Bridge in Lower Manhattan, the Seaport Inn caters to both tourists and business travelers. The former enjoy its location in the popular South Street Seaport area, now known for its museums, shops and galleries. The latter find the hotel well situated for their business dealings in the Financial District. Both appreciate the inn's reasonable prices.

Inside this brick building you'll find clean, well-kept rooms sporting country-style furnishings, floral prints, and in-room safes and refrigerators. Some guestrooms even feature a terrace and a whirlpool tub. Complimentary high-speed Internet access is available throughout the hotel. In the morning, guests enjoy a continental breakfast, and in the afternoon, fresh-baked cookies are set out; both are included in the room rate.

Ask for a room on the 6th or 7th floor, where you'll have a private terrace overlooking the East River and the Financial District skyscrapers. And why not bring the family along? At the Seaport Inn, children 17 and under stay free in their parents' room.

The Ritz-Carlton, Battery Park

002

2 West St. (at Battery Pl.)

Subway: Bowling Green
Phone: 212-344-0800 or 800-241-3333
Fax: 212-344-3801
Web: www.ritzcarlton.com
Prices: **$$$$**

259 Rooms
39 Suites

The Ritz-Carlton Hotel

Rising 39 stories above Battery Park in its glass and brick tower, the Ritz commands a stunning view of the Statue of Liberty and New York Harbor. Rooms with harbor views are equipped with high-powered telescopes so you can better take in the dramatic waterscapes. If your room doesn't have a harbor view, don't despair; you can enjoy the same striking panorama—and a cocktail—from the Rise Bar on the 14th floor.

Guests here nestle in spacious rooms amid soothing pale colors, luxurious fabrics, Frette linens and marble bathrooms. Say the word and a butler will draw you a relaxing bath. Stay on the Club Level and you'll be treated to a complimentary breakfast and evening cocktails and hors d'oeuvres.

After a workout at the hotel's 2,500-square-foot health club, you can justify a caloric splurge at 2 West restaurant, which prides itself on its prime Angus beef. While you're here, walk through the hotel's Art Deco-style public areas to see the impressive collection of modern art.

Wall Street is only a five-minute walk from the Ritz, and sightseers can catch ferries to the Statue of Liberty and Ellis Island right across the street.

Wall Street Inn

003

9 S. William St. (bet. Beaver & Broad Sts.)

Subway: Wall St (William St.)
Phone: 212-747-1500 or 877-747-1500
Fax: 212-747-1900
Web: www.thewallstreetinn.com
Prices: $$

46 Rooms

The Wall Street Inn

Tucked into one of the narrow streets laid out by the Dutch in the 17th century, this hotel fills two landmark buildings (1895 and 1920), previously occupied by Lehman Brothers. First-time guests soon become regulars here, drawn back time after time by the warm welcoming staff, well-appointed rooms, and moderate prices for the location.

Cheery chambers are tastefully done in period reproductions, and accented with fresh flowers and plants. All rooms have marble baths, and larger rooms on the 7th floor boast Jacuzzi tubs. Guest rooms on the back of the hotel overlook Stone Street, which can get noisy at night with revelers partying at popular watering holes.

The location, right down the block from the New York Stock Exchange, and near South Street Seaport, is great for business travelers as well as families. Amenities such as in-room refrigerators, a small business center offering a full range of services, free high-speed Internet access, and a small fitness facility, make the Wall Street Inn a good value for the price. And don't forget the complimentary continental breakfast.

The Carlton

001

88 Madison Ave. (at 29th St.)

Subway: 28 St (Park Ave. South)
Phone: 212-532-4100 or 800-601-8500
Fax: 212-889-8683
Web: www.carltonhotelny.com
Prices: **$$$**

293 Rooms
23 Suites

The Carlton

A traditional Beaux-Arts hotel dating back to 1904, The Carlton sports a chic new look crafted by renowned interior designer David Rockwell. The 316-room hotel has an intimate European ambience, beginning with the polished woods and stylish mushroom and cream tones of the lobby, which boasts a two-story waterfall. Guestrooms and suites are awash in a palette of greens, browns and grays, and luxuriously equipped with Frette linens, mahogany furnishings and marble bathrooms. Pets are invited to tag along to this supremely comfortable hotel, where all rooms have iPod docking stations and complimentary wireless Internet access.

The Carlton's location just north of Madison Square Park, in the Gramercy/Flatiron neighborhood, affords views of the Empire State Building and busy Madison Avenue. Although The Carlton doesn't have an on-site gym, it does provide guests with complimentary access to Boom Fitness Center *(4 Park Ave.)*.

In addition to high style, The Carlton invites its guests to indulge in fine dining at Country *(see restaurant listing)*. This restaurant wins rave reviews from hotel guests and New Yorkers alike, and routinely draws an A-list clientele.

Gramercy Park Hotel

002

2 Lexington Ave. (at 21st St.)

Subway: 23 St (Park Ave. South)
Phone: 212-920-3300 or 866-784-1300
Fax: 212-673-5890
Web: www.gramercyparkhotel.com
Prices: **$$$$**

140 Rooms

44 Suites

Nikolas Koenig

The Gramercy Park has been hosting artists, writers and celebrities since 1925, but now its storied past is married to a fresh new look. With hip hotelier Ian Schrager and artist Julian Schnabel breathing new life into this property, the hotel is back and it's hot. Posh British-castle-meets-Gothic-Revival describes the dark lobby décor with its coffered ceiling, crystal chandeliers, and striking artwork by modern masters. Red velvet draperies and tapestry-print fabrics lend a masculine feel to the rooms. Thoughtful amenities range from a fully loaded iPod (upon request) to a key to Gramercy Park (impossible to access unless you live on the square overlooking the gated greensward).

Room service delivers a "best of" menu from famous area restaurants, just as bath products are chosen according to a "best of" list, with full-size versions available for purchase in the mini-bar.

Meanwhile, the celebutante scene at the Rose and Jade bars begs you to don your best Manolos, and the rooftop beckons the well-connected in warm weather. After a night of shameless partying, detox in the hotel's Aerospace gym, where views of the leafy park should soothe your throbbing head.

Inn at Irving Place

003

56 Irving Pl. (bet 17th & 18th Sts.)

Subway: 14 St - Union Sq
Phone: 212-533-4600 or 800-685-1447
Fax: 212-533-4611
Web: www.innatirving.com
Prices: $$$$

12 Rooms

The Inn at Irving Place/Roy Wright

Once you step inside the doors of this small, unmarked luxury hotel, you'll be immersed in a bygone day. Built in 1834, two single-family brownstones (which contained everything from a speakeasy to a day spa over the years) now house the Inn at Irving Place. The cozy, charming lobby welcomes guests to a world filled with 19th-century antiques and a quiet grace.

Twelve individually decorated rooms are named for famous turn-of-the-century New Yorkers, many of whom once lived in the neighborhood (actress Sarah Bernhardt, author Washington Irving; interior designer Elsie de Wolfe). Don't think, however, that you'll lack for 21st-century comforts; Frette linens, Penhaligon's bathroom amenities, Sony CD players, and wireless Internet connection come with each room.

In the morning, savor a continental breakfast in your room or in the parlor. Be sure to save time for afternoon tea (reservations required) in Lady Mendl's Victorian tea salon. Downstairs, clubby Cibar lounge offers a menu of martinis and light appetizers.

W - Union Square

004

201 Park Ave. South (at 17th St.)

Subway: 14 St - Union Sq
Phone: 212-253-9119 or 877-782-0027
Fax: 212-253-9229
Web: www.whotels.com
Prices: $$$$

257 Rooms

13 Suites

W Hotels

The granite and limestone Guardian Life Building (1911) has been reborn as a posh W hotel overlooking Union Square. Designed by David Rockwell, the interior sports a contemporary look, from the polished two-story lobby with its sweeping staircase to soundproofed rooms with sleek leather headboards.

Comfort abounds in contemporary and roomy guest quarters, where you'll find goose-down comforters and pillows, cushy velvet armchairs, bath products from Bliss Spa, and terrycloth-lined robes. As for service, how can you argue with a hotel whose philosophy is "whatever you want, whenever you want it?" Just press the button on your room phone for everything from netting hard-to-get Knicks tickets to scheduling an in-room massage.

Pets are welcome here, and your four-legged friend will be walked, groomed and pampered with special meals. Add Olives' tasty Mediterranean cuisine *(see restaurant listing)* and the hip, intimate Underbar, and you won't wonder why W-Union Square attracts a steady stream of visitors and locals alike.

Gansevoort

001

18 Ninth Ave. (at 13th St.)

Subway: 14 St - 8 Av
Phone: 212-206-6700 or 877-462-7386
Fax: 212-255-5858
Web: www.hotelgansevoort.com
Prices: **$$$$**

158 Rooms
20 Suites

Spa

heated

Hotel Gansevoort/David Joseph

Slick, sleek, swank: the upscale hotel in the Meatpacking District, the Gansevoort rises 14 stories above the burgeoning hip-dom of this once gritty area. Only the name, which belonged to the grandfather of Herman Melville, is historic. The lobby of this oh-so-cool property is outfitted in cherrywood paneling and Matisse-inspired carpet. Eelskin-covered columns and mohair panels add texture, and special attention has been paid to lighting effects throughout. Elegant rooms wear a dusky palette with touches of color, and huge windows overlook, from the high floors, the Hudson River and surrounding city. Bathrooms are large and luxurious.

Ono *(see restaurant listing)* offers a hip scene and contemporary Japanese cuisine, but the coup de grace is the hotel's rooftop, complete with its popular bar and 45-foot-long heated pool with underwater music.

Gansevoort's newest additions are the Hiro Salon and the GSpa and Lounge, both located in the basement. By day, you can pamper yourself with a multitude of treatments at the sultry spa; by night, the spa equipment is removed and the space morphs into a lounge. It's quite the neighborhood hotspot.

The Hotel on Rivington

001

107 Rivington St. (bet. Essex & Ludlow Sts.)

Subway: Delancey St
Phone: 212-475-2600 or 800-915-1537
Fax: 212-475-5959
Web: www.hotelonrivington.com
Prices: **$$$**

89 Rooms

21 Suites

Hotel on Rivington/Nikolas Koenig

The Hotel on Rivington has taken utmost advantage of its status as the first tall building in this swiftly gentrifying neighborhood. With floor-to-ceiling glass walls on at least two sides, rooms in its 21 stories offer stunning, unobstructed views of the surrounding cityscape.

The remarkable result of a collaboration of cutting-edge architects, designers, decorators and artists from around the world, this hotel combines sleek minimalist décor with ultramodern amenities, and, yes, comfort. If you notice anything but the view, you'll appreciate the Tempur-pedic mattresses, Frette linens, and wake-up calls synchronized with motorized curtains. The deluxe Italian-tile bathrooms are equipped with heated floors, steam showers and Japanese-style soaking tubs.

When you get hungry, check out the hotel's restaurant, Thor. In this airy space, topped by a soaring glass ceiling, you can savor market-fresh seasonal fare for breakfast, lunch, dinner, and weekend brunch.

You enter the lobby—accessible only to you and your invited guests—through the Eggtrance, designed as a deconstructed egg.

The Benjamin

001

125 E. 50th St. (bet. Lexington & Third Aves.)

Subway: 51 St
Phone: 212-715-2500 or 866-233-4642
Fax: 212-715-2525
Web: www.thebenjamin.com
Prices: **$$$$**

112 Rooms

79 Suites

The Benjamin

From its classic 1927 building (designed by Emery Roth and now beautifully restored) to its attentive service, The Benjamin serves up New York on a silver platter without a sterling-silver price tag.

This comfortable hotel hospitably accommodates business travelers, who appreciate practical details like kitchenettes, in-room business amenities, and 24-hour fitness center. It's the staff that makes the true difference here. Cheerful personnel go well beyond what passes for service at nearby business-oriented hotels, greeting guests by name and caring for them warmly. Dark wood furnishings and soft cream and taupe hues create a sophisticated haven from hurried Midtown, and rooms are amply appointed with lamps, hangers, Bose radios, and abundant towels in the small but elegant baths.

If stress has you tied in knots, visit The Benjamin's spa, where a comprehensive menu treats guests to a variety of ways to relax, rejuvenate and revive. The Benjamin restaurant and Emery Bar are convenient for a business meeting, and in addition to room service, with advance notice, the hotel will stock your fridge prior to your arrival with your favorite groceries and beverages.

Elysée

002

60 E. 54th St. (bet. Madison & Park Aves.)

Subway: 5 Av - 53 St
Phone: 212-753-1066 or 800-535-9733
Fax: 212-980-9278
Web: www.elyseehotel.com
Prices: **$$$**

89 Rooms

12 Suites

Elysée Hotel

Since the 1920s, the Elysée has earned a reputation as a discreetly private haven for writers, actors and musicians. Vladimir Horowitz once lived in the suite where his piano still stands; Tennessee Williams lived and died here (in the Sunset Suite); and Marlon Brando made this his New York home.

The period atmosphere lingers on in the Neoclassical-style furnishings, careful service and recently redecorated rooms—some with terraces, kitchenettes or solariums. Lovely bathrooms are clad in marble. Classic, yes, but modern conveniences like hotel-wide wireless Internet access, iPod docking stations, and two-line phones are available here, too.

Complimentary breakfast and evening wine and hors d'oeuvres are served in the second-floor Club Room. Since the hotel does not have an on-site fitness center, guests are offered complimentary use of the nearby NY Sports Club.

The Elysée may be best known—and loved—for its engaging Monkey Bar *(see restaurant listing)*, where murals of frolicking monkeys, olive-shaped barstools and piano music, along with a newly revamped menu of pan-Asian fare, draw an attractive clientele.

Four Seasons New York

003

57 E. 57th St. (bet. Madison & Park Aves.)

Subway: 59 St
Phone: 212-758-5700 or 800-487-3769
Fax: 212-350-6302
Web: www.fourseasons.com
Prices: **$$$$**

305 Rooms

63 Suites

Four Seasons New York

Noted architect I.M. Pei designed the monumentally elegant Four Seasons New York in 1993. Nothing is small about this property. The tallest hotel in the city, the limestone-clad tower soars 52 stories in a Postmodern style inspired by the 1920s. Inside the 57th Street entrance, you'll walk into a grand foyer decorated with temple-like pillars, marble floors and a 33-foot backlit onyx ceiling.

The hotel also boasts some of the city's largest rooms, which, at 600 square feet, are doubtless among the most luxurious as well. A recent refurbishment installed plasma-screen TVs in the opulent bathrooms, which also feature marble soaking tubs that fill in just 60 seconds. Top-drawer service includes a 24-hour concierge, perks for pets and children, and a fabulous newly redesigned spa offering a full spectrum of massages, facials and body treatments. You'll find state-of-the-art exercise equipment, along with a whirlpool, steam room and sauna in the fitness facility.

In summer 2006, the Four Seasons welcomed its eagerly anticipated new restaurant, L'Atelier de Joël Robuchon *(see restaurant listing)*. This great addition to the New York dining scene features contemporary French cuisine by the renowned French chef.

Library

004

299 Madison Ave. (at 41st St.)

Subway: Grand Central - 42 St
Phone: 212-983-4500 or 877-793-7323
Fax: 212-499-9099
Web: www.libraryhotel.com
Prices: **$$$**

60 Rooms

Library Hotel

Nothing warms a room like books, and the Library Hotel proves the point. Steps from the New York Public and the Pierpont Morgan libraries, this boutique inn makes great use of its collection of 6,000 volumes. Each floor is numbered after a category in the Dewey Decimal system, and rooms contain books on a particular subject. History buff? Request the Biography room on the 9th floor. Literature your thing? Head to the 8th floor.

Furnishings are simple, and, though small, rooms are comfortable and quiet. Well equipped for business travelers, the hotel provides in-room high-speed Internet access, and computer stations in its business center. Enjoy a continental breakfast daily, snacks throughout the day and a wine reception on weekday evenings. Bottled spring water and Belgian chocolates come with each room, as does a VCR. Guests can choose their favorite movies from the hotel's video library of the American Film Institute's Top 100.

The hotel's pleasant public spaces, including the Writer's Den with its fireplace and comfy chairs, and the terrace Poetry Garden, are perfect for—what else?—reading.

New York Palace

005

455 Madison Ave. (bet. 50th & 51st Sts.)

Subway: 51 St
Phone: 212-888-7000 or 800-697-2522
Fax: 212-303-6000
Web: www.newyorkpalace.com
Prices: **$$$$**

807 Rooms
86 Suites

New York Palace

The opulent Palace joins the historic 1882 Villard town houses with a contemporary 55-story tower built in 1980. The hotel's public spaces occupy the lavishly restored town homes built in the Italian Renaissance style, which you can enter through the lovely carriage courtyard on Madison Avenue. Fifth Avenue shopping, Rockefeller Center and Midtown cultural attractions all lie within easy walking distance.

Modern hotel rooms in the tower (floors 41 through 54), including 86 suites, are done in either traditional or modern style and provide all the amenities. The Palace houses a 7,000-square-foot spa and fitness club along with 22,000 square feet of excellent conference facilities. West-facing rooms have a stunning view of St. Patrick's Cathedral, just across Madison Avenue.

Gilt *(see restaurant listing)*, the Palace's acclaimed restaurant, offers cutting-edge cuisine and classic service in the space formerly occupied by Le Cirque 2000. Stop by the adjacent Gilt Bar and Lounge for a sophisticated cocktail in a striking contemporary setting.

Roger Smith

006

501 Lexington Ave. (at 47th St.)

Subway: 51 St
Phone: 212-755-1400 or 800-445-0277
Fax: 212-758-4061
Web: www.rogersmithhotel.com
Prices: $$

102 Rooms

28 Suites

Roger Smith

Full of playful character—and art—the Roger Smith offers a casual, warm ambience cultivated by an attentive and welcoming young staff. In the public spaces, you'll find rotating exhibits of original artwork, and the hotel even owns and operates its own contemporary art gallery at the corner of 47th Street.

Spacious rooms in the bed-and-breakfast vein are individually decorated in crisp American country style, some with wrought-iron bed frames, and some with antique four-poster beds. Bathrooms remain in good condition, despite the fact that the building dates to 1929. Sunny junior suites claim coveted corner locations and come equipped with pull-out sofas for extra guests.

By special agreement, Roger Smith guests have access to a nearby fitness club (for a fee), and the hotel provides an iMac in the lobby for accessing your e-mail. Pets and children are welcome; kids 16 and under stay for free in their parents' room. All in all, the Roger Smith offers a good rate for its comfort, convenience and atmosphere.

Roger Williams

007

131 Madison Ave. (at 31st St.)

Subway: 33 St
Phone: 212-448-7000 or 888-448-7788
Fax: 212-448-7007
Web: www.hotelrogerwilliams.com
Prices: **$$$**

191 Rooms

2 Suites

Hotel Roger Williams

Clean lines and pure color best describe the freshly renovated Roger Williams. In a departure from fashionable dark woods and minimalist palettes of gray and beige, colorful highlights accent the furnishings here. Light fills the lobby through 20-foot-high windows, and comfortable seating areas provide a classy meeting place.

Simple interior design and furniture give "the Roger" a distinctly Scandinavian air. The rooms, 15 with terraces (nice for romantic alfresco dining), feature flat-screen TVs, wireless high-speed Internet access, and modern bathrooms, though some only have showers (no tubs). Thoughtful touches include Egyptian cotton linens, Aveda toiletries, mini-bars and umbrellas. Most rooms have spectacular views of the nearby Empire State Building.

A "help-yourself" European-style breakfast (stocking everything from fresh-baked pastries to meats and cheeses) is available in the Breakfast Pantry each morning, and jazz plays by candlelight several evenings a week in the lounge. Located at 31st Street, the Roger is convenient to Madison Square Garden, Macy's and the trendy shops and restaurants of Midtown.

70 Park Avenue

008

70 Park Ave. (at 38th St.)

Subway: Grand Central - 42 St
Phone: 212-973-2400 or 877-707-2752
Fax: 212-973-2401
Web: www.70parkave.com
Prices: **$$$**

201 Rooms
4 Suites

Kimpton New York/David Phelps

In elegance and style, this Kimpton hotel lives up to the fashionable residential neighborhood it occupies. A few blocks from Grand Central Station, and convenient to Madison and Fifth avenues, 70 Park takes its design cue from its historic façade. The interior color scheme, from lobby to guest rooms, ranges from limestone gray to shimmery bronze and light cocoa brown; a sandstone and limestone fireplace makes a notable centerpiece in the lobby.

Très chic, yes, but all set in a friendly and relaxing atmosphere. The rooms, comfortably contemporary, brim with electronic amenities, including CD/DVD players, and 42-inch flat-screen TVs with a yoga channel for hotel guests (yoga mats are available upon request). There's Wi-Fi Internet access throughout the property as well.

Tea and coffee are set out in the bar each morning, and after a hard day at work or play, you can mix and mingle at the evening wine receptions. Located off the lobby, Silverleaf Tavern serves a short menu of pub grub, as well as a full bar and a good selection of wines by the glass. As is the case at most Kimpton properties, pets are welcome here.

The St. Regis

009

2 E. 55th St. (at Fifth Ave.)

Subway: 5 Av - 53 St
Phone: 212-753-4500 or 800-759-7550
Fax: 212-787-3447
Web: www.stregis.com/newyork
Prices: $$$$

186 Rooms

70 Suites

The St. Regis Hotel

Stylish and elegant, and with service close to perfection, the St. Regis reigns among the city's finest hotels. Commissioned by John Jacob Astor in 1904, this Beaux-Arts confection at the corner of Fifth Avenue is located just blocks from Central Park, MoMA and other Midtown attractions. Its public spaces and lobby, from the painted ceilings to the marble staircase, are steeped in Gilded Age opulence.

A recent redesign updated the elegant guestrooms with silk wall coverings and custom-made furniture. Guests in the spacious suites (the smallest is 600 square feet; they range up to 3,400 square feet) are cosseted with extra luxuries, such as a bouquet of fresh roses delivered daily. Unparalleled service includes a butler you can call on 24 hours a day, an on-site florist, complimentary garment pressing when you arrive, and the on-site Remède spa. Their signature massage calms jangled nerves with a mix of Shiatsu, Swedish, deep-tissue and reflexology.

Be sure to stop in the King Cole Bar to peek at Maxfield Parrish's famous mural, and to sip a Bloody Mary, which was introduced here in the 1920s.

The Vincci Avalon

16 E. 32nd St. (bet. Fifth & Madison Aves.)

Subway: 33 St
Phone: 212-299-7000 or 888-442-8256
Fax: 212-299-7001
Web: www.theavalonny.com
Prices: $$$

80 Rooms

20 Suites

The Vincci Avalon

A classic European-style boutique property, the Avalon appeals especially to business travelers whose work takes them to the nearby Gramercy Park, lower Madison, Flatiron and Murray Hill areas. The lobby is elegant, if busy with pillars, patterns and paneling. Withdraw to the library/club room, complete with fireplace, for a bit more tranquility.

In addition to its superior rooms, the hotel has 2 large suites boasting traditional comforts designed in a conventional European style. They are particularly well outfitted for professionals, with two-line telephones equipped with dataports and speaker capability, and T1 lines for Internet access. Many rooms enjoy a view of the Empire State Building. Each guestroom has two 27-inch television sets, as well. Jacuzzi tubs, bidets and double sinks furnish the Italian-marble baths in the larger suites. Guests enjoy complimentary access to Bally's Sports Club and health spa.

A full American breakfast is available in the Avalon Bar and Grill, which also serves lunch and dinner.

The Waldorf=Astoria

011

301 Park Ave. (bet. 49th & 50th Sts.)

Subway: 51 St
Phone: 212-355-3000 or 800-925-3673
Fax: 212-872-7272
Web: www.waldorfastoria.com
Prices: $$$$

1235 Rooms
208 Suites

The Waldorf=Astoria

Nothing says New York high society like the Waldorf=Astoria. Built in 1931, the hotel blends exquisite Art Deco ornamentation and lavish Second Empire furnishings. The original Waldorf, built in 1893, was demolished along with its companion, the Astoria, to make room for the Empire State Building. The huge "new" hotel (including its boutique counterpart with a private entrance, the Waldorf Towers) occupies the entire block between Park and Lexington avenues at 49th Street. Its lobby features a striking inlaid-tile mosaic and Art Deco chandelier. A $400-million renovation refreshed the grand dame, and deluxe fabrics and classic furniture dress the richly appointed and beautifully maintained rooms and suites, all outfitted with sumptuous marble baths.

With 1,500 employees, a full-service spa, four bars, and four restaurants—including Inagiku *(see restaurant listing)* for Japanese specialties, the Bull and Bear *(see restaurant listing)* for steak, and elegant Peacock Alley—you'll want for little here.

W - The Tuscany

012

120 E. 39th St. (bet. Lexington & Park Aves.)

Subway: Grand Central - 42 St
Phone: 212-686-1600 or 888-627-7189
Fax: 212-779-7822
Web: www.whotels.com
Prices: $$$

113 Rooms

7 Suites

Starwood Hotels & Resorts

Tucked away on tree-lined 39th Street, not far from Grand Central Station, The Tuscany (not to be confused with its sister spot, W New York—The Court, located on the same block and designed for business travelers) cultivates a sensual, relaxed atmosphere. It begins in the cozy lobby (or "living room" in W speak) done up in luxuriant purples, greens and browns. Velvets and satins, rich woods and supple leather add to the lush feeling of the space, which beckons as a comfortable spot for a drink or a private conversation.

Spacious rooms, highlighted by bold, deep colors and textures, feature original contemporary furnishings. Pillow-top mattresses, goose-down duvets, and spa robes make for a comfy stay. Bathrooms, however, are on the small side. In-room electronics include access to a CD/DVD library (high-speed Internet access is available for a fee). W's signature "Whatever, Whenever" service is available 24/7 by pressing "0" on your cordless, dual-line phone.

Athletic types will want to visit Sweat, the on-site fitness center. Before or after your workout, you can grab a quick bite at the Audrey Cafe.

Algonquin

001

59 W. 44th St. (bet. Fifth & Sixth Aves.)

Subway: 42 St - Bryant Pk
Phone: 212-840-6800
Fax: 212-944-1419
Web: www.algonquinhotel.com
Prices: $$$

150 Rooms

24 Suites

Algonquin Hotel

New York's oldest operating hotel was fully renovated in 2004 but remains true to its classically elegant roots and timeless aura. Best known for the the circle of literati, including Dorothy Parker and Robert Benchley, who lunched in the Round Table Room in the years after World War I, the Algonquin preserves the feel and look of a fine Edwardian club.

Rooms have been smartly upgraded to include all modern amenities (tastefully hidden); top-quality fabrics and fittings lend rich jewel tones to the accommodations. You may not want to arise from your pillow-top mattress, 350-thread-count linen sheets, down pillows, and the famous "Algonquin Bed." (Order one for home, if you like.) Each of the suites adds a fully stocked refrigerator.

For a taste of 1930s cafe society, step into the Oak Room, the legendary cabaret where famous audiences and performers (crooners Harry Connick Jr. and Diana Krall got their starts here) made merry. The mood lingers, and the shows still go on, with such talent as Andrea Marcovicci and Jack Jones. In the intimate Blue Bar, you'll find artwork by the late Al Hirschfeld, who was a regular.

Casablanca

002

147 W. 43rd St. (bet. Broadway & Sixth Ave.)

Subway: 42 St - Bryant Pk
Phone: 212-869-1212 or 888-922-7225
Fax: 212-391-7585
Web: www.casablancahotel.com
Prices: $$

43 Rooms

5 Suites

Casablanca Hotel

No surprises here—except perhaps that the concept of designing a hotel after the famous Bogart movie works without being kitschy or overdone. The illusion begins as you enter through the ornate doors into the small tiled lobby, and while there is no nightclub on the premises, up a flight of stairs you'll find a tamer version of the famous Rick's. Complimentary continental breakfast is served here, or you can relax by the fireplace later for tea or champagne. A pianist—not necessarily named Sam—entertains on Fridays. You'll find a computer here to surf or check your e-mail, and high-speed Internet access comes complimentary in each room.

The Casablanca ambience extends into the fair-sized rooms as well, which are furnished with Moroccan-inspired fabrics and carved headboards. Bathrooms are done up nicely in dark and light tile, just exotic enough to evoke a more remote setting than Midtown. Despite the hotel's Times Square location, most rooms are surprisingly quiet. From Monday through Saturday beginning at 5pm (until 8pm), guests are treated to a cheese and Champagne reception in the common area.

Chambers

003

15 W. 56th St. (bet. Fifth & Sixth Aves.)

Subway: 57 St
Phone: 212-974-5656 or 866-204-5656
Fax: 212-974-5657
Web: www.chambershotel.com
Prices: $$$

72 Rooms
5 Suites

Chambers Hotel

Behind its latticework door, the soaring lobby of this sophisticate sets the mood. It's all about art here: the hotel displays over 500 original pieces by young artists. Lobby furnishings and design details in various textures—warm wood floors, leather rugs, velvet sofas—complete the look of a swank town home. On the mezzanine, roving waiters provide refreshments all day, while books, art, and stylish seating create a comfortable atmosphere.

Explore the hotel's 14 floors, as each hallway houses a site-specific work of art. Guestrooms resemble urbane loft spaces with wide-plank hardwood floors and an eclectic but handsome blend of warm and cool materials—gray-washed oak furniture and details in blackened steel, chenille, leather, glass and artist's canvas. Ask and you'll receive; services include babysitters, a car and driver, in-room massage, and even a personal trainer on call.

For sophisticated contemporary fare, make dinner reservations at Town *(see restaurant listing);* this restaurant also provides the hotel's room service.

City Club

004

55 W. 44th St. (bet. Fifth & Sixth Aves.)

Subway: 42 St - Bryant Pk
Phone: 212-921-5500
Fax: 212-944-5544
Web: www.cityclubhotel.com
Prices: **$$$**

62 Rooms
3 Suites

City Club Hotel

What started life in 1904 as a gentleman's club is now an urbane and sophisticated hotel. The City Club prides itself on its small, private lobby, more like the entryway to an exclusive residence than to a hotel.

Rooms are small but set about with pillows and other accessories that make them feel like guestrooms in a swank private home. Handsome black-marble bathrooms include spacious tubs or showers with bidets, a telephone and TV speakers. All guests enjoy complimentary high-speed Internet access as well as in-room DVD players and electronic safe-deposit boxes. Truly spectacular are the hotel's three duplex suites, decked out with private terraces and circular stairways that lead up to the sleeping room from a well-appointed sitting room below.

For kicked-up brasserie fare, try Daniel Boulud's DB Bistro Moderne *(see restaurant listing)*, which connects to the lobby via a paneled wine bar.

Iroquois

49 W. 44th St. (bet. Fifth & Sixth Aves.)

Subway: 42 St - Bryant Pk
Phone: 212-840-3080 or 888-332-7220
Fax: 212-719-0006
Web: www.iroquoisny.com
Prices: $$$

105 Rooms

9 Suites

The Iroquois

Well-known, well-kept and comfortable, the historic Iroquois evokes the mood of a private mansion. Modern European furnishings added during a recent renovation suit its 1923 vintage. A convenient library offers a computer with high-speed Internet access as well as a small selection of books.

Remodeled guestrooms are swathed in chocolate-brown, and offer luxuries like Frette linens, Simmons Beautyrest mattresses and goose-down pillows. Italian marble bathrooms sparkle in peach and cream. All rooms have both tub and shower, while the suites are equipped with Jacuzzi tubs. If you're sleeping in, press the button on your doorknob for privacy. Given the hotel's queenly grace, it's ironic to remember that bad boy James Dean lived in suite 803 from 1951 to 1953.

Amenities include a 24-hour exercise room featuring a Finnish sauna for the ultimate in relaxation (if you're planning to use the sauna, contact the front desk 30 minutes in advance). To savor the contemporary American cuisine at Triomphe restaurant, be sure to make a reservation; the intimate room is tiny and popular with theatergoers.

Jumeirah Essex House

006

160 Central Park South (bet. Sixth & Seventh Aves.)

Subway: 57 St - 7 Av
Phone: 212-247-0300 or 888-645-5697
Fax: 212-315-1839
Web: www.jumeirahessexhouse.com
Prices: $$$$

448 Rooms

67 Suites

Jumeirah Essex House

This well-known Art Deco landmark opened in 1931 in its commanding site at the very foot of Central Park. Within easy walking distance of Carnegie Hall and the shops and restaurants of Fifth Avenue and the Time Warner Center, the Jumeirah Essex House welcomes guests in its impressive marble lobby.

A change in ownership passed this former Westin hostelry into the hands of the Dubai-based Jumeirah hospitality group. A major makeover is in the process of bestowing a new style on the hotel, whose lobby now sports an elegant Art Deco look, complete with sleek white leather arm chairs and two large photographs of Central Park, commissioned by the hotel from artist Atta Kim.

Warm, comfortable rooms are being refreshed (as of this writing, the renovation is only about half completed) with textured wall coverings and white damask linens. On one bedside table, a touch-screen-activated phone controls the room's lighting. The desk, with its halogen lamp, speedy Internet, and leather swivel chair, isn't a bad place to catch up on email.

Amenities include a fitness center, courtesy car service within a 10-block radius, and bicycles to ride through nearby Central Park.

Le Parker Meridien

118 W. 57th St. (bet. Sixth & Seventh Aves.)

Subway: 57 St
Phone: 212-245-5000 or 800-543-4300
Fax: 212-307-1776
Web: www.parkermeridien.com
Prices: $$$$

510 Rooms

221 Suites

Le Parker Meridien/Andrew Bordwin

The Parker Meridien underwent a complete refurbishment recently. Its grand Neoclassical lobby has been updated with modern touches in lighting, seating and carpeting. While the large lobby suits the hotel's size, the service is surprisingly personal.

Ergonomic, well-planned accommodations bear the touch of a hotel-savvy designer. They are reasonable in size and uncluttered—streamlined, in fact—with Aeron desk chairs and Scandinavian-style cherry and cedar wood furniture. Showers are big enough for two, and desks allow ample room to work, if you must. In the suites, televisions are cleverly mounted to swivel for viewing from any angle.

Get your workout in at Gravity, the resident fitness club, offering spa services, and group fitness classes. You can do your laps at the penthouse pool. Fuel up first at Norma's, known for serving tasty breakfast dishes until mid-afternoon. For dinner try Seppi's, a French-style bistro, or, for a great burger, check out the rough-and-ready Burger Joint.

The London NYC

151 W. 54th St. (bet. Sixth & Seventh Aves.)

Subway: 57 St
Phone: 212-307-5000 or 866-690-2029
Fax: 212-468-8747
Web: www.thelondonnyc.com
Prices: **$$$$**

549 Rooms

13 Suites

The London NYC

The London NYC is like a hop across the Pond without the guilt of those pesky carbon emissions. Formerly the Righa Royal Hotel, The London with its ivy-covered façade rises 54 stories above Midtown.

Guest suites epitomize modern sophistication with Italian linens, limed oak flooring, sectional sofas, and embossed-leather desks. Tones of soft gray, plum, sky-blue and crisp white dominate. Styled by Waterworks, bathrooms have the last word in luxury, with white marble mosaic-tile floors, double rain showerheads, and sumptuous towels and bathrobes.

Since service is a hallmark of The London, the expert concierge services of Quintessentially are on hand to assist you with any business or personal requests. Novel extras include complimentary cleaning of your workout wear, and an iPod docking station in each room.

The London NYC is also known as the American home of celebrity chef Gordon Ramsay. He may be infamous for his cantankerous spirit, but Gordon Ramsay at The London *(see restaurant listing)* impresses with its polished service and contemporary cuisine. For a casual alternative, try Maze for Ramsay's menu of small plates served in a sleek brasserie setting.

Metro

009

45 W. 35th St. (bet. Fifth & Sixth Aves.)

Subway: 34 St - Herald Sq
Phone: 212-947-2500 or 800-356-3870
Fax: 212-279-1310
Web: www.hotelmetronyc.com
Prices: **$$**

179 Rooms

3 Suites

Hotel Metro/Linda Davis

Though not hip or stylish, the Hotel Metro is nonetheless a good stay for the money. Located in the heart of the Garment District, near Penn Station (light sleepers take note that the hotel's location is not a quiet one), the building was constructed in 1901. An Art Deco-inspired lobby leads into a spacious breakfast room/lounge where complimentary breakfasts are served each morning, and tea and coffee are available during the day.

Guest rooms have been recently refurbished (the Metro opened its doors in 1995) and are equipped with mini-bars, and upgraded "plush-top" mattresses. Many of the marble bathrooms benefit from natural light, and the overall standard of housekeeping is good. The hotel now offers high-speed wireless Internet access, as well as a small business center. Rates include a complimentary continental breakfast served in the lounge area.

From the large rooftop bar (open from May through September), you'll have stunning views of the Empire State Building and the surrounding neighborhood, which includes Macy's, for all you hard-core shoppers.

The Michelangelo

010

152 W. 51th St. (at Seventh Ave.)

Subway: 50 St (Broadway)
Phone: 212-765-1900 or 800-237-0990
Fax: 212-541-6604
Web: www.michelangelohotel.com
Prices: **$$$**

163 Rooms

15 Suites

The Michelangelo Hotel

Convenient to Times Square, the Theater District, Rockefeller Center and Midtown offices, The Michelangelo caters to both leisure and business travelers. A recent renovation has polished the two-story lobby, regal in its liberal use of marble, rich fabric panels, and crystal chandeliers.

Winding hallways have been freshened with new paint and carpeting; shelves of books add a homey touch. Attractively appointed with marble foyers, small sitting areas, down pillows and Bose radio/CD players, guest rooms are generous for Manhattan, with a standard king measuring about 325 square feet (upgrades get bigger from there). Marble bathrooms come equipped with hair dryers, make-up mirrors, deep soaking tubs, terrycloth robes, and even a small TV. Part of an Italian hotel chain, The Michelangelo interprets hospitality with *gusto di vivere italiano*. Turndown service, a complimentary continental breakfast, a small fitness center, and limo service to Wall Street on weekday mornings number among the amenities.

Chef/partner Marco Canora (also of Hearth) has added a touch of urbane flair to the hotel's erstwhile dining room with Insieme *(see restaurant listing)*.

The Peninsula New York

011

700 Fifth Ave. (at 55th St.)

Subway: 5 Av - 53 St
Phone: 212-956-2888 or 800-262-9467
Fax: 212-903-3949
Web: www.peninsula.com
Prices: **$$$$**

185 Rooms

54 Suites

The Peninsula, New York

Still sparkling from its $45-million restoration in 1998, this magnificent 1905 hotel serves beautifully as Peninsula's flagship U.S. property. When built as The Gotham, it was the city's tallest skyscraper, towering 23 stories.
Plush rooms exude a timeless elegance, and Art Nouveau accents complement their rich colors and appointments. Ample in size and well conceived for business travelers, each guest room provides a silent fax machine, wireless Internet access, and a bottled-water bar (with your choice of still or sparkling water). Service is a particularly strong suit at the Peninsula, and the smartly liveried staff effortlessly execute your every request.
You could spend hours in the 35,000-square-foot, three-story Peninsula Spa and Health Club, complete with its Jacuzzi, sauna, steam rooms, and luxurious indoor pool, but don't be late for afternoon tea or cocktails at the intimate Gotham Lounge. Ascend to the Pen-Top Bar and Terrace before retiring to intimate Fives restaurant (on the second floor) for a romantic meal.

Hotel QT

012

125 W. 45th St. (bet. Sixth & Seventh Aves.)

Subway: Times Sq - 42 St
Phone: 212-354-2323
Fax: 212-302-8585
Web: www.hotelqt.com
Prices: **$$$**

140 Rooms

Nikolas Koenig

The good life doesn't have to come at a high price. This unique, contemporary hotel brings cheap chic to the heart of Times Square, and offers an uncommonly good value in a city well known for its outrageously priced guest quarters.

Owned by Andre Balazs, who runs such hip hotels as The Mercer in New York and Chateau Marmont in Los Angeles, Hotel QT is a fantastic choice for those with Champagne tastes and beer budgets. Guestrooms are simply decorated in a modern monastic style and boast flat-screen TVs, high-speed Internet access and platform and bunk beds topped with Egyptian cotton sheets. Complimentary buffet breakfast is included with each stay.

A youthful vibe penetrates the QT, where a sleek steel kiosk stocked with sundries serves as the reception desk. On the lobby level, the pool with its swim-up bar boasts a great scene of young urban professionals on business and holiday; meanwhile, the mezzanine lounge pulses with nightly DJ performances. A small fitness center with steam room and sauna is available to guests 24 hours a day, and in lieu of a restaurant or room service, the hotel stocks a library of take-out menus from area restaurants.

The Ritz-Carlton, Central Park

013

50 Central Park South (at Sixth Ave.)

Subway: 5 Av - 59 St
Phone: 212-308-9100 or 800-826-8129
Fax: 212-207-8831
Web: www.ritzcarlton.com
Prices: **$$$$**

213 Rooms

47 Suites

The Ritz-Carlton Hotel

Renovated as the city's newest Ritz-Carlton in 2002, this classic Central Park hotel was built in 1929 as the St. Moritz. The reception lobby remains intimate to invoke a small luxury property, but the lobby lounge opens into a grand two-story space.

The facelift cut the number of guestrooms in half to create sumptuous accommodations of generous size. Steeped in Old World elegance, they offer the best in electronic amenities rivaled only by old-fashioned touches such as a bath butler, a telescope to explore Central Park, and, in the top-end suites, a choice of fine bed linens. For that extra personalized service, reserve a room on the Club Level, where guests have access to the exclusive Club Lounge that offers complimentary food and beverages daily.

Jet lag got you down? A visit to La Prairie provides the ultimate in spa treatments and pampering. Stop by the hotel's plush Star Lounge for proper afternoon tea or a well-shaken pre- or post-dinner martini.

Sofitel

45 W. 44th St. (bet. Fifth & Sixth Aves.)

Subway: 47-50 Sts - Rockefeller Ctr
Phone: 212-354-8844 or 877-565-9240
Fax: 212-354-2480
Web: www.sofitel-newyork.com
Prices: **$$$$**

346 Rooms

52 Suites

Sofitel

Combining the best of French and American sensibilities, the Sofitel doesn't feel like a modern, 30-story tower hotel. Rich marble and leather greet guests in a spacious lobby filled with sofas and armchairs. Nicely sized guest rooms are attractively decorated with large windows (ask for a room on a higher floor for better views) and artwork that relates to both New York and Paris. Exceptional marble bathrooms include separate shower and tub. Wi-Fi Internet access and an on-site fitness center complete the picture. Pets are welcome here, too.
For cocktails, try Gaby Bar, a stylish lounge in the Art Deco tradition, with plenty of tables and comfortable chairs. Its companion restaurant, Gaby, serves French cuisine with Asian accents. The Sofitel's ideal location, between Rockefeller Center and the Empire State Building, and just east of Times Square and the Theater District, is equally convenient for business and leisure travelers.

The Warwick

015

65 W. 54th St. (at Sixth Ave.)

Subway: 57 St
Phone: 212-247-2700 or 800-203-3232
Fax: 212-247-2725
Web: www.warwickhotelny.com
Prices: **$$$**

359 Rooms
66 Suites

The Warwick Hotel

Newspaper magnate William Randolph Hearst built the Warwick in 1927 so that his lady friend, Marion Davies, could host their band of Hollywood and theatrical friends in style. Convenient to MoMA and the Theater District, the 33-story hotel underwent a facelift in 2001, and the smart guest rooms haven't lost their traditional feeling. Larger than many city hotel quarters, rooms here incorporate slick modern touches such as temperature controls that sense your presence. Go for broke and book the Suite of the Stars, where Cary Grant lived for 12 years; it boasts 1,200 square feet of space and its own wrap-around terrace.

For business travelers, high-speed Internet access is available throughout the hotel, and the business center in the lobby offers 24-hour fax and copying services. There's also an on-site fitness facility.

After working, or working out, treat yourself to a meal at Murals on 54, in full view of Dean Cornwall's wonderful murals depicting the history of Sir Walter Raleigh. Commissioned by Hearst in 1937 for the hotel's former Raleigh Room, these paintings have now been restored to their original luster.

Washington Jefferson Hotel

016

318 W. 51st St. (bet. Eighth & Ninth Aves.)

Subway: 50 St (Eighth Ave.)
Phone: 212-246-7550 or 888-567-7550
Fax: 212-246-7622
Web: www.wjhotel.com
Prices: $

135 Rooms

Washington Jefferson Hotel

Fresh, contemporary design at a decent price in Manhattan was once a pipe dream, but the Washington Jefferson Hotel delivers style without a high price tag. Located in the up-and-coming neighborhood of Hell's Kitchen, the hotel is close to the bright lights of the Theater District.

The lobby is warm and welcoming, and the staff ensures that all guests feel at home from the moment they step inside the doors. Rooms are somewhat Spartan, with platform beds dressed in crisp white linens, yet provide all the necessary amenities (TV with premium channels, radio/CD player). Clean lines extend to the bathrooms, outfitted with slate flooring and slate-tiled tubs. While standard rooms are on the small side, comfort is never sacrificed. Guests have 24-hour access to a small exercise room on-site, while serious athletes can take advantage of the reduced-price daily pass to Gold's Gym, available at the hotel's front desk.

Although there is no room service, you can enjoy lunch and dinner at the hotel's restaurant, Shimuzu. Sushi is a popular component here, but for those who prefer their fish cooked, the restaurant offers a delightful array of traditional Japanese dishes.

The Mercer

001

147 Mercer St. (at Prince St.)

Subway: Prince St
Phone: 212-966-6060
Fax: 212-965-3838
Web: www.mercerhotel.com
Prices: **$$$$**

67 Rooms
8 Suites

The Mercer/ Thomas Loof

Even if your name isn't Leonardo DiCaprio, Cher or Calvin Klein, you'll be equally welcome at The Mercer. Housed in a striking Romanesque Revival-style building erected in 1890, the hotel caters to the glitterati with discreet, personalized service and intimate elegance. The modern lobby feels like your stylish friend's living room, complete with comfy seating, appealing coffee-table books and an Apple computer for guests' use.

A Zen vibe pervades the guestrooms, fashioned by Parisian interior designer Christian Liaigre with high, loft-like ceilings, large windows that open, soothing neutral palettes, and Asian decorative touches. You'll find everything you need for business or leisure travel in your room, right down to scented candles and oversize bath products. Forgot something? The hotel's warm staff will gladly accommodate you with a laptop, a cell phone or a fax machine in your room.

Sure, the hotel offers 24-hour room service, but in this case the food comes from Jean-Georges Vongerichten's Mercer Kitchen *(see restaurant listing),* located in the basement. Don't fret if you get a room facing the street; soundproofing filters out the noise.

60 Thompson

002

60 Thompson St. (bet. Broome & Spring Sts.)

Subway: Spring St (Sixth Ave.)
Phone: 212-431-0400 or 877-431-0400
Fax: 212-431-0200
Web: www.60thompson.com
Prices: $$$$

85 Rooms
13 Suites

Thompson Hotels

With its spare 1940s look inspired by French designer Jean-Michel Frank, 60 Thompson absolutely oozes SoHo style. The lobby, decorated in gray, brown, and moss-green tones, is accented by bouquets of fresh flowers, and natural light floods in from floor-to-ceiling windows.

Room sizes vary, but all sport a minimalist look, with crisp, white Frette linens standing out against a wall of dark, paneled leather. Amenities include flat-screen TVs in all the rooms, and high-speed wireless Internet access. (Business travelers take note that 60 Thompson has replaced the requisite in-room desk with a sitting area in its standard rooms.) Bathrooms are tiled with chocolate-colored marble and stocked with spa products by Fresh. For those who don't appreciate the smell of cigarette smoke in their room, the hotel devotes two entire floors to non-smoking chambers.

Check out the rooftop bar on the 12th floor, where you can sip a cocktail while you drink in great city views. In good weather, the rooftop scene is a hot one, whereas the lobby bar bustles year-round with a cool crowd. Downstairs, Kittichai restaurant *(see restaurant listing)* specializes in Thai cuisine.

Soho Grand

003

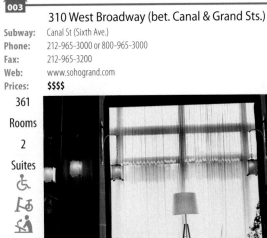

310 West Broadway (bet. Canal & Grand Sts.)

Subway: Canal St (Sixth Ave.)
Phone: 212-965-3000 or 800-965-3000
Fax: 212-965-3200
Web: www.sohogrand.com
Prices: **$$$$**

361 Rooms
2 Suites

Soho Grand

The architecture of this hip hotel (opened in 1996) recalls SoHo's industrial past, from the exposed-brick walls to the superb suspended steel staircase that connects the ground floor to the main lobby.

Two metal dog statues stand near the elevator, reminding guests of the Soho Grand's pet-friendly policy—what else would you expect from the same folks who own Hartz Mountain Industries? There's even a fish bowl in every room; if you grow attached to your new fishy friend, you're welcome to take him home with you.

And speaking of rooms, they're done in tones of gray and gold, with large picture windows overlooking the neighborhood. You'll relax in state-of-the-art style with Bose Wave CD/radios, in-room fax machines and broadband Internet connections. Feel like splurging? Reserve one of the airy, two-bedroom penthouse loft suites. They boast their own wrap-around terraces for enjoying the awesome cityscape.

If you can't get a reservation at the Soho Grand, the hotel's nearby sister, the Tribeca Grand *(see hotel listing)*, may be able to accommodate you.

Cosmopolitan

95 West Broadway (at Chambers St.)

Subway: Chambers St (West Broadway)
Phone: 212-566-1900 or 888-895-9400
Fax: 212-566-6909
Web: www.cosmohotel.com
Prices: $

125 Rooms

Cosmopolitan

Located in the heart of TriBeCa, the Cosmopolitan ranks as the longest continually operated hotel in New York City, dating back to 1853. This well-run, no-frills hotel pulls in a big business-travel and European clientele; fans of the Cosmopolitan tend to come back year after year.

Renovated rooms may be small, simple and practical, but they are perfectly maintained. (One caveat: the entire hotel is smoking-friendly.) All guest quarters have private bathrooms and color TVs; ask for a room on the back side of the hotel, if you're worried about the street noise. Although the Cosmopolitan doesn't have a restaurant, the Soda Shop, located in the same building, serves breakfast, lunch and dinner in a charming soda-fountain setting. Of course, TriBeCa's myriad restaurants are nearby.

The hotel lies just a five-minute walk from Wall Street, SoHo and Chinatown, and the Chambers Street subway station is practically right outside the door. Don't expect fawning service or a multitude of amenities—although guests do receive free passes to the New York Sports Club—and you won't be disappointed. The cleanliness, location and modest price are reasons enough to stay here.

Tribeca Grand

2 Sixth Ave. (at Church St.).

Subway: Canal St (Sixth Ave.)
Phone: 212-519-6600 or 877-519-6600
Fax: 212-519-6700
Web: www.tribecagrand.com
Prices: **$$$**

196 Rooms

7 Suites

Tribeca Grand

Swanky, hip and Eurocentric, the Tribeca Grand fits its trendy neighborhood like a glove. Inside, the soaring open atrium lends the lobby an airy feel, and a wall of lit votive candles stands in for a fireplace. Also in this space, the Church Lounge draws a crowd in the evening for light fare and libations. In warm weather, outdoor seating spills out onto Sixth Avenue.

Rooms in this sister to the Soho Grand are large, comfortable and equally well equipped for business and leisure travelers. The desk, accompanied by an ergonomic chair, is big enough to actually work on. Wi-Fi Internet access and a fax/printer/copier are available in each room. The hotel says welcome with a long-stemmed rose on the bed and a dish of strawberries and chocolate, while a good-night's sleep awaits you on the comfortable bed. Modern amenities include a flat-screen TV, a DVD player (the hotel owns a vast library of videos) and a Bose Wave radio. But if you prefer to read, the wing chair by the window is the perfect place to do so.

Lest you think this is an adults-only property, the hotel welcomes children of all ages as well as pets, with customized programs for both.

Bentley

001

500 E. 62nd St. (at York Ave.)

Subway: Lexington Av - 59 St
Phone: 212-644-6000 or 888-664-6835
Fax: 212-207-4800
Web: www.nychotels.com
Prices: $$

161 Rooms

36 Suites

Bentley Hotel

Trendy it's not, but the Bentley nevertheless offers oversize rooms for a good price in an area that's within walking distance of the subway, the shops and myriad of restaurants, and the attractions of Central Park. The Art Deco lobby makes a sleek first impression, with its beige and brown furnishings, boxy lamps and geometric-print area rugs.

Belgian linens, down comforters, and streamlined furnishings highlight the comfortable, contemporary-style rooms. In many of them, large windows—especially on the south side—take in views of the East River and the nearby Queensboro Bridge. For families, the Bentley's suites are a particularly good value; these spacious rooms include pull-out sofas or futons. All guests receive free passes to a nearby health club.

If you're not up for going out for dinner, the hotel's rooftop restaurant offers a limited menu and affords a glittering nighttime panorama of the City That Never Sleeps. The Bentley doesn't serve breakfast, but guests do have complimentary access to the cappuccino bar (located off the lobby) 24 hours a day.

The Carlyle

002

35 E. 76th St. (at Madison Ave.)

Subway: 77 St
Phone: 212-744-1600 or 800-227-5737
Fax: 212-717-4682
Web: www.thecarlyle.com
Prices: **$$$$**

123 Rooms

58 Suites

The Carlyle

Since it opened across from Central Park in 1930, The Carlyle has hosted every American president since Truman, along with a roster of foreign dignitaries from Prime Minister Nehru to Princess Diana—how's that for an A-list?

Named for British historian Thomas Carlyle, the hotel epitomizes luxury with its fine artwork, Baccarat crystal light fixtures, and marble baths (despite the presence of silver everywhere, the service could use some polishing). The individually decorated classic (Carlyle-speak for "standard") rooms are dressed in Louis XVI style with original Audubon prints, 440-thread-count Italian linens, elegant carpets over wood floors and bright marble baths. Some of the Carlyle's roomy suites feature a Steinway or a Baldwin baby-grand piano for those who wish to tickle the ivories.

For entertainment, there's Café Carlyle, where Woody Allen regularly jams with the Eddie Davis New Orleans jazz band. Legendary Bemelmans Bar, renowned for its whimsical mural of characters from artist Ludwig Bemelmans' famous *Madeline* series of children's books, is a popular place for a cocktail. Bring the kids by for Madeline Tea, served from noon until 4pm.

The Lowell

003

28 E. 63rd St. (bet. Madison & Park Aves.)

Subway: Lexington Av - 63 St
Phone: 212-838-1400 or 800-221-4444
Fax: 212-319-4230
Web: www.lowellhotel.com
Prices: $$$$

23 Rooms

47 Suites

The Lowell

A block from Central Park and close to Madison Avenue boutiques, The Lowell occupies a landmark 1928 building on a tree-lined Upper East Side street. The hotel's intimate size, discreet staff and sumptuous ambience are the reasons most fans give for coming back time after time.

From the moment you step inside the silk-paneled lobby, you'll sense the European elegance that defines The Lowell. Guests here are cosseted in lavish suites, most of which have working fireplaces and private terraces (the Garden Suite has two terraces) and iPod docking stations. A recent renovation added new marble-clad baths—complete with mini TVs and Bulgari toiletries—king size, half-canopy beds, new designer fabrics and upgraded kitchens to all accommodations.

The well-equipped fitness room adds thoughtful touches like magazines, cool towels, and fruit. If it's aerobics classes or an indoor pool you want, guests have complimentary access to the posh Equinox Fitness Club nearby.

Savor a hearty steak in the hotel's clubby Post House restaurant, or drop by the aristocratic Pembroke Room, all swagged in English chintz, for breakfast, afternoon tea or weekend brunch.

The Pierre

004

2 E. 61st St. (at Fifth Ave.)

Subway: 5 Av - 59 St
Phone: 212-838-8000 or 800-743-7734
Fax: 212-940-8109
Web: www.tajhotels.com/pierre
Prices: **$$$$**

149 Rooms

51 Suites

The Pierre

Opened in 1930 by Charles Pierre Casalasco, The Pierre (now a Taj hotel) has pampered the crème de la crème of New York society for decades. The location of the Neoclassical-style building is unparalleled: overlooking lovely Central Park, The Pierre stands near the prestigious shops of Fifth Avenue—a big plus for hard-core shoppers. Inside, handmade carpets, silk draperies, and ebullient bouquets of fresh flowers are just a sampling of the luxury that awaits you. Murals abound, from The Rotunda tea room and lounge to the 1,600-square-foot fitness center (which even has a room for massage therapy). Outfitted with wingback chairs, mahogany furnishings, and black and white marble baths, rooms have an old-fashioned elegance. Several of the 51 suites feature terraces with awesome city or Central Park views.

Elevator operators wearing white gloves epitomize the quality of service at a hotel where the business center and the concierge are available 24 hours a day. Oenophiles dining at the Cafe Pierre will be happy to know that the hotel boasts a 10,000-bottle wine cellar.

The Regency

540 Park Ave. (at 61st St.)

Subway: Lexington Av - 63 St
Phone: 212-759-4100 or 800-233-2356
Fax: 212-826-5674
Web: www.loewshotels.com
Prices: **$$$$**

267 Rooms

86 Suites

The Regency, A Loews Hotel

A multimillion-dollar renovation spiffed up this flagship of Loew's hotel properties, just two blocks east of Central Park. Lush fabrics, Frette linens, CD players, TVs in the bathrooms, and double-paned windows are a few of the amenities you'll find in the contemporary-style rooms—the smallest of which is 225 square feet. Even Fido gets the royal treatment here with his own room-service menu and a dog-walking service.

Boasting a staff-to-guest ratio of 1 to 1, the hotel delights in serving its guests. Forget your reading glasses? Need a humidifier in your room? The Regency's staff is only too happy to oblige. Business travelers will appreciate rooms equipped with large writing desks, fax/printers, and high-speed Internet access. And if you need a haircut before that big meeting, there's even a beauty salon and barbershop on-site.

For that power breakfast, you need not go any farther than the hotel's 540 Park restaurant. For night owls, Feinstein's at The Regency (named for its owner, pop vocalist and songwriter Michael Feinstein) offers big-name cabaret acts six nights a week.

Hotel Wales

006

1295 Madison Ave. (bet. 92nd & 93rd Sts.)

Subway: 96 St (Lexington Ave.)
Phone: 212-876-6000 or 866-925-3746
Fax: 212-860-7000
Web: www.waleshotel.com
Prices: **$$$**

46 Rooms 41 Suites

Hotel Wales

Built in 1902, the Hotel Wales sits atop Carnegie Hill, on the same block with the mansion of steel magnate Andrew Carnegie. Close to Upper East Side museums (including the Metropolitan Museum of Art), the hotel exudes a countryside feel in its soothing lobby, complete with a fireplace, marble staircase, coffered ceiling and mosaic floor.

All rooms profited from its recent renovation, which preserved the turn-of-the-century spirit with period furnishings, Belgian linens, down comforters, fresh flowers, and sepia-tone photographs of the neighborhood. Bathrooms are on the small side.

Spend some time on the rooftop terrace taking in the city views, or squeeze in a workout at the hotel's fitness studio. Continental breakfast is served each morning in the Pied Piper Room, decorated as a Victorian-era parlor. The Wales also includes Sarabeth's restaurant, loved by locals for its homemade breads, pastries and fruit preserves (available for sale), as well as its weekend brunch.

Excelsior

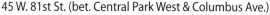

45 W. 81st St. (bet. Central Park West & Columbus Ave.)

Subway: 81 St - Museum of Natural History
Phone: 212-362-9200
Fax: 212-580-3972
Web: www.excelsiorhotelny.com
Prices: $$

120 Rooms
80 Suites

Excelsior

Located within a dinosaur bone's throw from the American Museum of Natural History, the 16-story Excelsior sits in the center of the action of the Upper West Side touring scene. Parents can charge their hearts' delight at the shops on nearby Columbus Avenue, then let the kids lead the charge through Central Park.

A country-French motif characterizes the décor of the reasonably priced standard rooms and one- and two-bedroom suites, while the renovated bathrooms, sporting sparkling white tiles, remind you of why you love to stay in hotels. Bear in mind that while the street-view bedrooms are brighter, the rooms on the back side of the hotel offer peace and quiet. Wi-Fi Internet access is available throughout the property, and if you forgot your laptop, an Internet station is available for guests in the Excelsior's lobby.

The concierge will gladly arrange for theater tickets and restaurant reservations. But after a day of museum-hopping, why not retire to the Entertainment Room, where you can work out in the fitness center, peruse the books in the well-stocked library, or simply relax in front of the TV?

Mandarin Oriental

002

80 Columbus Circle (at 60th St.)

Subway: 59 St - Columbus Circle
Phone: 212-805-8800 or 866-801-8880
Fax: 212-805-8888
Web: www.mandarinoriental.com
Prices: **$$$$**

202 Rooms

46 Suites

Mandarin Oriental Hotel/George Apostolidis

Occupying floors 35 to 54 in the north tower of the Time Warner Center, the Mandarin Oriental affords sweeping views of Central Park and the city, while bathing its guests in über-luxury. If the views from the floor-to-ceiling windows in your room don't do it for you, walk across the marble-floored lobby to the Lobby Lounge and take in the dramatic panorama while you sip—what else?—a Manhattan.

All of the 248 soundproofed guest rooms reflect subtle elegance with their Asian color schemes and 1940s-style furniture; most bathrooms are equipped with soaking tubs set near picture windows. Flat-panel LCD televisions can be found in both the bedroom and bath. And don't forget about the fitness center with its indoor lap pool, or the 14,500-square-foot, full-service spa. The latter is equipped with amethyst-crystal steam rooms, and a private VIP spa suite complete with its own sauna and fireplace.

Granted, the Time Warner Center contains some must-try restaurants, but why leave the hotel floors when you can enjoy contemporary Asian cuisine as well as stellar views on the 35th floor at Asiate *(see restaurant listing)?*

On the Ave

003

2178 Broadway (at 77th St.)

Subway: 79 St
Phone: 212-362-1100 or 800-497-6028
Fax: 212-787-9521
Web: www.ontheave.com
Prices: $$

242 Rooms

27 Suites

On the Ave

Only a short walk away from Lincoln Center and Central Park, this early 20th-century structure has been renovated and updated with early 21st-century accommodations. Flat-screen plasma TVs, CD players, wireless Internet access, and black marble bathrooms will appeal to the cool in you, while Frette robes, down duvets, and the complimentary Belgian chocolates left on your pillow at turndown will leave you feeling appropriately pampered. Suite amenities include homemade cookies delivered to your room, and private balconies (in some suites).

Nightly piano music in the lobby makes a nice prelude to a refreshing sleep in feather beds adorned with 310-thread-count Italian cotton linens. Rooms on the top three floors boast balconies and afford views of the Hudson River or the trees of Central Park. If your room doesn't have a view, take the elevator to the landscaped balcony on the 16th floor; this pleasant space is equipped with Adirondack chairs for relaxing. All this, plus the pet-friendly hotel has a 24-hour business center, too.

Trump International Hotel & Tower

004

1 Central Park West (at Columbus Circle)

Subway: 59 St - Columbus Circle
Phone: 212-299-1000 or 888-448-7867
Fax: 212-299-1150
Web: www.trumpintl.com
Prices: **$$$$**

38 Rooms
129 Suites

Trump International Hotel & Tower

Don't let the diminutive lobby fool you; the accommodations here are oh-so-The Donald. Inhabiting the 3rd through the 17th floors of this 52-story tower, the hotel offers luxurious guest rooms and suites that promise spectacular views of Manhattan through their floor-to-ceiling windows.

Appropriate for business or pleasure, lodgings at Trump International are that perfect mix of posh yet approachable. Shades of cinnamon, paprika or sage define the décor, while marble bathrooms, complete with Jacuzzi tubs, invite you for a relaxing soak above the hustle and bustle of the Big Apple. Or, for an even more "at home in the city" feel, choose a suite with a sleek European-style kitchen.

Over-the-top amenities include 42-inch plasma TVs, CD and DVD players, personalized business cards, a 6,000-square-foot fitness center equipped with a pool, a spa, and personal trainers. Not to mention in-room catering from the hotel's stellar restaurant Jean-Georges (*see restaurant listing*). Last, but not least, the property's signature Attaché Service provides each guest with their own concierge—would you expect anything less from The Donald?

Notes

Notes

Notes

Notes

Notes

Notes

Notes

Notes

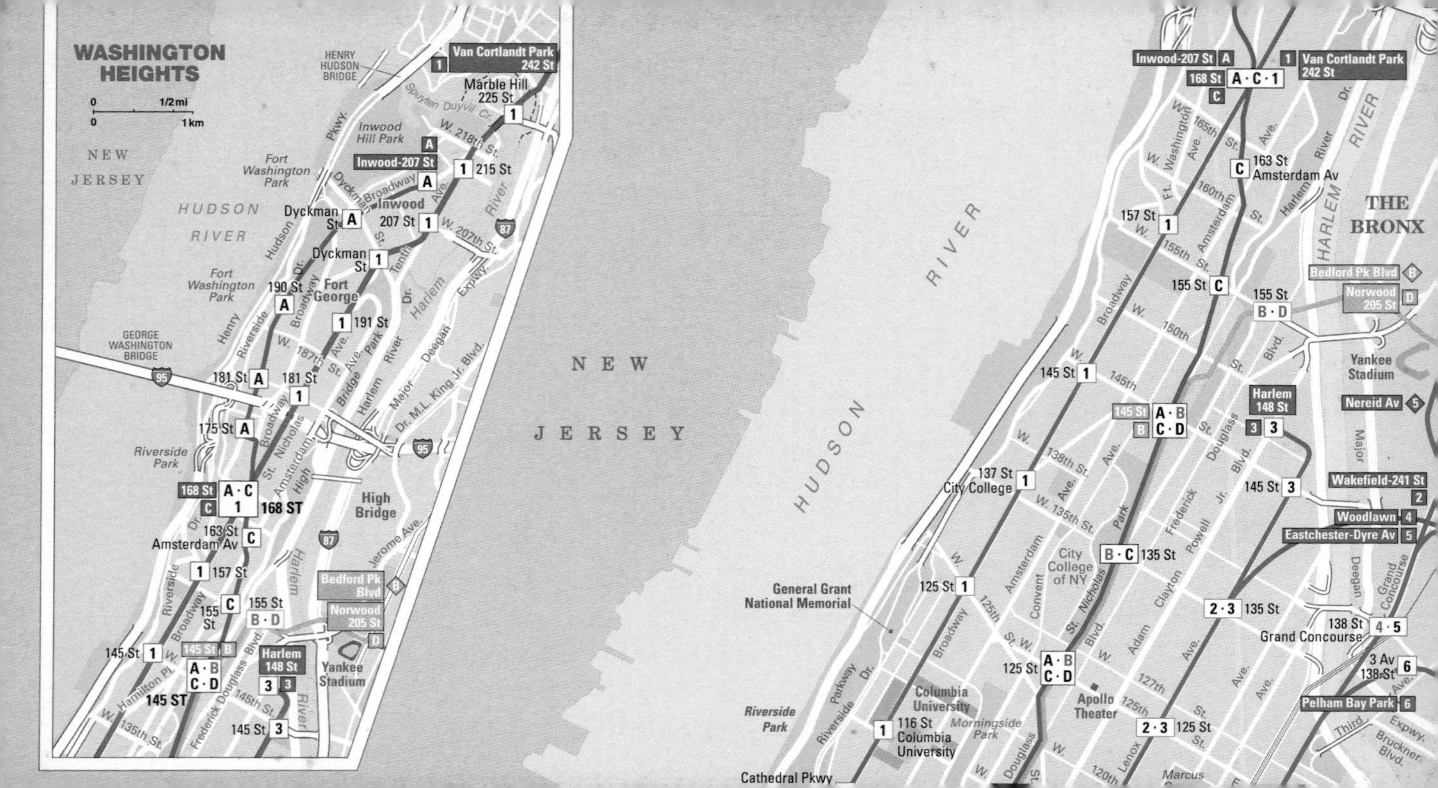
WASHINGTON HEIGHTS
0 1/2 mi
0 1 km
NEW JERSEY
HUDSON RIVER
HENRY HUDSON BRIDGE
Van Cortlandt Park 242 St
Marble Hill 225 St
Spuyten Duyvil Cr.
Inwood Hill Park
Inwood-207 St
215 St
Fort Washington Park
Inwood
207 St
Dyckman St
Fort George
190 St
191 St
GEORGE WASHINGTON BRIDGE
181 St
175 St
Riverside Park
168 St
168 ST
163 St Amsterdam Av
157 St
155 St
145 St
145 ST
Harlem 148 St
Yankee Stadium
Bedford Pk Blvd
Norwood 205 St
High Bridge
Harlem River
NEW JERSEY
HUDSON RIVER
THE BRONX
HARLEM RIVER
137 St City College
City College of NY
135 St
125 St
116 St Columbia University
Columbia University
Morningside Park
Apollo Theater
General Grant National Memorial
Riverside Park
Cathedral Pkwy
Nereid Av
Wakefield-241 St
Woodlawn
Eastchester-Dyre Av
138 St Grand Concourse
3 Av 138 St
Pelham Bay Park